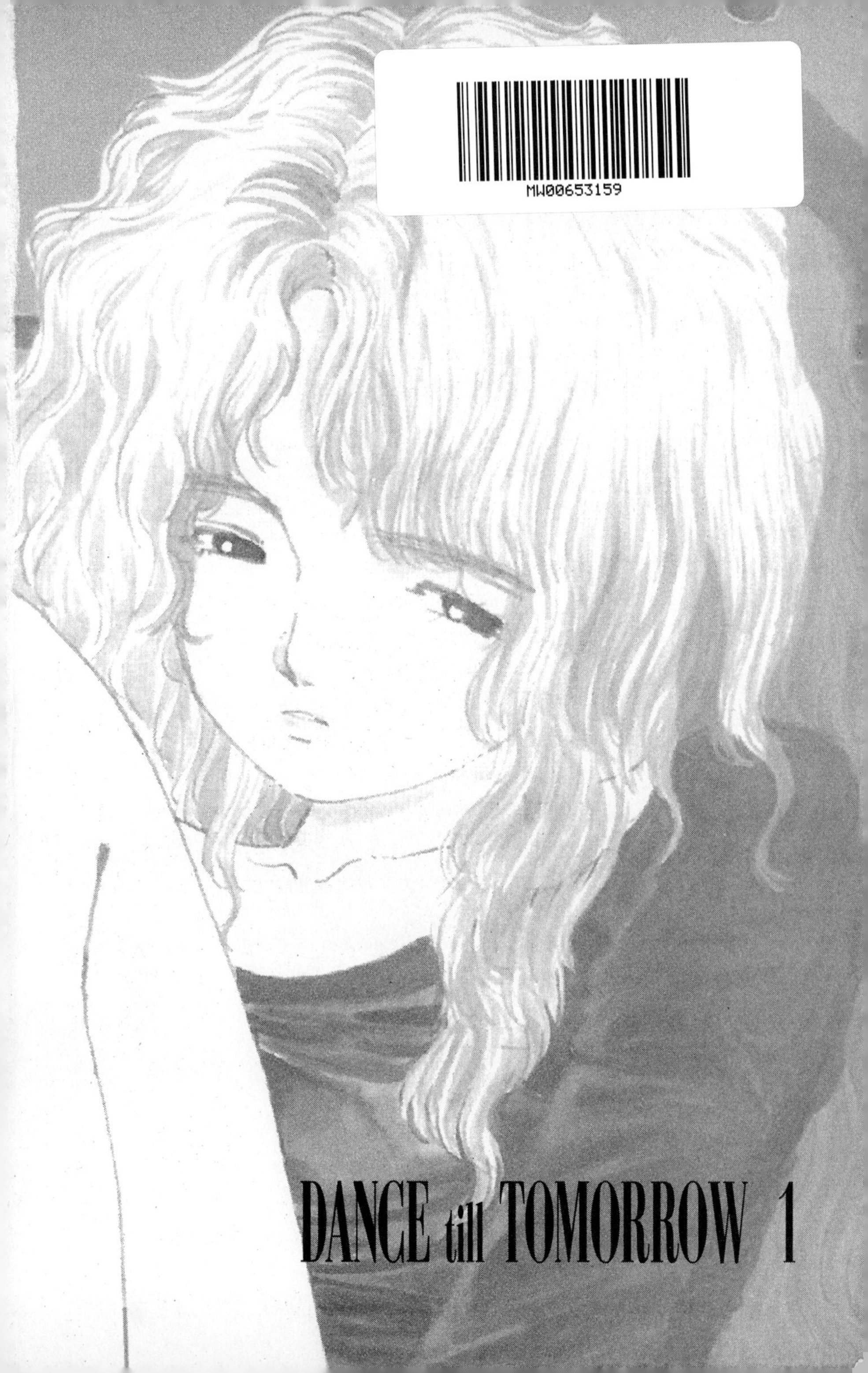
DANCE till TOMORROW 1

DANCE TILL TOMORROW VOL. 1

**IF COLLEGE STUDENT SUEKICHI GRA-
DUATES FROM COLLEGE, HE'LL COL-
LECT A $4.5 MILLION INHERITANCE
FROM HIS GREAT-GRANDFATHER....
BUT SEXY AYA WOULD RATHER GIVE
HIM AN ADVANCED EDUCATION IN
THE ARTS OF LOVE!**

Suekichi prefers his work as the producer
of an avant-garde theater troupe to studying—perhaps because he has a big crush on
the troupe's dedicated leader, Ms.
Shimomura. At the same time, Suekichi
can't resist the seductive charms of Aya,
even though he suspects she's only in love
with his money....

DANCE till TOMORROW

STORY AND ART BY NAOKI YAMAMOTO

PULP GRAPHIC NOVEL

vol.1

STORY & ART BY
NAOKI YAMAMOTO

**ENGLISH ADAPTATION BY
MATT THORN &
ANNETTE ROMAN**

Translation/Matt Thorn, Lillian Olsen &
Kaori Kawakubo
Touch-Up Art & Lettering/Dan Nakrosis
Cover Design/Izumi Evers
Editor/Annette Roman

Managing Editor/Hyoe Narita
Editor-in-Chief/Satoru Fujii
Publisher/Seiji Horibuchi

Printed in Canada

Published by Viz Communications, Inc.
P.O. Box 77010 · San Francisco, CA 94107

10 9 8 7 6 5 4 3 2 1
First printing, September 1998

Vizit our web sites at www.viz.com,
www.pulp-mag.com,
www.animerica-mag.com, and our Internet
magazine at www.j-pop.com !

CONTENTS

This volume contains the DANCE TILL TOMORROW installments from
PULP Vol. 1. No. 1 through Vol. 2, No. 6 in their entirety.

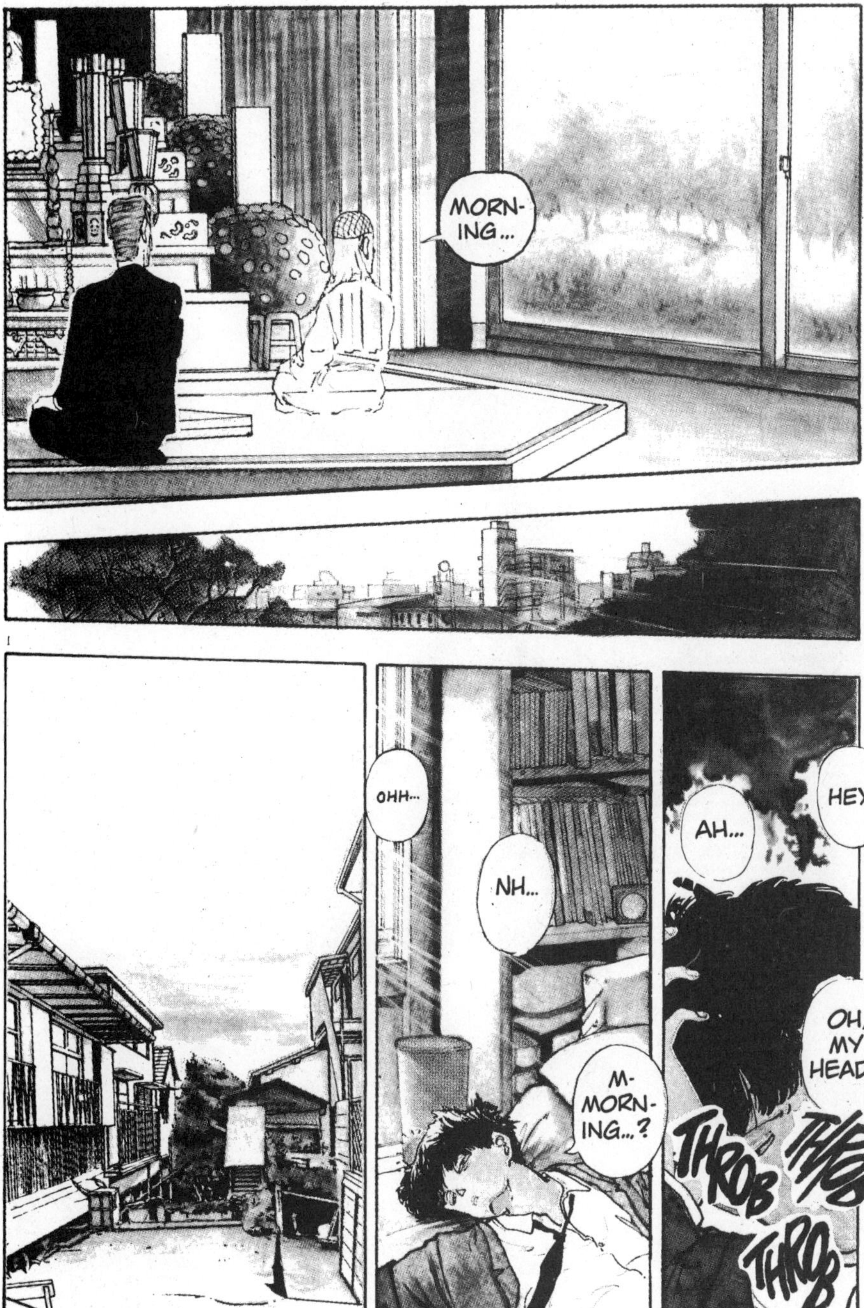
MORN-
ING...
OHH...
NH...
M-
MORN-
ING...?
AH...
HEY!
OH,
MY
HEAD.
THROB
THROB
THROB

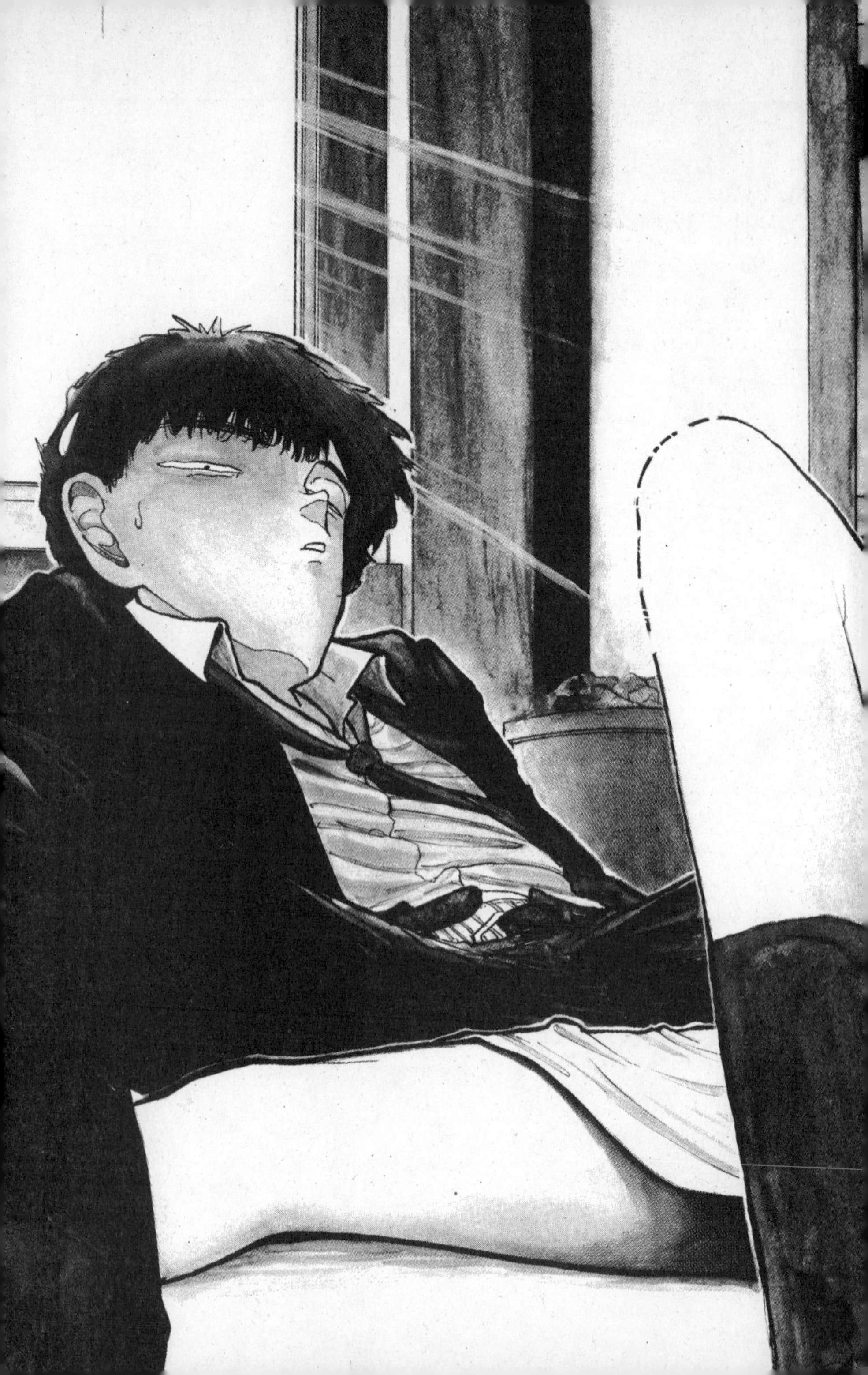

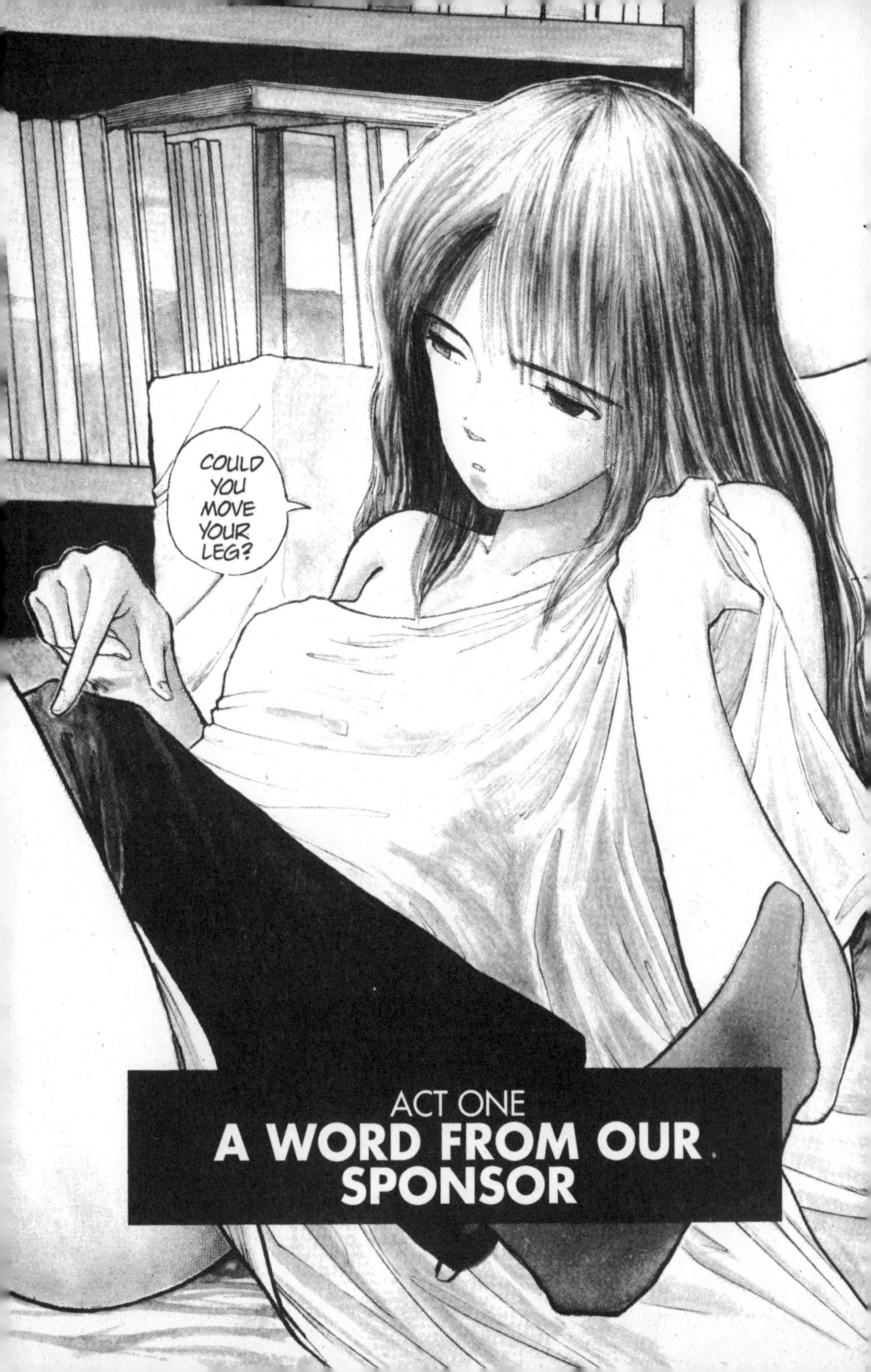
COULD YOU MOVE YOUR LEG?

ACT ONE
A WORD FROM OUR SPONSOR

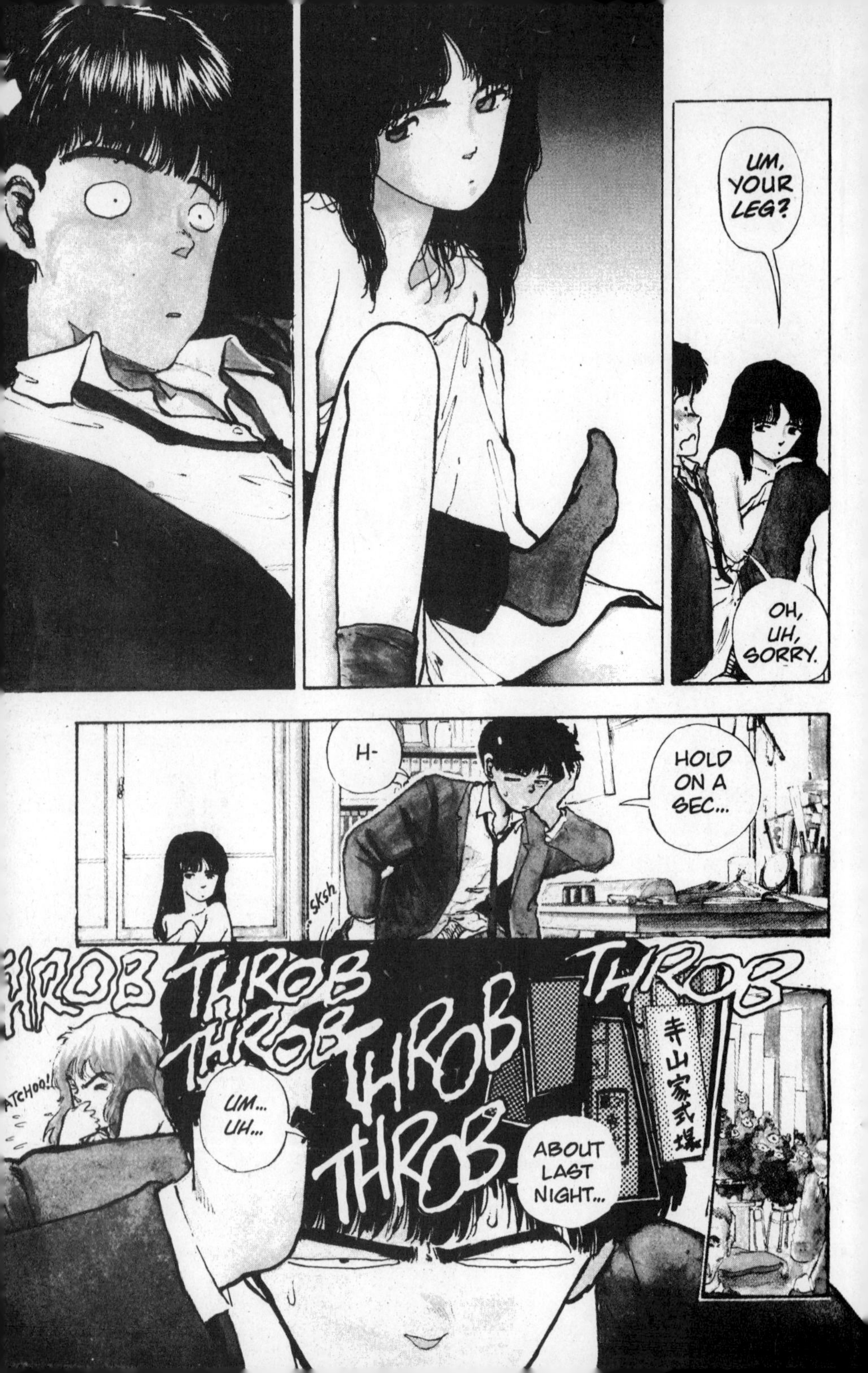
UM, YOUR LEG?
OH, UH, SORRY.
H-
HOLD ON A SEC...
SKSH
THROB THROB
THROB
THROB
THROB
THROB
ATCHOO!!
UM... UH...
寺山家式場
ABOUT LAST NIGHT...

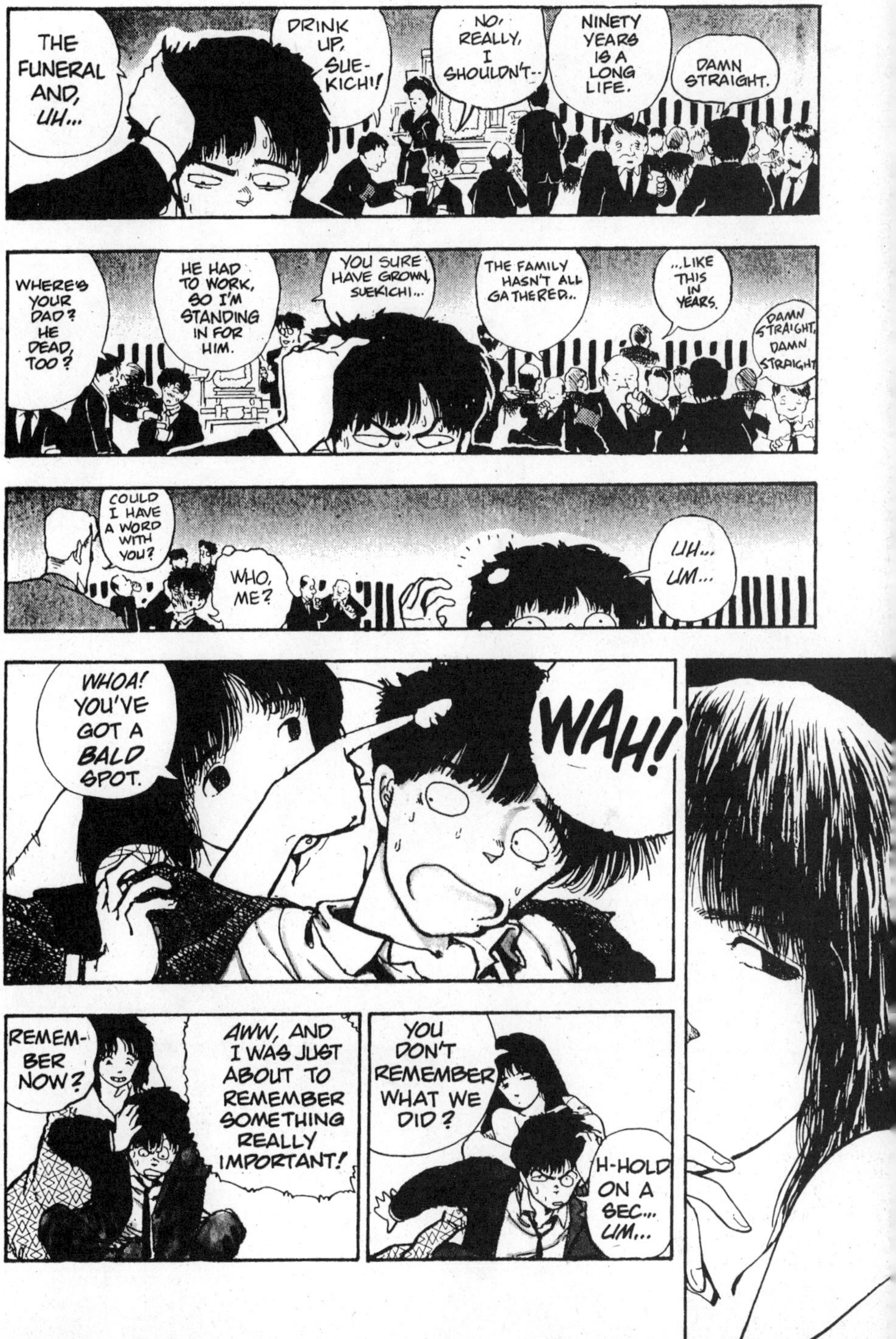
THE FUNERAL AND, UH...
DRINK UP, SUE-KICHI!
NO, REALLY, I SHOULDN'T...
NINETY YEARS IS A LONG LIFE.
DAMN STRAIGHT.
WHERE'S YOUR DAD? HE DEAD, TOO?
HE HAD TO WORK, SO I'M STANDING IN FOR HIM.
YOU SURE HAVE GROWN, SUEKICHI...
THE FAMILY HASN'T ALL GATHERED...
...LIKE THIS IN YEARS.
DAMN STRAIGHT, DAMN STRAIGHT
COULD I HAVE A WORD WITH YOU?
WHO, ME?
UH... UM...
WHOA! YOU'VE GOT A BALD SPOT.
WAH!
REMEM-BER NOW?
AWW, AND I WAS JUST ABOUT TO REMEMBER SOMETHING REALLY IMPORTANT!
YOU DON'T REMEMBER WHAT WE DID?
H-HOLD ON A SEC... UM...

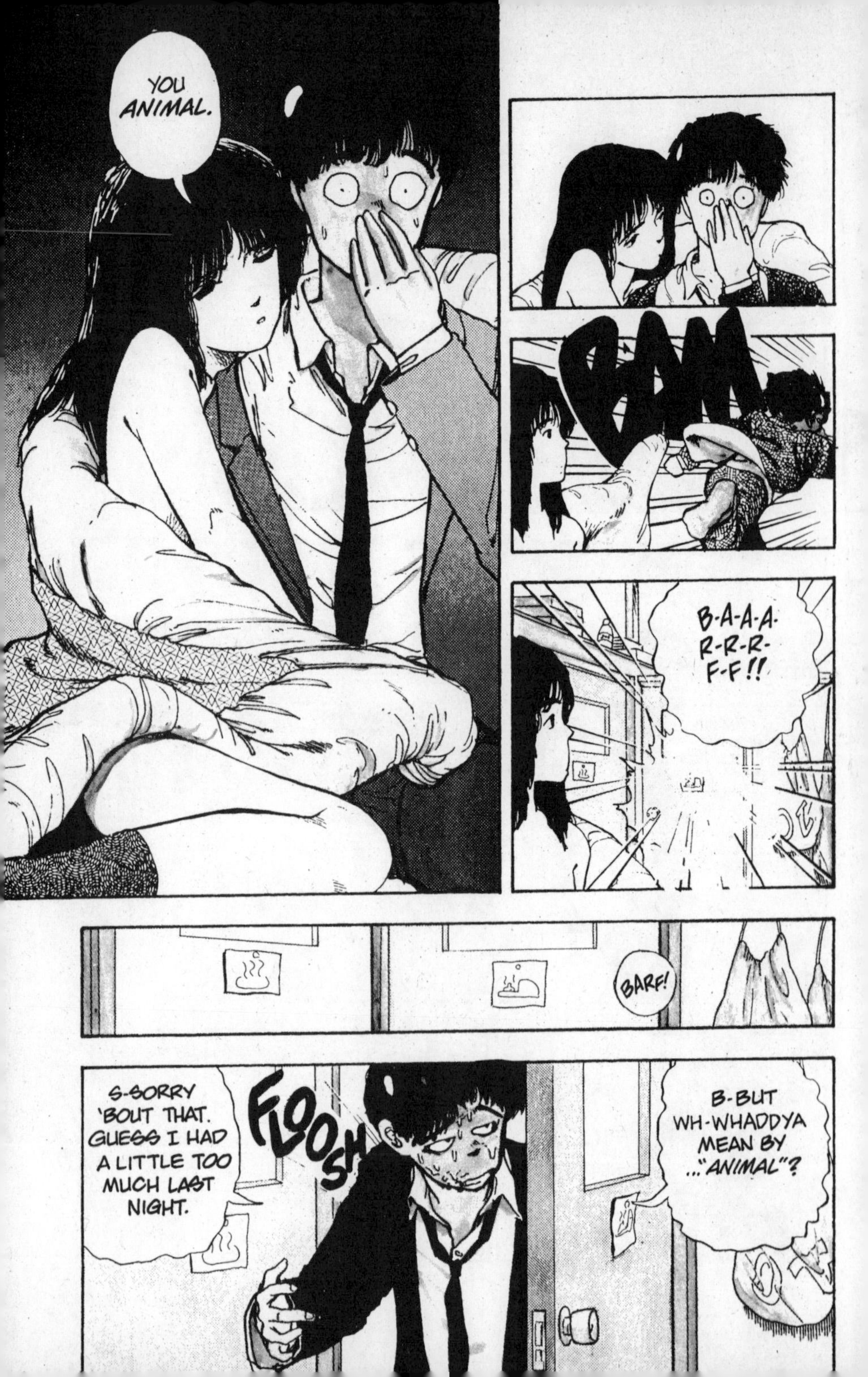
YOU ANIMAL.
B-A-A-A-R-R-R-F-F!!
BARF!
S-SORRY 'BOUT THAT. GUESS I HAD A LITTLE TOO MUCH LAST NIGHT.
FLOOSH
B-BUT WH-WHADDYA MEAN BY ..."ANIMAL"?

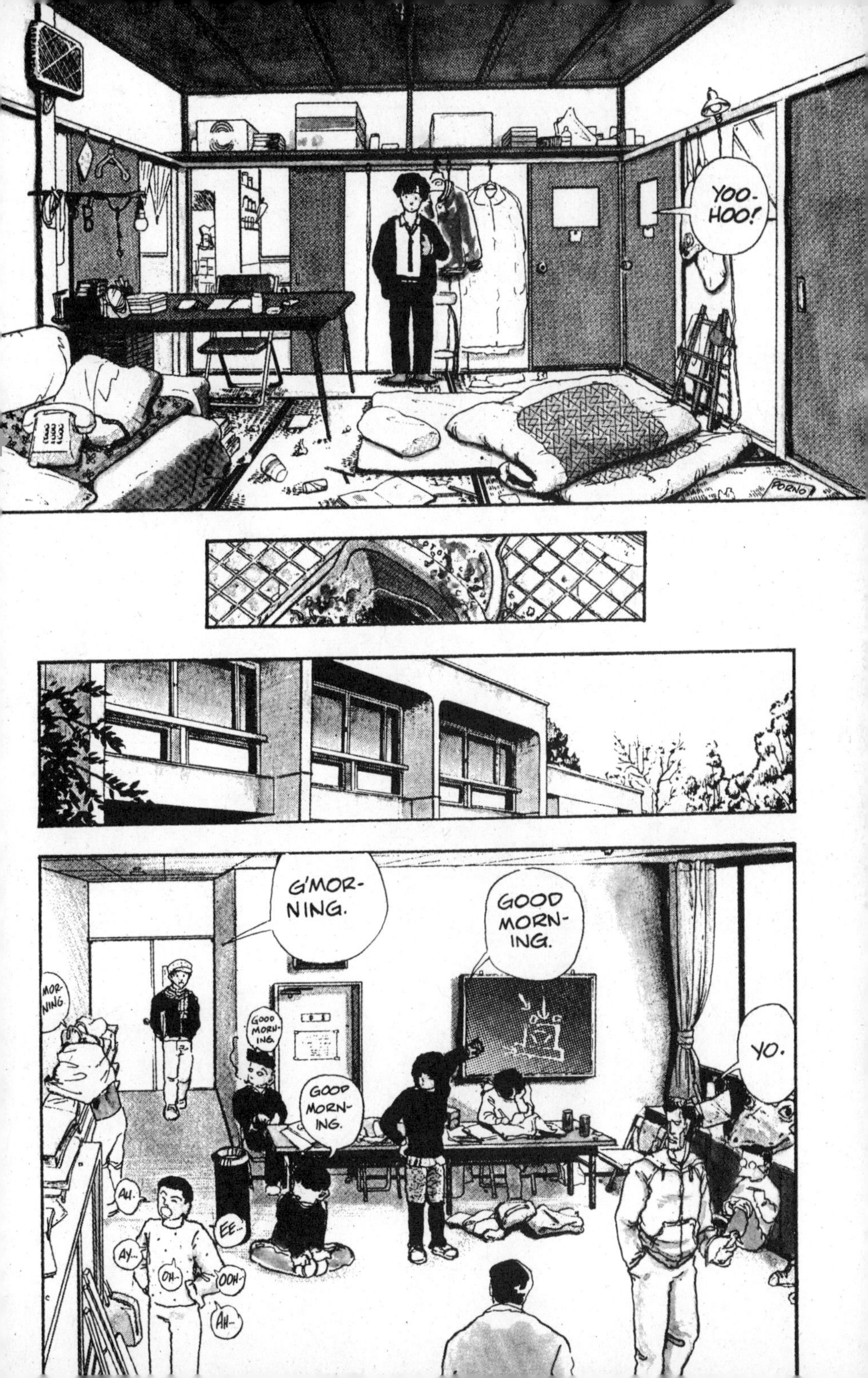
YOO-HOO!
PORNO
MORNING.
G'MORNING.
GOOD MORNING.
GOOD MORNING.
GOOD MORNING.
YO.
AH..
EE..
AY...
OH-
OOH-
AH...

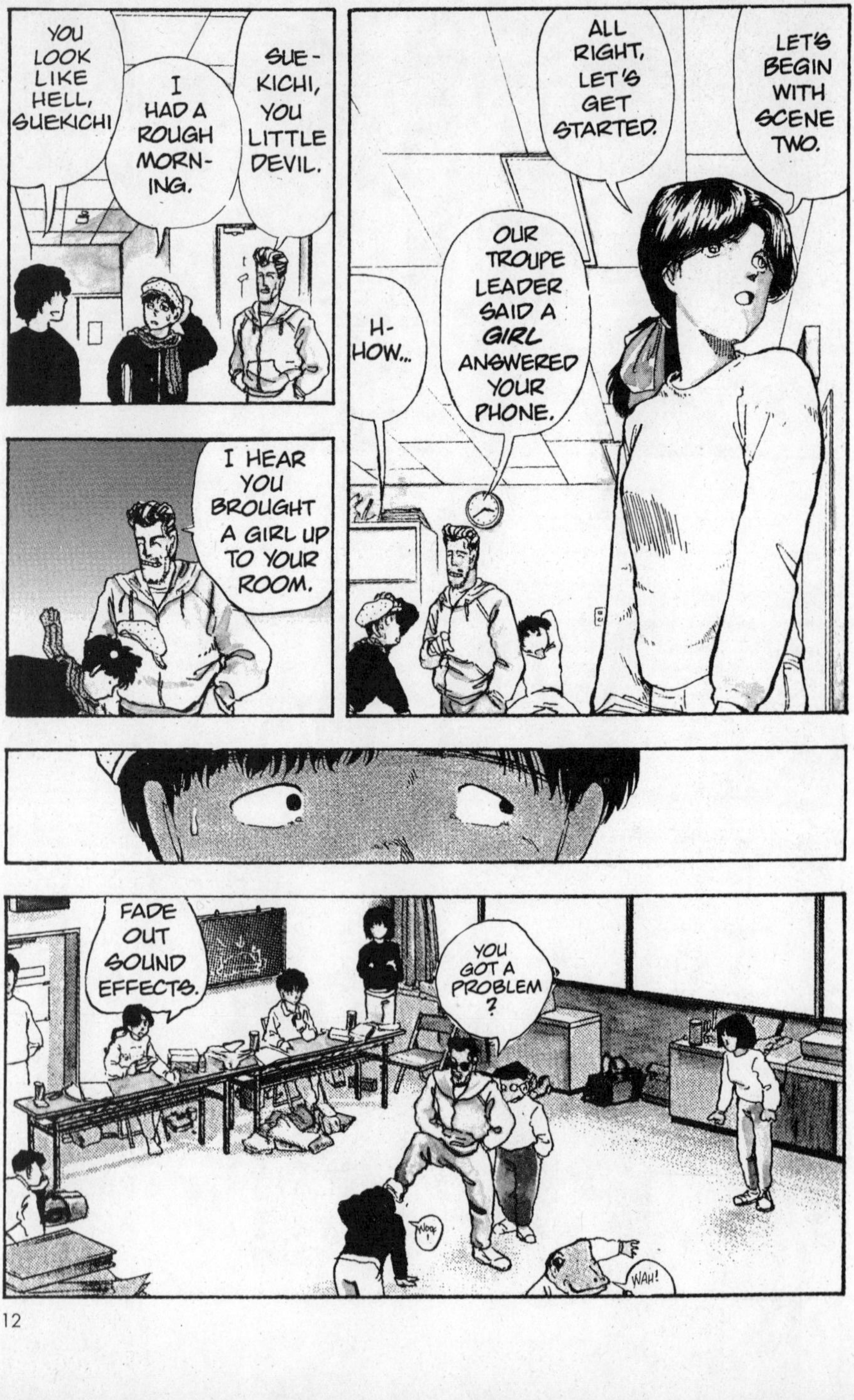
YOU LOOK LIKE HELL, SUEKICHI
I HAD A ROUGH MORNING.
SUE-KICHI, YOU LITTLE DEVIL.
I HEAR YOU BROUGHT A GIRL UP TO YOUR ROOM.
ALL RIGHT, LET'S GET STARTED.
LET'S BEGIN WITH SCENE TWO.
H-HOW...
OUR TROUPE LEADER SAID A GIRL ANSWERED YOUR PHONE.
FADE OUT SOUND EFFECTS.
YOU GOT A PROBLEM ?
WOOF !
WAH!

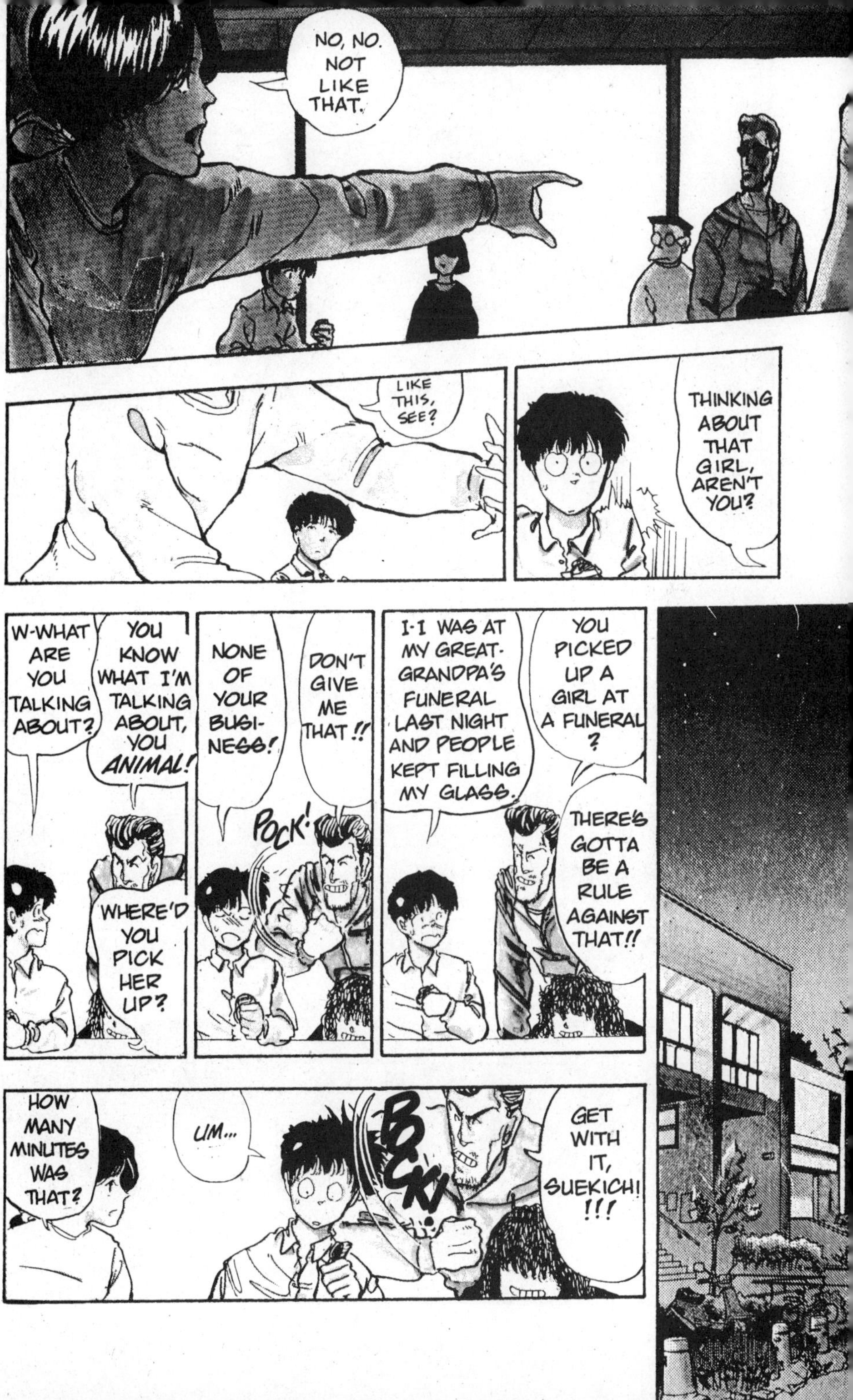
NO, NO. NOT LIKE THAT.
LIKE THIS, SEE?
THINKING ABOUT THAT GIRL, AREN'T YOU?
W-WHAT ARE YOU TALKING ABOUT?
YOU KNOW WHAT I'M TALKING ABOUT, YOU ANIMAL!
WHERE'D YOU PICK HER UP?
NONE OF YOUR BUSI-NESS!
DON'T GIVE ME THAT!!
POCK!
I-I WAS AT MY GREAT-GRANDPA'S FUNERAL LAST NIGHT AND PEOPLE KEPT FILLING MY GLASS.
YOU PICKED UP A GIRL AT A FUNERAL?
THERE'S GOTTA BE A RULE AGAINST THAT!!
HOW MANY MINUTES WAS THAT?
UM...
BOCK!
GET WITH IT, SUEKICH!
!!!

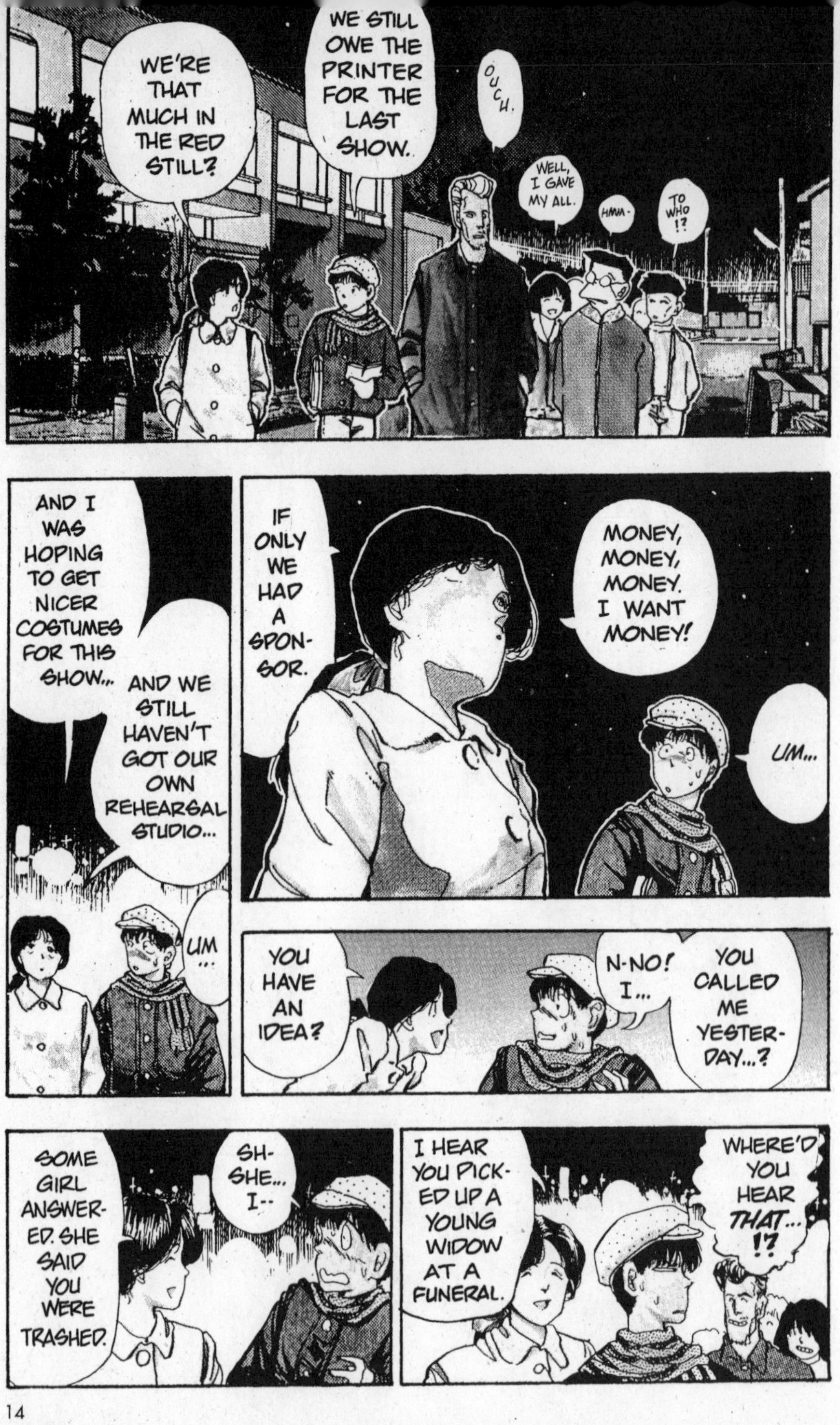
WE'RE THAT MUCH IN THE RED STILL?
WE STILL OWE THE PRINTER FOR THE LAST SHOW.
OUCH.
WELL, I GAVE MY ALL.
HMM.
TO WHO !?
AND I WAS HOPING TO GET NICER COSTUMES FOR THIS SHOW...
AND WE STILL HAVEN'T GOT OUR OWN REHEARSAL STUDIO...
IF ONLY WE HAD A SPON-SOR.
MONEY, MONEY, MONEY. I WANT MONEY!
UM...
UM ...
YOU HAVE AN IDEA?
N-NO! I...
YOU CALLED ME YESTER-DAY...?
SOME GIRL ANSWER-ED. SHE SAID YOU WERE TRASHED.
SH-SHE... I--
I HEAR YOU PICK-ED UP A YOUNG WIDOW AT A FUNERAL.
WHERE'D YOU HEAR *THAT*... !?

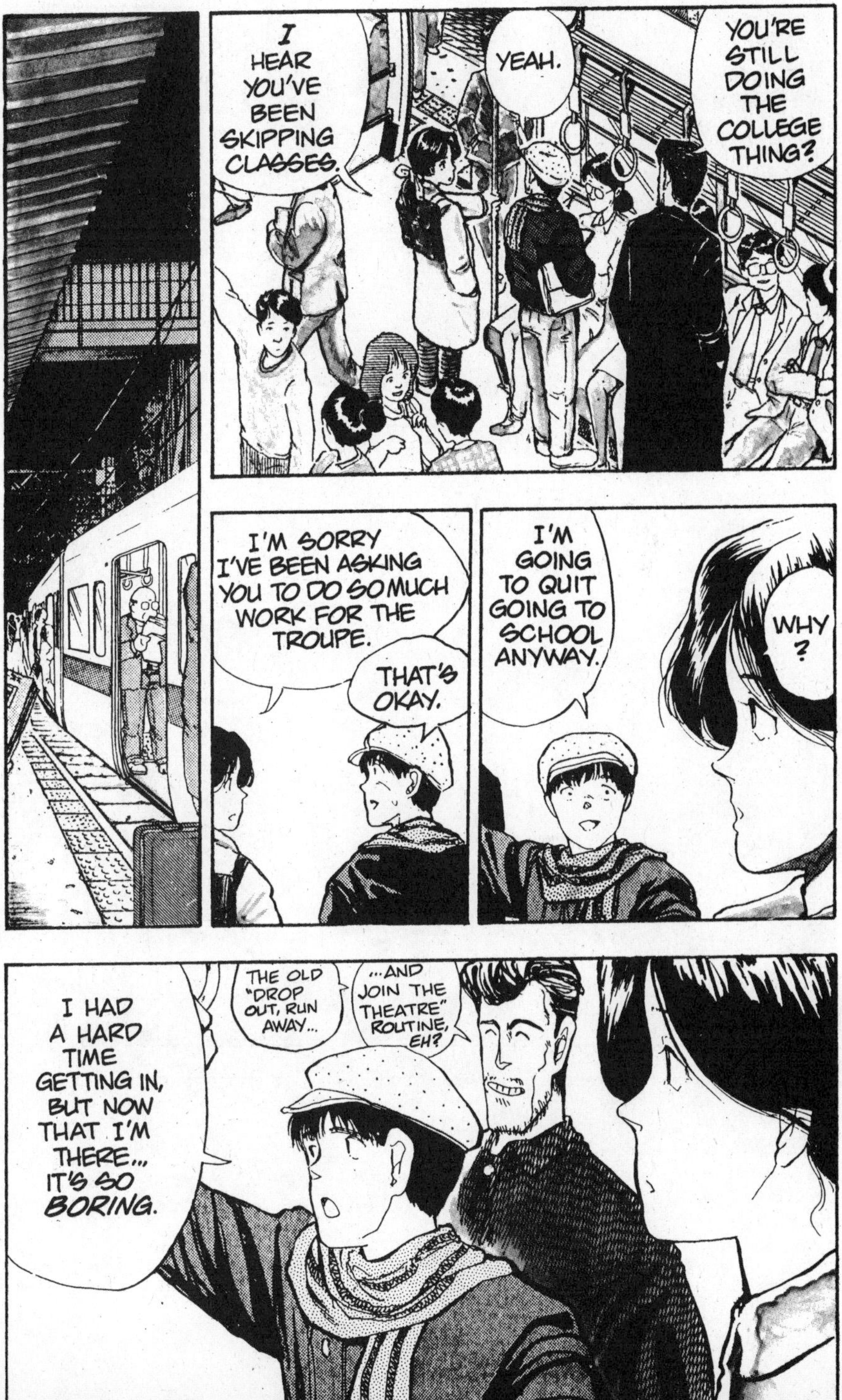
I HEAR YOU'VE BEEN SKIPPING CLASSES.
YEAH.
YOU'RE STILL DOING THE COLLEGE THING?
I'M SORRY I'VE BEEN ASKING YOU TO DO SO MUCH WORK FOR THE TROUPE.
THAT'S OKAY.
I'M GOING TO QUIT GOING TO SCHOOL ANYWAY.
WHY?
I HAD A HARD TIME GETTING IN, BUT NOW THAT I'M THERE... IT'S SO BORING.
THE OLD "DROP OUT, RUN AWAY...
...AND JOIN THE THEATRE" ROUTINE, EH?

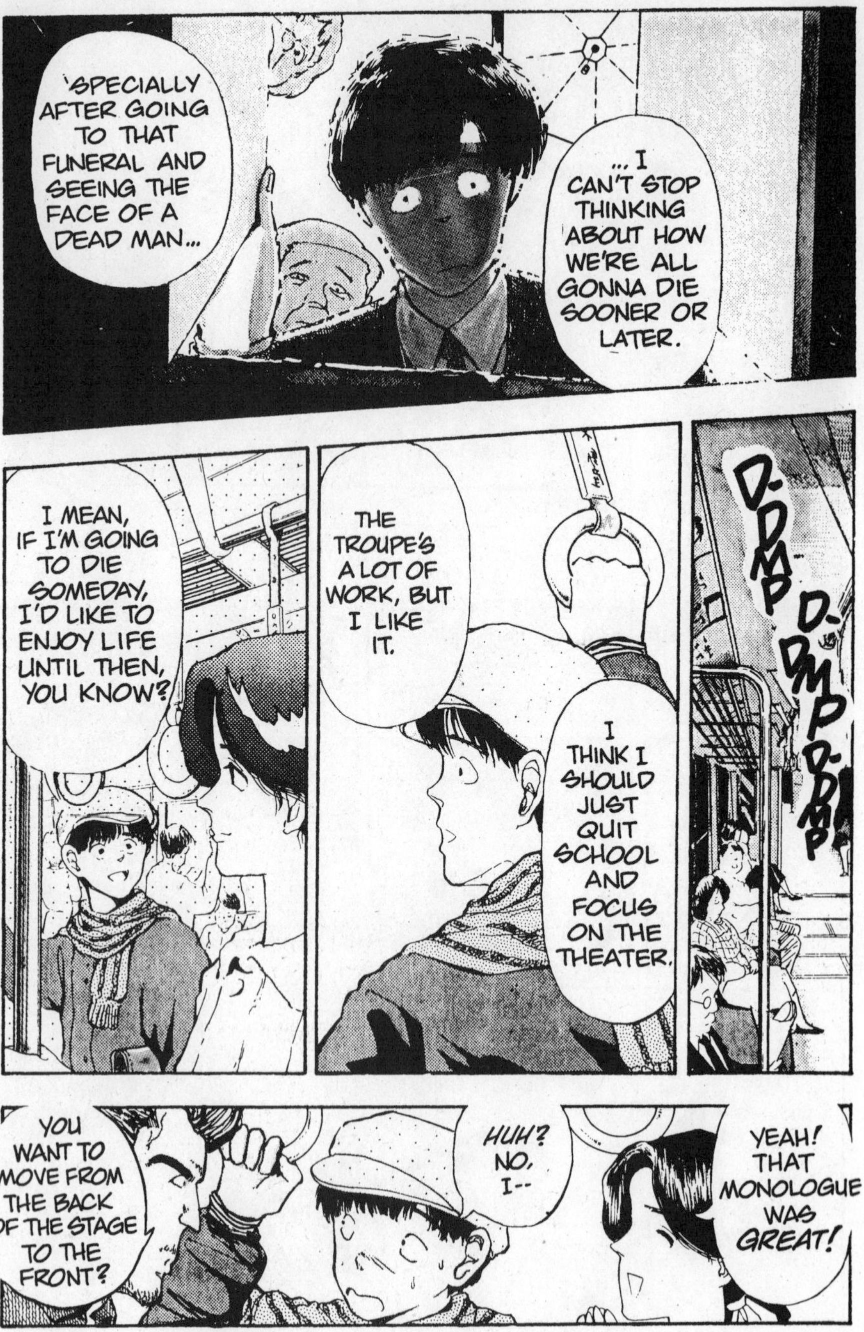
'SPECIALLY AFTER GOING TO THAT FUNERAL AND SEEING THE FACE OF A DEAD MAN...
... I CAN'T STOP THINKING ABOUT HOW WE'RE ALL GONNA DIE SOONER OR LATER.
I MEAN, IF I'M GOING TO DIE SOMEDAY, I'D LIKE TO ENJOY LIFE UNTIL THEN, YOU KNOW?
THE TROUPE'S A LOT OF WORK, BUT I LIKE IT.
I THINK I SHOULD JUST QUIT SCHOOL AND FOCUS ON THE THEATER.
D-DMP D-DMP D-DMP
YOU WANT TO MOVE FROM THE BACK OF THE STAGE TO THE FRONT?
HUH? NO, I--
YEAH! THAT MONOLOGUE WAS GREAT!

FORGET ABOUT COLLEGE.

COLLEGE IS MEAN-INGLESS. IT'S A WASTE OF TIME.

JUST SITTING ON YOUR ASS FOR FOUR YEARS SO YOU CAN GET A JOB. NO DREAMS!

A PLACE LIKE THAT'LL JUST SAP THE LIFE RIGHT OUT OF YOU!

WHAT'S HE GOT AGAINST COLLEGE STUDENTS?

HIS GIRL JUST DUMPED HIM FOR ONE.

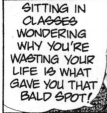

SITTING IN CLASSES WONDERING WHY YOU'RE WASTING YOUR LIFE IS WHAT GAVE YOU THAT BALD SPOT!

HEY!

GIMME MY HAT BACK!

YOU SURE YOU DON'T WANT TO BE AN ACTOR!?

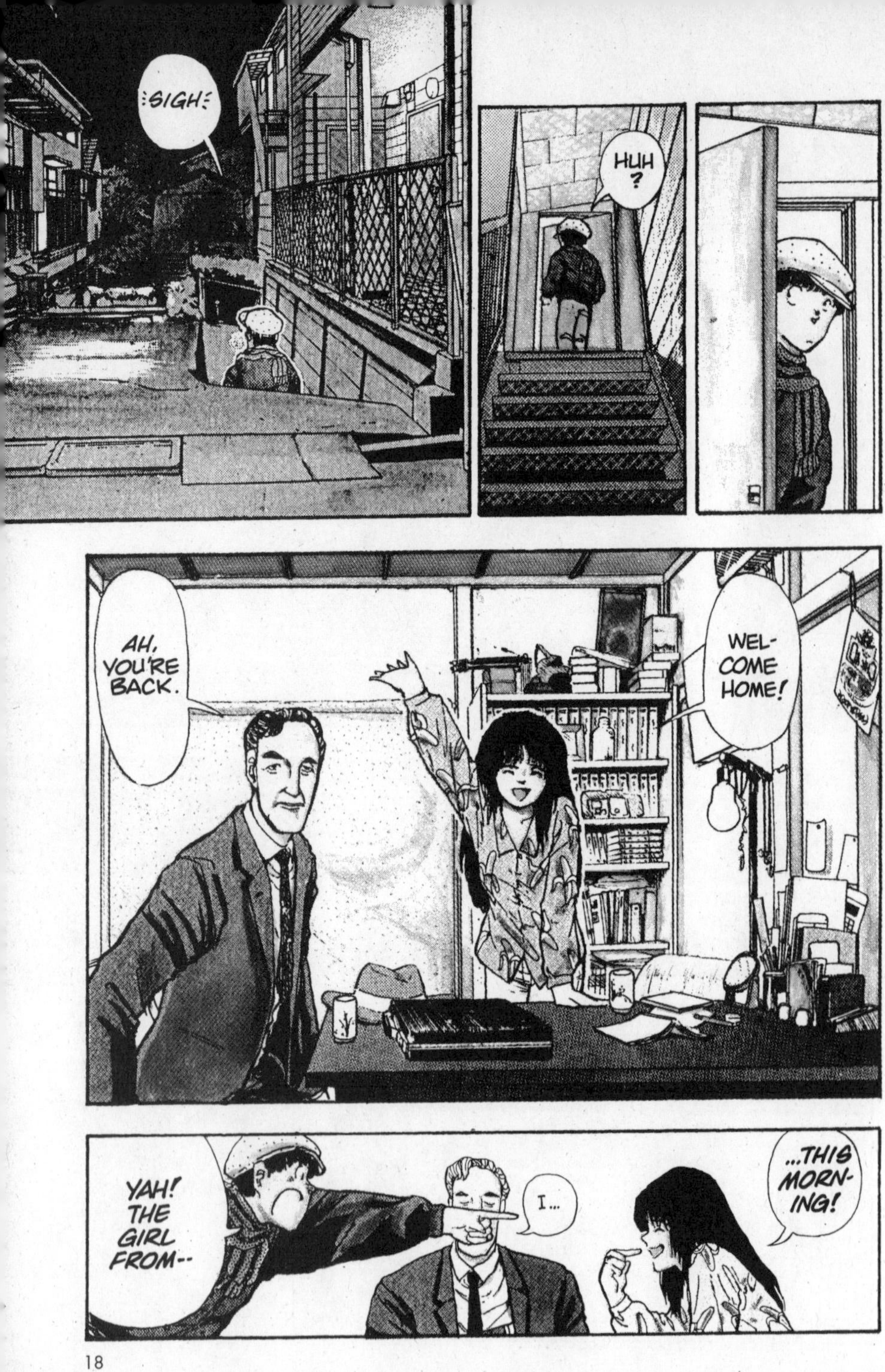
SIGH
HUH?
AH, YOU'RE BACK.
WEL-COME HOME!
YAH! THE GIRL FROM--
I...
...THIS MORN-ING!

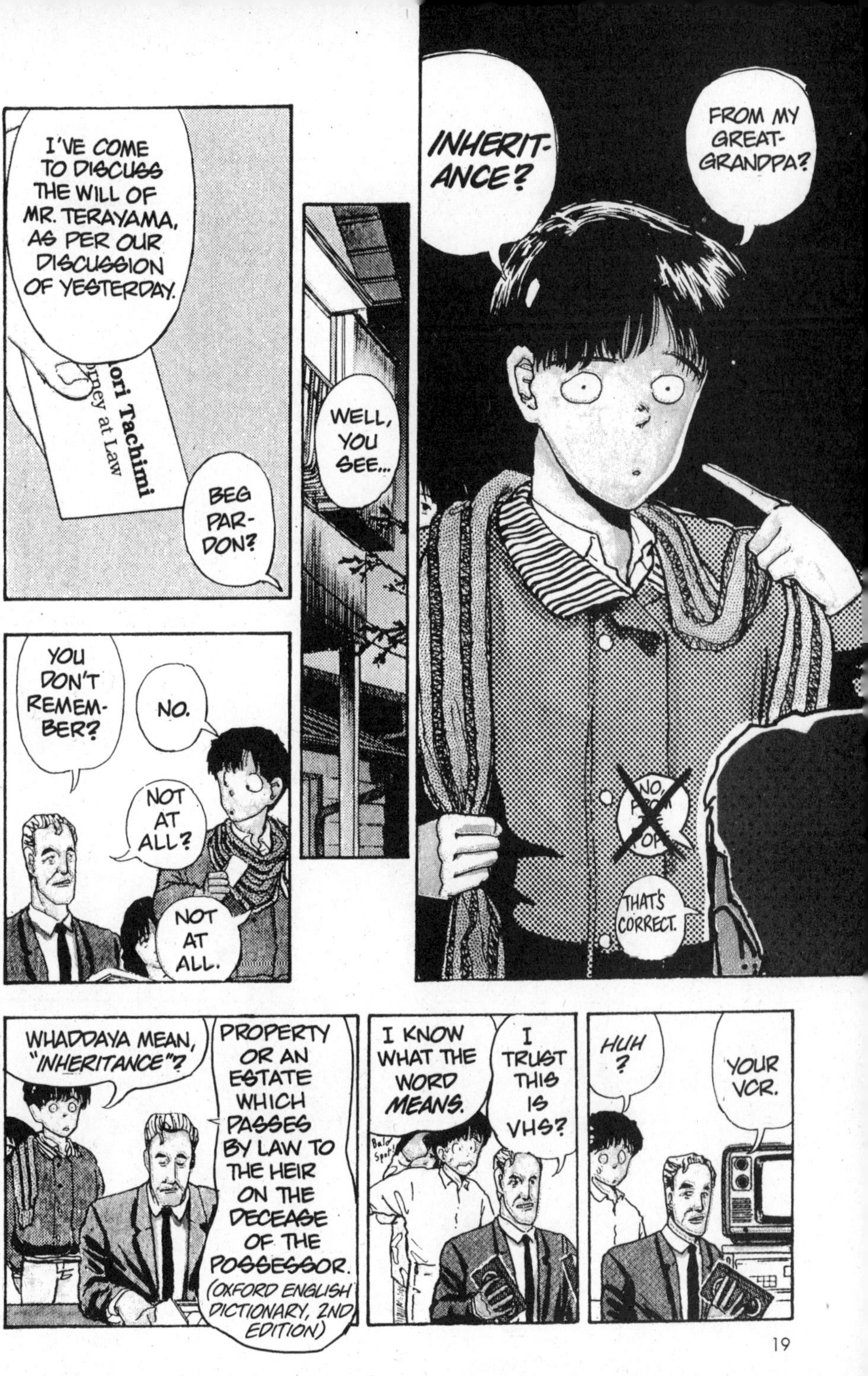

I'VE COME TO DISCUSS THE WILL OF MR. TERAYAMA, AS PER OUR DISCUSSION OF YESTERDAY.
BEG PAR-DON?
YOU DON'T REMEM-BER?
NO.
NOT AT ALL?
NOT AT ALL.
WELL, YOU SEE...
INHERIT-ANCE?
FROM MY GREAT-GRANDPA?
THAT'S CORRECT.
WHADDAYA MEAN, "INHERITANCE"?
PROPERTY OR AN ESTATE WHICH PASSES BY LAW TO THE HEIR ON THE DECEASE OF THE POSSESSOR. (OXFORD ENGLISH DICTIONARY, 2ND EDITION)
I KNOW WHAT THE WORD MEANS.
Bald Spot!
I TRUST THIS IS VHS?
HUH?
YOUR VCR.

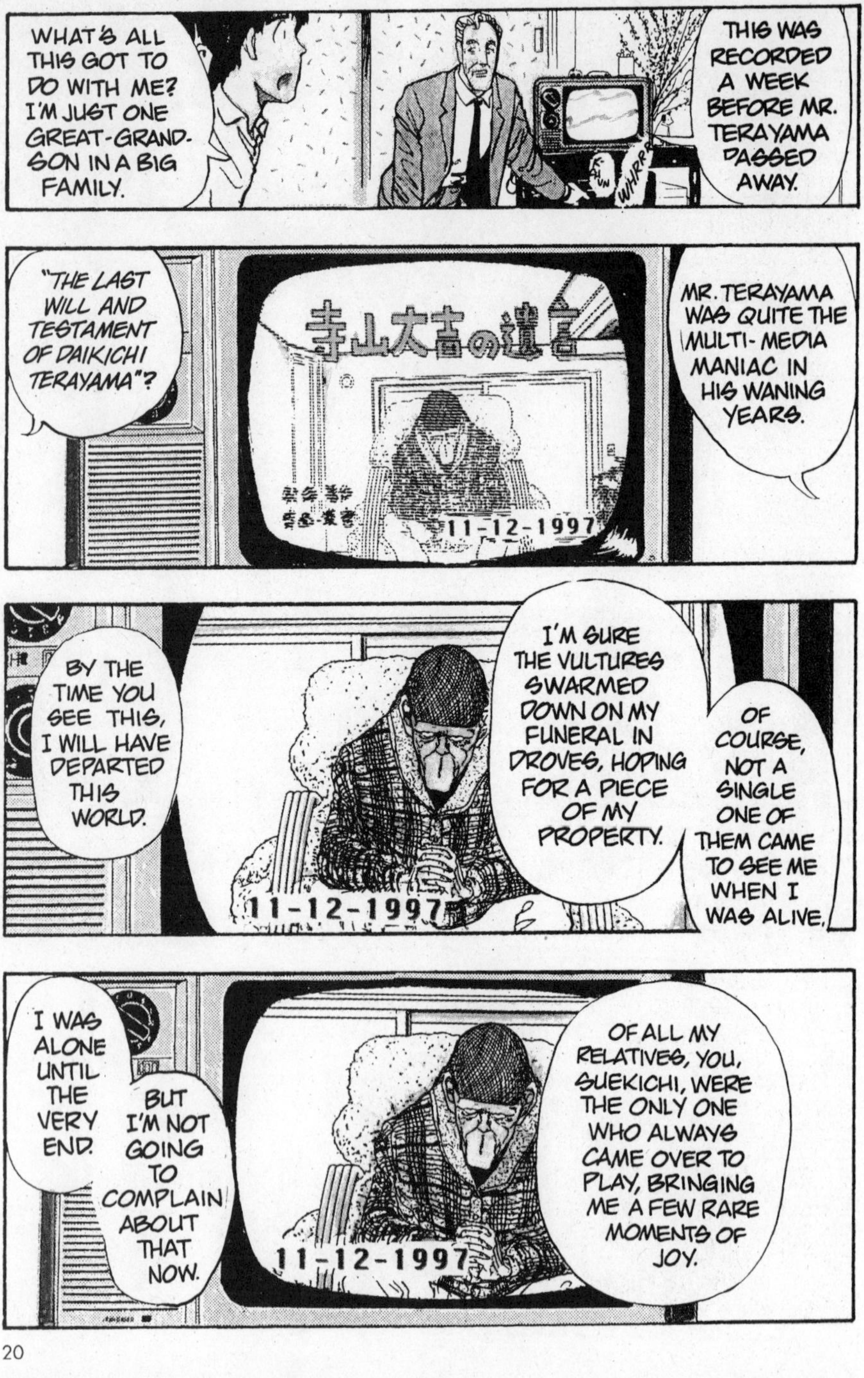
WHAT'S ALL THIS GOT TO DO WITH ME? I'M JUST ONE GREAT-GRANDSON IN A BIG FAMILY.
THIS WAS RECORDED A WEEK BEFORE MR. TERAYAMA PASSED AWAY.
WHRRR
"THE LAST WILL AND TESTAMENT OF DAIKICHI TERAYAMA"?
寺山大吉の遺言
11-12-1997
MR. TERAYAMA WAS QUITE THE MULTI-MEDIA MANIAC IN HIS WANING YEARS.
BY THE TIME YOU SEE THIS, I WILL HAVE DEPARTED THIS WORLD.
I'M SURE THE VULTURES SWARMED DOWN ON MY FUNERAL IN DROVES, HOPING FOR A PIECE OF MY PROPERTY.
OF COURSE, NOT A SINGLE ONE OF THEM CAME TO SEE ME WHEN I WAS ALIVE.
11-12-1997
I WAS ALONE UNTIL THE VERY END.
BUT I'M NOT GOING TO COMPLAIN ABOUT THAT NOW.
11-12-1997
OF ALL MY RELATIVES, YOU, SUEKICHI, WERE THE ONLY ONE WHO ALWAYS CAME OVER TO PLAY, BRINGING ME A FEW RARE MOMENTS OF JOY.

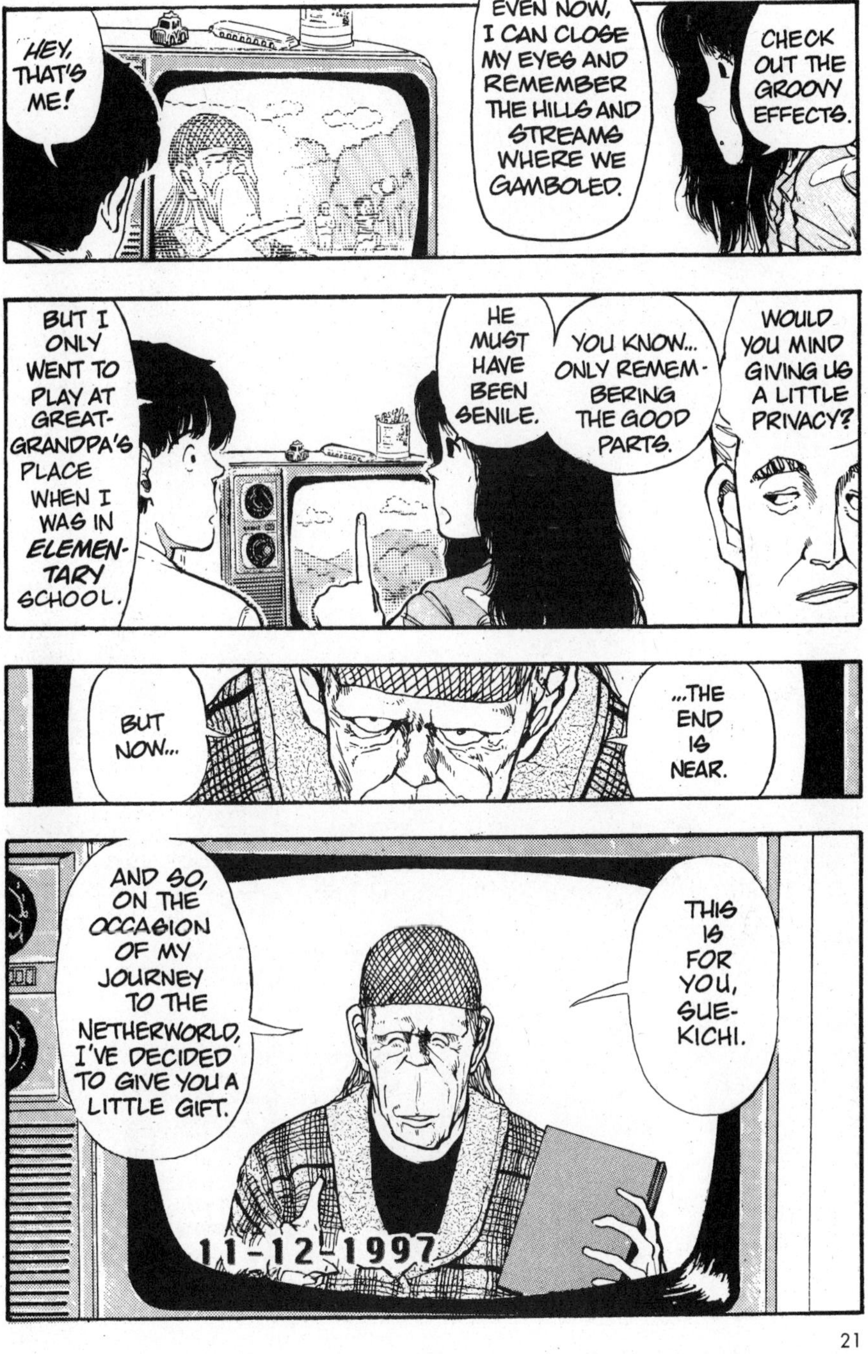
HEY, THAT'S ME!
EVEN NOW, I CAN CLOSE MY EYES AND REMEMBER THE HILLS AND STREAMS WHERE WE GAMBOLED.
CHECK OUT THE GROOVY EFFECTS.
BUT I ONLY WENT TO PLAY AT GREAT-GRANDPA'S PLACE WHEN I WAS IN *ELEMENTARY* SCHOOL.
HE MUST HAVE BEEN SENILE.
YOU KNOW... ONLY REMEMBERING THE GOOD PARTS.
WOULD YOU MIND GIVING US A LITTLE PRIVACY?
BUT NOW...
...THE END IS NEAR.
AND SO, ON THE OCCASION OF MY JOURNEY TO THE NETHERWORLD, I'VE DECIDED TO GIVE YOU A LITTLE GIFT.
THIS IS FOR YOU, SUE-KICHI.
11-12-1997

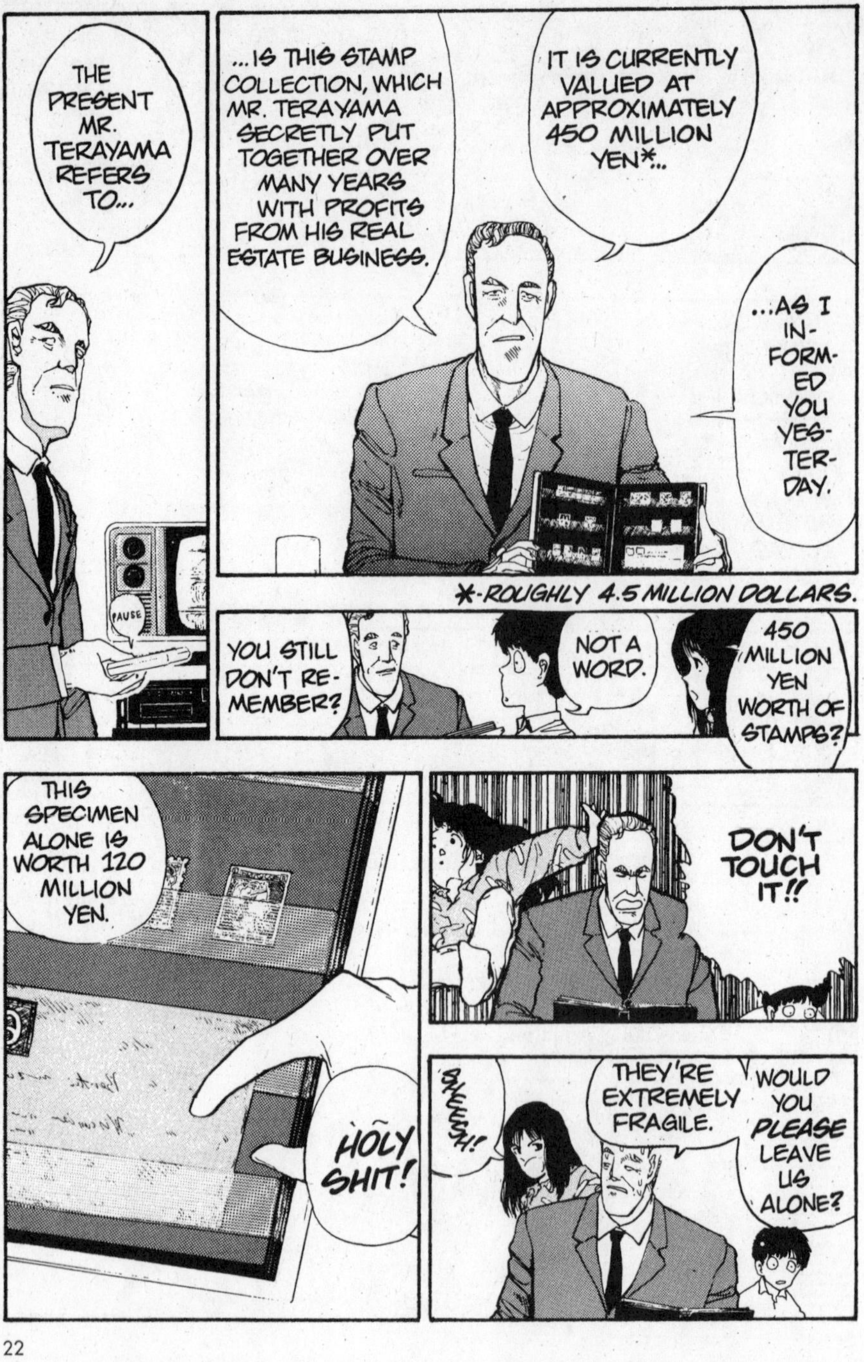
THE PRESENT MR. TERAYAMA REFERS TO...
PAUSE
...IS THIS STAMP COLLECTION, WHICH MR. TERAYAMA SECRETLY PUT TOGETHER OVER MANY YEARS WITH PROFITS FROM HIS REAL ESTATE BUSINESS.
IT IS CURRENTLY VALUED AT APPROXIMATELY 450 MILLION YEN*...
...AS I IN-FORM-ED YOU YES-TER-DAY.
*-ROUGHLY 4.5 MILLION DOLLARS.
YOU STILL DON'T RE-MEMBER?
NOT A WORD.
450 MILLION YEN WORTH OF STAMPS?
THIS SPECIMEN ALONE IS WORTH 120 MILLION YEN.
HOLY SHIT!
DON'T TOUCH IT!!
SHEESH!
THEY'RE EXTREMELY FRAGILE.
WOULD YOU *PLEASE* LEAVE US ALONE?

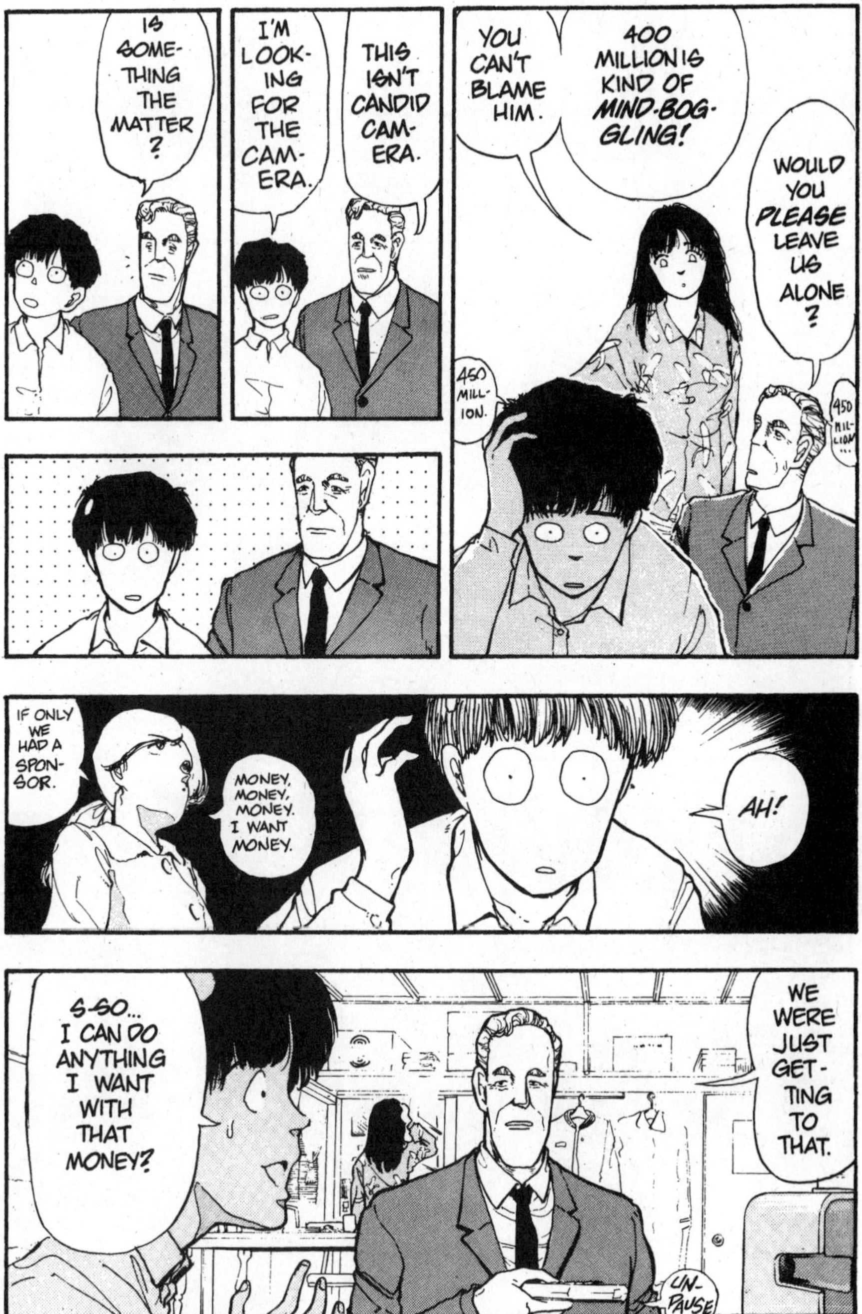
IS SOMETHING THE MATTER?
I'M LOOKING FOR THE CAMERA.
THIS ISN'T CANDID CAMERA.
YOU CAN'T BLAME HIM.
400 MILLION IS KIND OF MIND-BOGGLING!
WOULD YOU PLEASE LEAVE US ALONE?
450 MILLION.
450 MILLION...
IF ONLY WE HAD A SPONSOR.
MONEY, MONEY, MONEY. I WANT MONEY.
AH!
S-SO... I CAN DO ANYTHING I WANT WITH THAT MONEY?
WE WERE JUST GETTING TO THAT.
UN-PAUSE

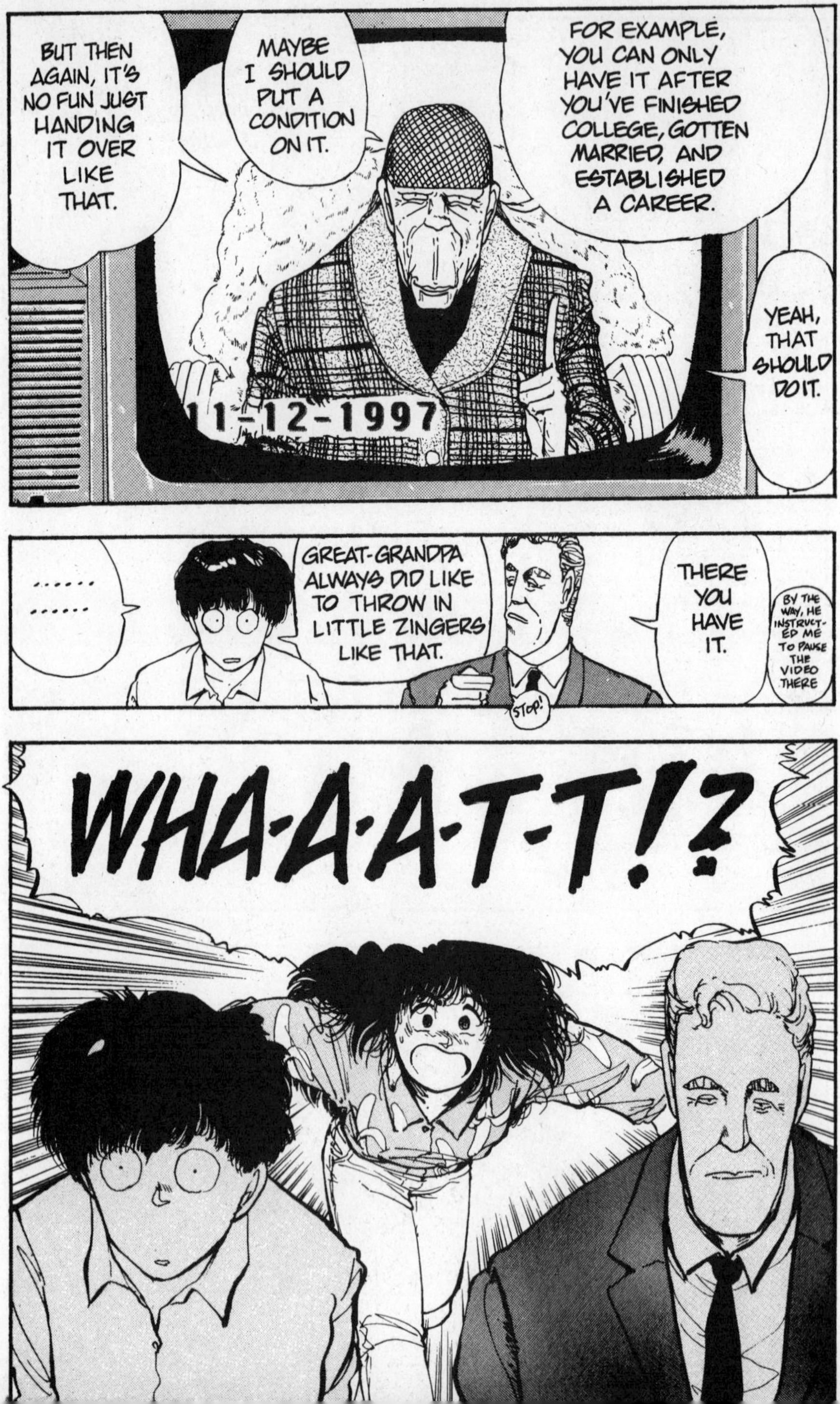

BUT THEN AGAIN, IT'S NO FUN JUST HANDING IT OVER LIKE THAT.
MAYBE I SHOULD PUT A CONDITION ON IT.
FOR EXAMPLE, YOU CAN ONLY HAVE IT AFTER YOU'VE FINISHED COLLEGE, GOTTEN MARRIED, AND ESTABLISHED A CAREER.
11-12-1997
YEAH, THAT SHOULD DO IT.
......
......
GREAT-GRANDPA ALWAYS DID LIKE TO THROW IN LITTLE ZINGERS LIKE THAT.
THERE YOU HAVE IT.
BY THE WAY, HE INSTRUCTED ME TO PAUSE THE VIDEO THERE
STOP!
WHA-A-A-T-T!?

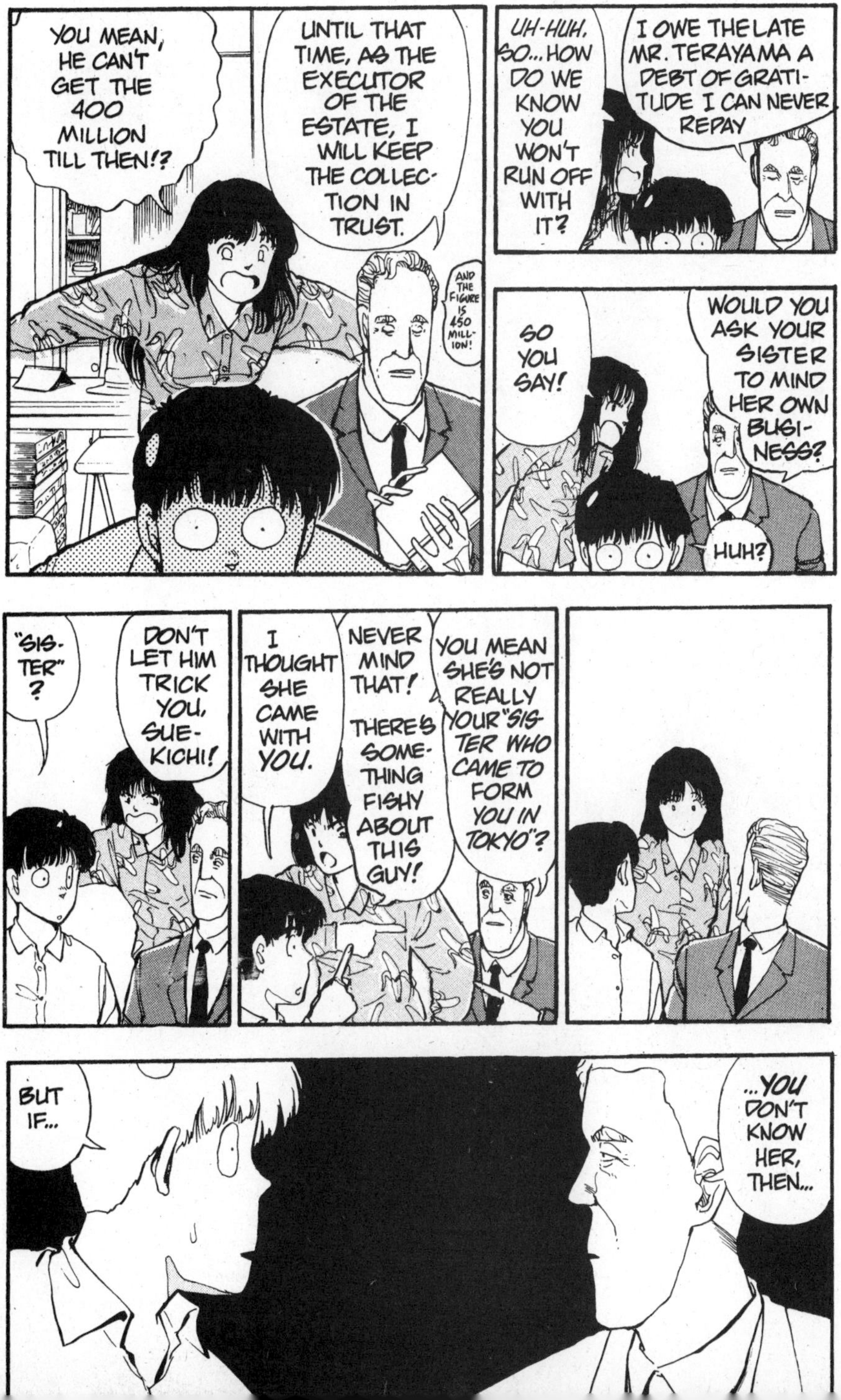
YOU MEAN, HE CAN'T GET THE 400 MILLION TILL THEN!?
UNTIL THAT TIME, AS THE EXECUTOR OF THE ESTATE, I WILL KEEP THE COLLECTION IN TRUST.
AND THE FIGURE IS 450 MILLION!
UH-HUH. SO... HOW DO WE KNOW YOU WON'T RUN OFF WITH IT?
I OWE THE LATE MR. TERAYAMA A DEBT OF GRATITUDE I CAN NEVER REPAY
SO YOU SAY!
WOULD YOU ASK YOUR SISTER TO MIND HER OWN BUSINESS?
HUH?
"SISTER"?
DON'T LET HIM TRICK YOU, SUEKICHI!
I THOUGHT SHE CAME WITH YOU.
NEVER MIND THAT!
THERE'S SOMETHING FISHY ABOUT THIS GUY!
YOU MEAN SHE'S NOT REALLY YOUR "SISTER WHO CAME TO FORM YOU IN TOKYO"?
BUT IF...
...YOU DON'T KNOW HER, THEN...

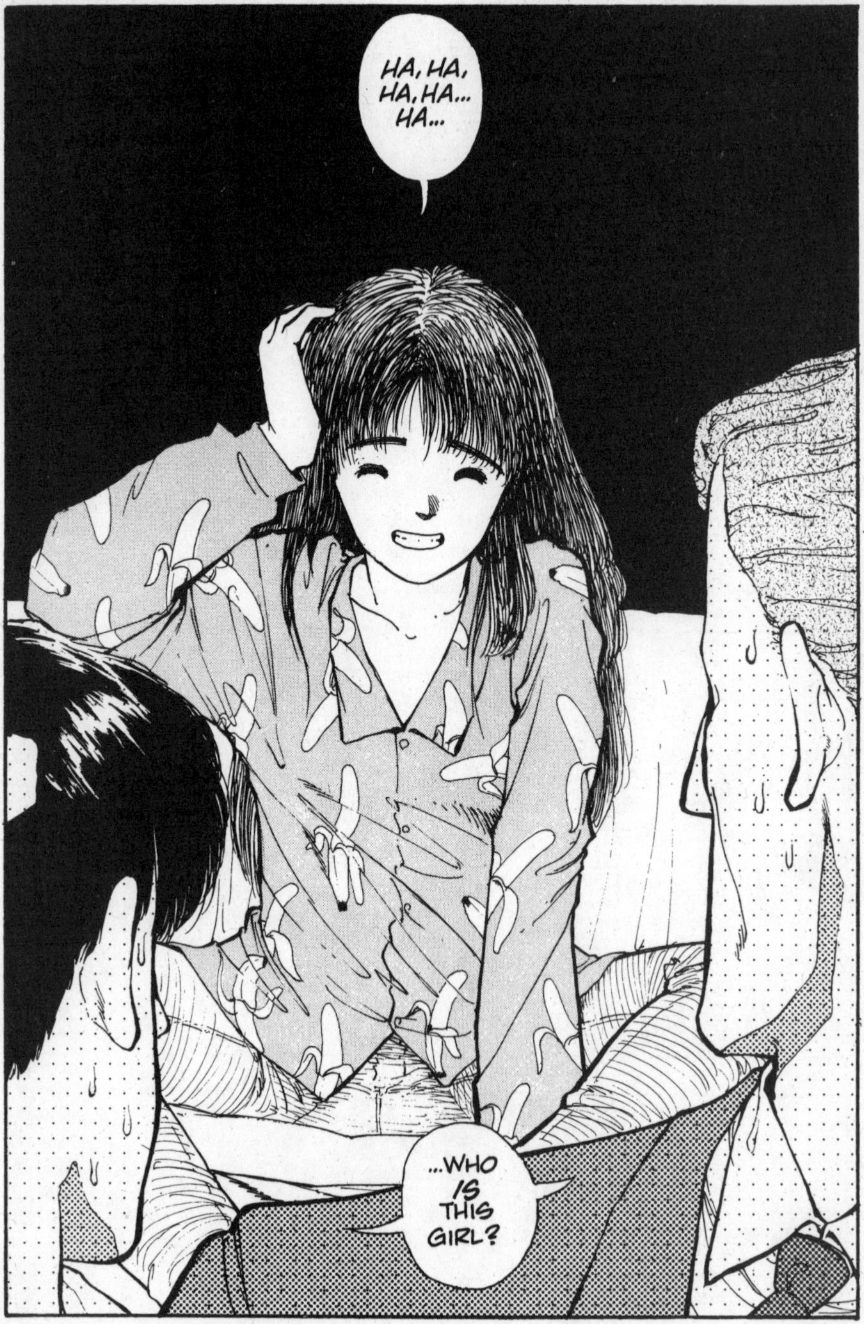
HA, HA, HA, HA... HA...
...WHO IS THIS GIRL?

ACT TWO
THE LUCKIEST MAN IN TOKYO

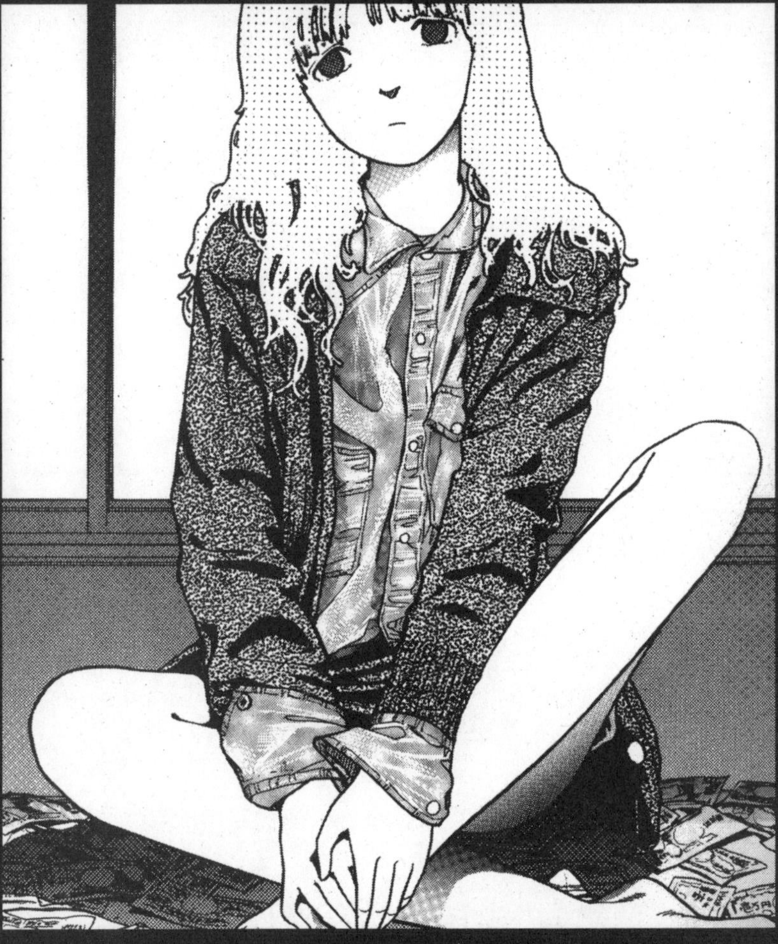

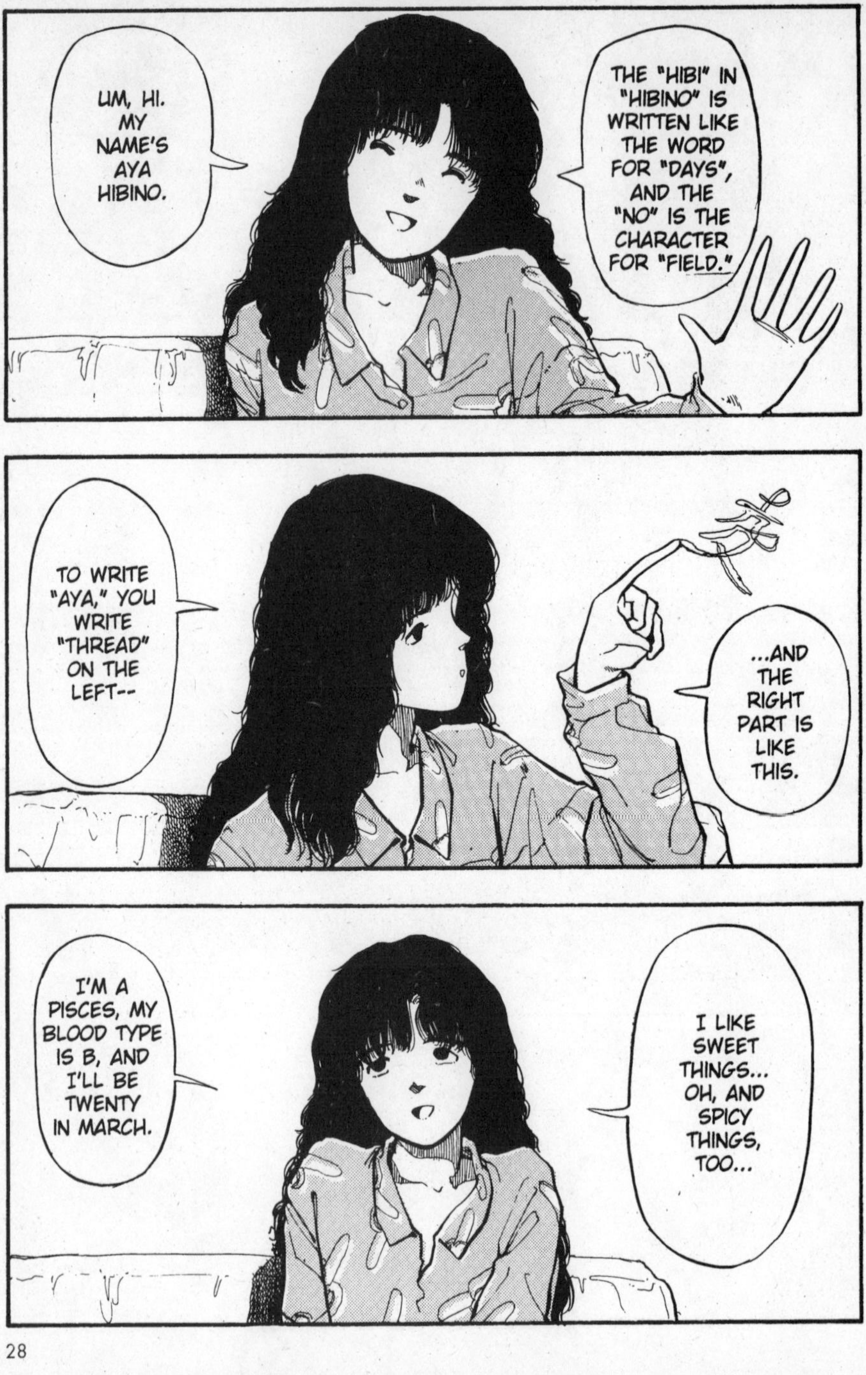
UM, HI. MY NAME'S AYA HIBINO.
THE "HIBI" IN "HIBINO" IS WRITTEN LIKE THE WORD FOR "DAYS", AND THE "NO" IS THE CHARACTER FOR "FIELD."
TO WRITE "AYA," YOU WRITE "THREAD" ON THE LEFT--
...AND THE RIGHT PART IS LIKE THIS.
I'M A PISCES, MY BLOOD TYPE IS B, AND I'LL BE TWENTY IN MARCH.
I LIKE SWEET THINGS... OH, AND SPICY THINGS, TOO...

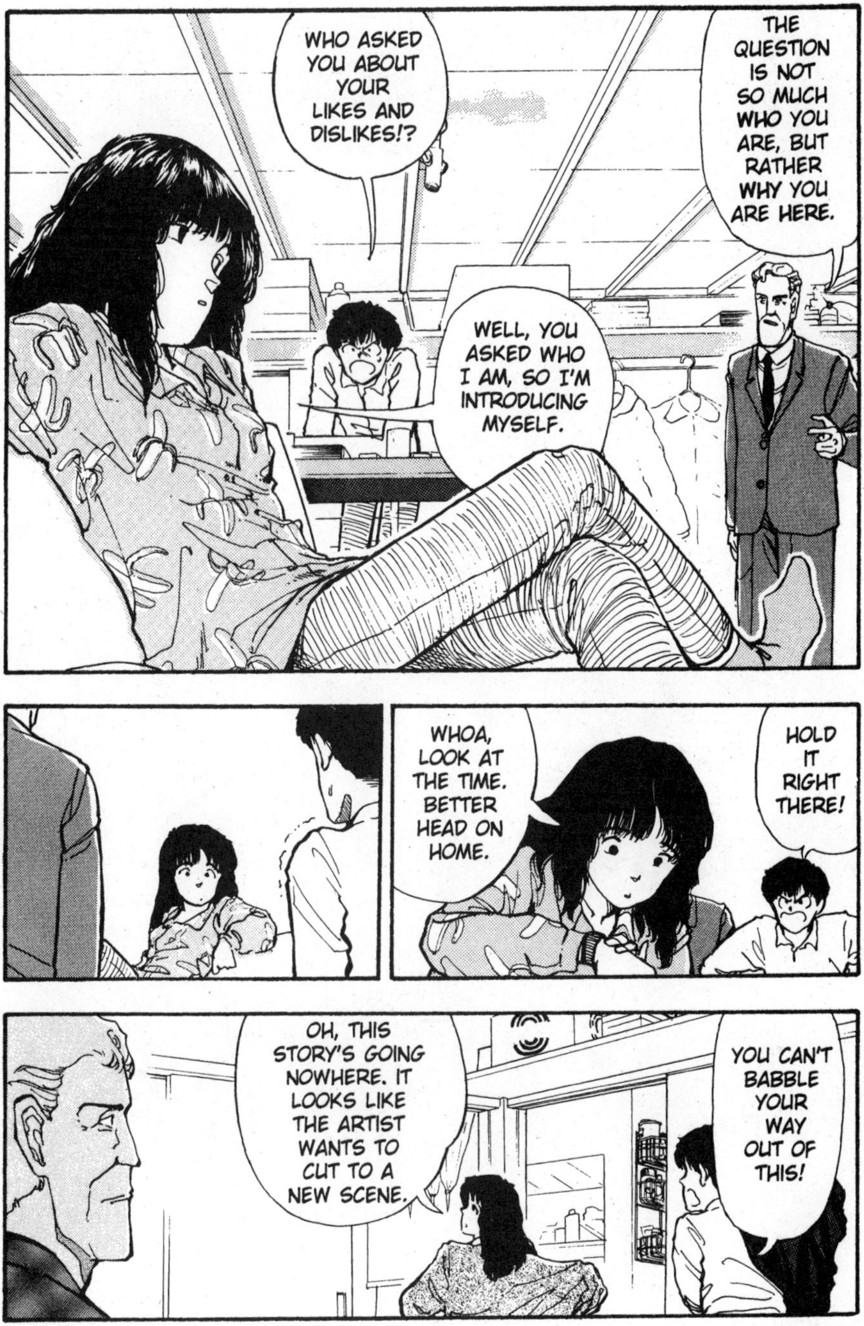
WHO ASKED YOU ABOUT YOUR LIKES AND DISLIKES!?
THE QUESTION IS NOT SO MUCH WHO YOU ARE, BUT RATHER WHY YOU ARE HERE.
WELL, YOU ASKED WHO I AM, SO I'M INTRODUCING MYSELF.
WHOA, LOOK AT THE TIME. BETTER HEAD ON HOME.
HOLD IT RIGHT THERE!
OH, THIS STORY'S GOING NOWHERE. IT LOOKS LIKE THE ARTIST WANTS TO CUT TO A NEW SCENE.
YOU CAN'T BABBLE YOUR WAY OUT OF THIS!

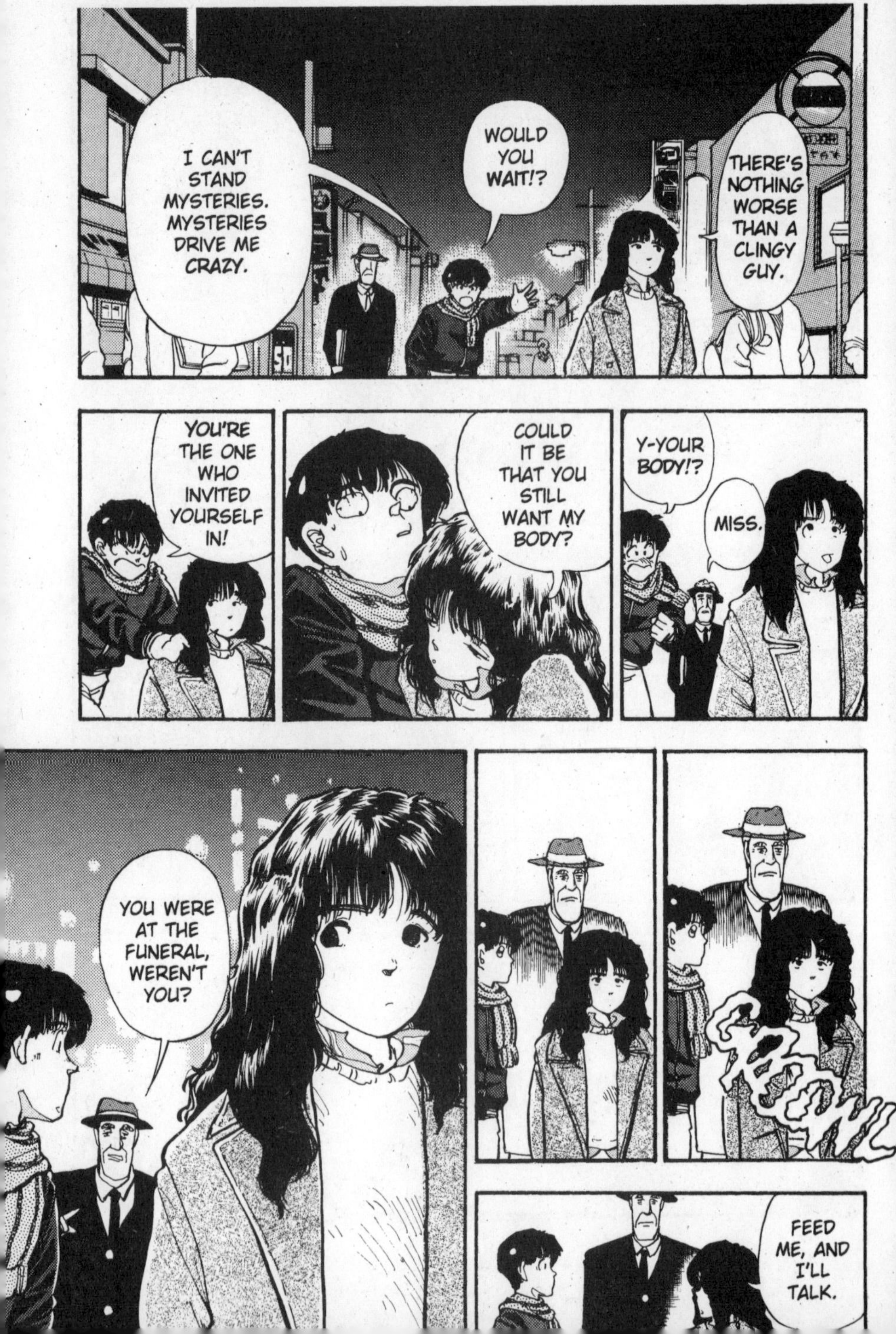
I CAN'T STAND MYSTERIES. MYSTERIES DRIVE ME CRAZY.
WOULD YOU WAIT!?
THERE'S NOTHING WORSE THAN A CLINGY GUY.
YOU'RE THE ONE WHO INVITED YOURSELF IN!
COULD IT BE THAT YOU STILL WANT MY BODY?
Y-YOUR BODY!?
MISS.
YOU WERE AT THE FUNERAL, WEREN'T YOU?
FEED ME, AND I'LL TALK.

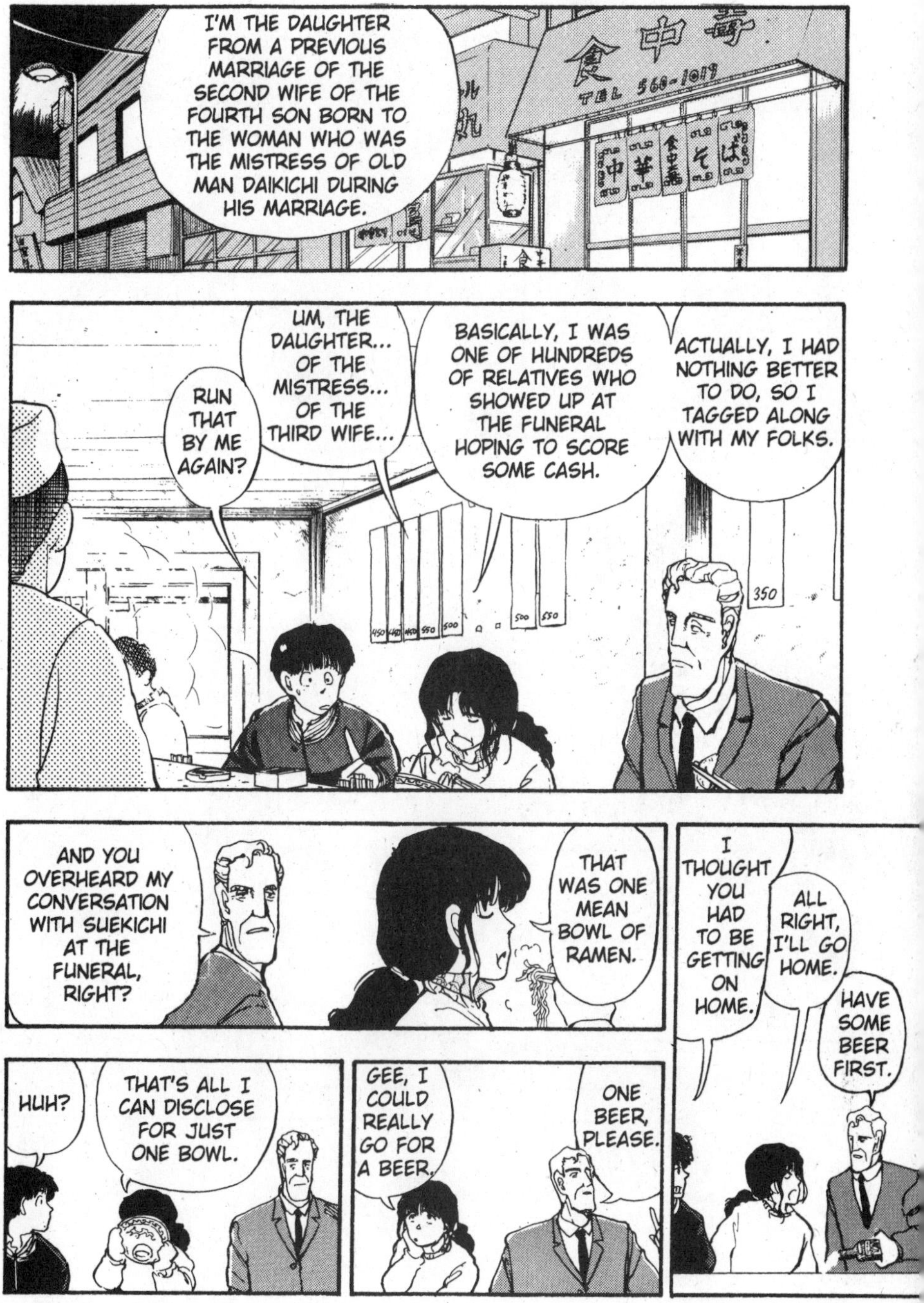
I'M THE DAUGHTER FROM A PREVIOUS MARRIAGE OF THE SECOND WIFE OF THE FOURTH SON BORN TO THE WOMAN WHO WAS THE MISTRESS OF OLD MAN DAIKICHI DURING HIS MARRIAGE.
TEL 560-1019
RUN THAT BY ME AGAIN?
UM, THE DAUGHTER... OF THE MISTRESS... OF THE THIRD WIFE...
BASICALLY, I WAS ONE OF HUNDREDS OF RELATIVES WHO SHOWED UP AT THE FUNERAL HOPING TO SCORE SOME CASH.
ACTUALLY, I HAD NOTHING BETTER TO DO, SO I TAGGED ALONG WITH MY FOLKS.
AND YOU OVERHEARD MY CONVERSATION WITH SUEKICHI AT THE FUNERAL, RIGHT?
THAT WAS ONE MEAN BOWL OF RAMEN.
HUH?
THAT'S ALL I CAN DISCLOSE FOR JUST ONE BOWL.
GEE, I COULD REALLY GO FOR A BEER.
ONE BEER, PLEASE.
I THOUGHT YOU HAD TO BE GETTING ON HOME.
ALL RIGHT, I'LL GO HOME.
HAVE SOME BEER FIRST.

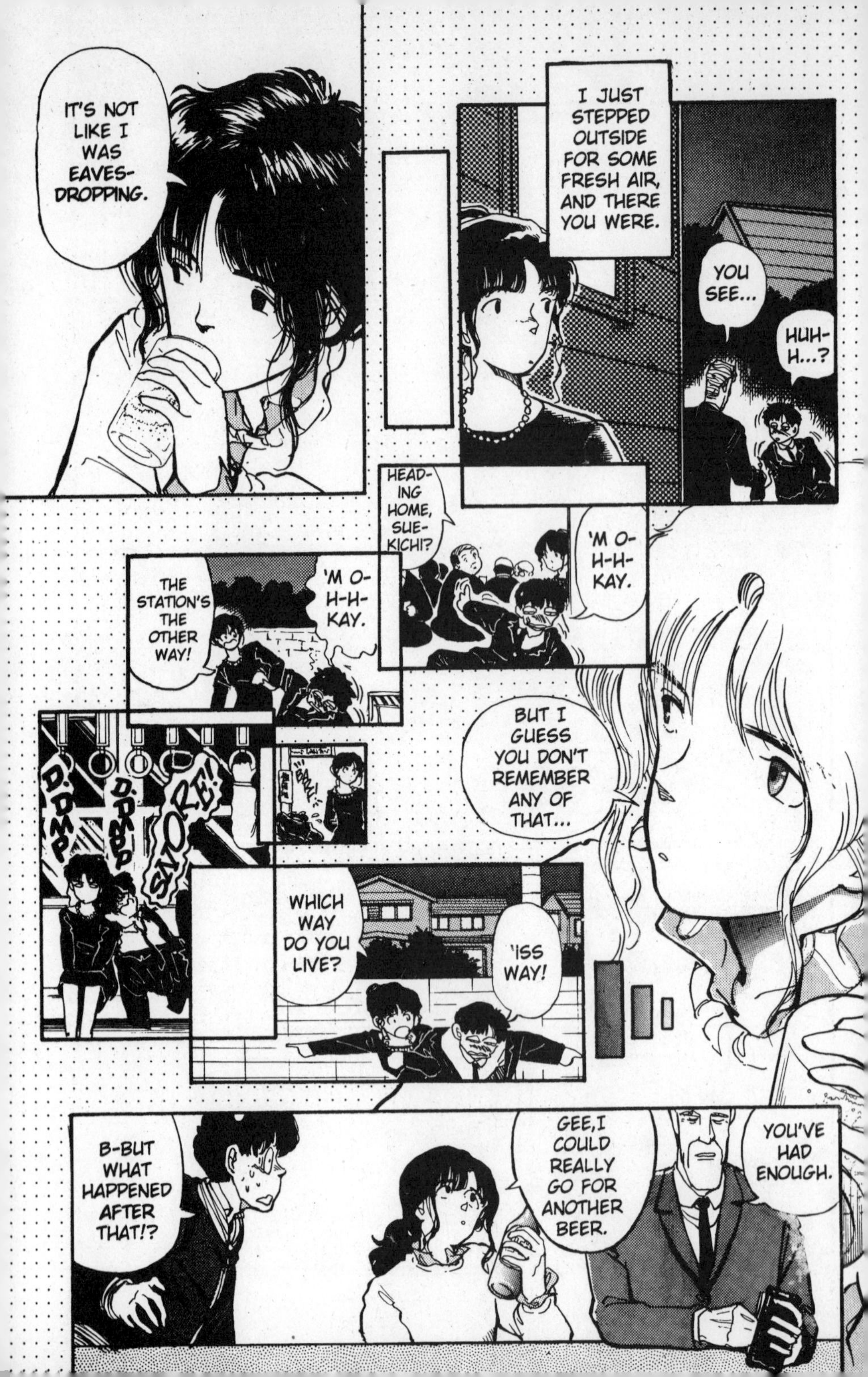
IT'S NOT LIKE I WAS EAVES-DROPPING.
I JUST STEPPED OUTSIDE FOR SOME FRESH AIR, AND THERE YOU WERE.
YOU SEE...
HUH-H...?
HEAD-ING HOME, SUE-KICHI?
'M O-H-H-KAY.
THE STATION'S THE OTHER WAY!
'M O-H-H-KAY.
D-DMP
D-DMP
SNORE!
BUT I GUESS YOU DON'T REMEMBER ANY OF THAT...
WHICH WAY DO YOU LIVE?
'ISS WAY!
B-BUT WHAT HAPPENED AFTER THAT!?
GEE, I COULD REALLY GO FOR ANOTHER BEER.
YOU'VE HAD ENOUGH.

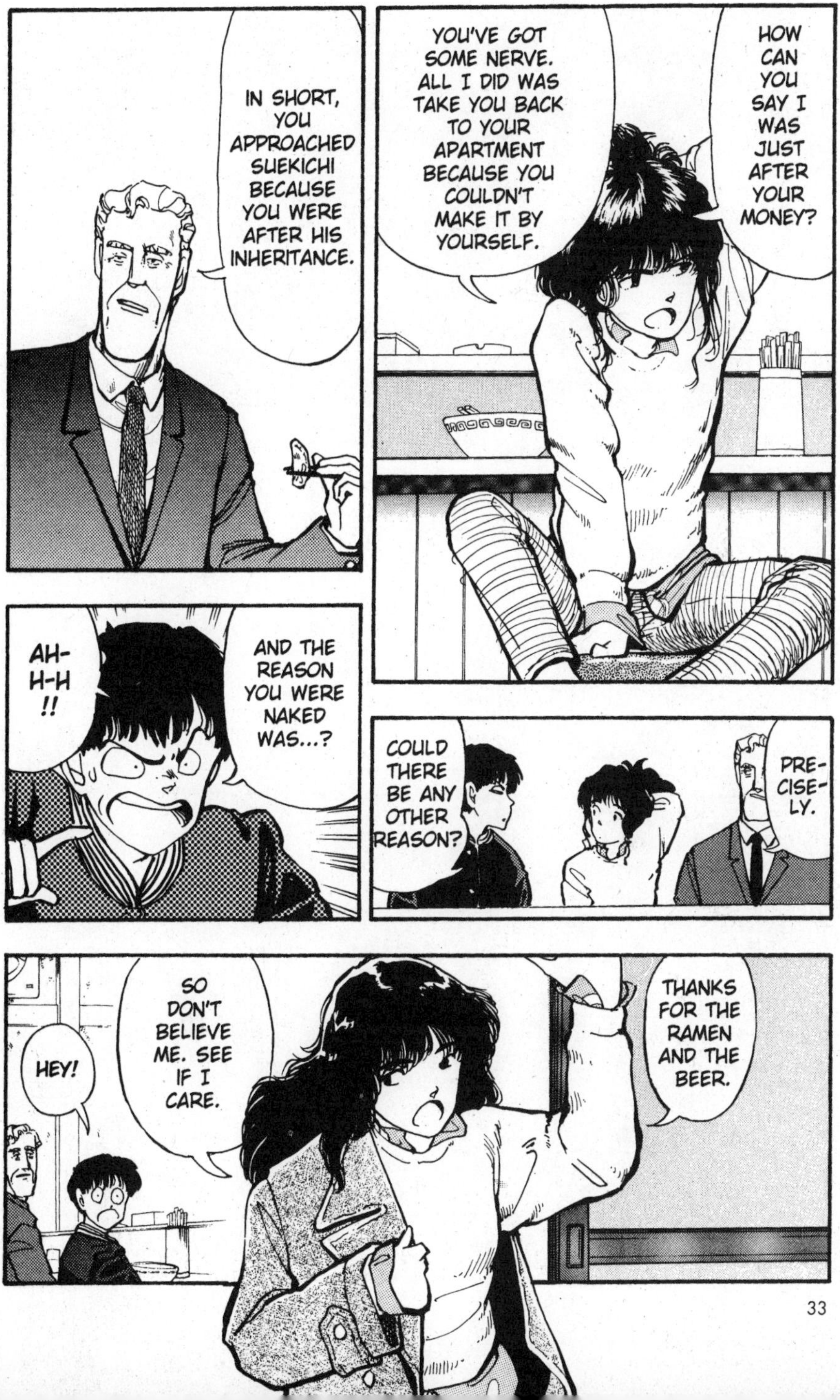
IN SHORT, YOU APPROACHED SUEKICHI BECAUSE YOU WERE AFTER HIS INHERITANCE.
YOU'VE GOT SOME NERVE. ALL I DID WAS TAKE YOU BACK TO YOUR APARTMENT BECAUSE YOU COULDN'T MAKE IT BY YOURSELF.
HOW CAN YOU SAY I WAS JUST AFTER YOUR MONEY?
AH-H-H !!
AND THE REASON YOU WERE NAKED WAS...?
COULD THERE BE ANY OTHER REASON?
PRE-CISE-LY.
HEY!
SO DON'T BELIEVE ME. SEE IF I CARE.
THANKS FOR THE RAMEN AND THE BEER.

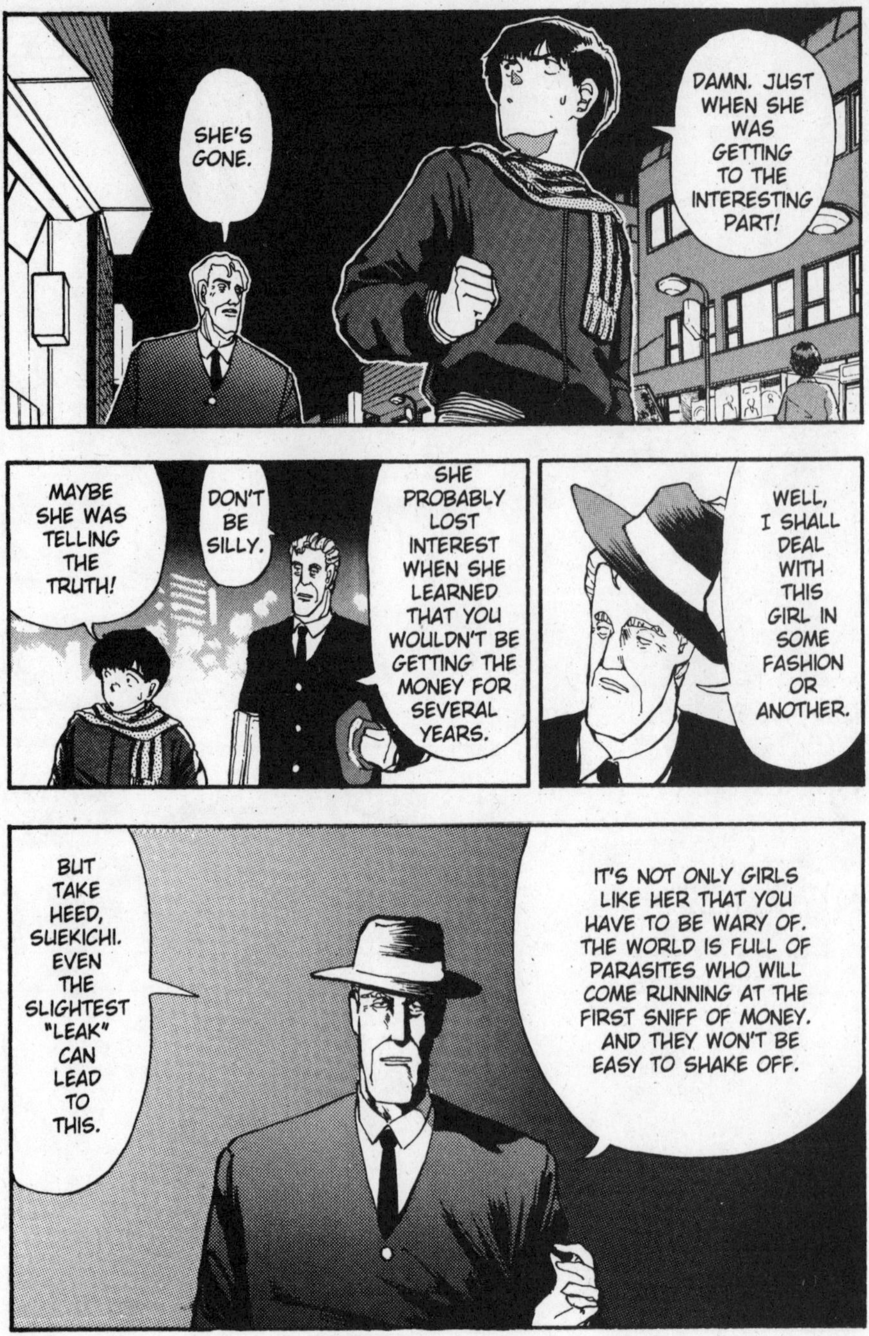

SHE'S GONE.
DAMN. JUST WHEN SHE WAS GETTING TO THE INTERESTING PART!
MAYBE SHE WAS TELLING THE TRUTH!
DON'T BE SILLY.
SHE PROBABLY LOST INTEREST WHEN SHE LEARNED THAT YOU WOULDN'T BE GETTING THE MONEY FOR SEVERAL YEARS.
WELL, I SHALL DEAL WITH THIS GIRL IN SOME FASHION OR ANOTHER.
BUT TAKE HEED, SUEKICHI. EVEN THE SLIGHTEST "LEAK" CAN LEAD TO THIS.
IT'S NOT ONLY GIRLS LIKE HER THAT YOU HAVE TO BE WARY OF. THE WORLD IS FULL OF PARASITES WHO WILL COME RUNNING AT THE FIRST SNIFF OF MONEY. AND THEY WON'T BE EASY TO SHAKE OFF.

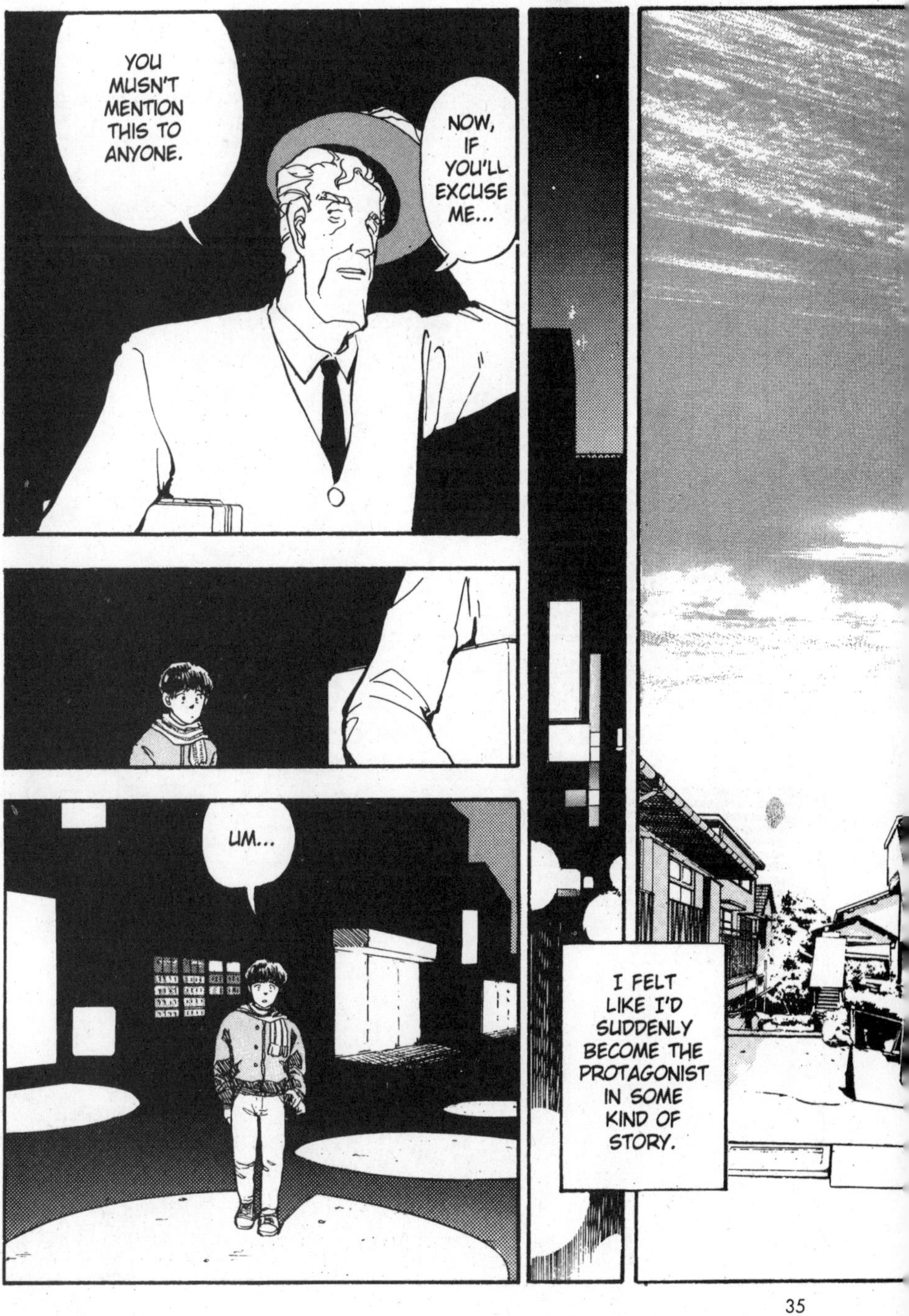
YOU MUSN'T MENTION THIS TO ANYONE.
NOW, IF YOU'LL EXCUSE ME...
UM...
I FELT LIKE I'D SUDDENLY BECOME THE PROTAGONIST IN SOME KIND OF STORY.

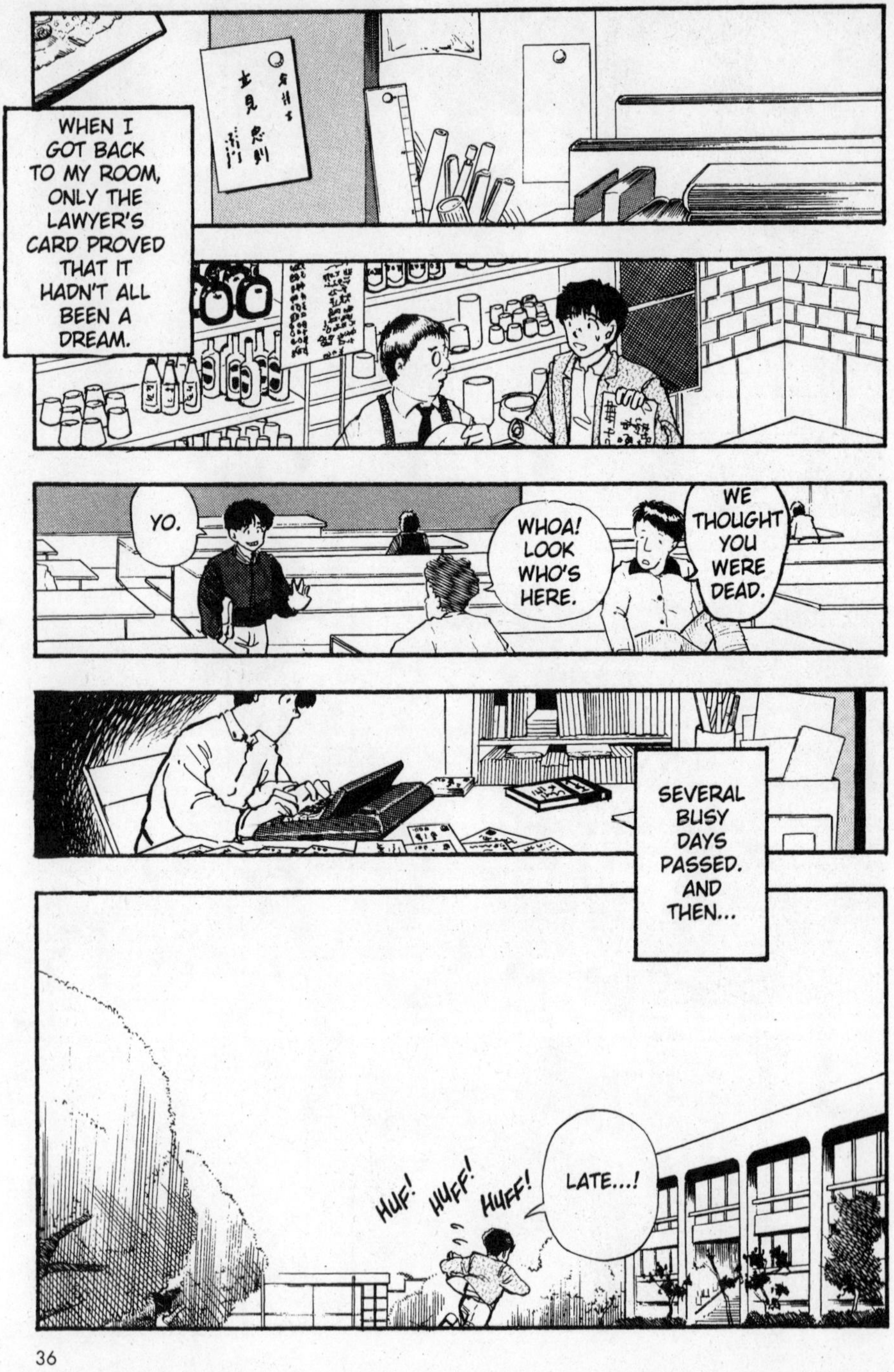
WHEN I GOT BACK TO MY ROOM, ONLY THE LAWYER'S CARD PROVED THAT IT HADN'T ALL BEEN A DREAM.
YO.
WHOA! LOOK WHO'S HERE.
WE THOUGHT YOU WERE DEAD.
SEVERAL BUSY DAYS PASSED. AND THEN...
HUF! HUFF! HUFF!
LATE...!

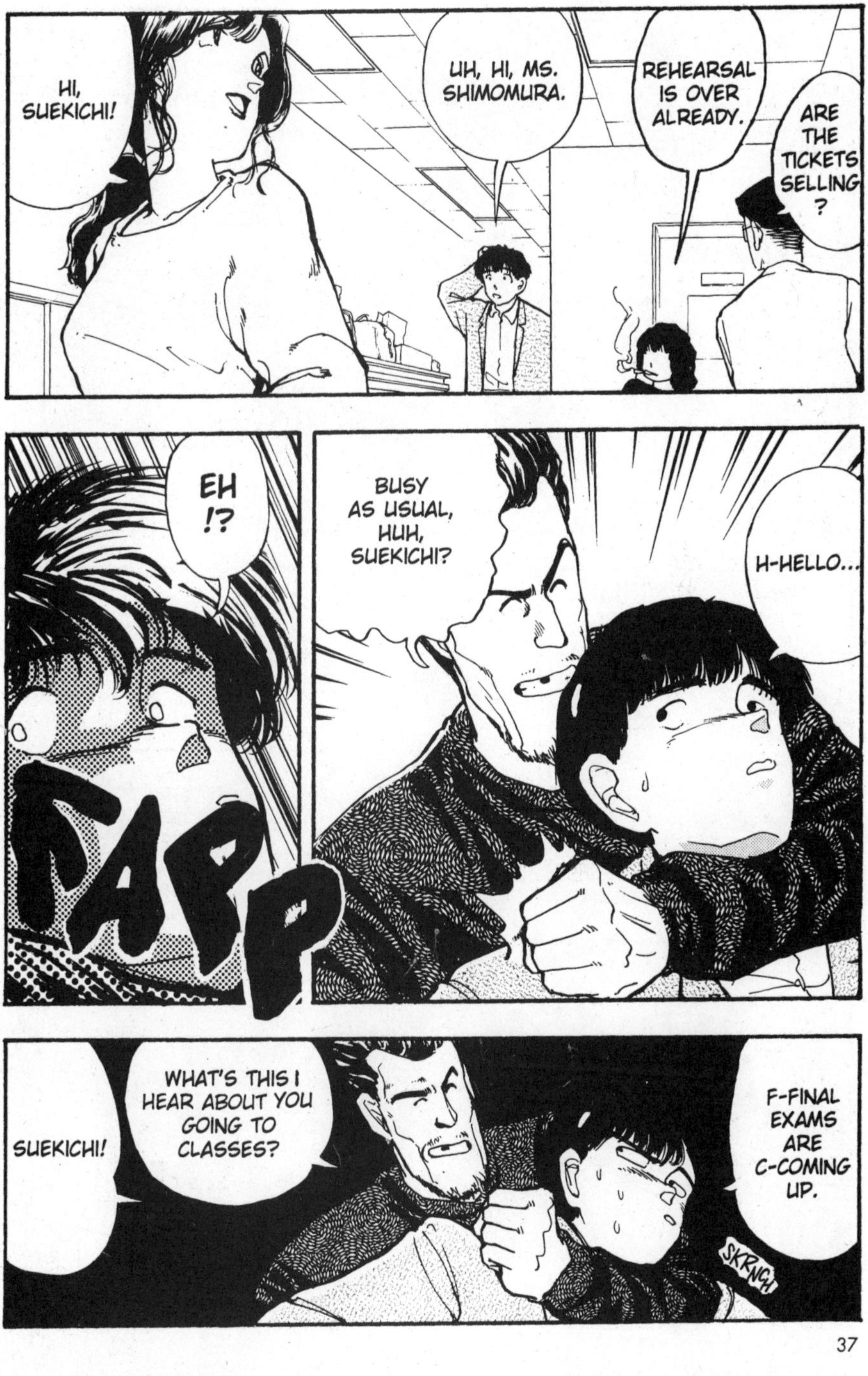
HI, SUEKICHI!
UH, HI, MS. SHIMOMURA.
REHEARSAL IS OVER ALREADY.
ARE THE TICKETS SELLING ?
EH !?
TAPP
BUSY AS USUAL, HUH, SUEKICHI?
H-HELLO...
SUEKICHI!
WHAT'S THIS I HEAR ABOUT YOU GOING TO CLASSES?
F-FINAL EXAMS ARE C-COMING UP.
SKRNCH

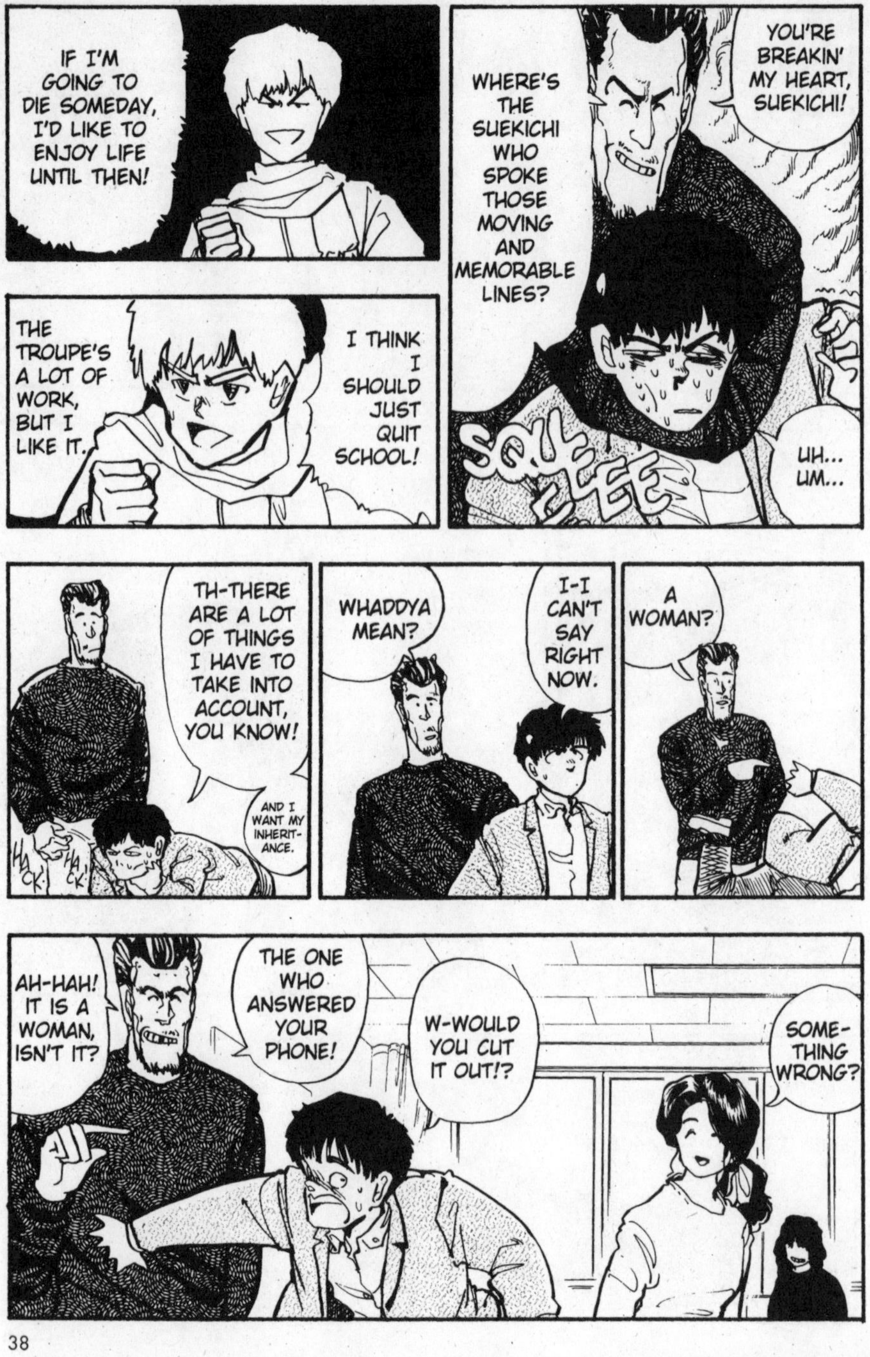
IF I'M GOING TO DIE SOMEDAY, I'D LIKE TO ENJOY LIFE UNTIL THEN!
THE TROUPE'S A LOT OF WORK, BUT I LIKE IT.
I THINK I SHOULD JUST QUIT SCHOOL!
WHERE'S THE SUEKICHI WHO SPOKE THOSE MOVING AND MEMORABLE LINES?
YOU'RE BREAKIN' MY HEART, SUEKICHI!
UH... UM...
TH-THERE ARE A LOT OF THINGS I HAVE TO TAKE INTO ACCOUNT, YOU KNOW!
AND I WANT MY INHERITANCE.
HACK HACK
WHADDYA MEAN?
I-I CAN'T SAY RIGHT NOW.
A WOMAN?
AH-HAH! IT IS A WOMAN, ISN'T IT?
THE ONE WHO ANSWERED YOUR PHONE!
W-WOULD YOU CUT IT OUT!?
SOME-THING WRONG?

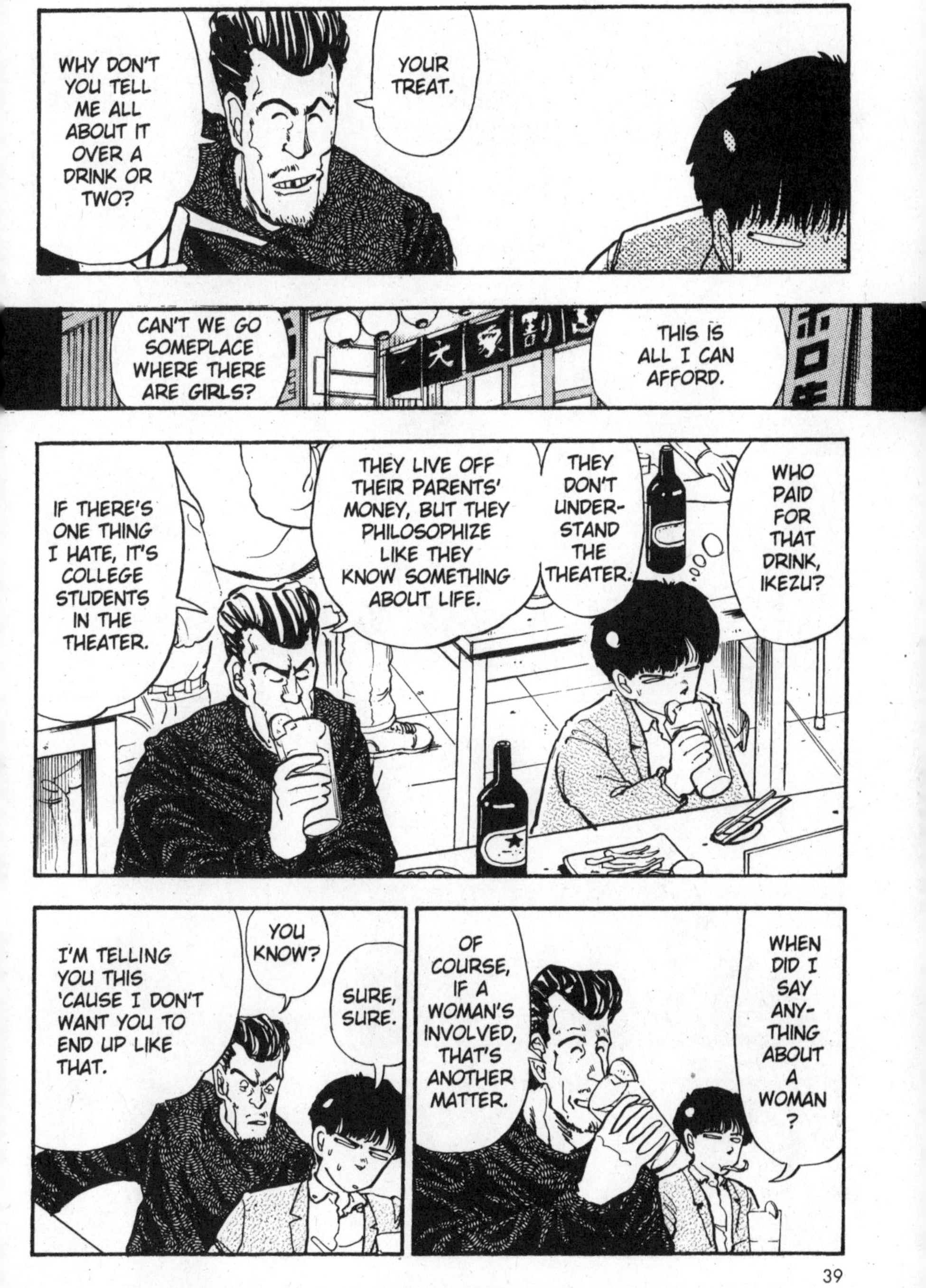
WHY DON'T YOU TELL ME ALL ABOUT IT OVER A DRINK OR TWO?
YOUR TREAT.
CAN'T WE GO SOMEPLACE WHERE THERE ARE GIRLS?
THIS IS ALL I CAN AFFORD.
IF THERE'S ONE THING I HATE, IT'S COLLEGE STUDENTS IN THE THEATER.
THEY LIVE OFF THEIR PARENTS' MONEY, BUT THEY PHILOSOPHIZE LIKE THEY KNOW SOMETHING ABOUT LIFE.
THEY DON'T UNDER-STAND THE THEATER.
WHO PAID FOR THAT DRINK, IKEZU?
I'M TELLING YOU THIS 'CAUSE I DON'T WANT YOU TO END UP LIKE THAT.
YOU KNOW?
SURE, SURE.
OF COURSE, IF A WOMAN'S INVOLVED, THAT'S ANOTHER MATTER.
WHEN DID I SAY ANY-THING ABOUT A WOMAN?

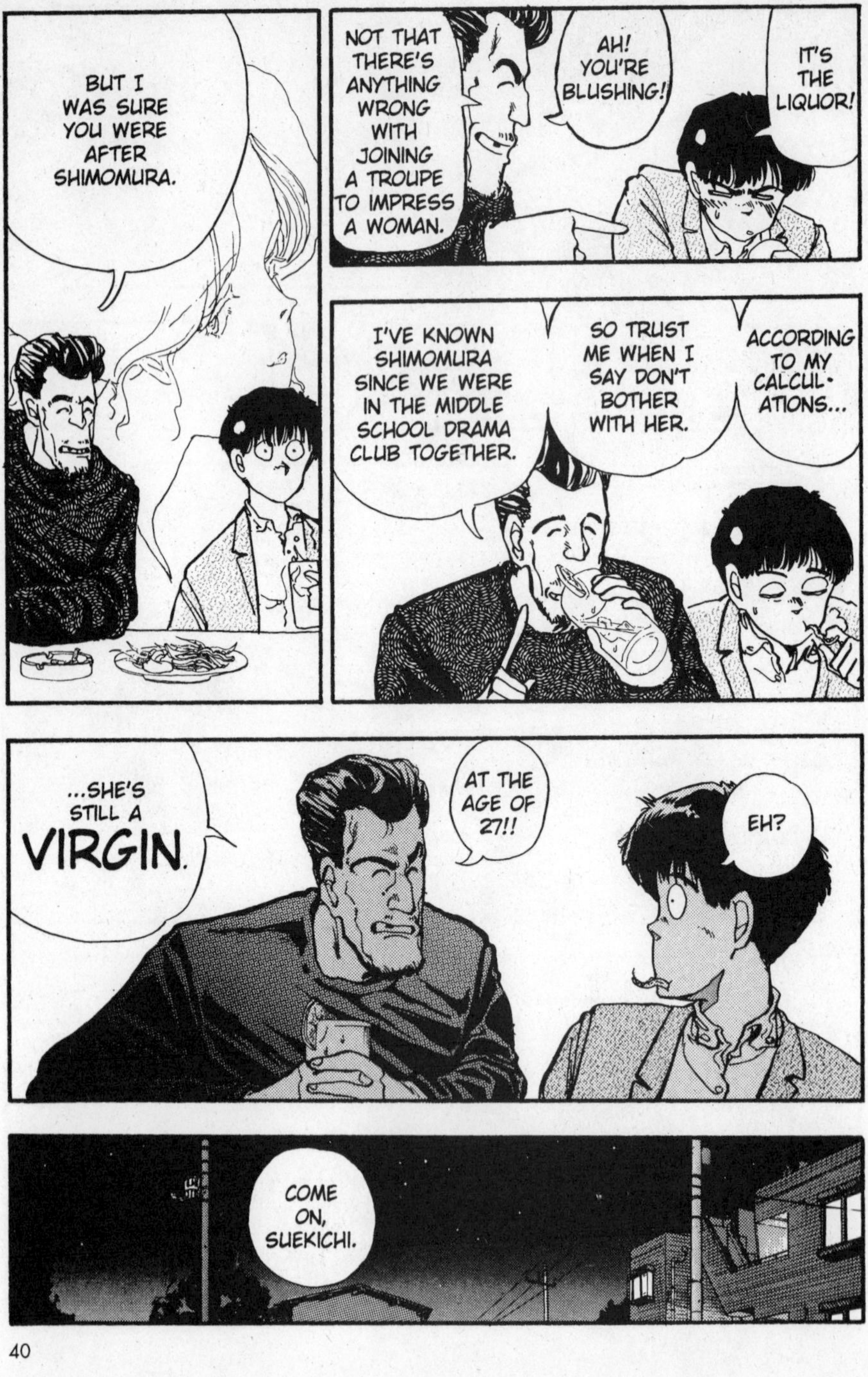
BUT I WAS SURE YOU WERE AFTER SHIMOMURA.
NOT THAT THERE'S ANYTHING WRONG WITH JOINING A TROUPE TO IMPRESS A WOMAN.
AH! YOU'RE BLUSHING!
IT'S THE LIQUOR!
I'VE KNOWN SHIMOMURA SINCE WE WERE IN THE MIDDLE SCHOOL DRAMA CLUB TOGETHER.
SO TRUST ME WHEN I SAY DON'T BOTHER WITH HER.
ACCORDING TO MY CALCUL-ATIONS...
...SHE'S STILL A VIRGIN.
AT THE AGE OF 27!!
EH?
COME ON, SUEKICHI.

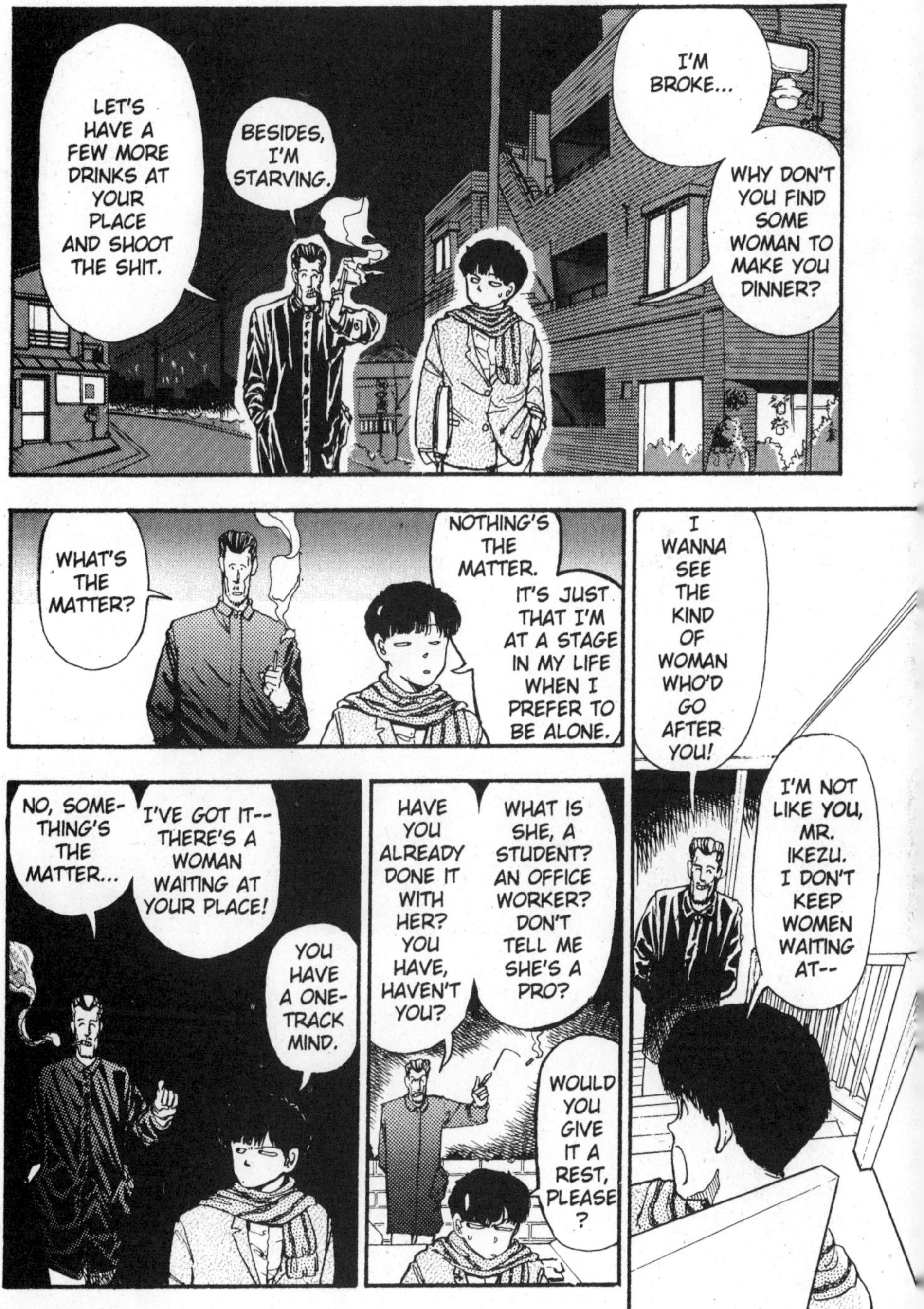
LET'S HAVE A FEW MORE DRINKS AT YOUR PLACE AND SHOOT THE SHIT.
BESIDES, I'M STARVING.
I'M BROKE...
WHY DON'T YOU FIND SOME WOMAN TO MAKE YOU DINNER?
WHAT'S THE MATTER?
NOTHING'S THE MATTER.
IT'S JUST THAT I'M AT A STAGE IN MY LIFE WHEN I PREFER TO BE ALONE.
NO, SOME-THING'S THE MATTER...
I'VE GOT IT-- THERE'S A WOMAN WAITING AT YOUR PLACE!
YOU HAVE A ONE-TRACK MIND.
HAVE YOU ALREADY DONE IT WITH HER? YOU HAVE, HAVEN'T YOU?
WHAT IS SHE, A STUDENT? AN OFFICE WORKER? DON'T TELL ME SHE'S A PRO?
WOULD YOU GIVE IT A REST, PLEASE?
I WANNA SEE THE KIND OF WOMAN WHO'D GO AFTER YOU!
I'M NOT LIKE YOU, MR. IKEZU. I DON'T KEEP WOMEN WAITING AT--

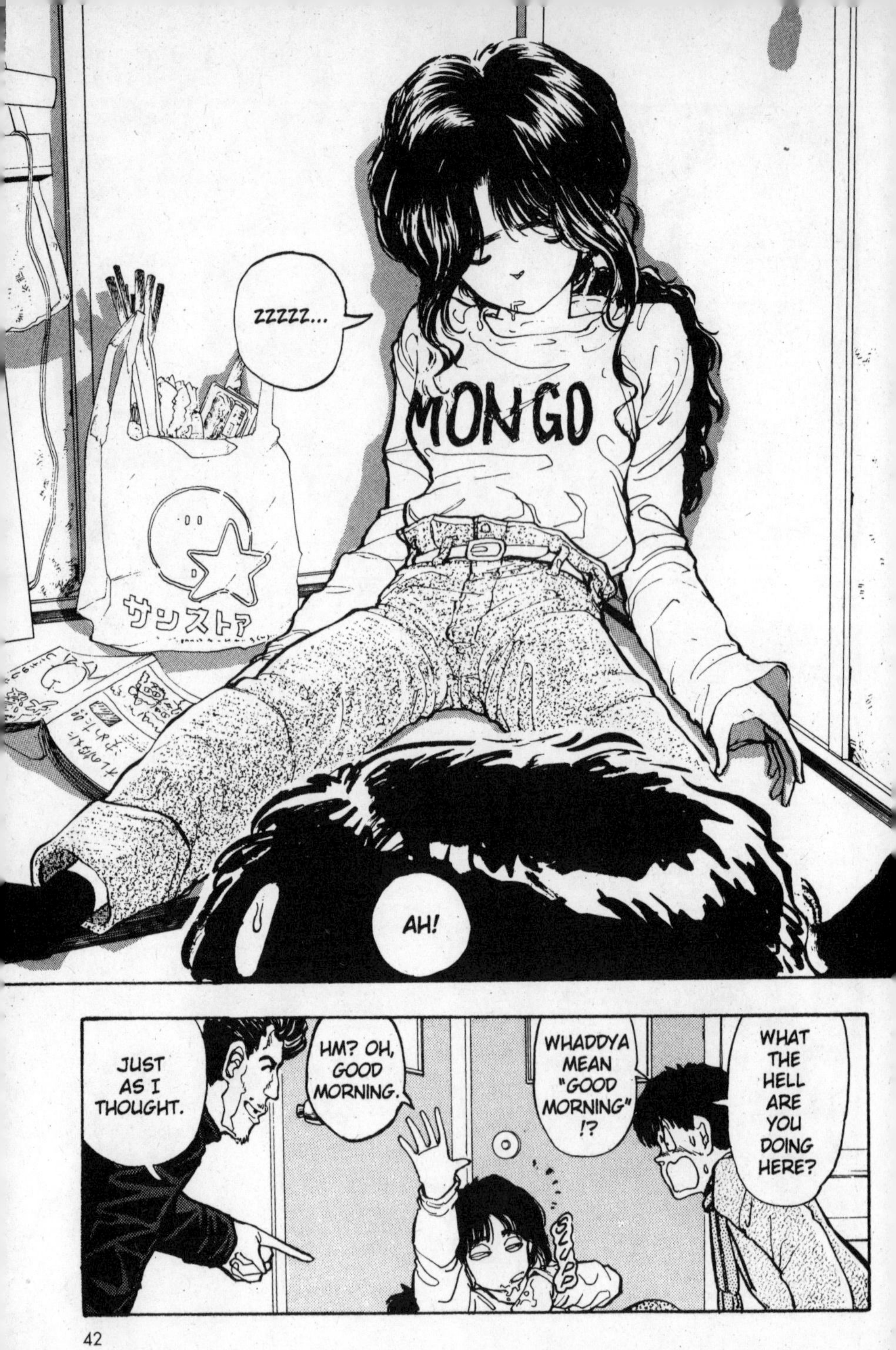
ZZZZZ...
MONGO
サンストア
AH!
JUST AS I THOUGHT.
HM? OH, GOOD MORNING.
SLUPP
WHADDYA MEAN "GOOD MORNING" !?
WHAT THE HELL ARE YOU DOING HERE?

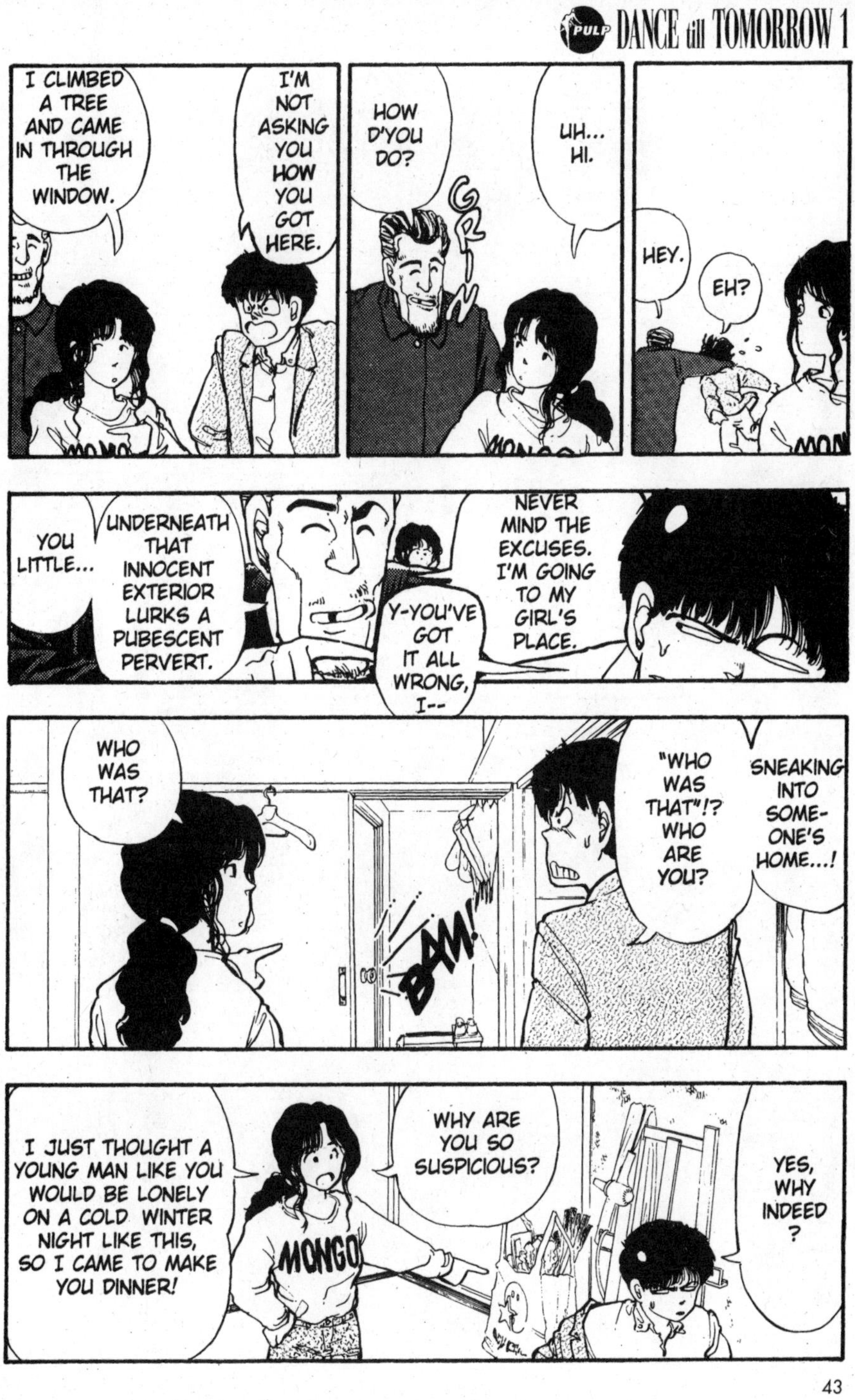
I CLIMBED A TREE AND CAME IN THROUGH THE WINDOW.
I'M NOT ASKING YOU HOW YOU GOT HERE.
HOW D'YOU DO?
GRIN
UH... HI.
HEY.
EH?
YOU LITTLE...
UNDERNEATH THAT INNOCENT EXTERIOR LURKS A PUBESCENT PERVERT.
Y-YOU'VE GOT IT ALL WRONG, I--
NEVER MIND THE EXCUSES. I'M GOING TO MY GIRL'S PLACE.
WHO WAS THAT?
BAM!
"WHO WAS THAT"!? WHO ARE YOU?
SNEAKING INTO SOME-ONE'S HOME...!
I JUST THOUGHT A YOUNG MAN LIKE YOU WOULD BE LONELY ON A COLD WINTER NIGHT LIKE THIS, SO I CAME TO MAKE YOU DINNER!
MONGO
WHY ARE YOU SO SUSPICIOUS?
YES, WHY INDEED?

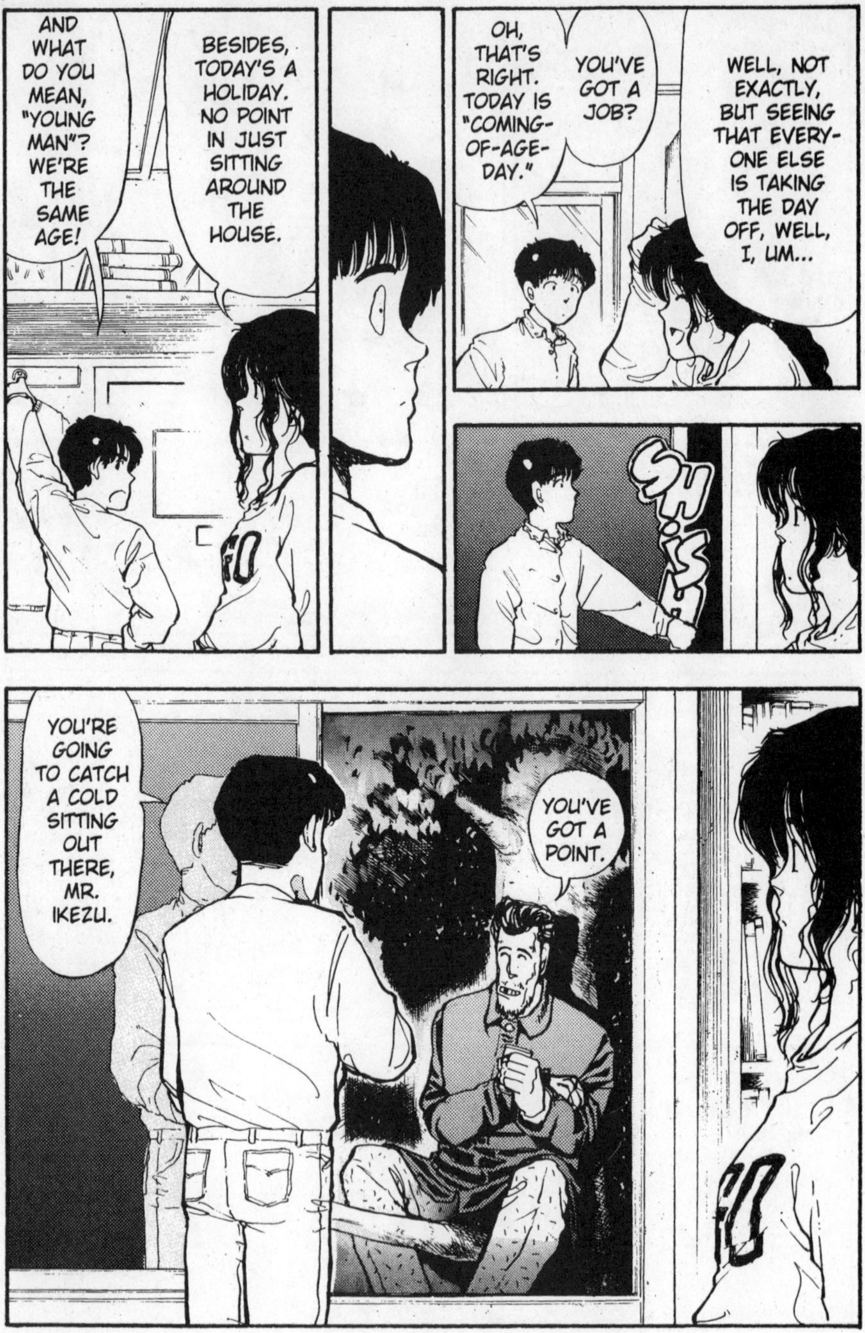
AND WHAT DO YOU MEAN, "YOUNG MAN"? WE'RE THE SAME AGE!
BESIDES, TODAY'S A HOLIDAY. NO POINT IN JUST SITTING AROUND THE HOUSE.
OH, THAT'S RIGHT. TODAY IS "COMING-OF-AGE-DAY."
YOU'VE GOT A JOB?
WELL, NOT EXACTLY, BUT SEEING THAT EVERYONE ELSE IS TAKING THE DAY OFF, WELL, I, UM...
SH.S.H
YOU'RE GOING TO CATCH A COLD SITTING OUT THERE, MR. IKEZU.
YOU'VE GOT A POINT.

ACT THREE

THE MIND SAYS NO, BUT THE LOINS SAY GO

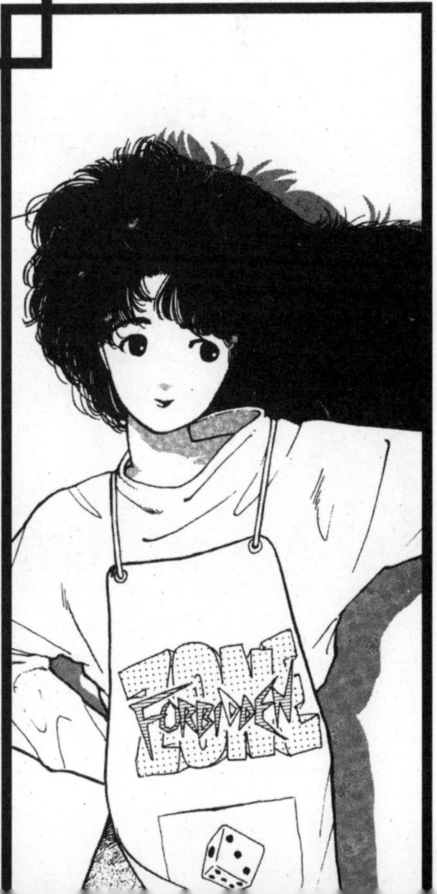
FORBIDDEN

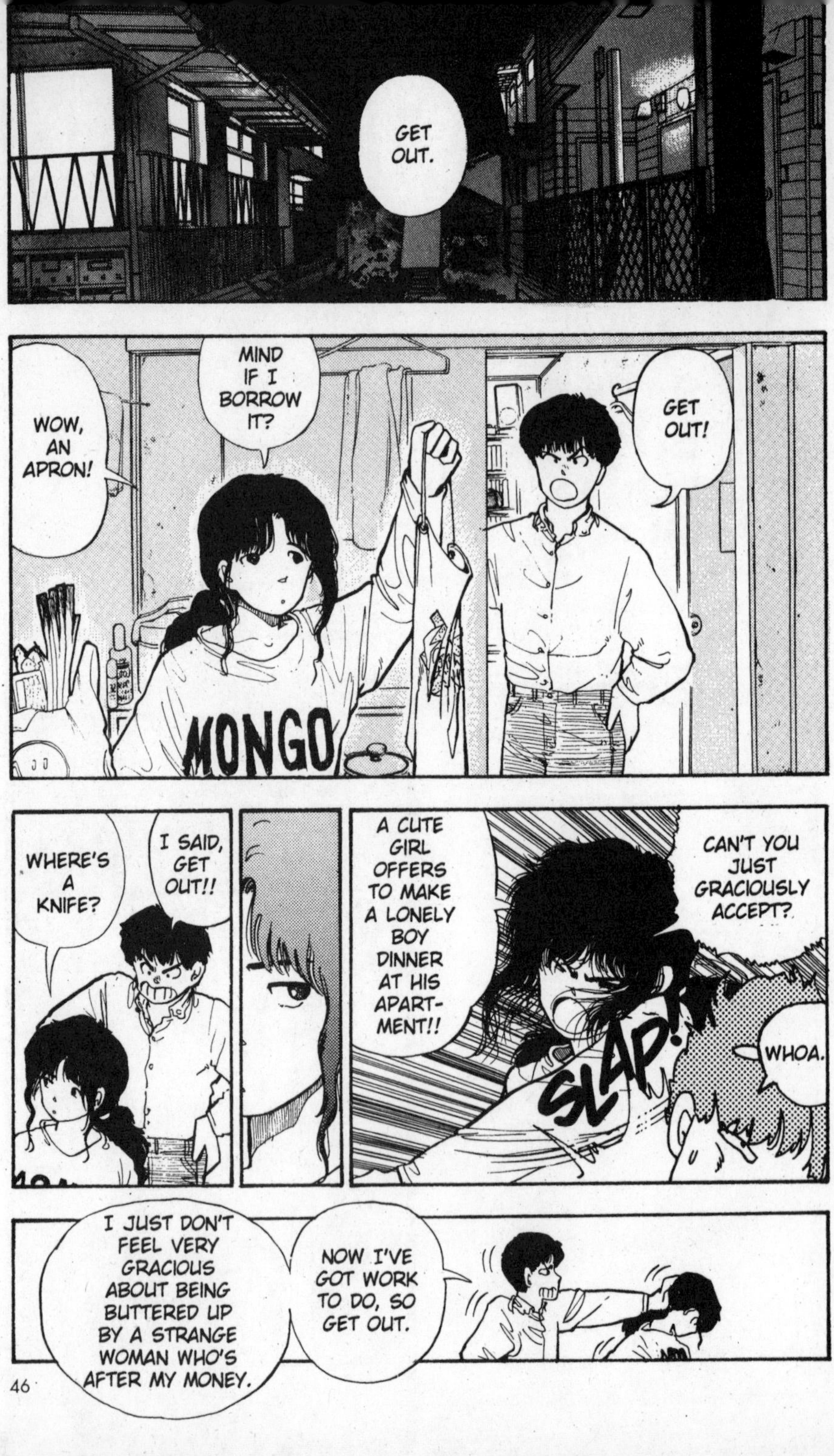
GET OUT.
WOW, AN APRON!
MIND IF I BORROW IT?
GET OUT!
WHERE'S A KNIFE?
I SAID, GET OUT!!
A CUTE GIRL OFFERS TO MAKE A LONELY BOY DINNER AT HIS APARTMENT!!
CAN'T YOU JUST GRACIOUSLY ACCEPT?
SLAP!!
WHOA.
I JUST DON'T FEEL VERY GRACIOUS ABOUT BEING BUTTERED UP BY A STRANGE WOMAN WHO'S AFTER MY MONEY.
NOW I'VE GOT WORK TO DO, SO GET OUT.
MONGO

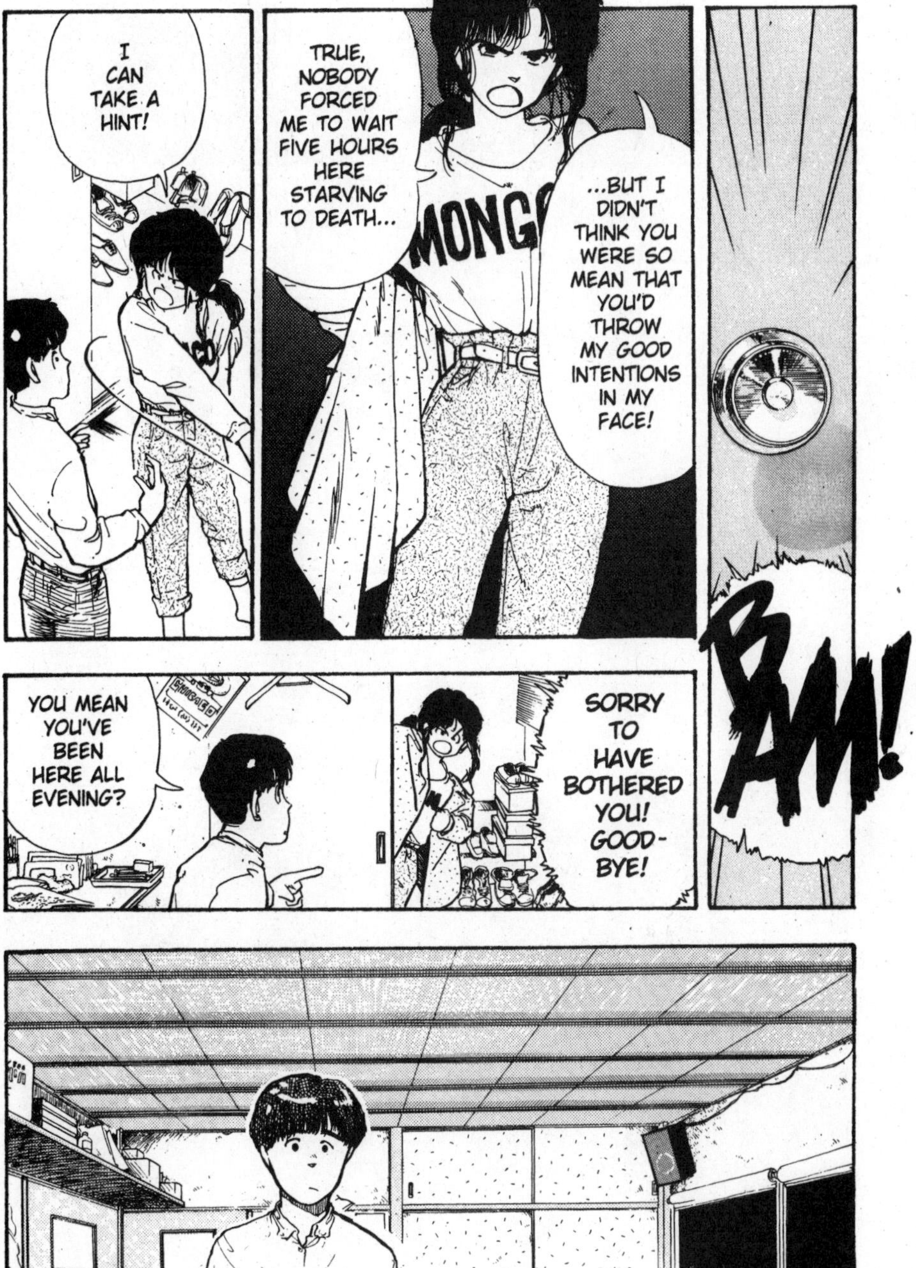
I CAN TAKE A HINT!
TRUE, NOBODY FORCED ME TO WAIT FIVE HOURS HERE STARVING TO DEATH...
...BUT I DIDN'T THINK YOU WERE SO MEAN THAT YOU'D THROW MY GOOD INTENTIONS IN MY FACE!
YOU MEAN YOU'VE BEEN HERE ALL EVENING?
SORRY TO HAVE BOTHERED YOU! GOOD-BYE!
BAM!

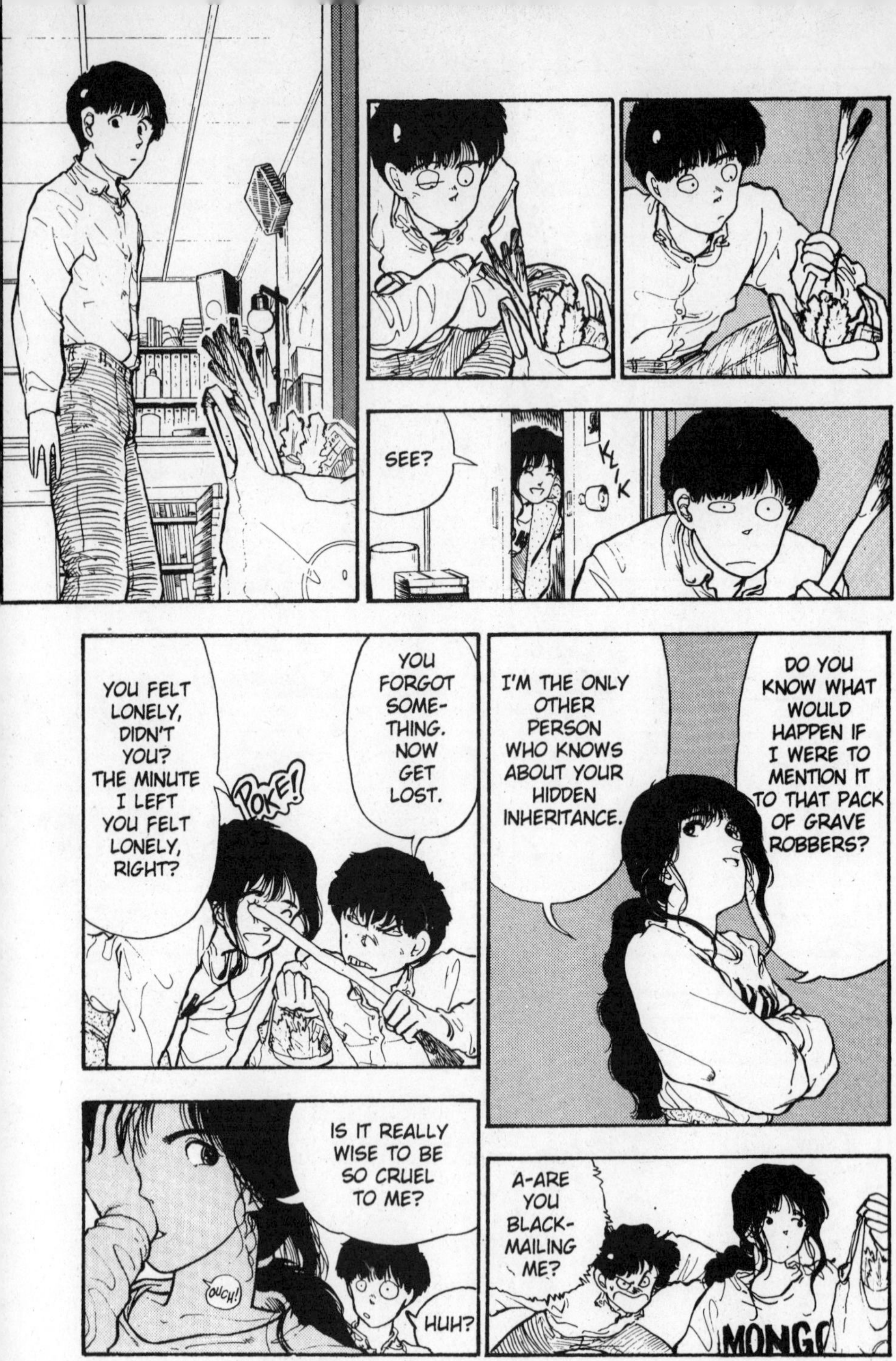
SEE?
KLIK
YOU FELT LONELY, DIDN'T YOU? THE MINUTE I LEFT YOU FELT LONELY, RIGHT?
POKE!
YOU FORGOT SOME-THING. NOW GET LOST.
I'M THE ONLY OTHER PERSON WHO KNOWS ABOUT YOUR HIDDEN INHERITANCE.
DO YOU KNOW WHAT WOULD HAPPEN IF I WERE TO MENTION IT TO THAT PACK OF GRAVE ROBBERS?
IS IT REALLY WISE TO BE SO CRUEL TO ME?
OUCH!
HUH?
A-ARE YOU BLACK-MAILING ME?
MONGO

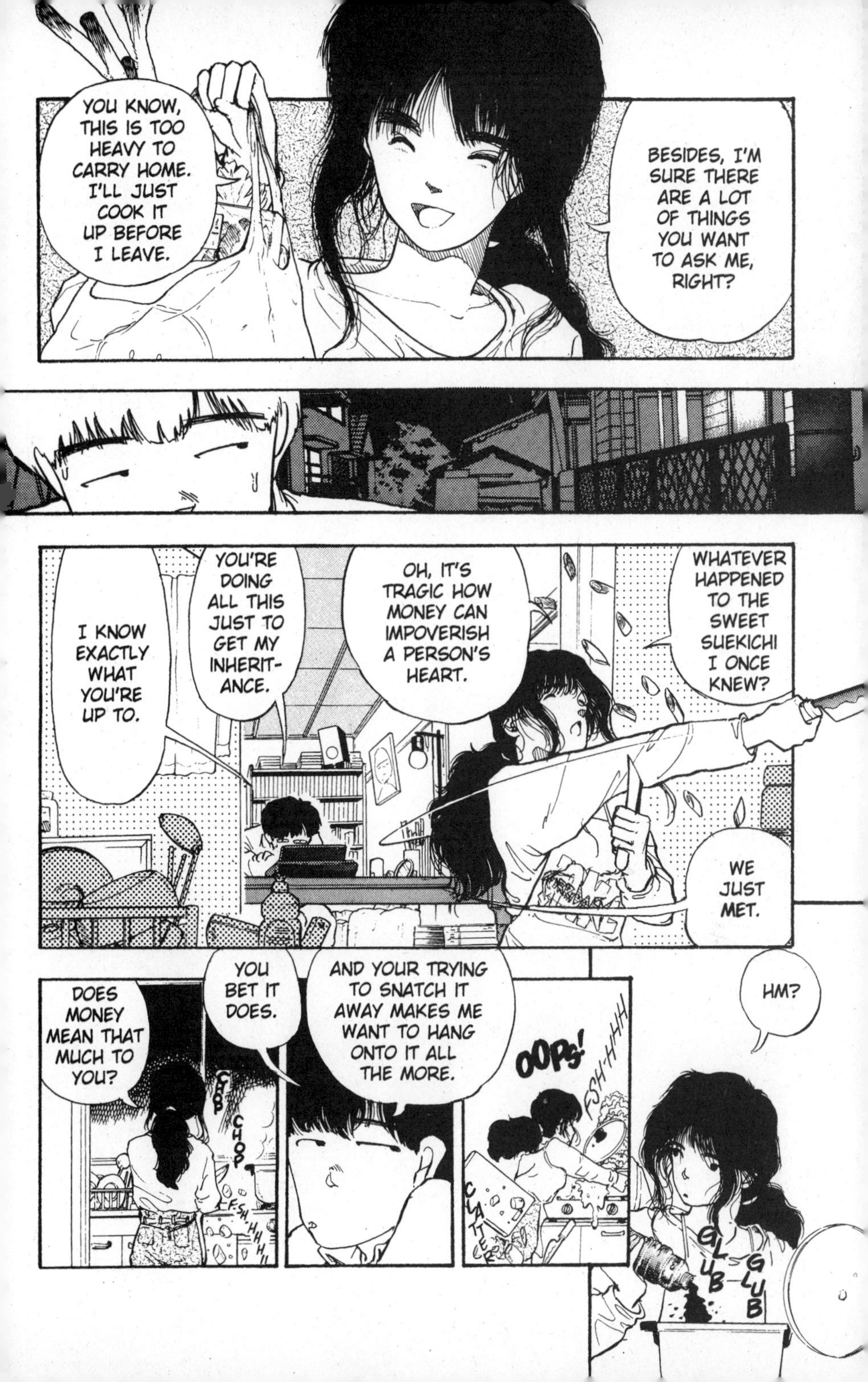
YOU KNOW, THIS IS TOO HEAVY TO CARRY HOME. I'LL JUST COOK IT UP BEFORE I LEAVE.
BESIDES, I'M SURE THERE ARE A LOT OF THINGS YOU WANT TO ASK ME, RIGHT?
I KNOW EXACTLY WHAT YOU'RE UP TO.
YOU'RE DOING ALL THIS JUST TO GET MY INHERIT-ANCE.
OH, IT'S TRAGIC HOW MONEY CAN IMPOVERISH A PERSON'S HEART.
WHATEVER HAPPENED TO THE SWEET SUEKICHI I ONCE KNEW?
WE JUST MET.
DOES MONEY MEAN THAT MUCH TO YOU?
CHOP
CHOP
F-SH-HHHH
YOU BET IT DOES.
AND YOUR TRYING TO SNATCH IT AWAY MAKES ME WANT TO HANG ONTO IT ALL THE MORE.
OOPS!
FSH-HHH
CLATTER
HM?
GLUB
GLUB

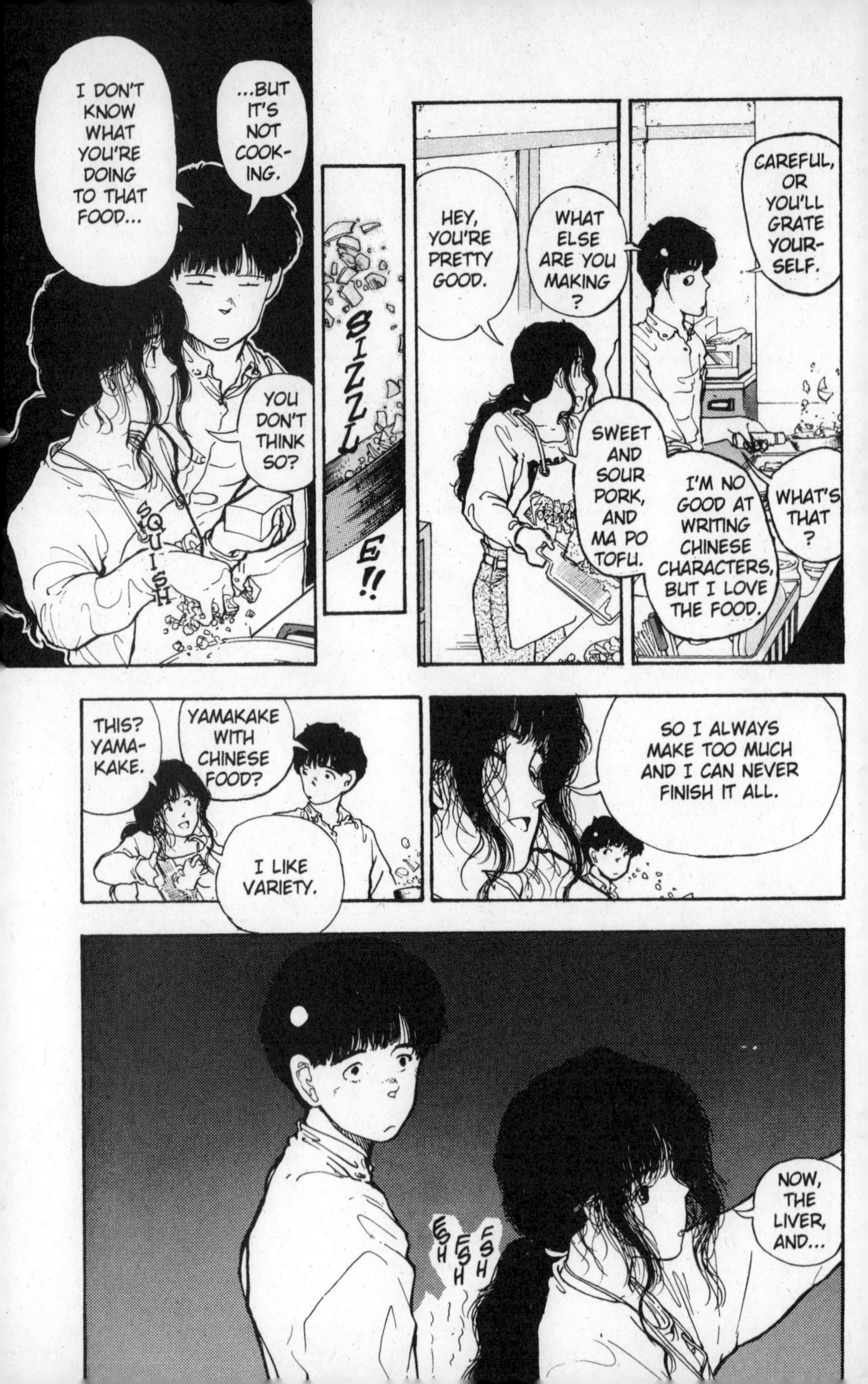
I DON'T KNOW WHAT YOU'RE DOING TO THAT FOOD...
...BUT IT'S NOT COOKING.
YOU DON'T THINK SO?
SQUISH
SIZZLE!!
HEY, YOU'RE PRETTY GOOD.
WHAT ELSE ARE YOU MAKING?
SWEET AND SOUR PORK, AND MA PO TOFU.
CAREFUL, OR YOU'LL GRATE YOURSELF.
I'M NO GOOD AT WRITING CHINESE CHARACTERS, BUT I LOVE THE FOOD.
WHAT'S THAT?
THIS? YAMAKAKE.
YAMAKAKE WITH CHINESE FOOD?
I LIKE VARIETY.
SO I ALWAYS MAKE TOO MUCH AND I CAN NEVER FINISH IT ALL.
FSH FSH FSH
NOW, THE LIVER, AND...

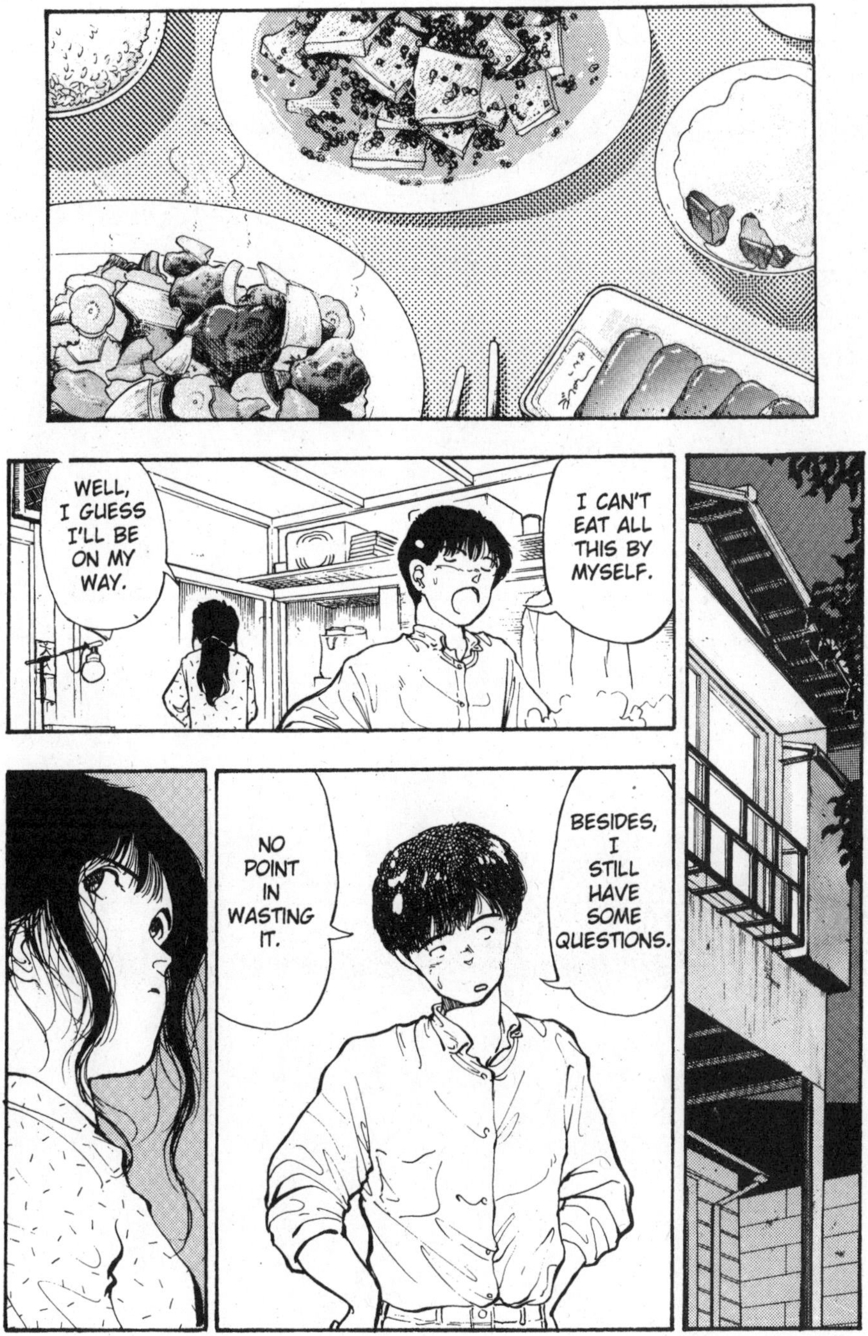
WELL, I GUESS I'LL BE ON MY WAY.
I CAN'T EAT ALL THIS BY MYSELF.
NO POINT IN WASTING IT.
BESIDES, I STILL HAVE SOME QUESTIONS.

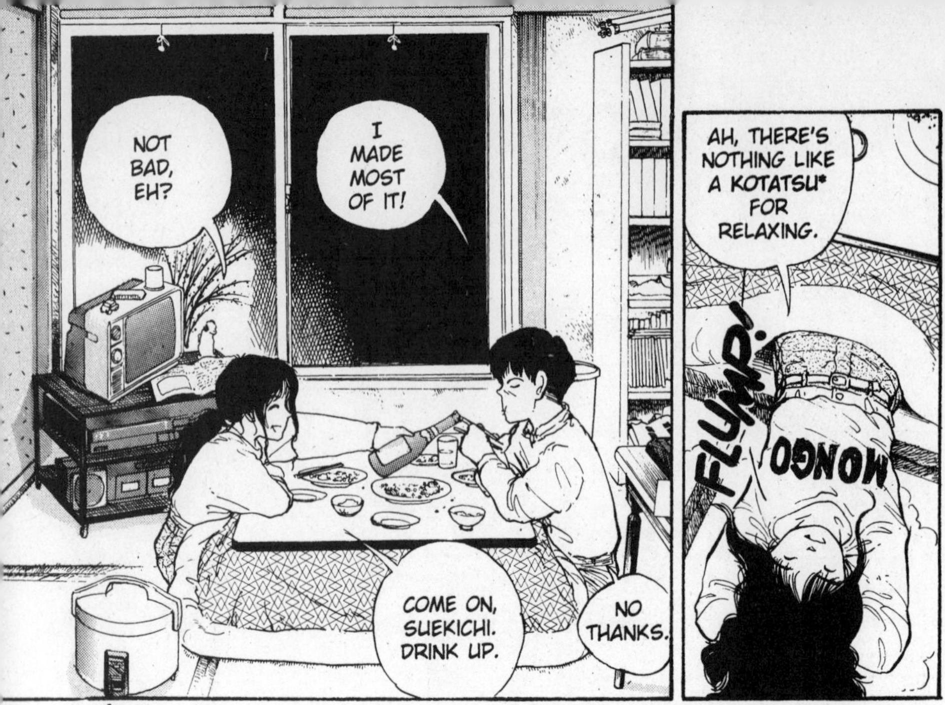
NOT BAD, EH?
I MADE MOST OF IT!
COME ON, SUEKICHI. DRINK UP.
NO THANKS.
AH, THERE'S NOTHING LIKE A KOTATSU* FOR RELAXING.
FLUMP!
MONGO

*KOTATSU: A LOW TABLE WITH A HEATER ON THE UNDERSIDE AND A QUILTED SKIRT TO KEEP IN THE WARMTH.

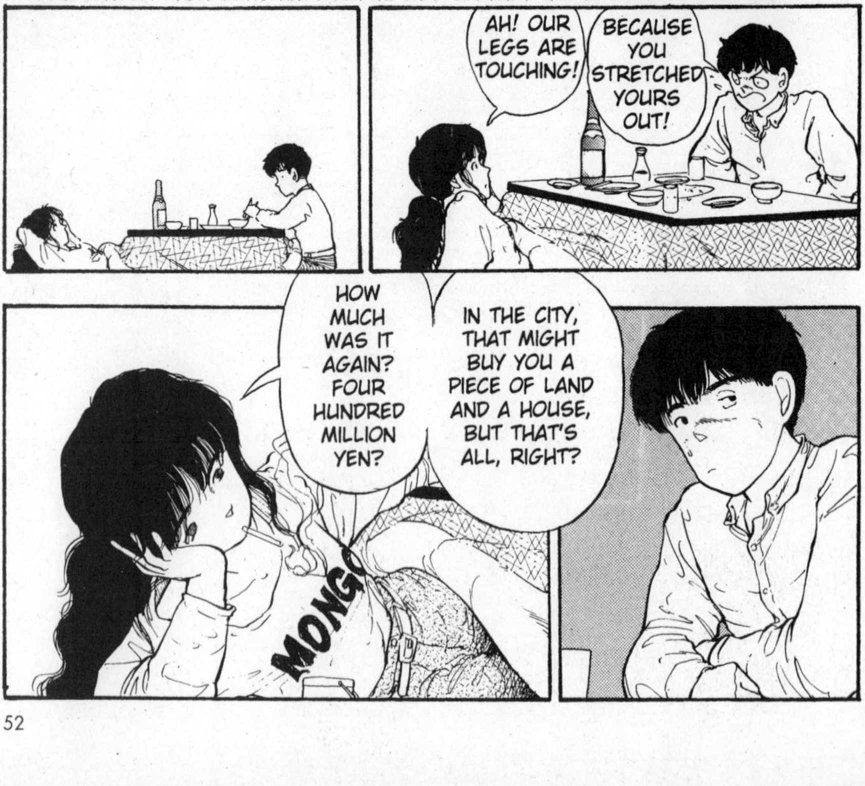
AH! OUR LEGS ARE TOUCHING!
BECAUSE YOU STRETCHED YOURS OUT!
HOW MUCH WAS IT AGAIN? FOUR HUNDRED MILLION YEN?
IN THE CITY, THAT MIGHT BUY YOU A PIECE OF LAND AND A HOUSE, BUT THAT'S ALL, RIGHT?
MONGO

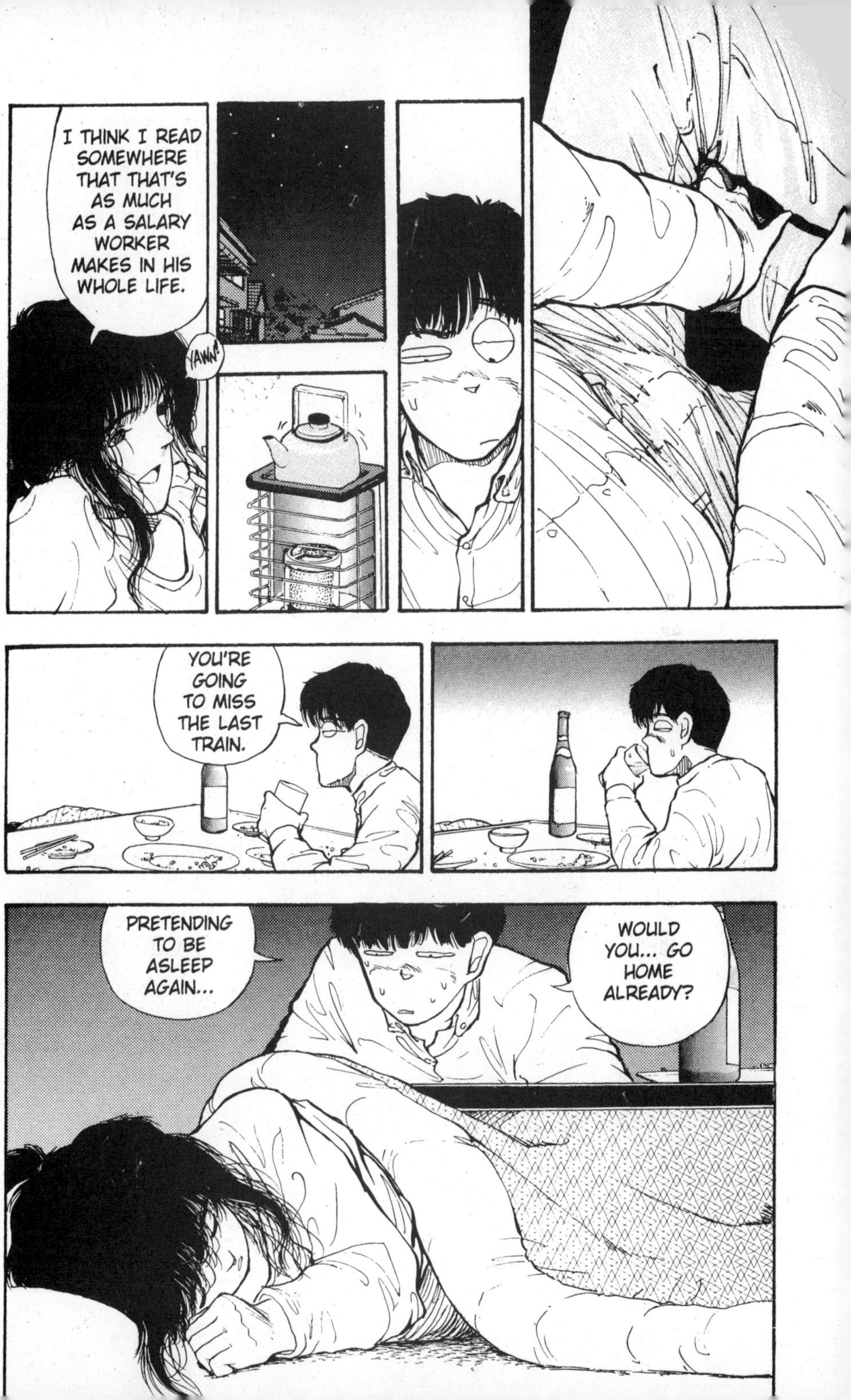
I THINK I READ SOMEWHERE THAT THAT'S AS MUCH AS A SALARY WORKER MAKES IN HIS WHOLE LIFE.
YAWN
YOU'RE GOING TO MISS THE LAST TRAIN.
PRETENDING TO BE ASLEEP AGAIN...
WOULD YOU... GO HOME ALREADY?

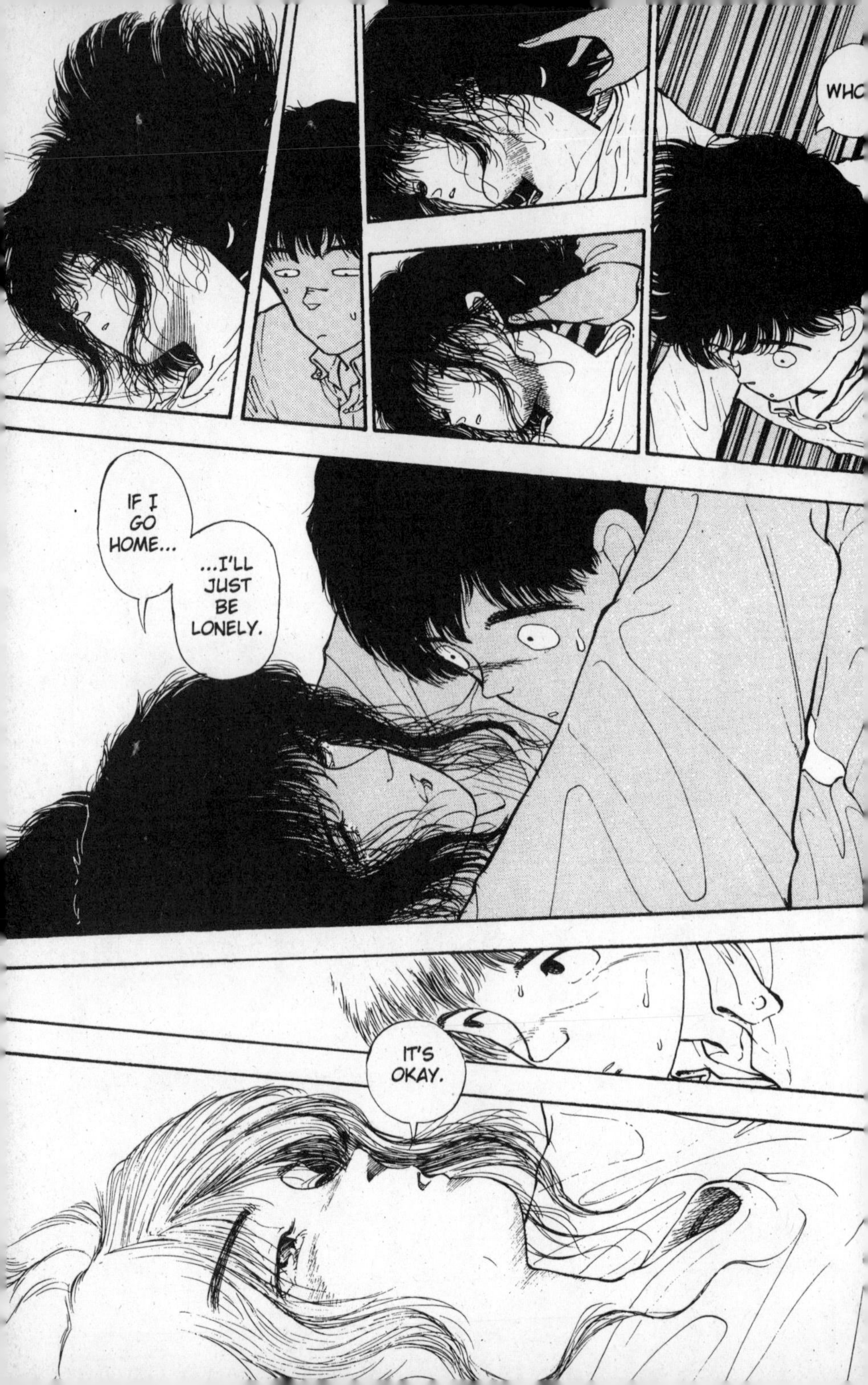
WHO
IF I GO HOME...
...I'LL JUST BE LONELY.
IT'S OKAY.

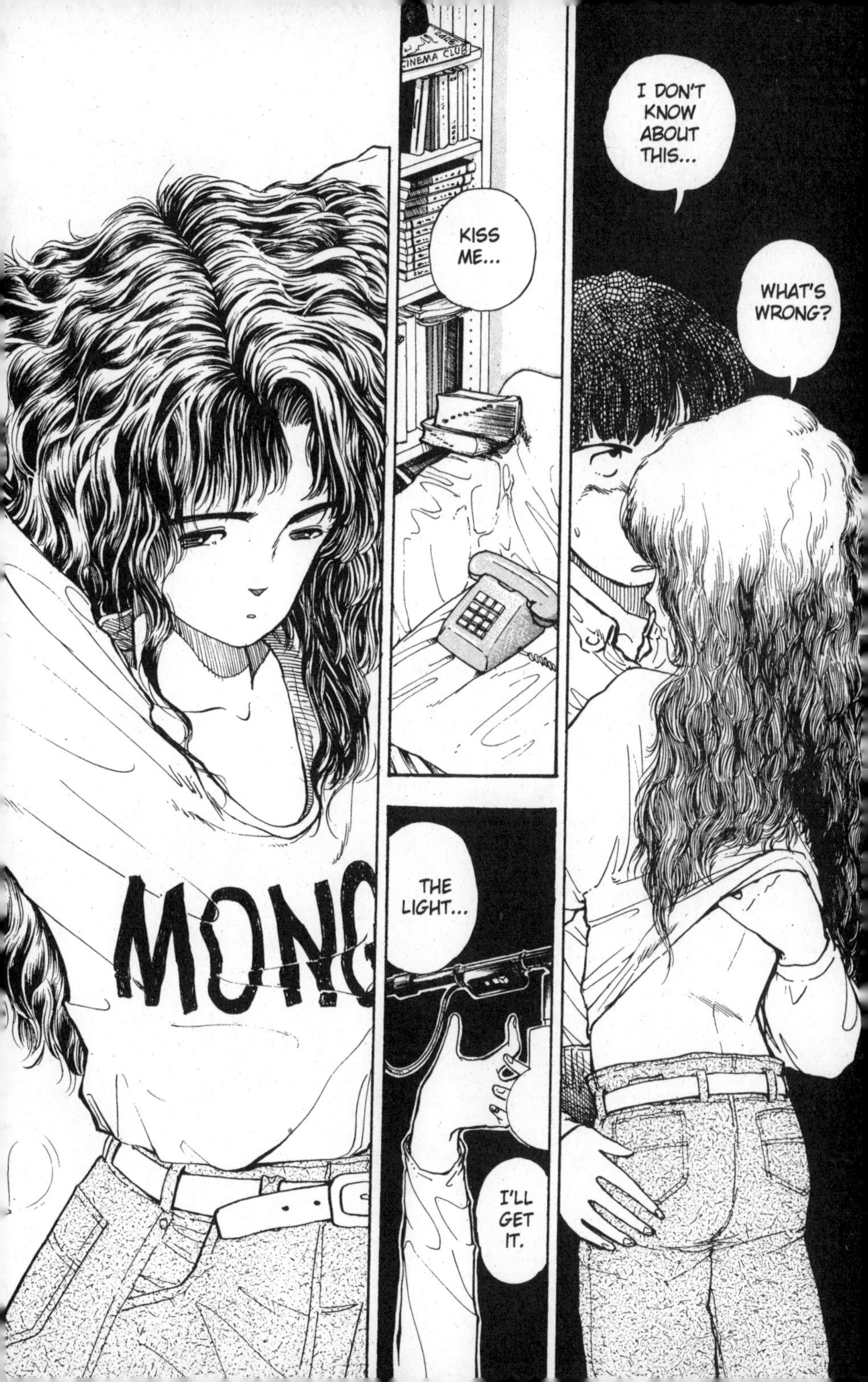
MONO
CINEMA CLUB
KISS ME...
THE LIGHT...
I'LL GET IT.
I DON'T KNOW ABOUT THIS...
WHAT'S WRONG?

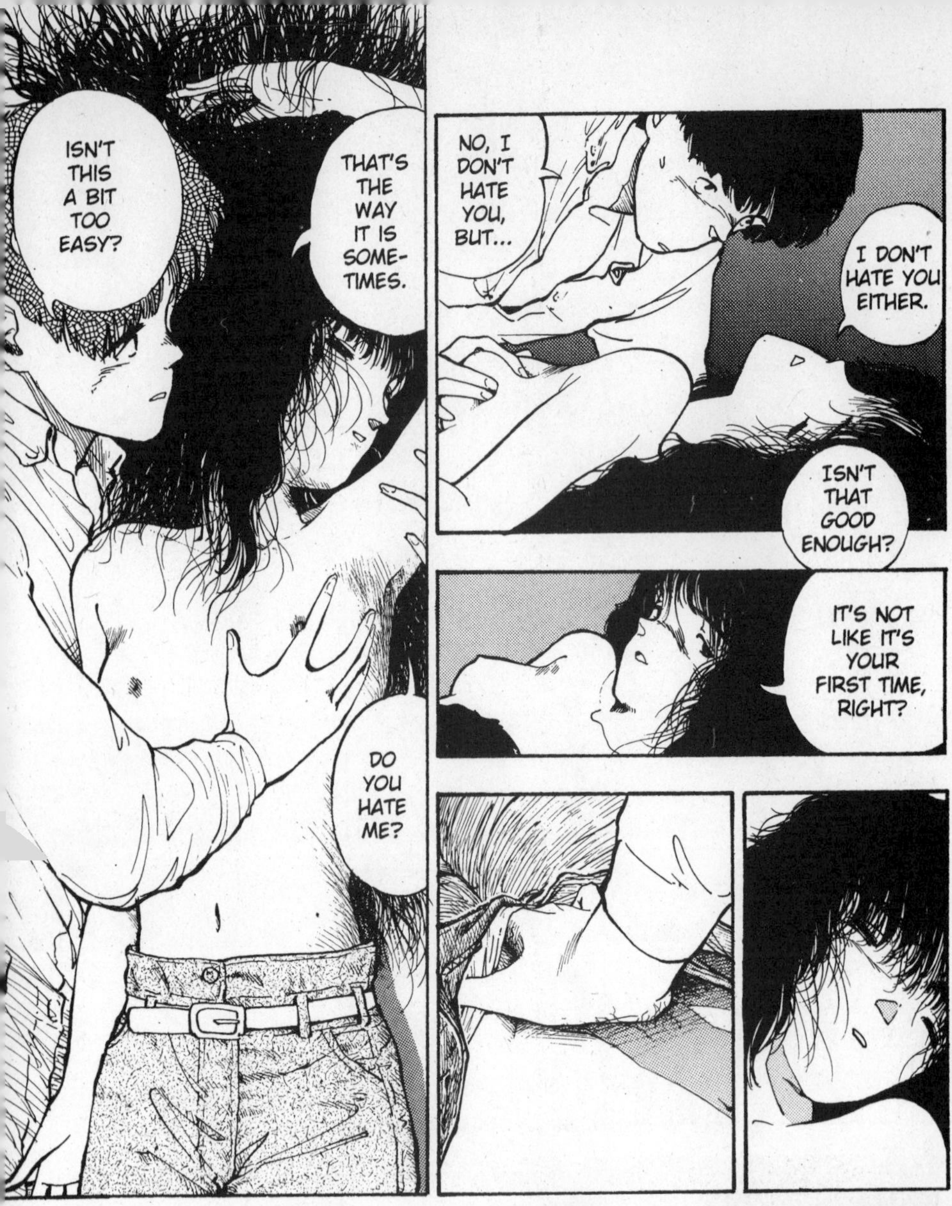
ISN'T THIS A BIT TOO EASY?
THAT'S THE WAY IT IS SOME-TIMES.
DO YOU HATE ME?
NO, I DON'T HATE YOU, BUT...
I DON'T HATE YOU EITHER.
ISN'T THAT GOOD ENOUGH?
IT'S NOT LIKE IT'S YOUR FIRST TIME, RIGHT?
DID I DO THIS LAST TIME,TOO?
...

AH.
WH-WHAT...
...ARE YOU...
...
AH!

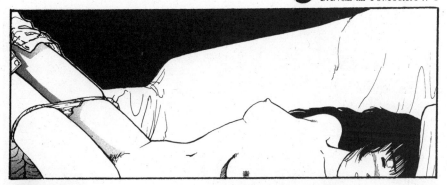

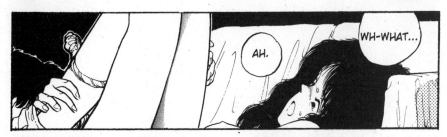

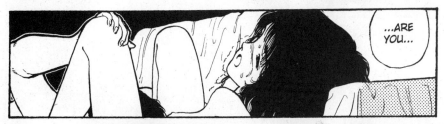

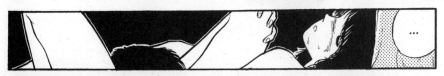

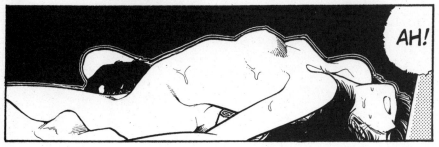

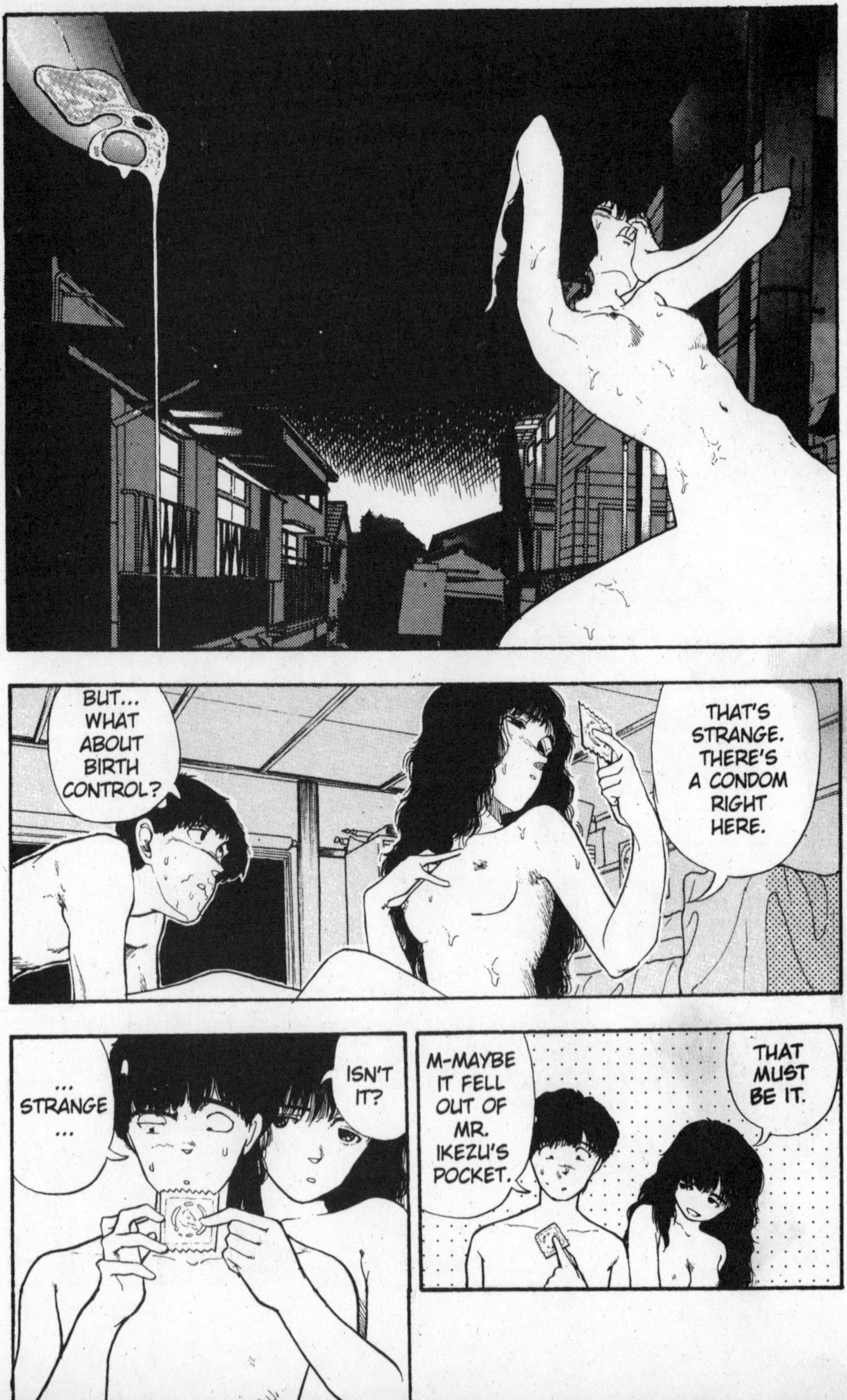
BUT... WHAT ABOUT BIRTH CONTROL?
THAT'S STRANGE. THERE'S A CONDOM RIGHT HERE.
... STRANGE ...
ISN'T IT?
M-MAYBE IT FELL OUT OF MR. IKEZU'S POCKET.
THAT MUST BE IT.

FUMBLE!
UH, LET'S SEE...
FUMBLE!
HM?
WHAT IS IT?

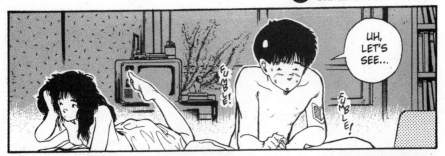

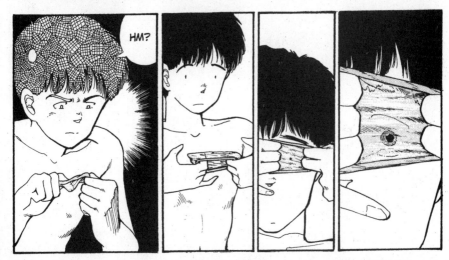

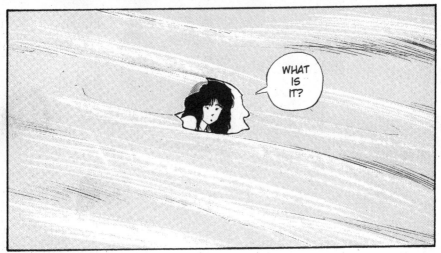

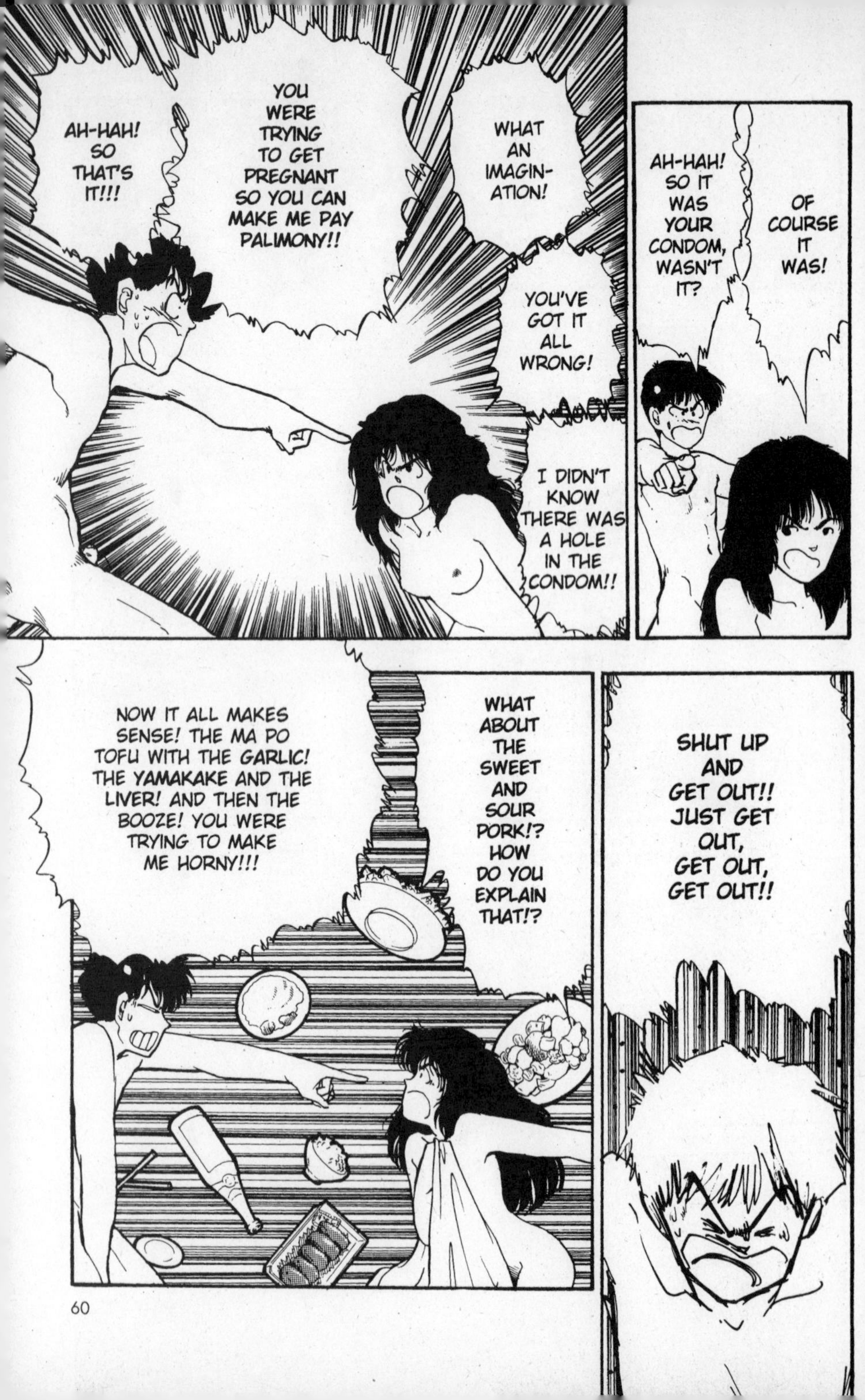
AH-HAH! SO THAT'S IT!!!
YOU WERE TRYING TO GET PREGNANT SO YOU CAN MAKE ME PAY PALIMONY!!
WHAT AN IMAGIN-ATION!
YOU'VE GOT IT ALL WRONG!
I DIDN'T KNOW THERE WAS A HOLE IN THE CONDOM!!
AH-HAH! SO IT WAS YOUR CONDOM, WASN'T IT?
OF COURSE IT WAS!
NOW IT ALL MAKES SENSE! THE MA PO TOFU WITH THE GARLIC! THE YAMAKAKE AND THE LIVER! AND THEN THE BOOZE! YOU WERE TRYING TO MAKE ME HORNY!!!
WHAT ABOUT THE SWEET AND SOUR PORK!? HOW DO YOU EXPLAIN THAT!?
SHUT UP AND GET OUT!! JUST GET OUT, GET OUT, GET OUT!!

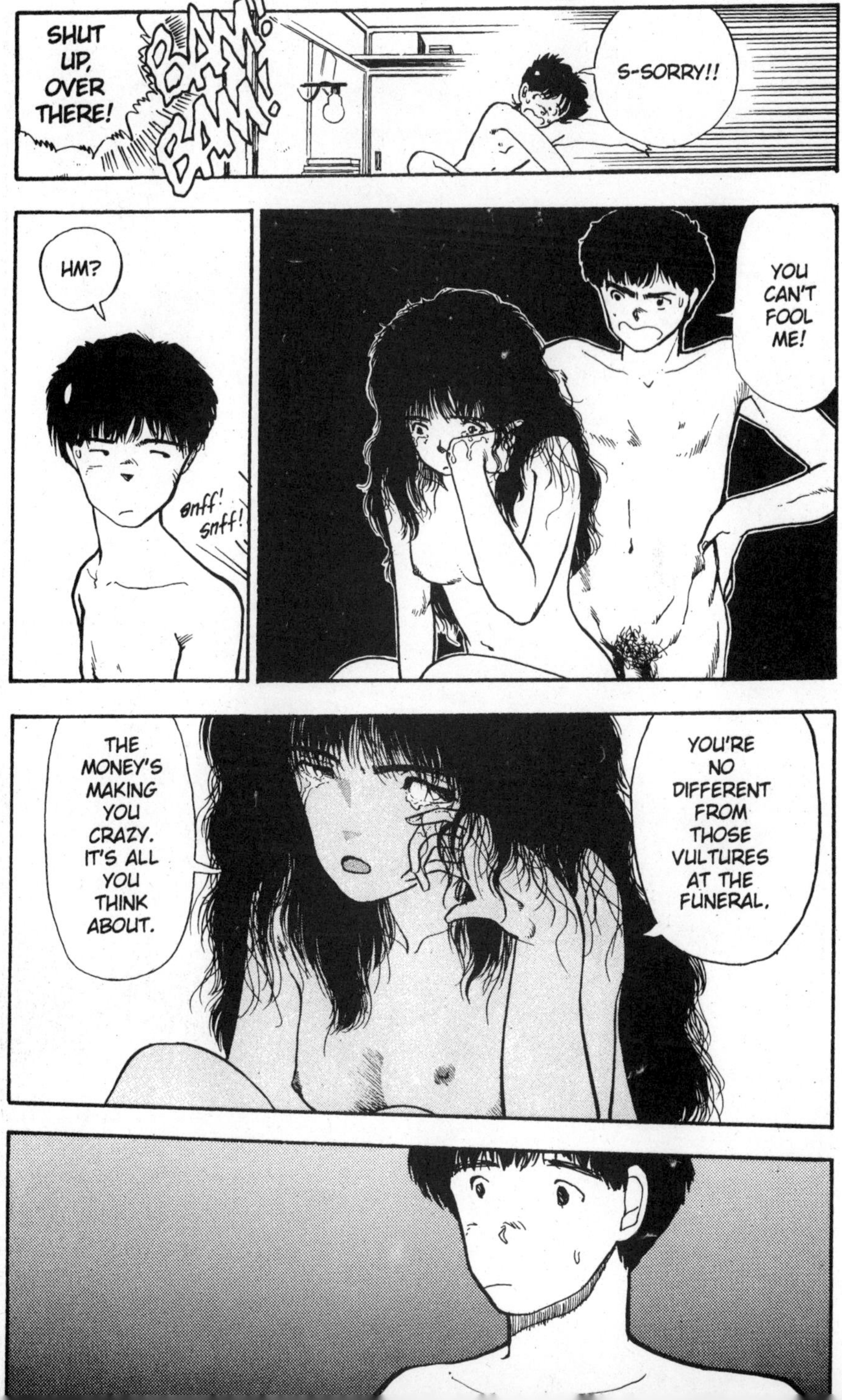
SHUT UP, OVER THERE!
BAM! BAM!
S-SORRY!!
HM?
snff! snff!
YOU CAN'T FOOL ME!
THE MONEY'S MAKING YOU CRAZY. IT'S ALL YOU THINK ABOUT.
YOU'RE NO DIFFERENT FROM THOSE VULTURES AT THE FUNERAL.

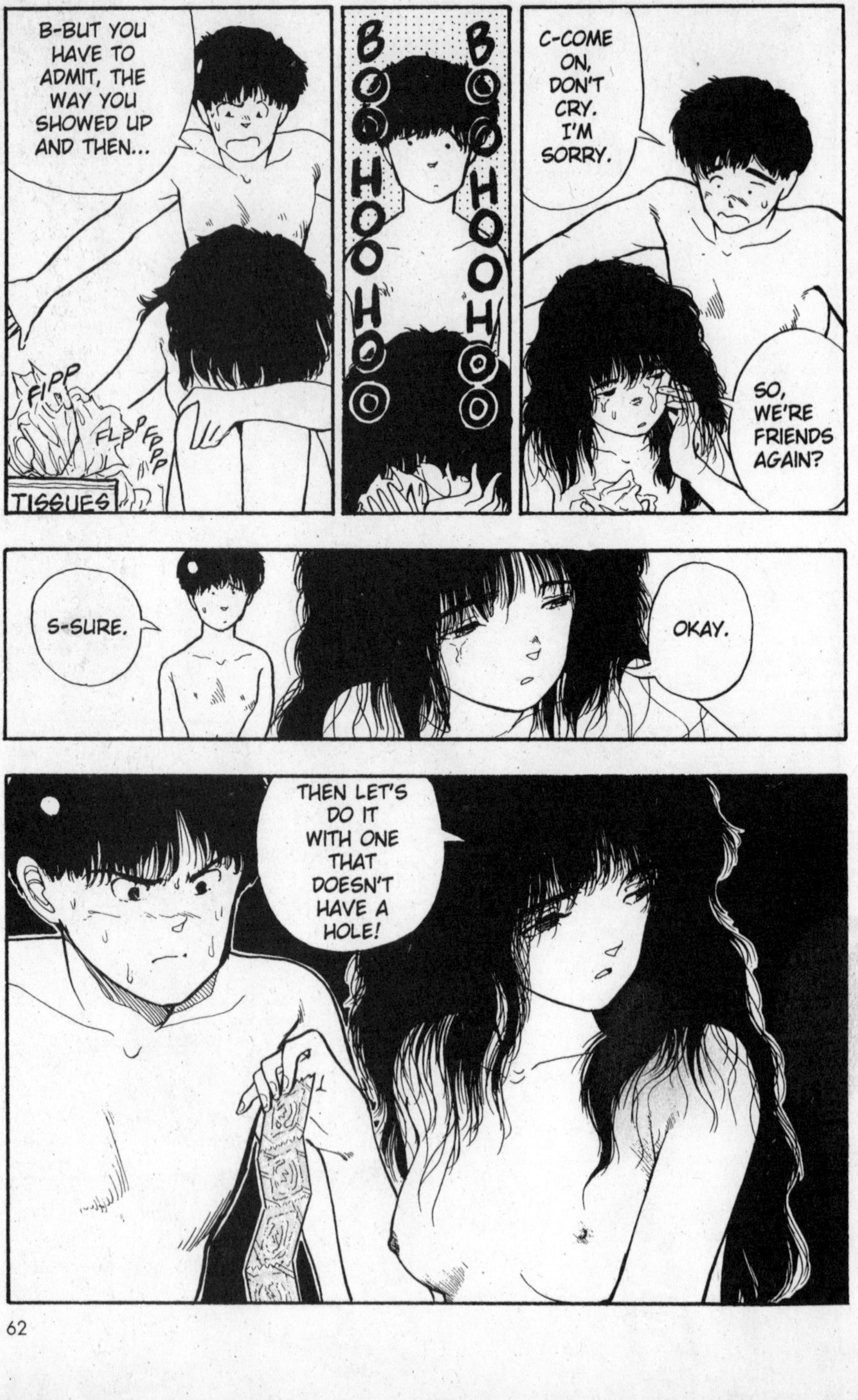
B-BUT YOU HAVE TO ADMIT, THE WAY YOU SHOWED UP AND THEN...
FLIPP
FLPPPPPP
TISSUES
BOOHOOHOO
BOOHOOHOO
C-COME ON, DON'T CRY. I'M SORRY.
SO, WE'RE FRIENDS AGAIN?
S-SURE.
OKAY.
THEN LET'S DO IT WITH ONE THAT DOESN'T HAVE A HOLE!

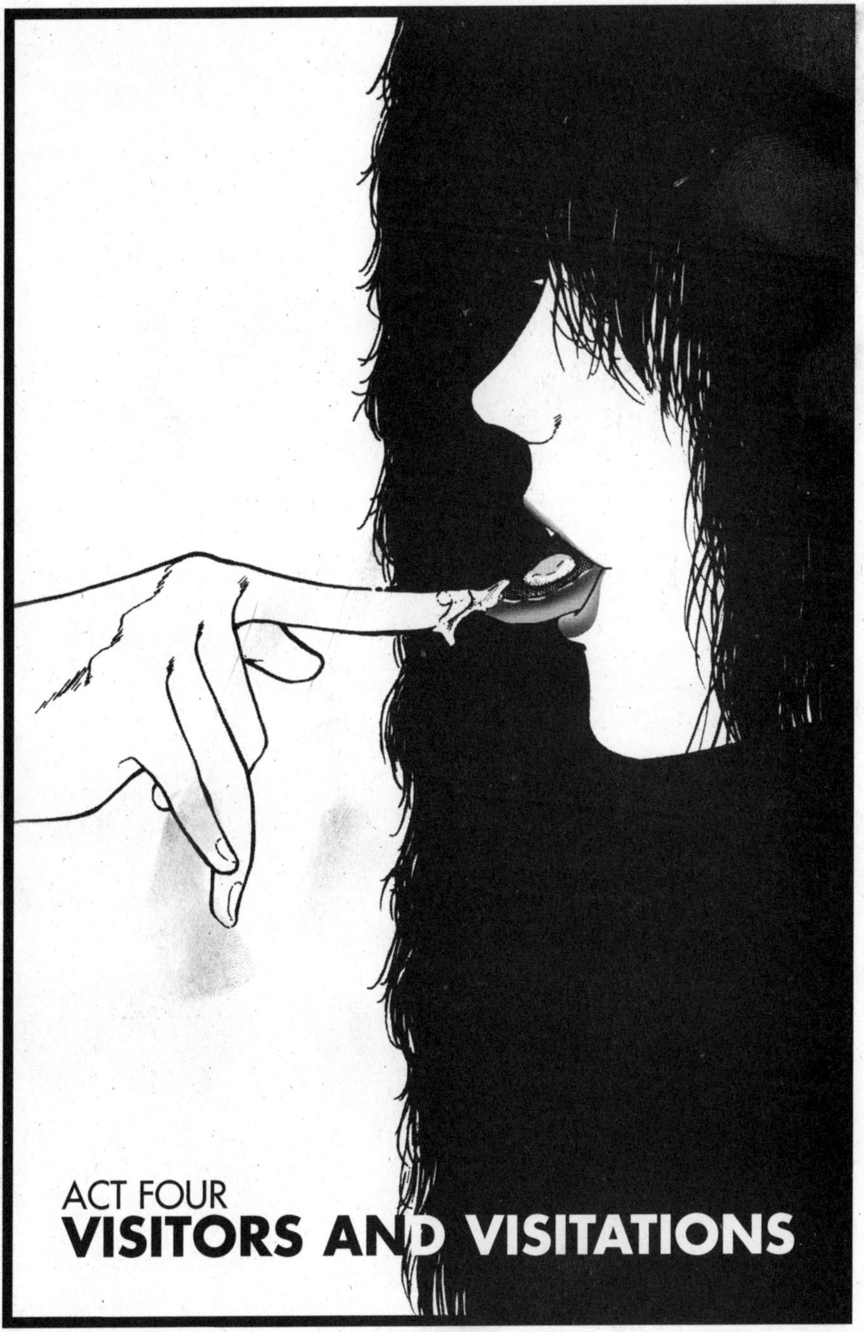

ACT FOUR
VISITORS AND VISITATIONS

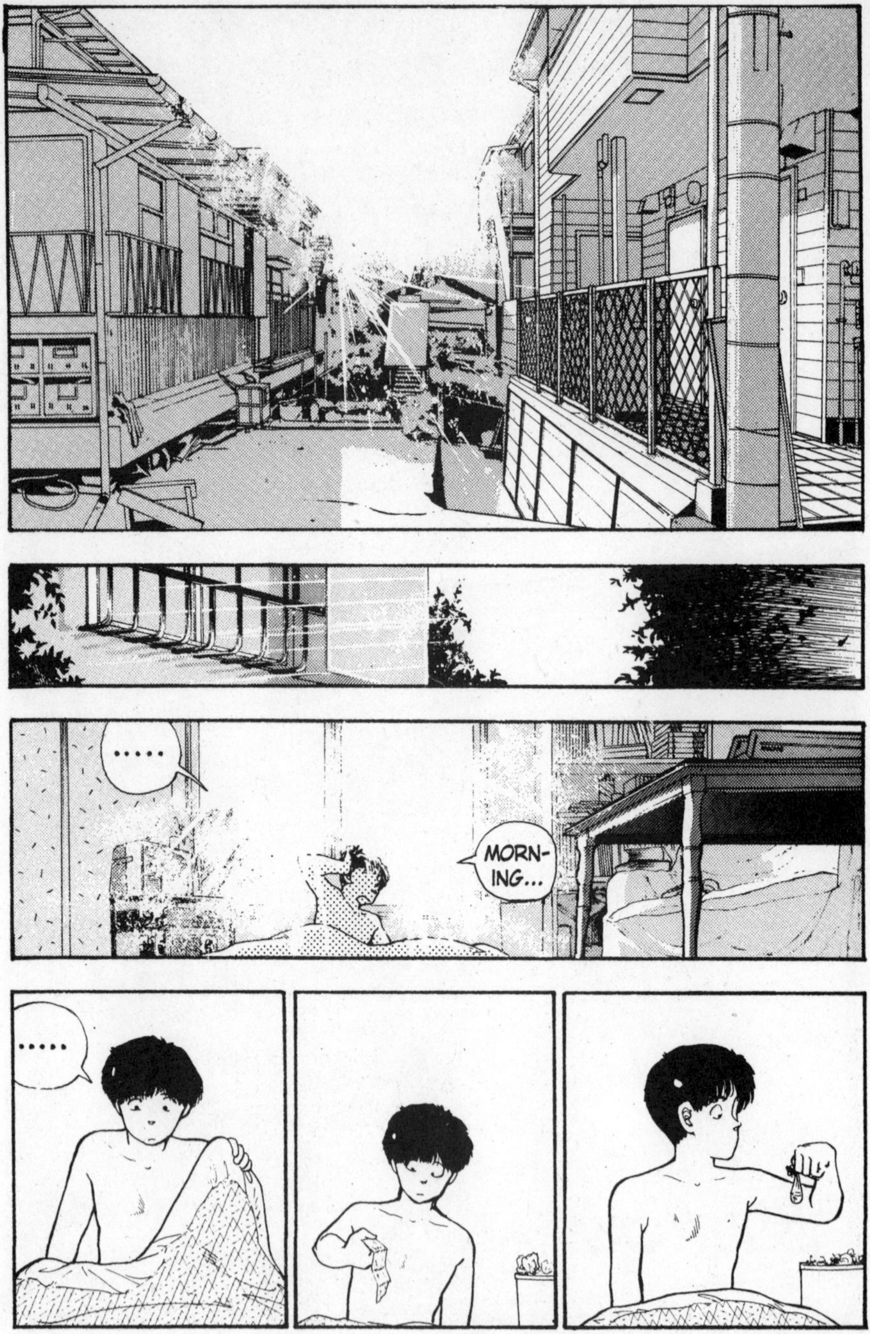
.....
MORN-
ING...
.....

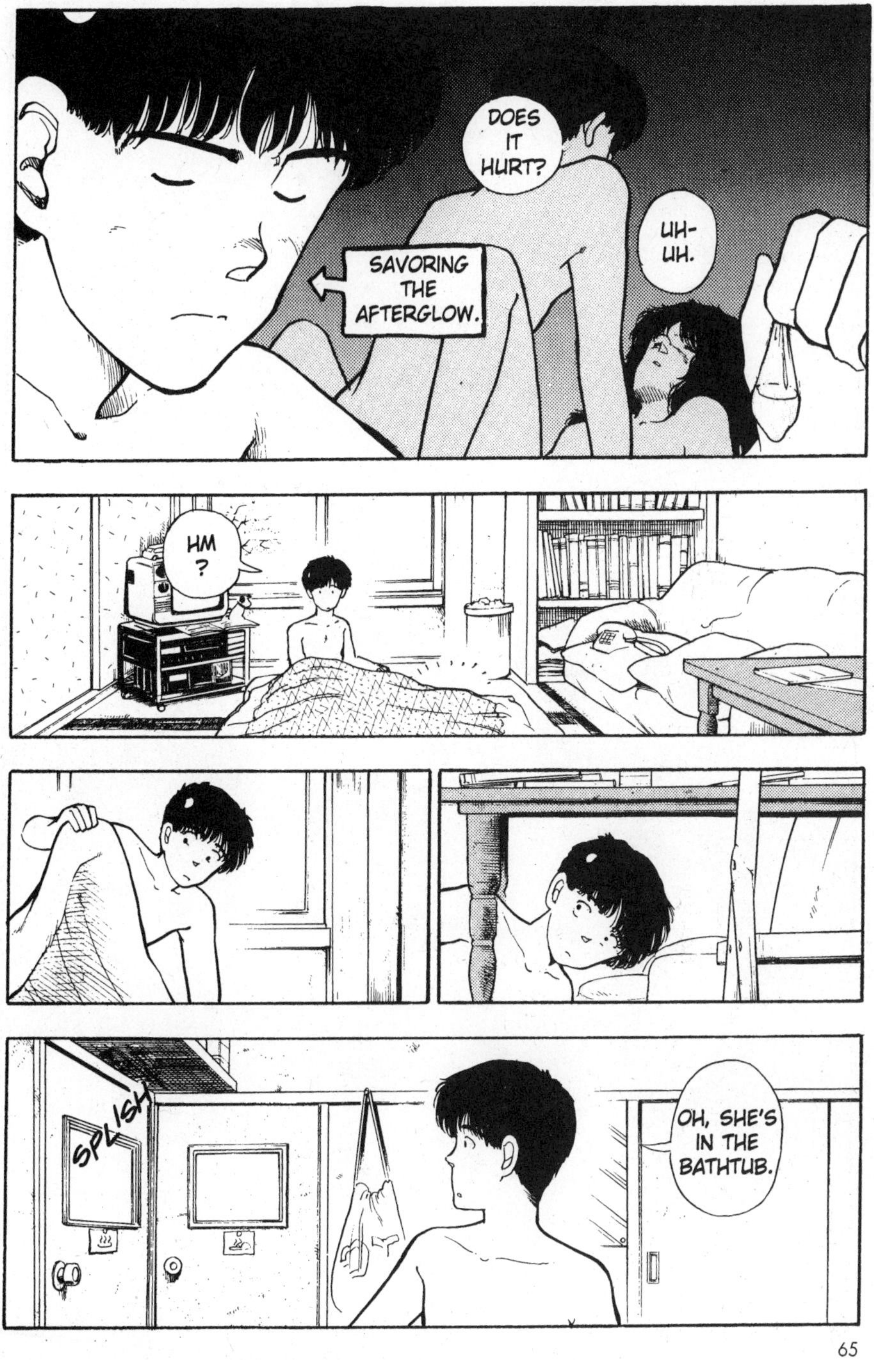
DOES IT HURT?
UH-UH.
SAVORING THE AFTERGLOW.
HM ?
SPLISH
OH, SHE'S IN THE BATHTUB.

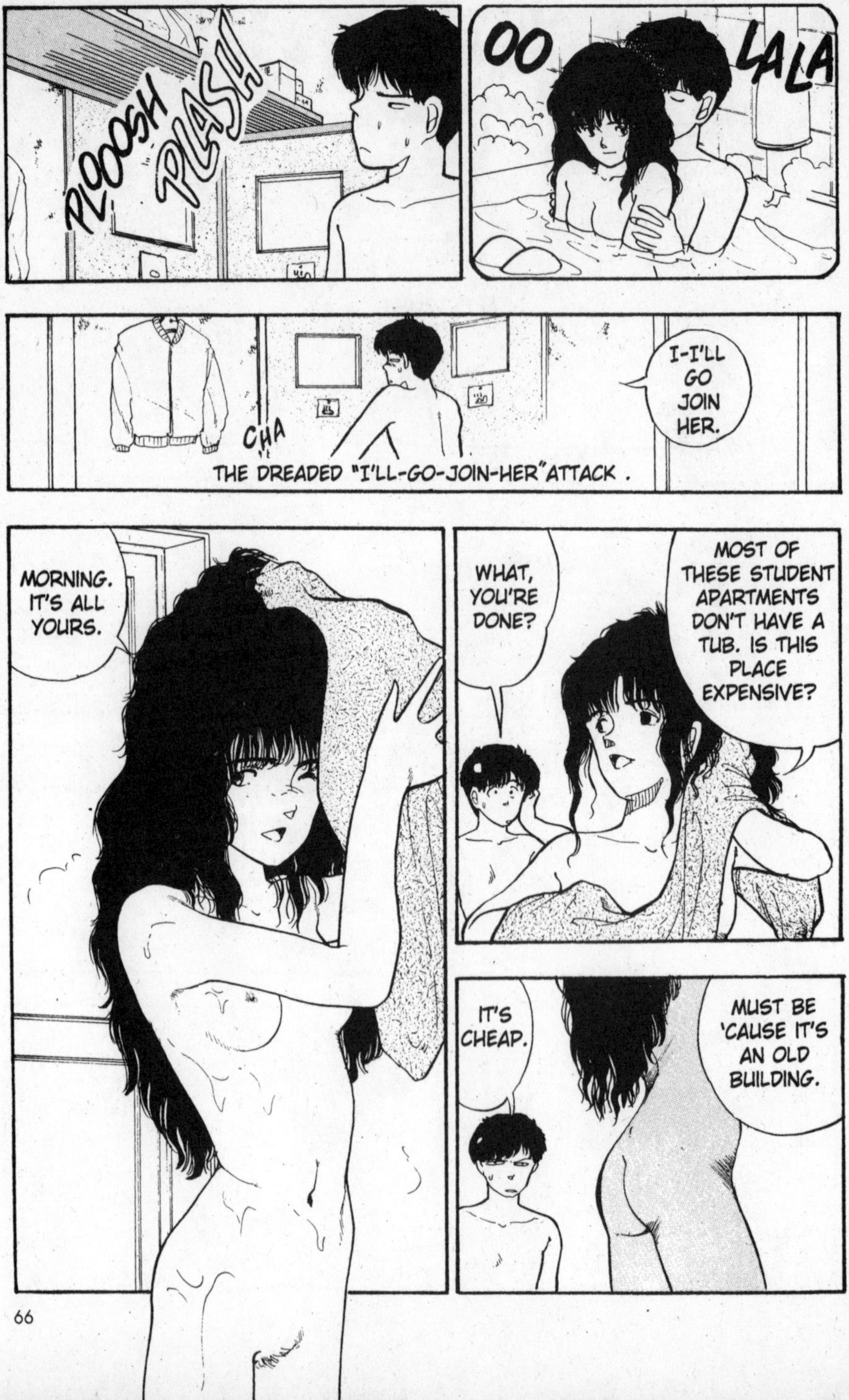
PLOOOSH
PLASH
OO LALA
CHA
I-I'LL GO JOIN HER.
THE DREADED "I'LL-GO-JOIN-HER" ATTACK .
MORNING. IT'S ALL YOURS.
WHAT, YOU'RE DONE?
MOST OF THESE STUDENT APARTMENTS DON'T HAVE A TUB. IS THIS PLACE EXPENSIVE?
IT'S CHEAP.
MUST BE 'CAUSE IT'S AN OLD BUILDING.

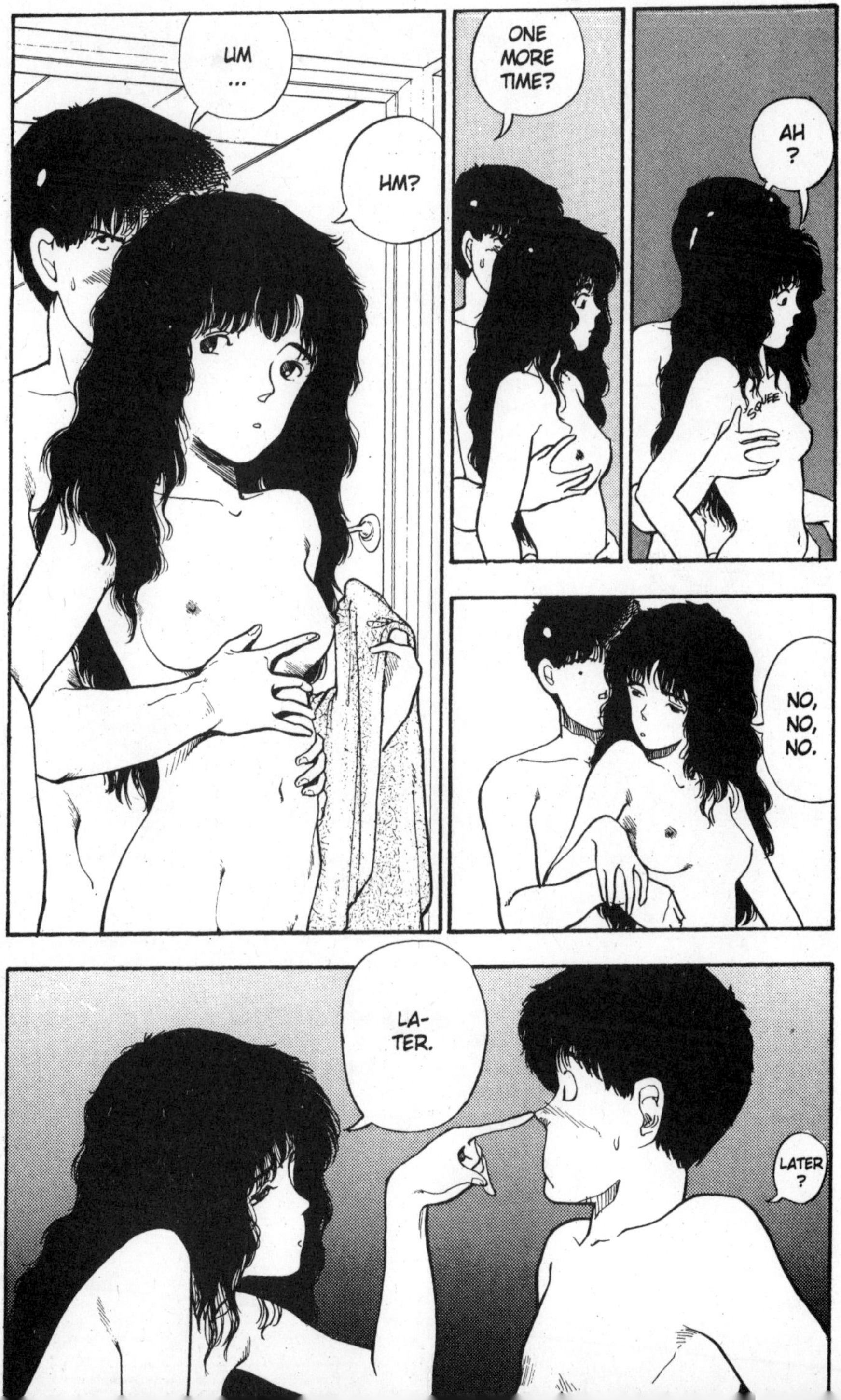
UM ...
HM?
ONE MORE TIME?
AH ?
SQUEE
NO, NO, NO.
LA-TER.
LATER ?

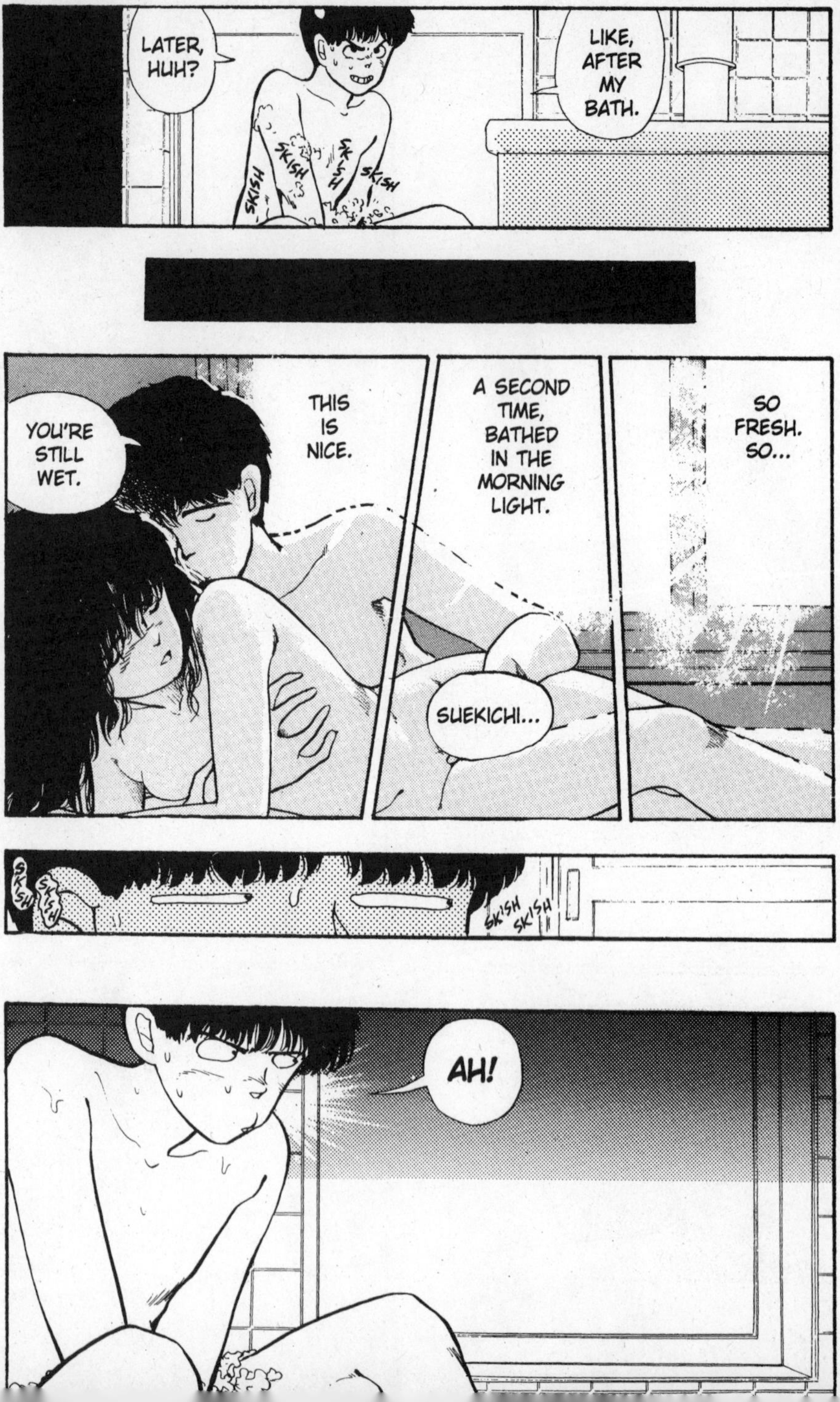
LATER, HUH?
SKISH SKISH SKISH SKISH
LIKE, AFTER MY BATH.
YOU'RE STILL WET.
THIS IS NICE.
A SECOND TIME, BATHED IN THE MORNING LIGHT.
SUEKICHI...
SO FRESH. SO...
SKISH SKISH SKISH SKISH
AH!

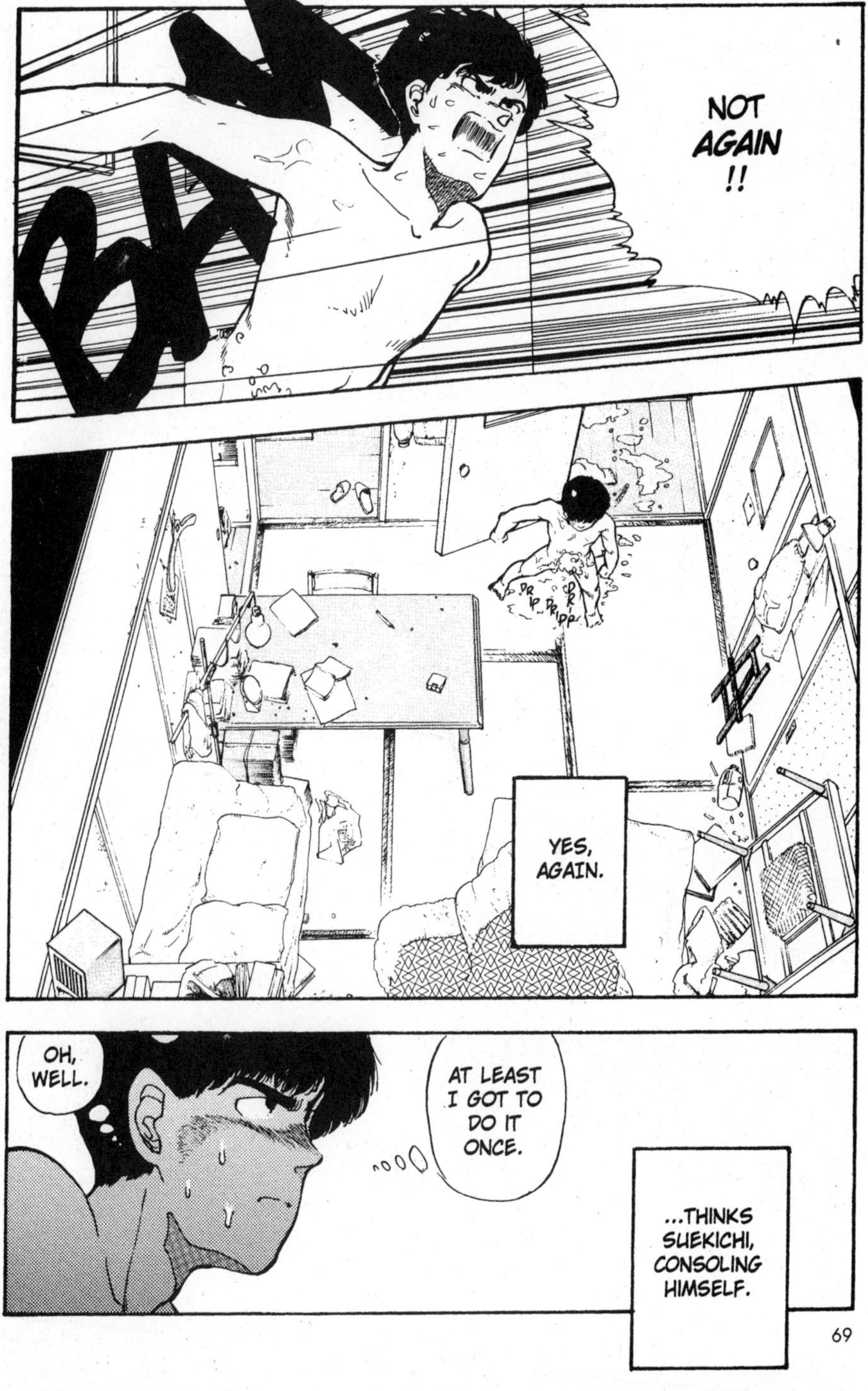
NOT AGAIN !!
YES, AGAIN.
OH, WELL.
AT LEAST I GOT TO DO IT ONCE.
...THINKS SUEKICHI, CONSOLING HIMSELF.

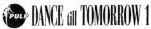

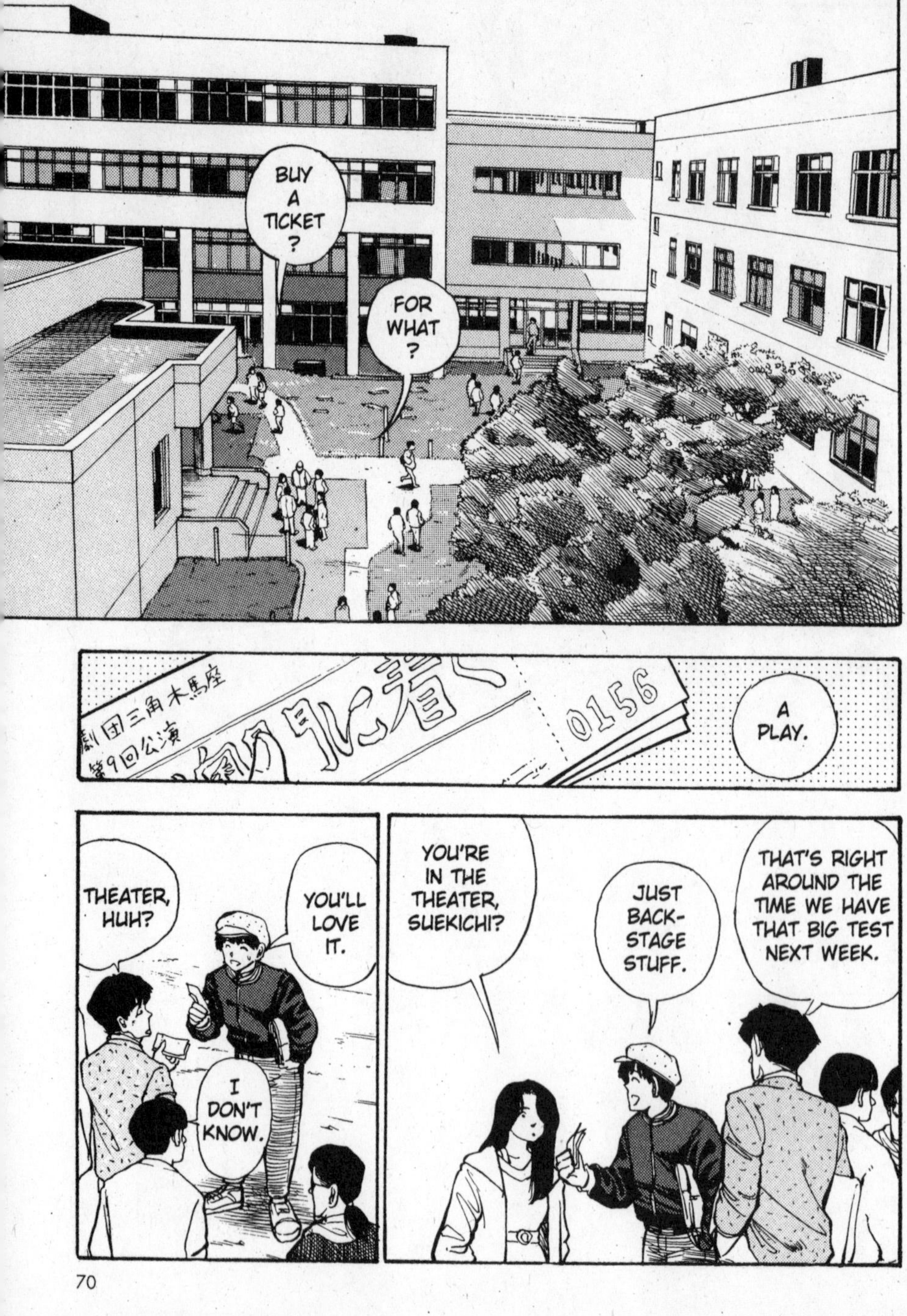
BUY A TICKET?
FOR WHAT?
劇団三角木馬座
第9回公演
0156
A PLAY.
THEATER, HUH?
YOU'LL LOVE IT.
I DON'T KNOW.
YOU'RE IN THE THEATER, SUEKICHI?
JUST BACKSTAGE STUFF.
THAT'S RIGHT AROUND THE TIME WE HAVE THAT BIG TEST NEXT WEEK.

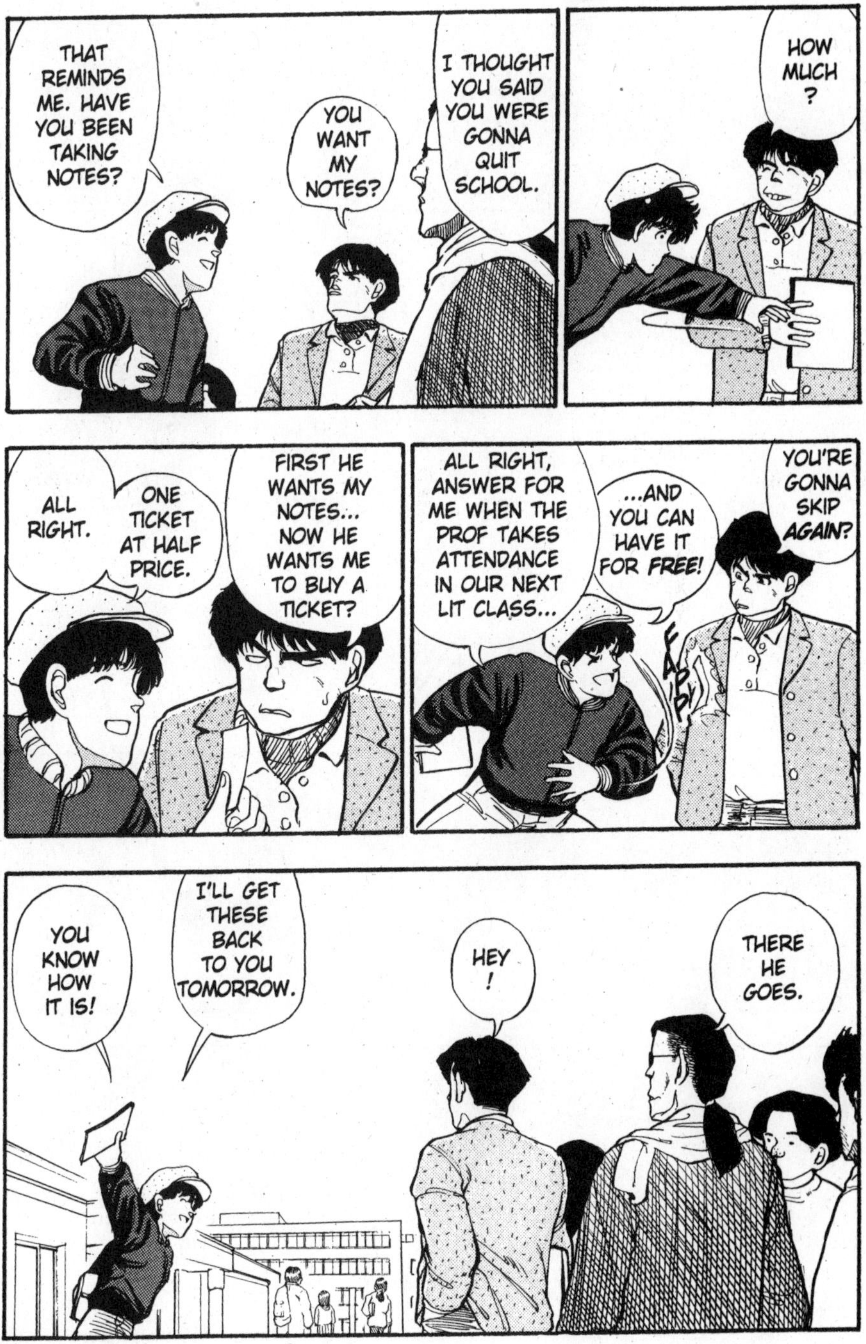
THAT REMINDS ME. HAVE YOU BEEN TAKING NOTES?
YOU WANT MY NOTES?
I THOUGHT YOU SAID YOU WERE GONNA QUIT SCHOOL.
HOW MUCH?
ALL RIGHT.
ONE TICKET AT HALF PRICE.
FIRST HE WANTS MY NOTES... NOW HE WANTS ME TO BUY A TICKET?
ALL RIGHT, ANSWER FOR ME WHEN THE PROF TAKES ATTENDANCE IN OUR NEXT LIT CLASS...
...AND YOU CAN HAVE IT FOR FREE!
YOU'RE GONNA SKIP AGAIN?
FAPP
YOU KNOW HOW IT IS!
I'LL GET THESE BACK TO YOU TOMORROW.
HEY!
THERE HE GOES.

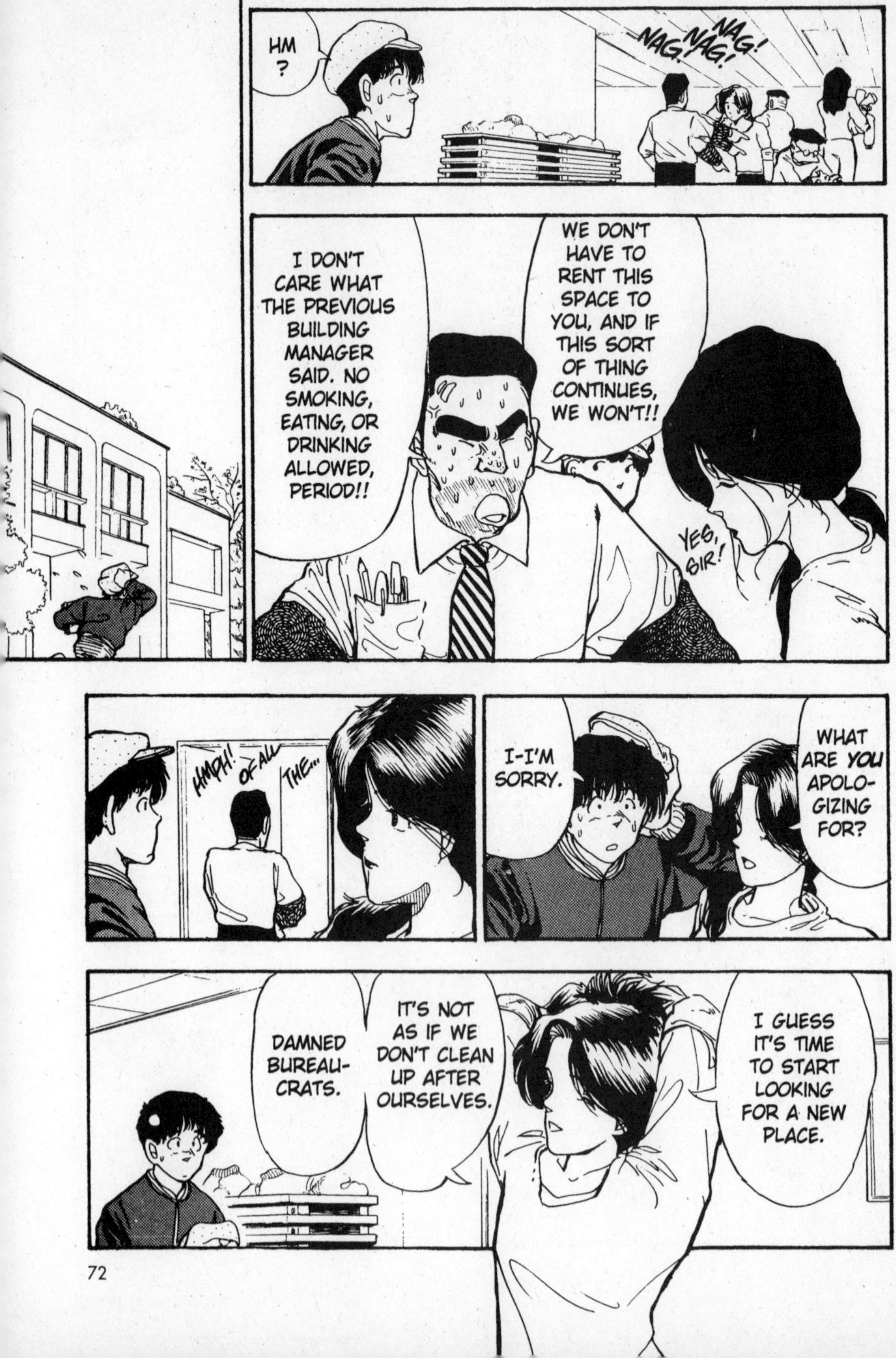
HM ?
NAG NAG NAG!
I DON'T CARE WHAT THE PREVIOUS BUILDING MANAGER SAID. NO SMOKING, EATING, OR DRINKING ALLOWED, PERIOD!!
WE DON'T HAVE TO RENT THIS SPACE TO YOU, AND IF THIS SORT OF THING CONTINUES, WE WON'T!!
YES, SIR!
HMPH! OF ALL THE...
I-I'M SORRY.
WHAT ARE *YOU* APOLOGIZING FOR?
DAMNED BUREAU-CRATS.
IT'S NOT AS IF WE DON'T CLEAN UP AFTER OURSELVES.
I GUESS IT'S TIME TO START LOOKING FOR A NEW PLACE.

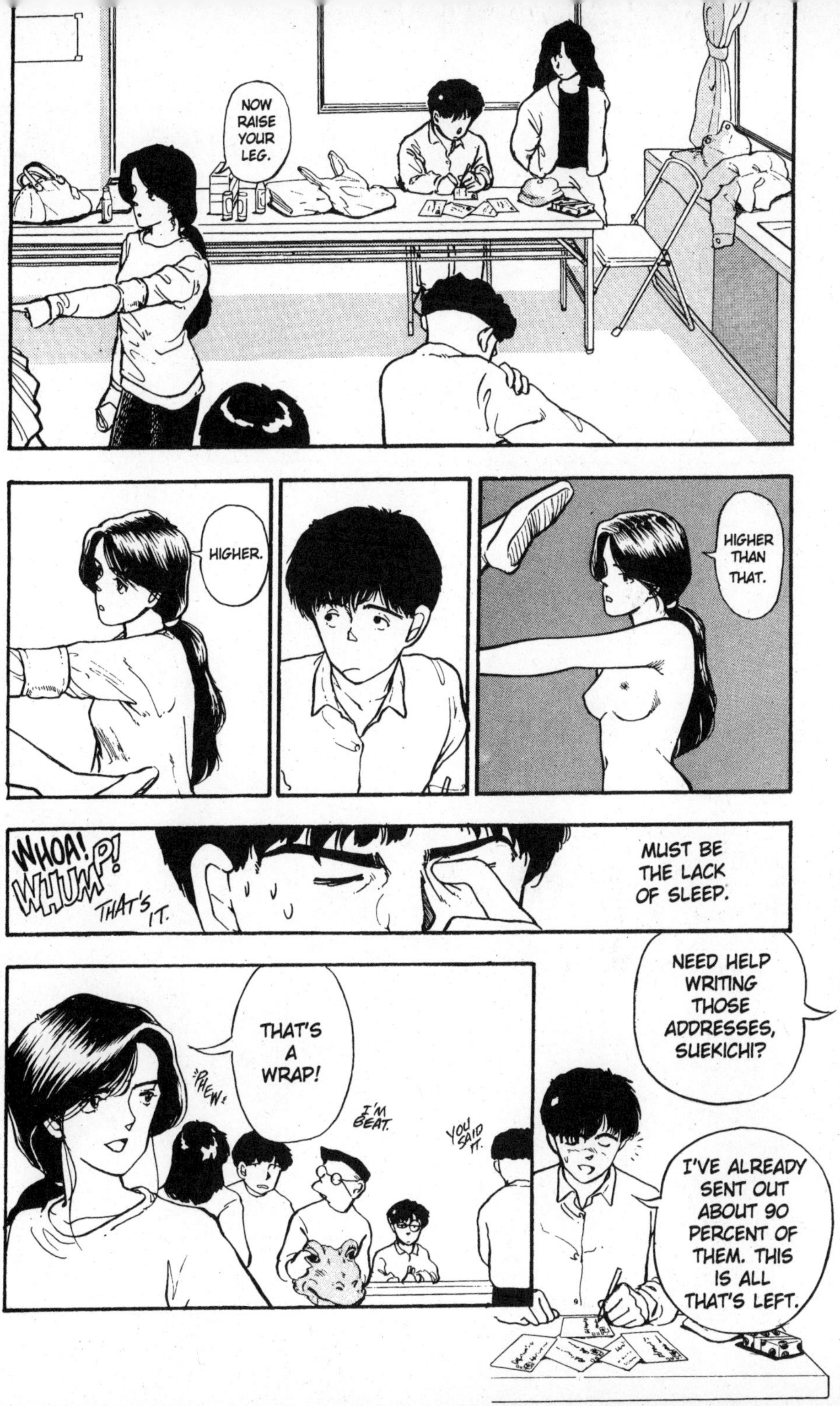
NOW RAISE YOUR LEG.
HIGHER.
HIGHER THAN THAT.
WHOA!
WHUMP!
THAT'S IT.
MUST BE THE LACK OF SLEEP.
PHEW
THAT'S A WRAP!
I'M BEAT.
YOU SAID IT.
NEED HELP WRITING THOSE ADDRESSES, SUEKICHI?
I'VE ALREADY SENT OUT ABOUT 90 PERCENT OF THEM. THIS IS ALL THAT'S LEFT.

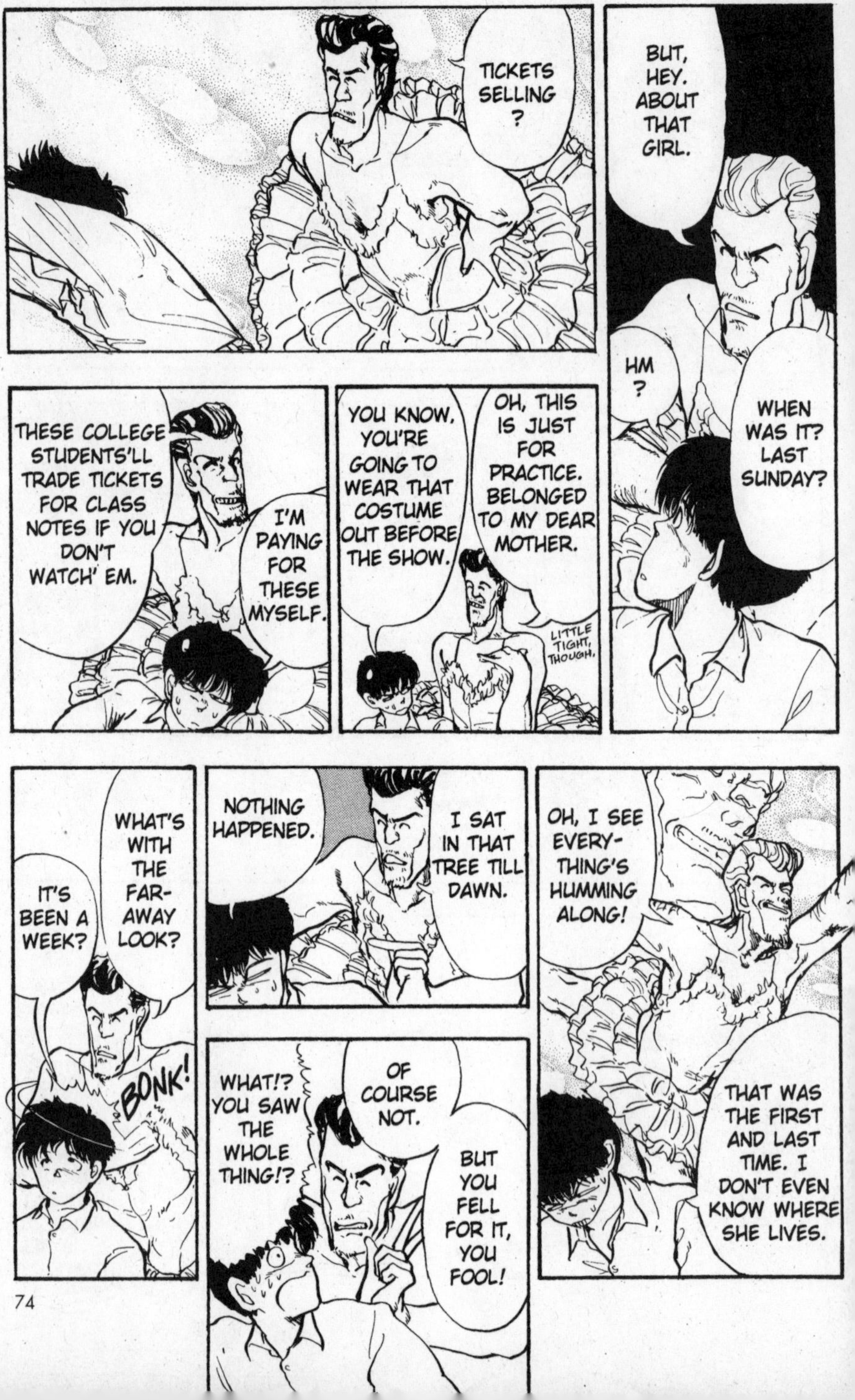
TICKETS SELLING ?
THESE COLLEGE STUDENTS'LL TRADE TICKETS FOR CLASS NOTES IF YOU DON'T WATCH' EM.
I'M PAYING FOR THESE MYSELF.
YOU KNOW, YOU'RE GOING TO WEAR THAT COSTUME OUT BEFORE THE SHOW.
OH, THIS IS JUST FOR PRACTICE. BELONGED TO MY DEAR MOTHER.
LITTLE TIGHT, THOUGH.
BUT, HEY. ABOUT THAT GIRL.
HM ?
WHEN WAS IT? LAST SUNDAY?
WHAT'S WITH THE FAR-AWAY LOOK?
IT'S BEEN A WEEK?
BONK!
NOTHING HAPPENED.
I SAT IN THAT TREE TILL DAWN.
WHAT!? YOU SAW THE WHOLE THING!?
OF COURSE NOT.
BUT YOU FELL FOR IT, YOU FOOL!
OH, I SEE EVERY-THING'S HUMMING ALONG!
THAT WAS THE FIRST AND LAST TIME. I DON'T EVEN KNOW WHERE SHE LIVES.

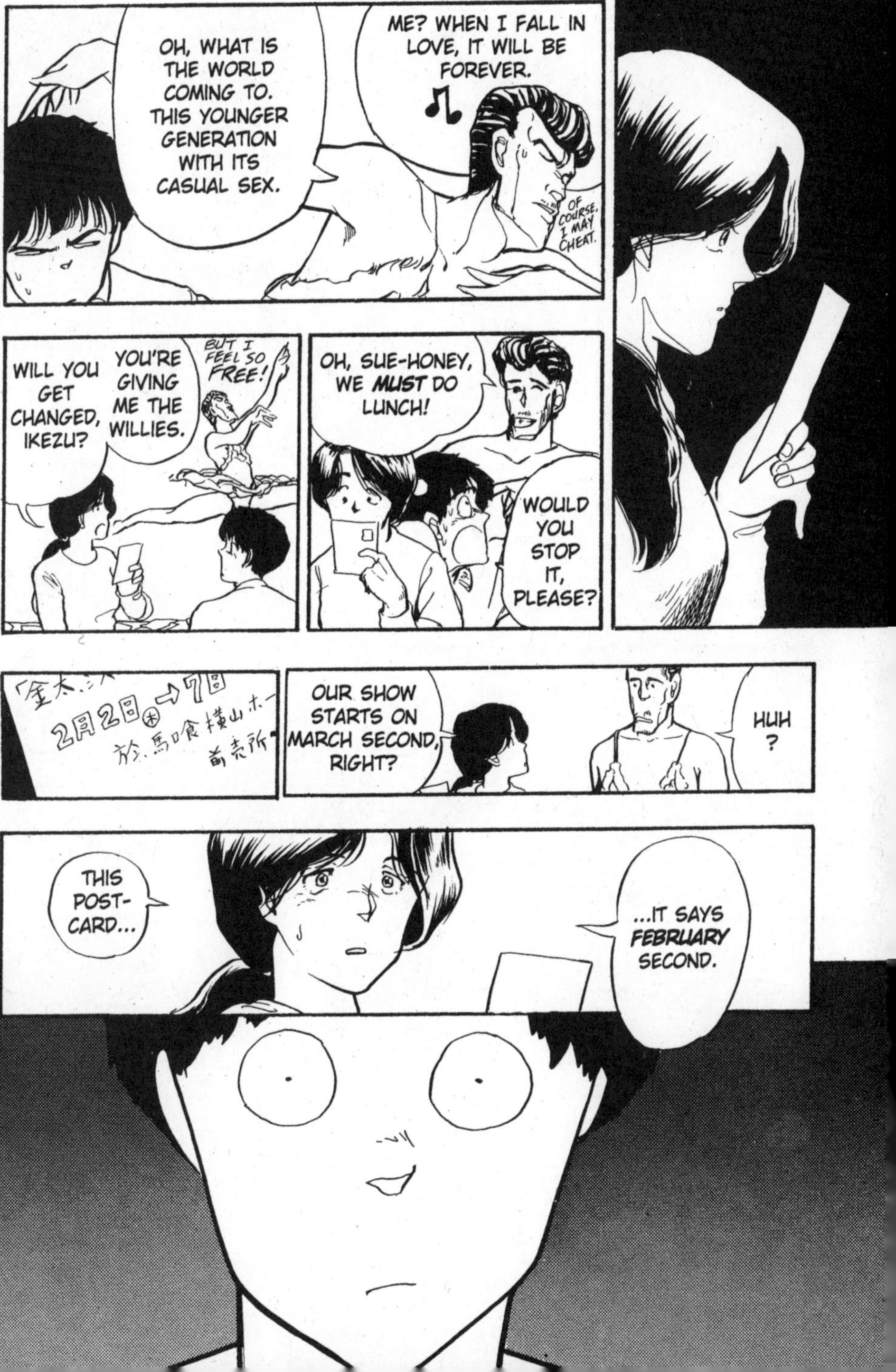
OH, WHAT IS THE WORLD COMING TO. THIS YOUNGER GENERATION WITH ITS CASUAL SEX.
ME? WHEN I FALL IN LOVE, IT WILL BE FOREVER.
OF COURSE, I MAY CHEAT.
WILL YOU GET CHANGED, IKEZU?
YOU'RE GIVING ME THE WILLIES.
BUT I FEEL SO FREE!
OH, SUE-HONEY, WE MUST DO LUNCH!
WOULD YOU STOP IT, PLEASE?
「金太
2月2日㊍→7日
於.馬喰横山ホー
前売所
OUR SHOW STARTS ON MARCH SECOND, RIGHT?
HUH?
THIS POST-CARD...
...IT SAYS FEBRUARY SECOND.

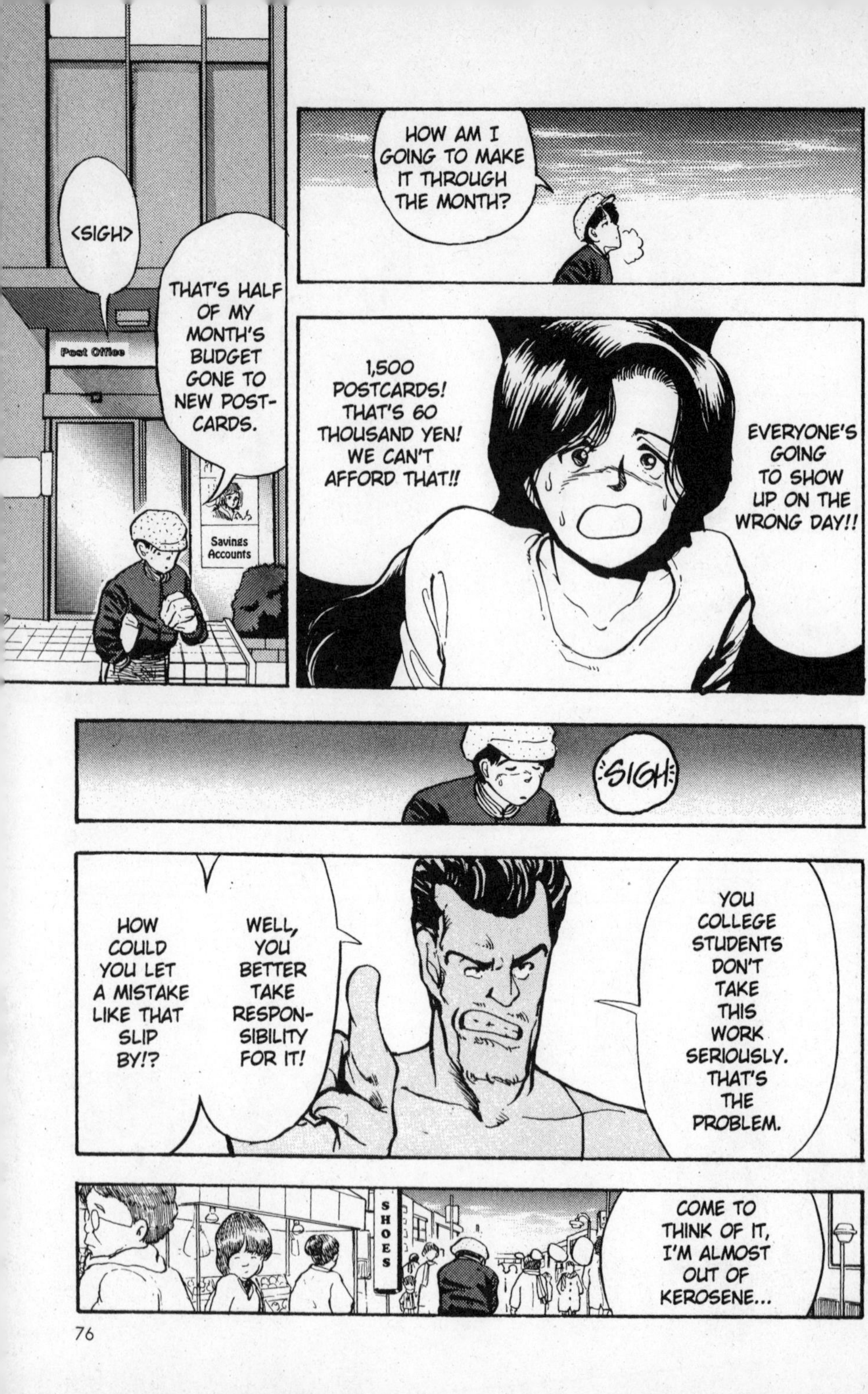

<SIGH>
Post Office
THAT'S HALF OF MY MONTH'S BUDGET GONE TO NEW POST-CARDS.
Savings Accounts
HOW AM I GOING TO MAKE IT THROUGH THE MONTH?
1,500 POSTCARDS! THAT'S 60 THOUSAND YEN! WE CAN'T AFFORD THAT!!
EVERYONE'S GOING TO SHOW UP ON THE WRONG DAY!!
SIGH
HOW COULD YOU LET A MISTAKE LIKE THAT SLIP BY!?
WELL, YOU BETTER TAKE RESPON-SIBILITY FOR IT!
YOU COLLEGE STUDENTS DON'T TAKE THIS WORK SERIOUSLY. THAT'S THE PROBLEM.
SHOES
COME TO THINK OF IT, I'M ALMOST OUT OF KEROSENE...

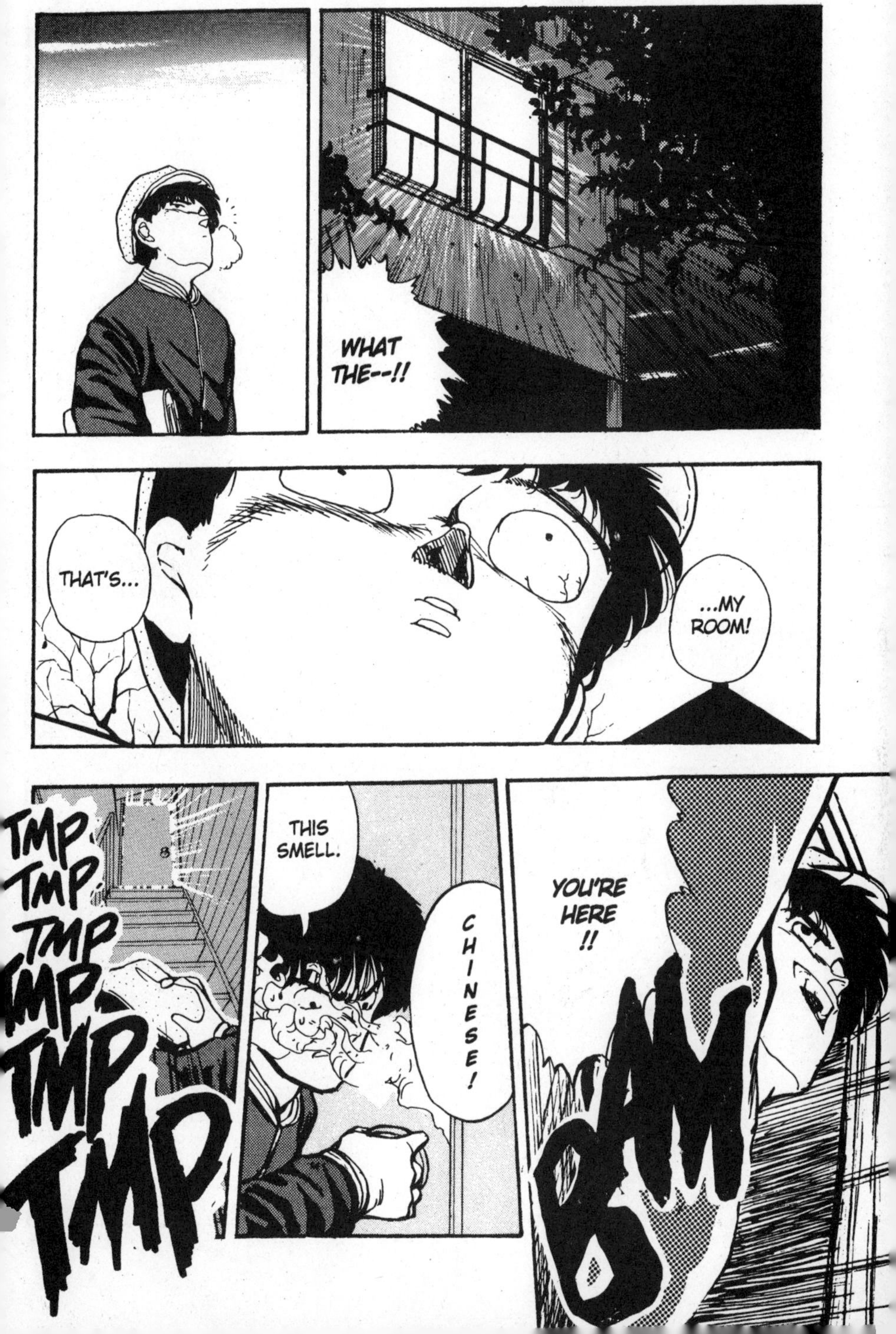
WHAT THE--!!
THAT'S...
...MY ROOM!
TMP TMP TMP TMP TMP TMP
THIS SMELL.
CHINESE!
YOU'RE HERE !!
BAM

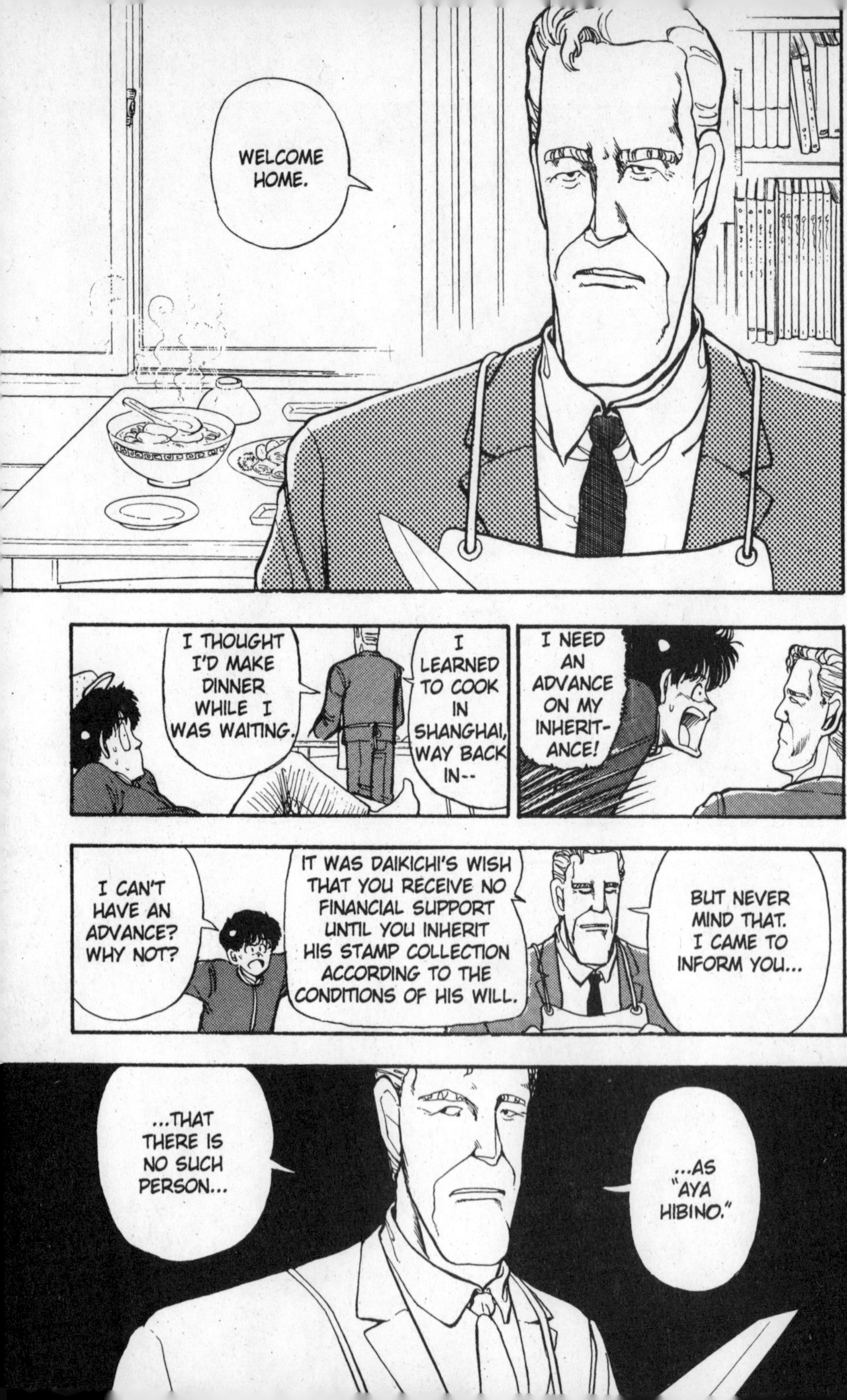
WELCOME HOME.
I THOUGHT I'D MAKE DINNER WHILE I WAS WAITING.
I LEARNED TO COOK IN SHANGHAI, WAY BACK IN--
I NEED AN ADVANCE ON MY INHERIT- ANCE!
I CAN'T HAVE AN ADVANCE? WHY NOT?
IT WAS DAIKICHI'S WISH THAT YOU RECEIVE NO FINANCIAL SUPPORT UNTIL YOU INHERIT HIS STAMP COLLECTION ACCORDING TO THE CONDITIONS OF HIS WILL.
BUT NEVER MIND THAT. I CAME TO INFORM YOU...
...THAT THERE IS NO SUCH PERSON...
...AS "AYA HIBINO."

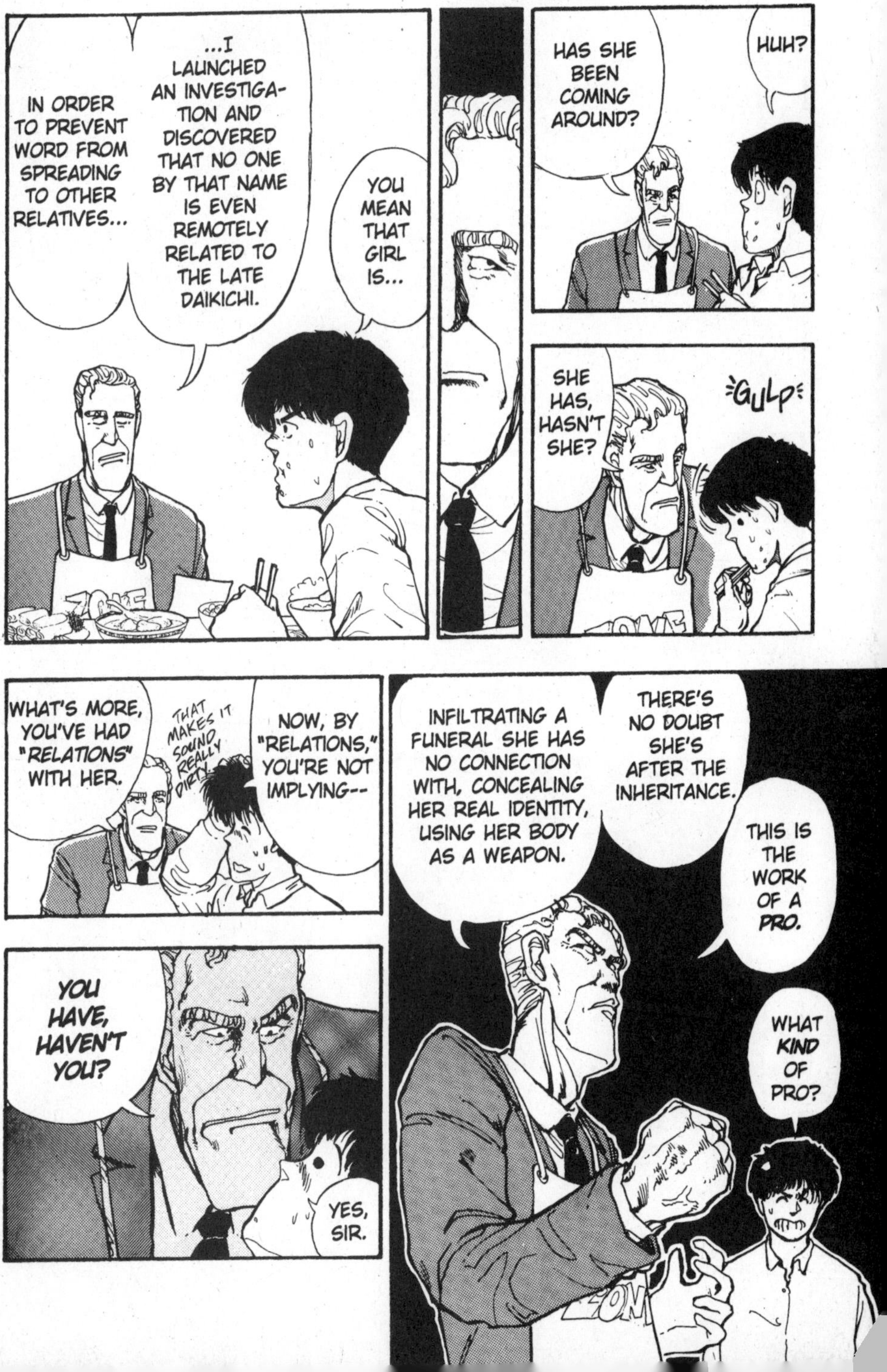
IN ORDER TO PREVENT WORD FROM SPREADING TO OTHER RELATIVES...
...I LAUNCHED AN INVESTIGATION AND DISCOVERED THAT NO ONE BY THAT NAME IS EVEN REMOTELY RELATED TO THE LATE DAIKICHI.
YOU MEAN THAT GIRL IS...
HAS SHE BEEN COMING AROUND?
HUH?
SHE HAS, HASN'T SHE?
GULP
WHAT'S MORE, YOU'VE HAD "RELATIONS" WITH HER.
THAT MAKES IT SOUND REALLY DIRTY
NOW, BY "RELATIONS," YOU'RE NOT IMPLYING--
YOU HAVE, HAVEN'T YOU?
YES, SIR.
INFILTRATING A FUNERAL SHE HAS NO CONNECTION WITH, CONCEALING HER REAL IDENTITY, USING HER BODY AS A WEAPON.
THERE'S NO DOUBT SHE'S AFTER THE INHERITANCE.
THIS IS THE WORK OF A PRO.
WHAT KIND OF PRO?

AT THIS RATE, THAT VIXEN IS SURE TO GET WHAT SHE'S AFTER.

THE ENEMY IS A PROFESSIONAL. IF SHE COMES HERE AGAIN, YOU ARE TO HAVE NOTHING TO DO WITH HER.

DON'T LET YOUR FEELINGS GET THE BEST OF YOU.

MR. TACHIMI...

I'LL BE OFF NOW.

I MUST PLAN A STRATEGY AT ONCE.

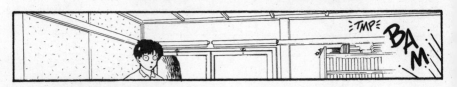

TMP

BAM

PHEW, IT'S AWFULLY STUFFY IN THERE.

SH SH

RED

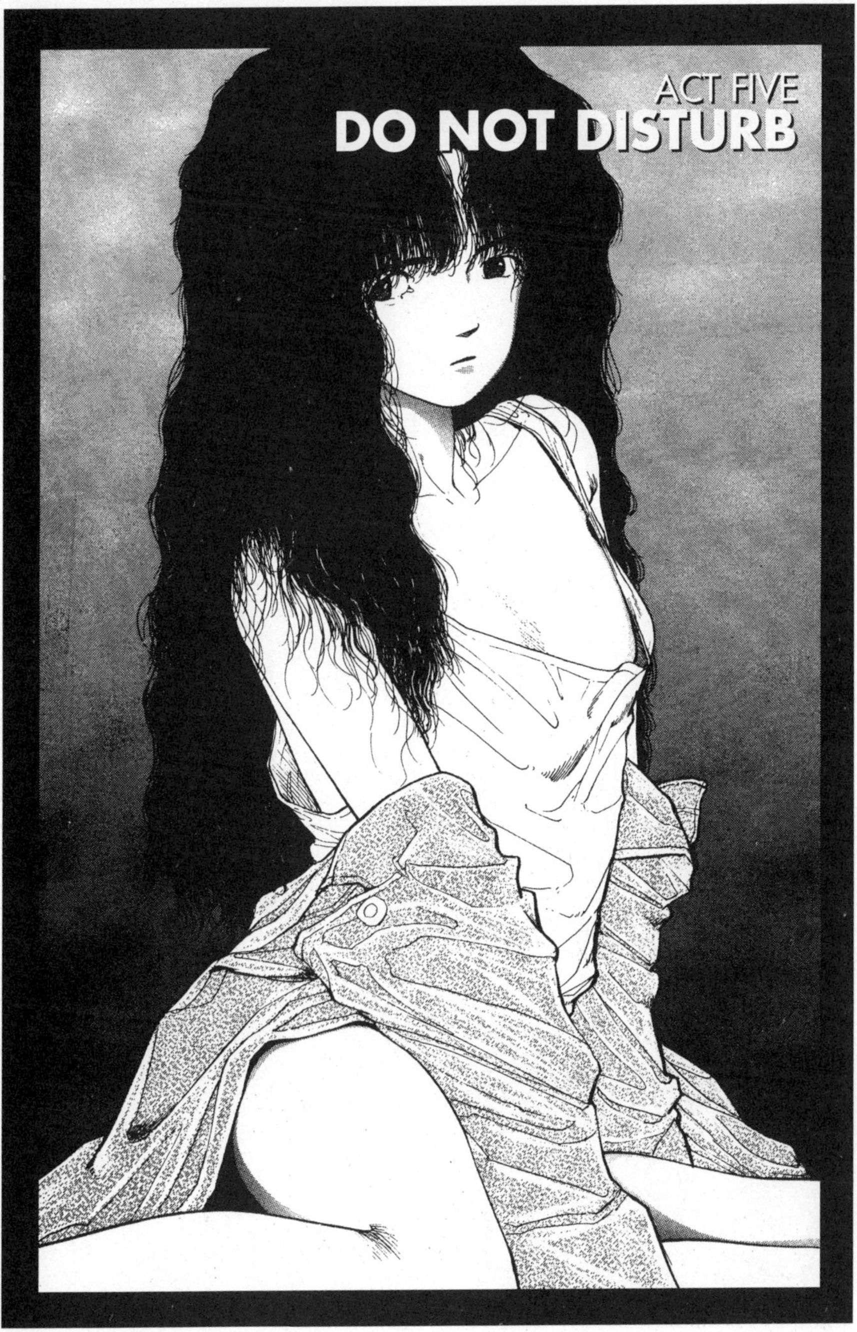
ACT FIVE
DO NOT DISTURB

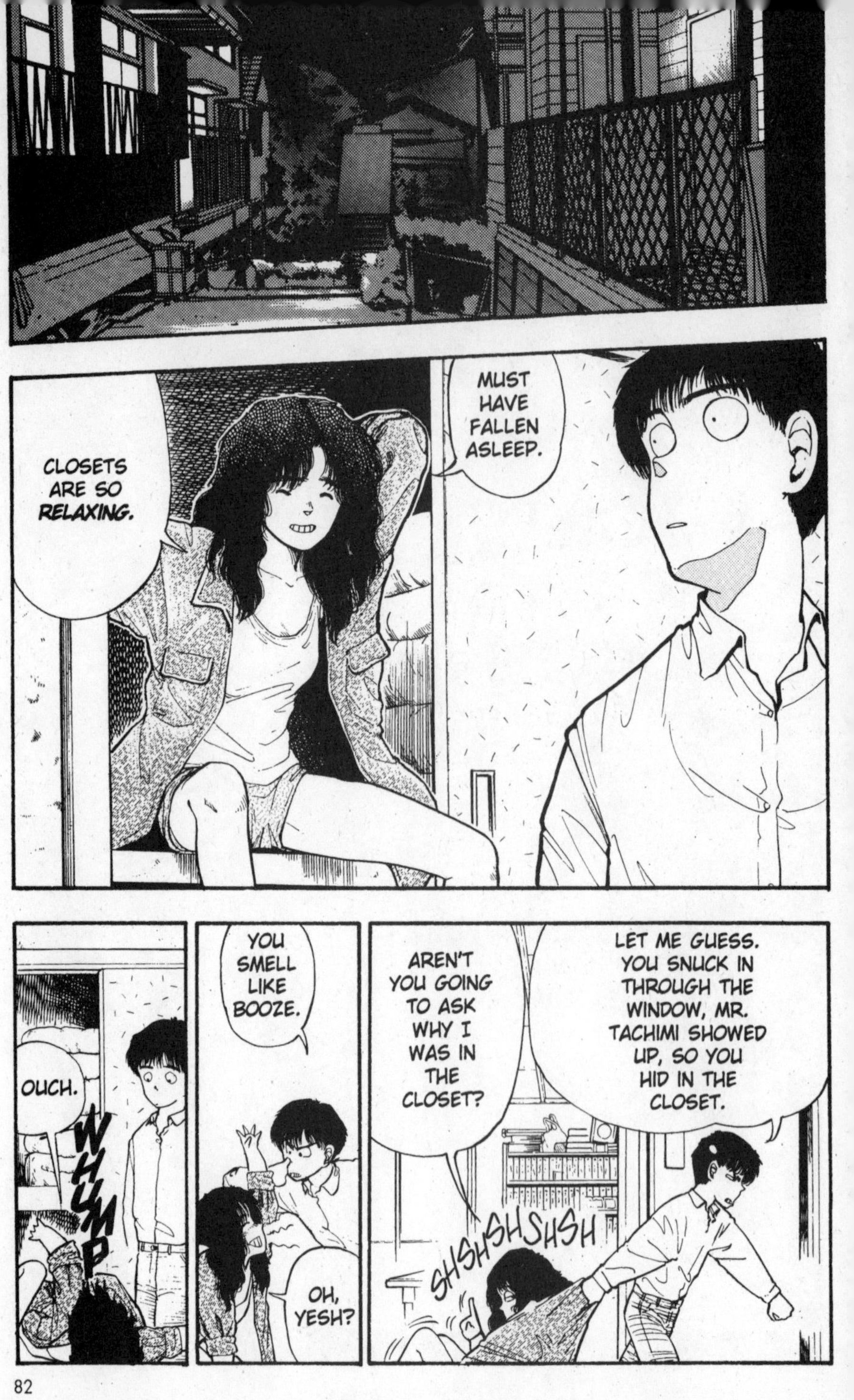
CLOSETS ARE SO RELAXING.
MUST HAVE FALLEN ASLEEP.
OUCH.
WHUMP
YOU SMELL LIKE BOOZE.
OH, YESH?
AREN'T YOU GOING TO ASK WHY I WAS IN THE CLOSET?
LET ME GUESS. YOU SNUCK IN THROUGH THE WINDOW, MR. TACHIMI SHOWED UP, SO YOU HID IN THE CLOSET.
SHSHSHSHSH

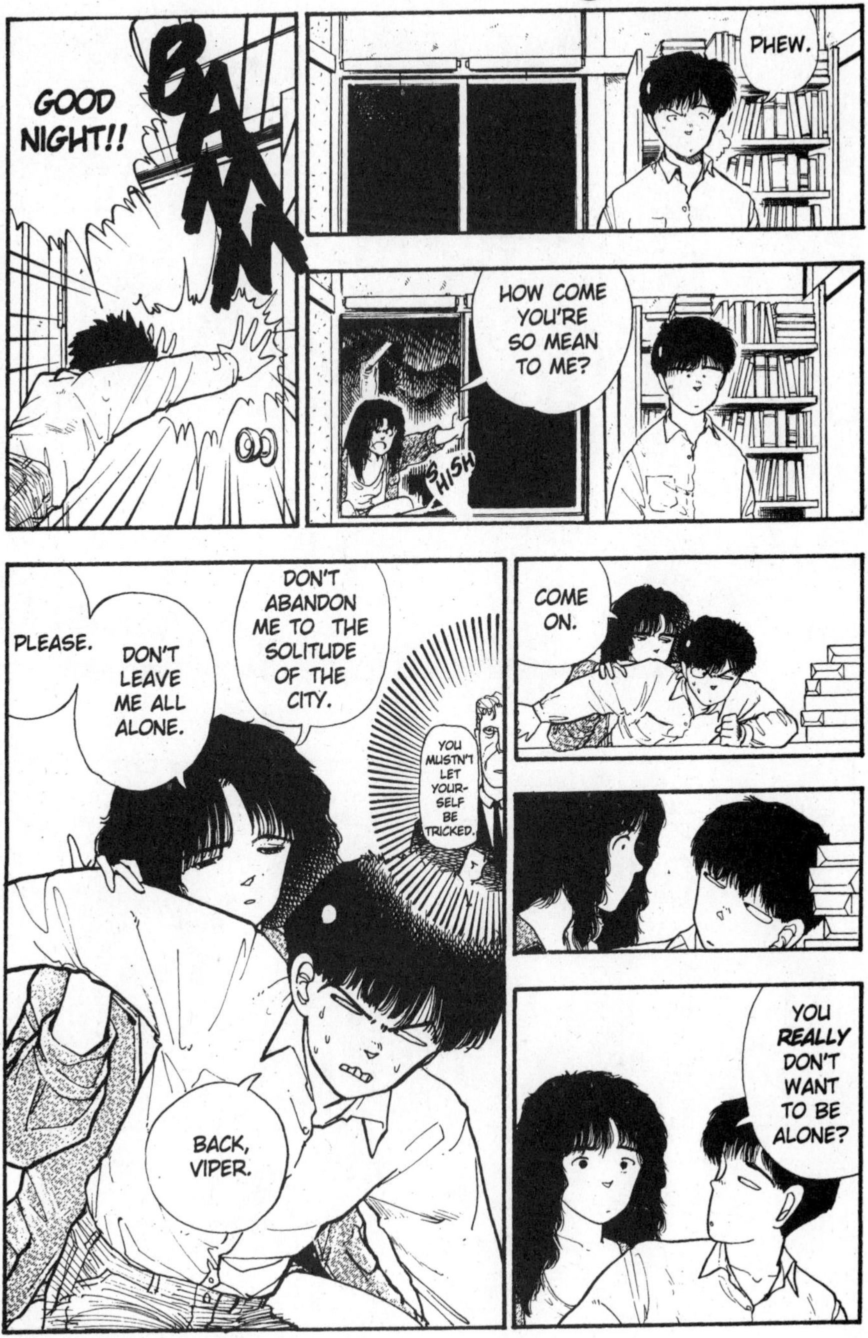
GOOD NIGHT!!
BAM
PHEW.
HOW COME YOU'RE SO MEAN TO ME?
SHISH
PLEASE.
DON'T LEAVE ME ALL ALONE.
DON'T ABANDON ME TO THE SOLITUDE OF THE CITY.
YOU MUSTN'T LET YOURSELF BE TRICKED.
BACK, VIPER.
COME ON.
YOU REALLY DON'T WANT TO BE ALONE?

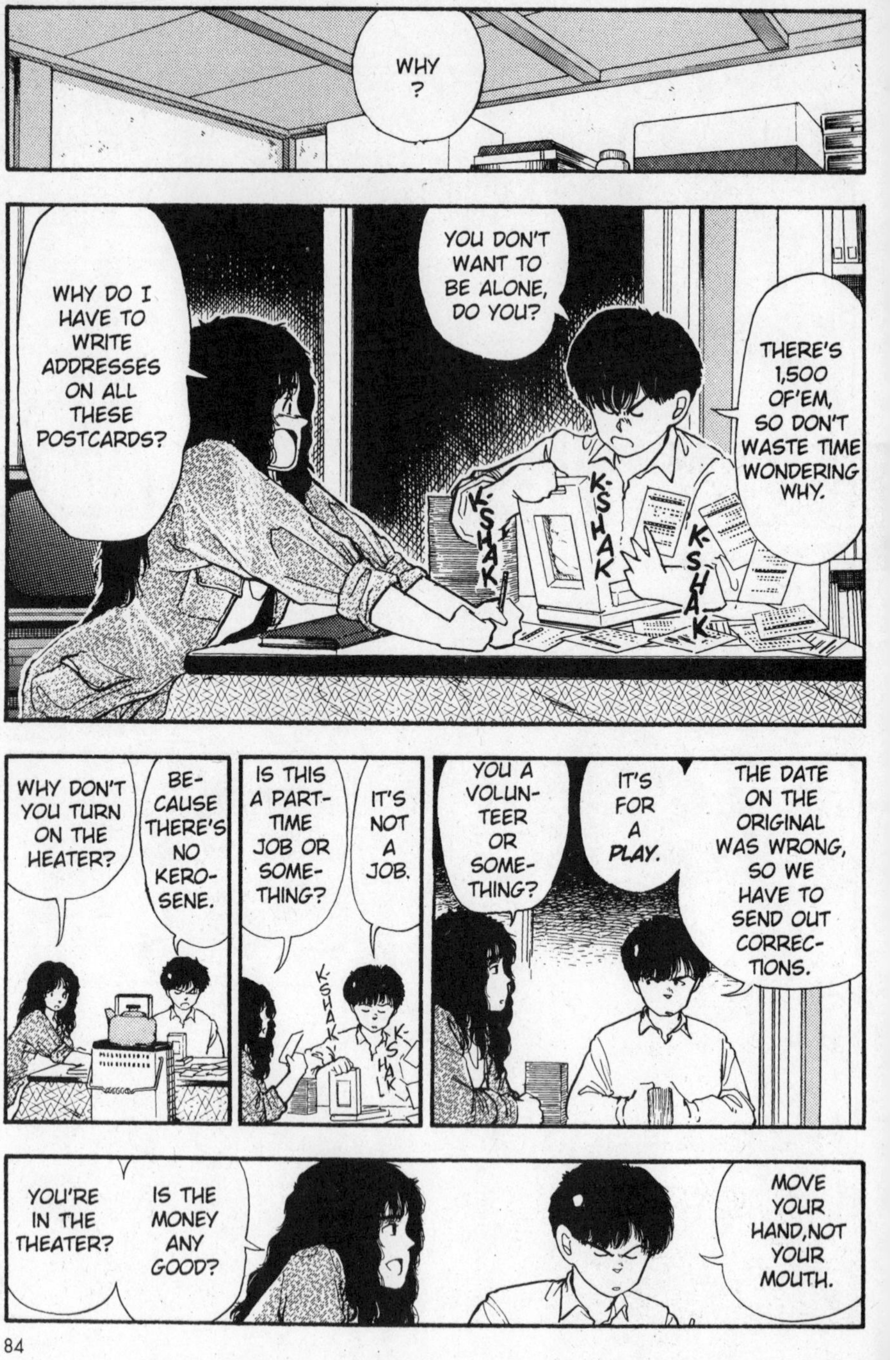
WHY ?
WHY DO I HAVE TO WRITE ADDRESSES ON ALL THESE POSTCARDS?
YOU DON'T WANT TO BE ALONE, DO YOU?
K-SHAK
K-SHAK
K-SHAK
THERE'S 1,500 OF'EM, SO DON'T WASTE TIME WONDERING WHY.
WHY DON'T YOU TURN ON THE HEATER?
BE-CAUSE THERE'S NO KERO-SENE.
IS THIS A PART-TIME JOB OR SOME-THING?
IT'S NOT A JOB.
K-SHAK
K-SHALK
YOU A VOLUN-TEER OR SOME-THING?
IT'S FOR A *PLAY*.
THE DATE ON THE ORIGINAL WAS WRONG, SO WE HAVE TO SEND OUT CORREC-TIONS.
YOU'RE IN THE THEATER?
IS THE MONEY ANY GOOD?
MOVE YOUR HAND,NOT YOUR MOUTH.

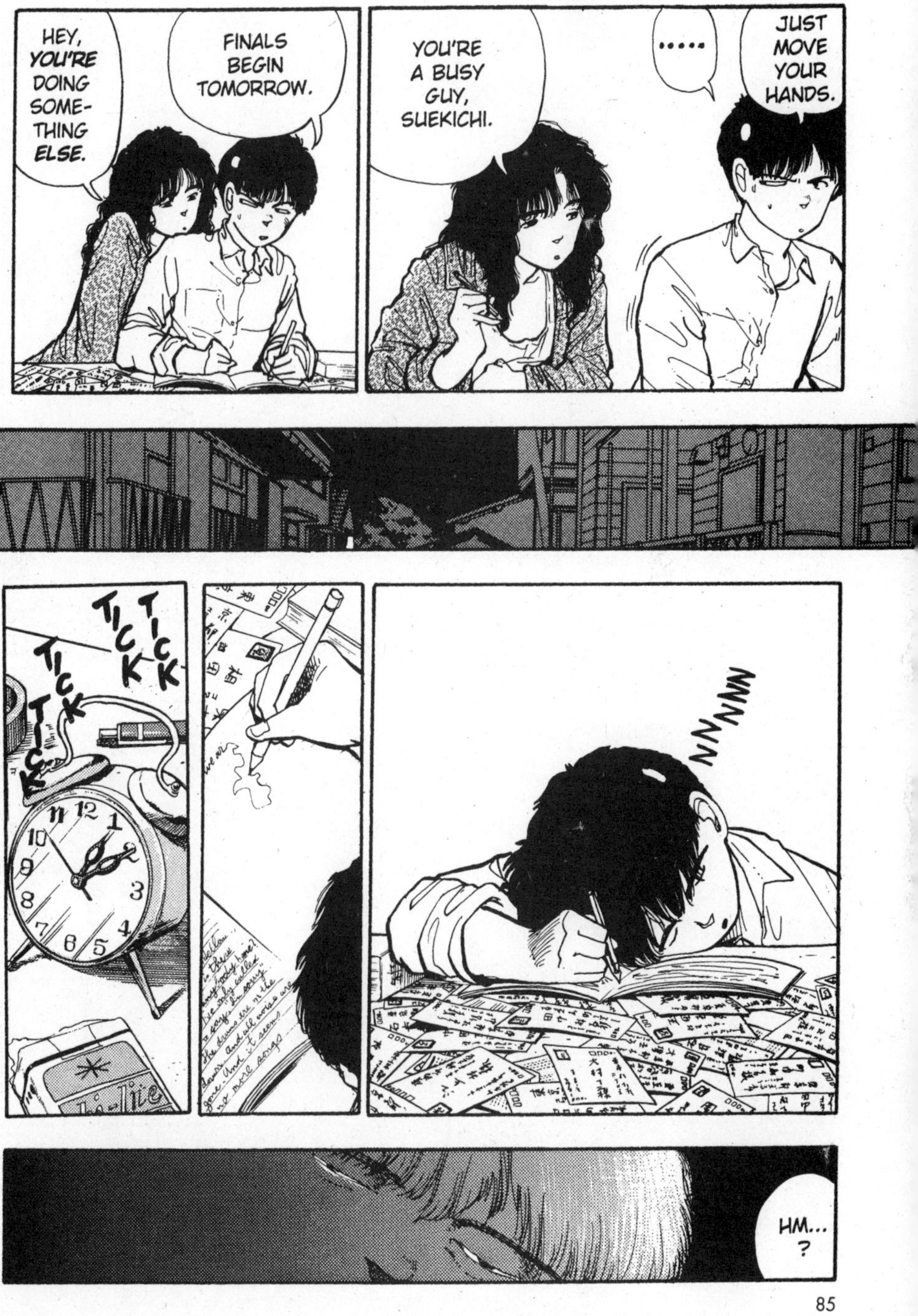
HEY, YOU'RE DOING SOME-THING ELSE.
FINALS BEGIN TOMORROW.
YOU'RE A BUSY GUY, SUEKICHI.
.....
JUST MOVE YOUR HANDS.
TICK TICK TICK TICK
NNNNNN
HM... ?

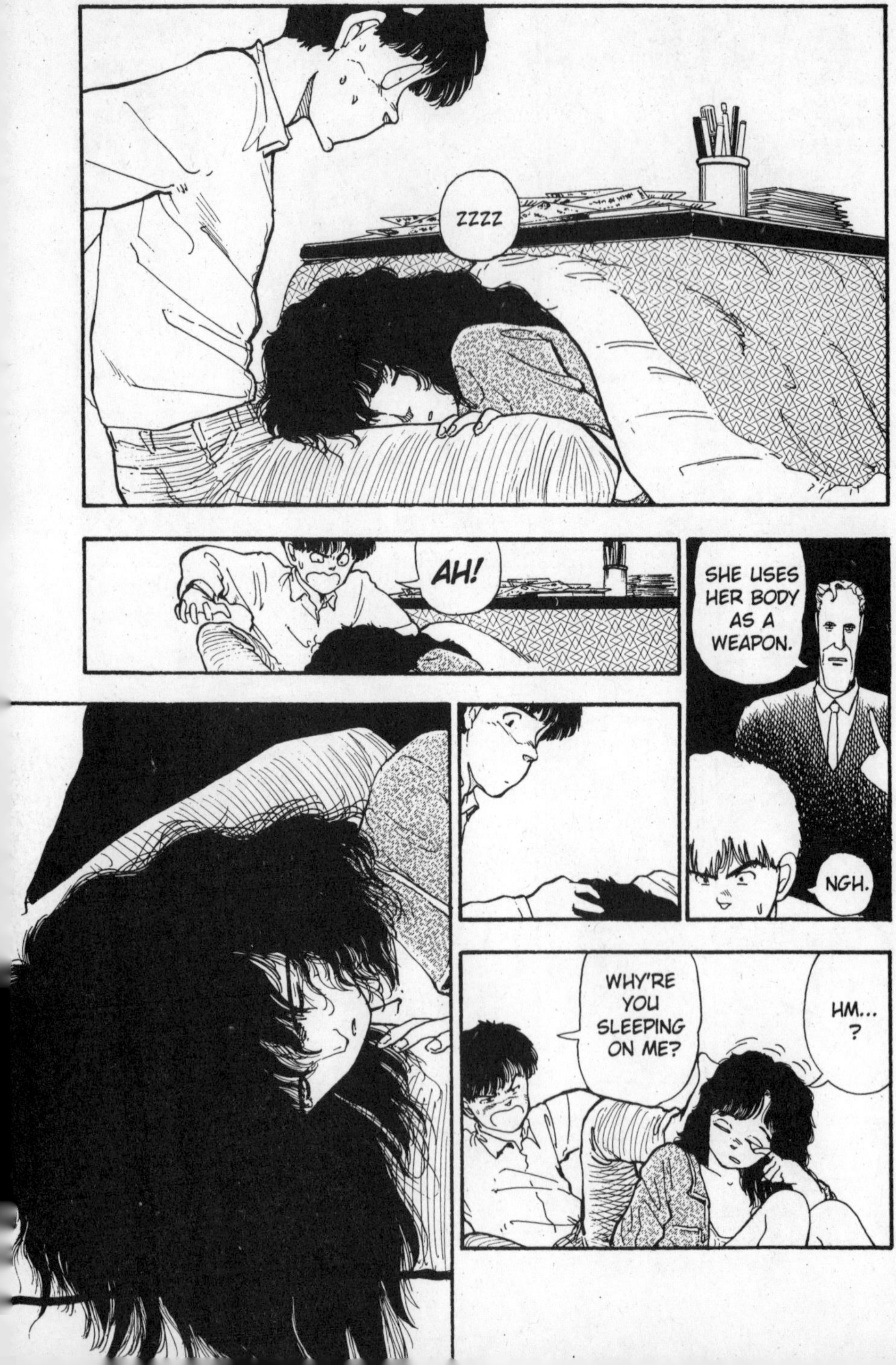
ZZZZ
AH!
SHE USES HER BODY AS A WEAPON.
NGH.
WHY'RE YOU SLEEPING ON ME?
HM... ?

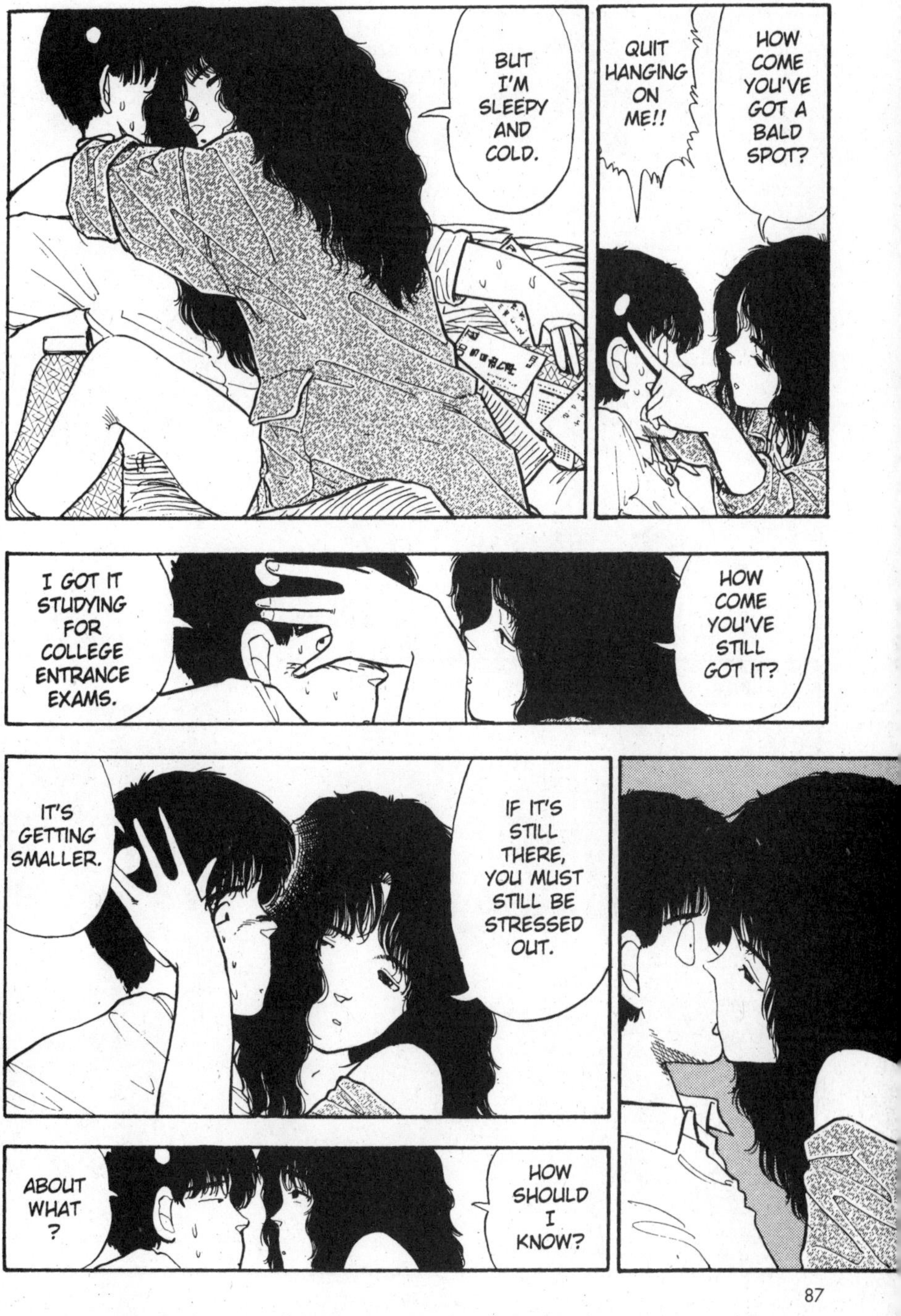
BUT I'M SLEEPY AND COLD.
QUIT HANGING ON ME!!
HOW COME YOU'VE GOT A BALD SPOT?
I GOT IT STUDYING FOR COLLEGE ENTRANCE EXAMS.
HOW COME YOU'VE STILL GOT IT?
IT'S GETTING SMALLER.
IF IT'S STILL THERE, YOU MUST STILL BE STRESSED OUT.
ABOUT WHAT ?
HOW SHOULD I KNOW?

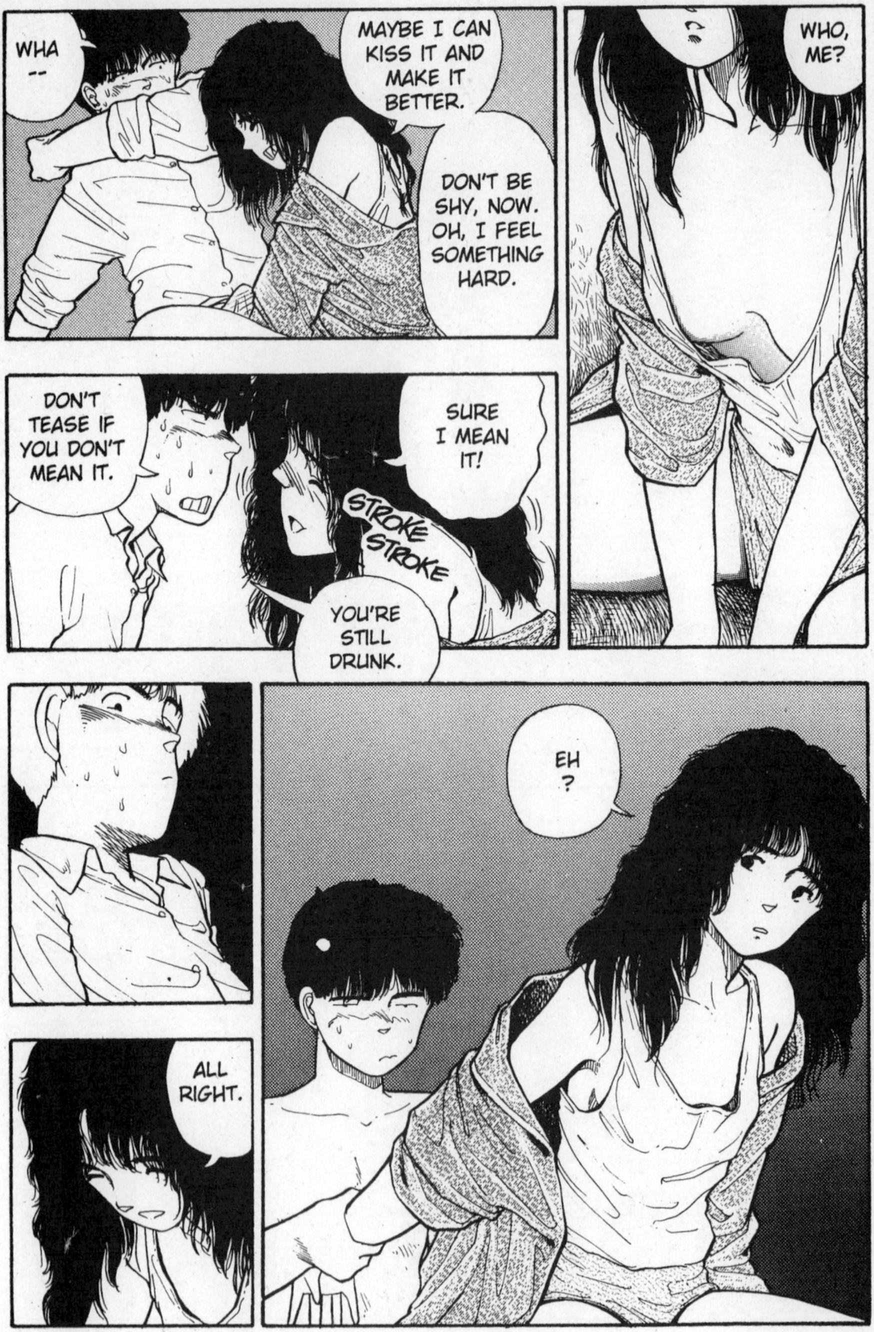
WHA --
MAYBE I CAN KISS IT AND MAKE IT BETTER.
DON'T BE SHY, NOW. OH, I FEEL SOMETHING HARD.
DON'T TEASE IF YOU DON'T MEAN IT.
SURE I MEAN IT!
STROKE STROKE
YOU'RE STILL DRUNK.
WHO, ME?
ALL RIGHT.
EH ?

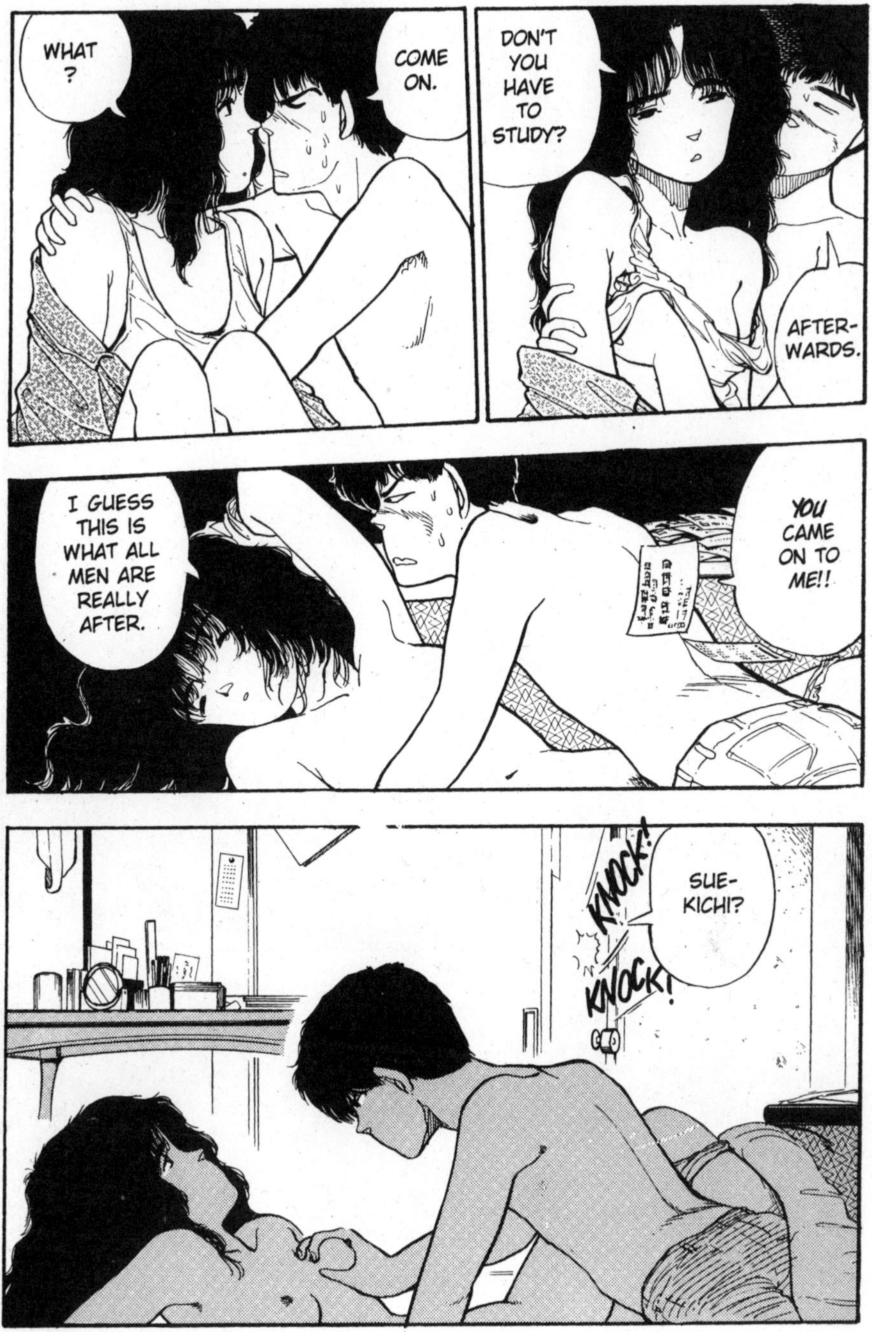
WHAT ?
COME ON.
DON'T YOU HAVE TO STUDY?
AFTER-WARDS.
I GUESS THIS IS WHAT ALL MEN ARE REALLY AFTER.
YOU CAME ON TO ME!!
KNOCK!
KNOCK!
SUE-KICHI?

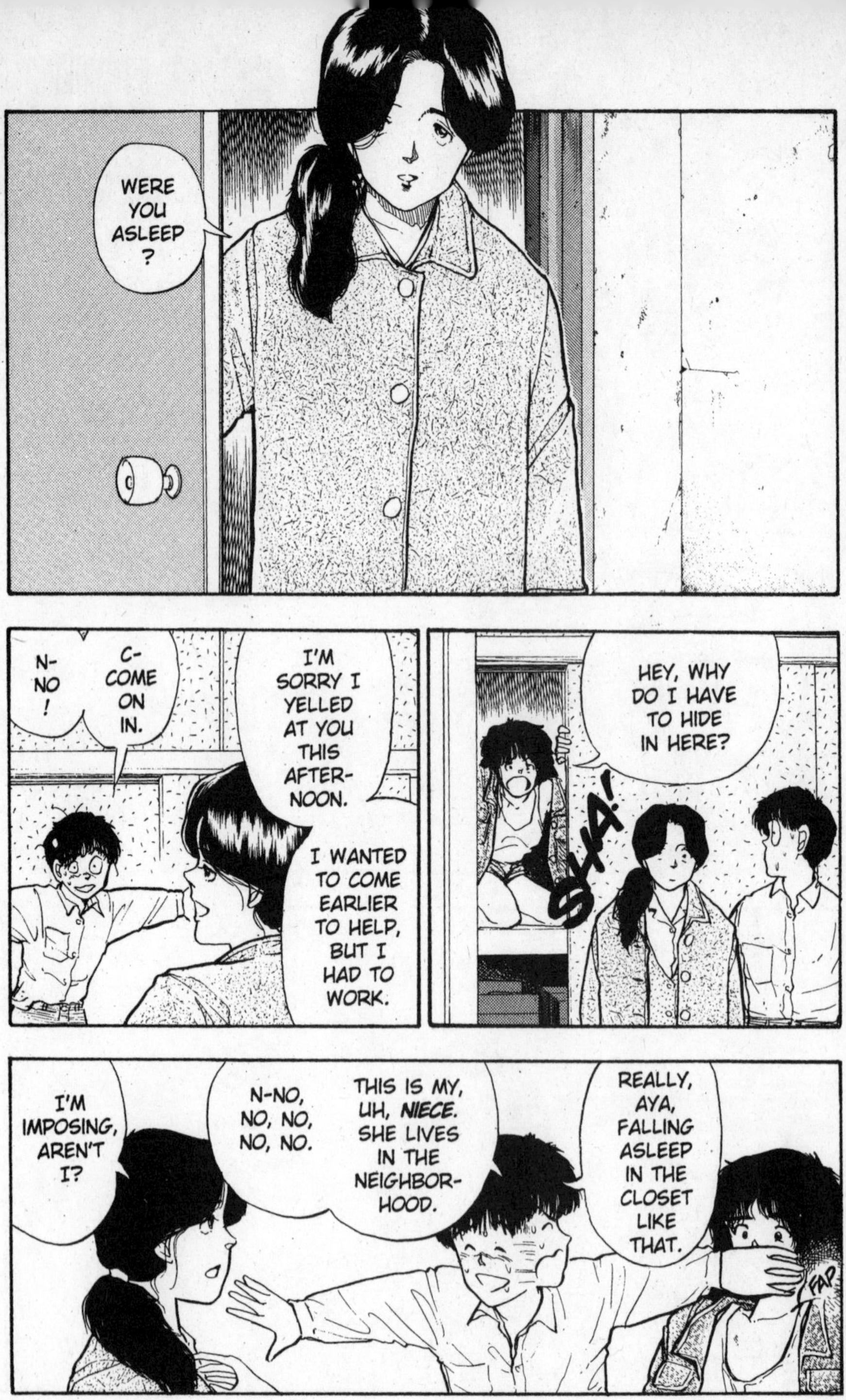
WERE YOU ASLEEP?
N-NO!
C-COME ON IN.
I'M SORRY I YELLED AT YOU THIS AFTERNOON.
I WANTED TO COME EARLIER TO HELP, BUT I HAD TO WORK.
HEY, WHY DO I HAVE TO HIDE IN HERE?
SHA!
I'M IMPOSING, AREN'T I?
N-NO, NO, NO, NO, NO.
THIS IS MY, UH, *NIECE*. SHE LIVES IN THE NEIGHBORHOOD.
REALLY, AYA, FALLING ASLEEP IN THE CLOSET LIKE THAT.
FAP

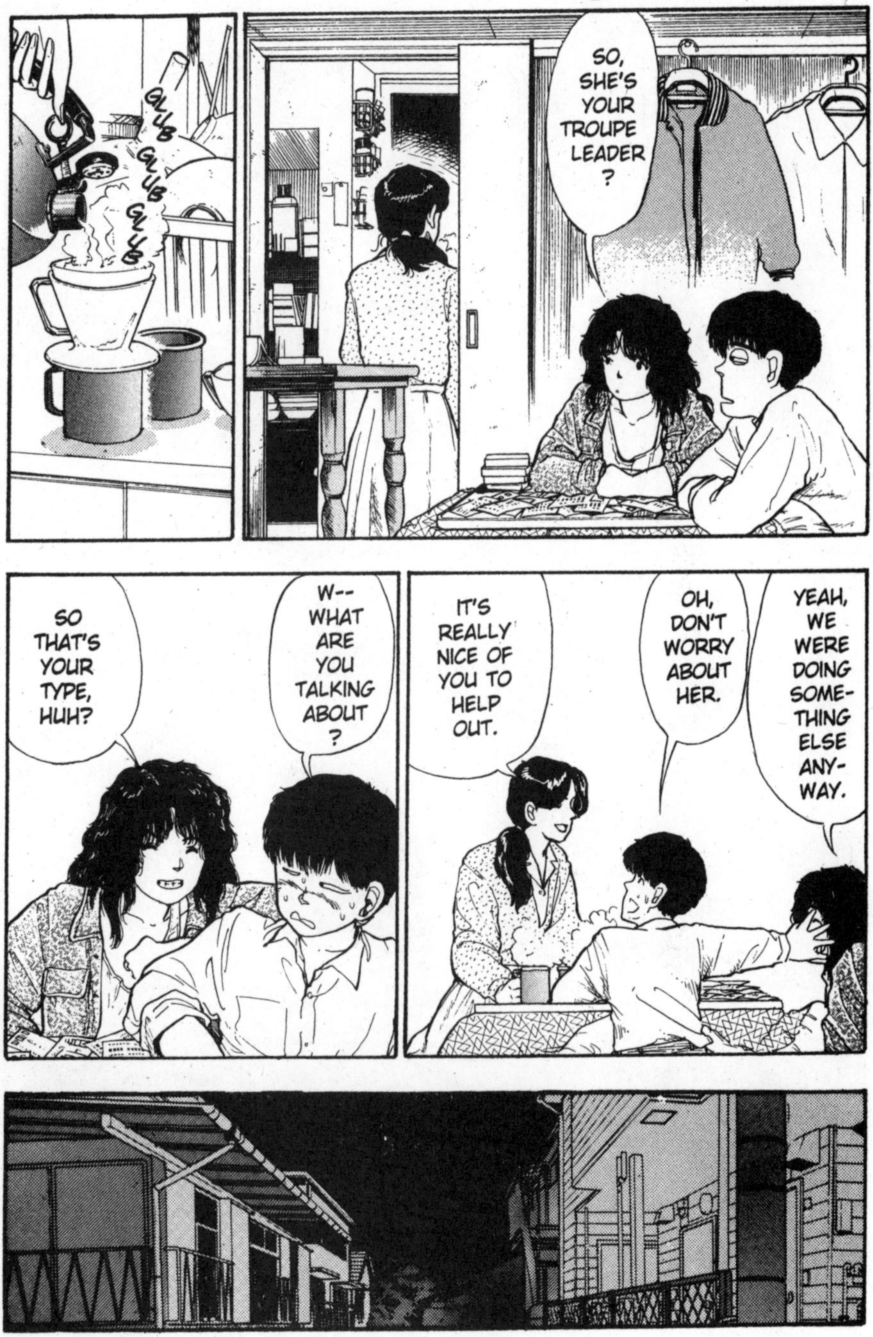
GLUB GLUB GLUB GLUB
SO, SHE'S YOUR TROUPE LEADER?
SO THAT'S YOUR TYPE, HUH?
W-- WHAT ARE YOU TALKING ABOUT?
IT'S REALLY NICE OF YOU TO HELP OUT.
OH, DON'T WORRY ABOUT HER.
YEAH, WE WERE DOING SOME-THING ELSE ANY-WAY.

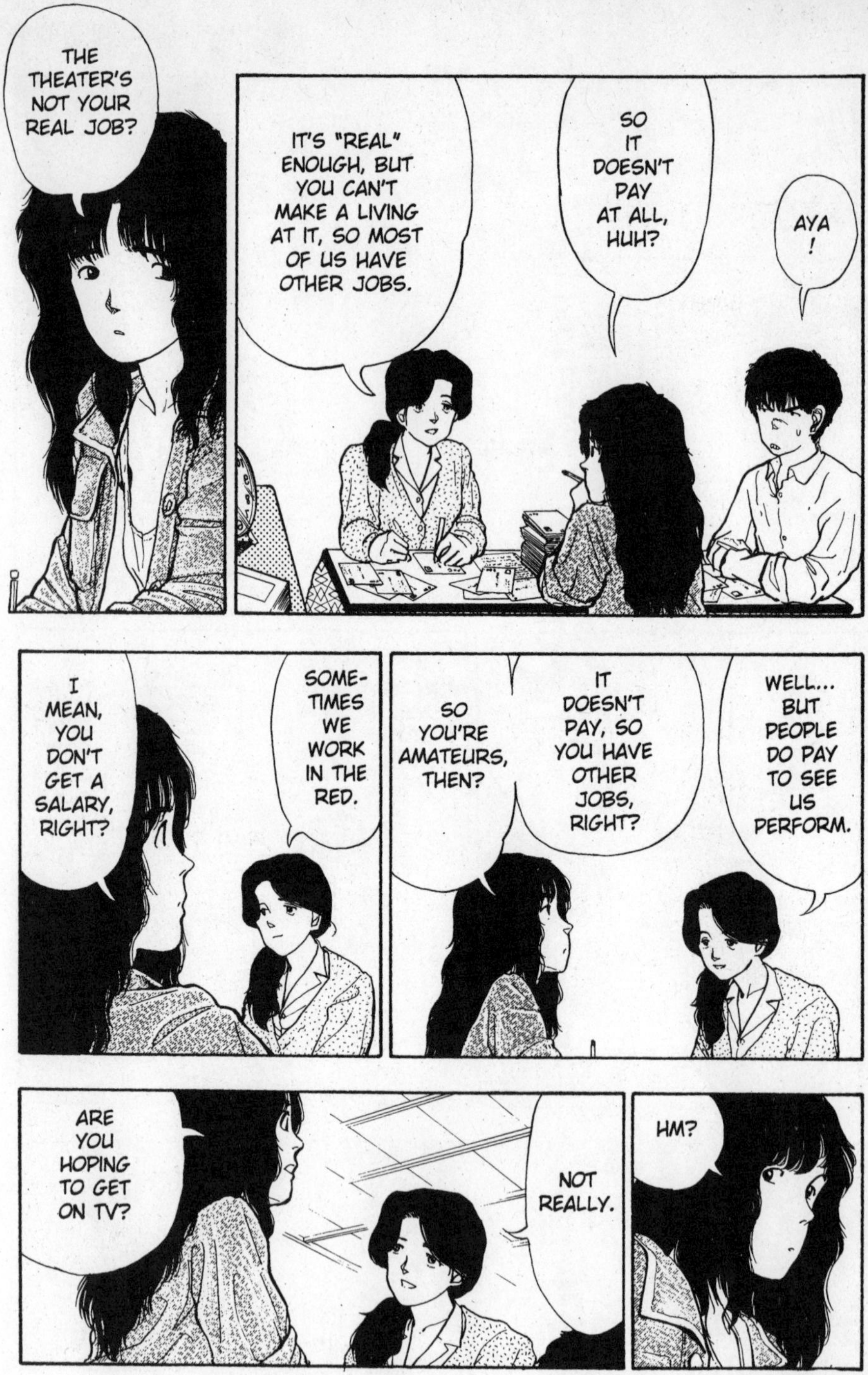
THE THEATER'S NOT YOUR REAL JOB?
IT'S "REAL" ENOUGH, BUT YOU CAN'T MAKE A LIVING AT IT, SO MOST OF US HAVE OTHER JOBS.
SO IT DOESN'T PAY AT ALL, HUH?
AYA!
I MEAN, YOU DON'T GET A SALARY, RIGHT?
SOME-TIMES WE WORK IN THE RED.
SO YOU'RE AMATEURS, THEN?
IT DOESN'T PAY, SO YOU HAVE OTHER JOBS, RIGHT?
WELL... BUT PEOPLE DO PAY TO SEE US PERFORM.
ARE YOU HOPING TO GET ON TV?
NOT REALLY.
HM?

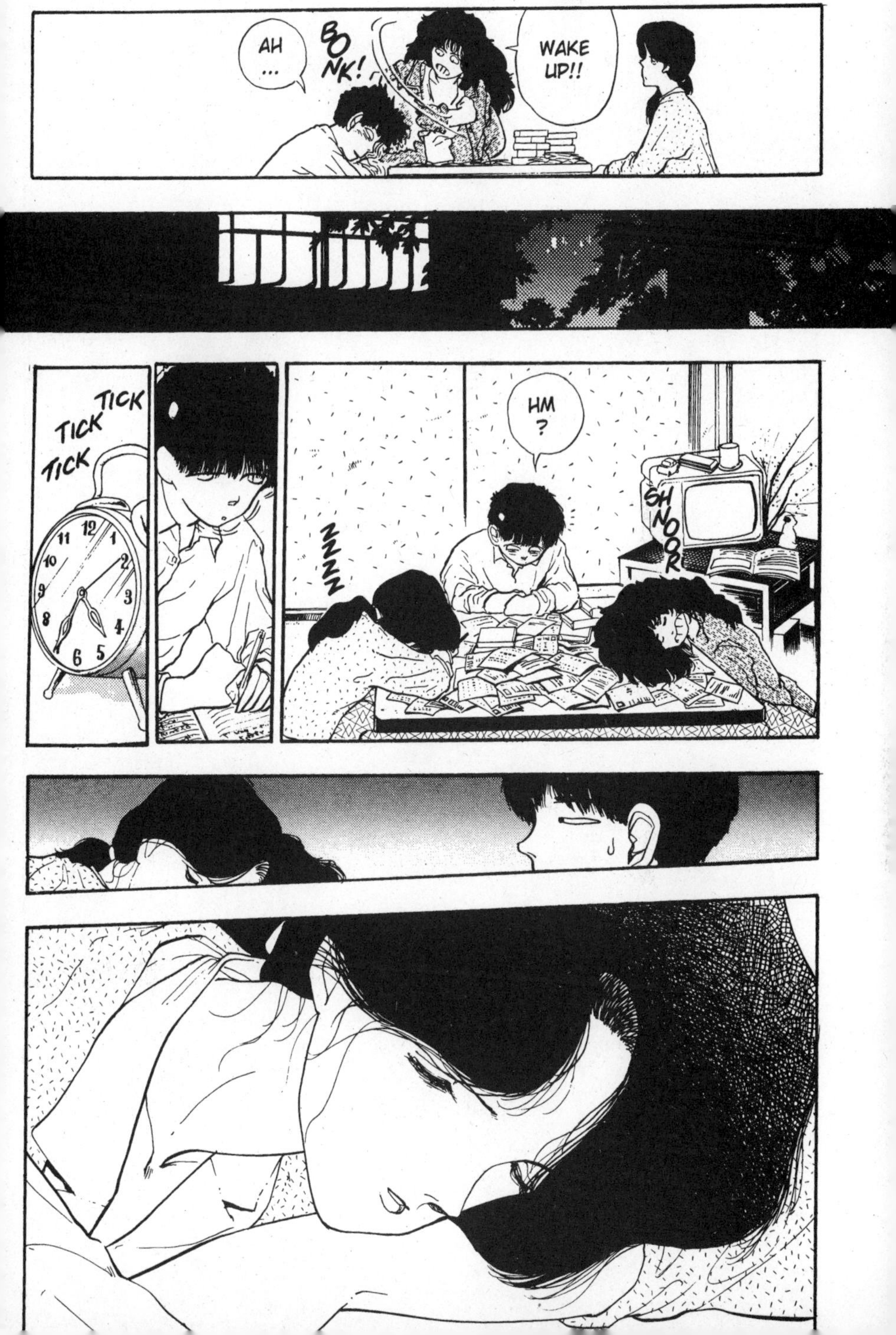
AH ...
BONK!
WAKE UP!!
TICK
TICK
TICK
HM ?
ZZZZ
SHNOOR

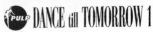

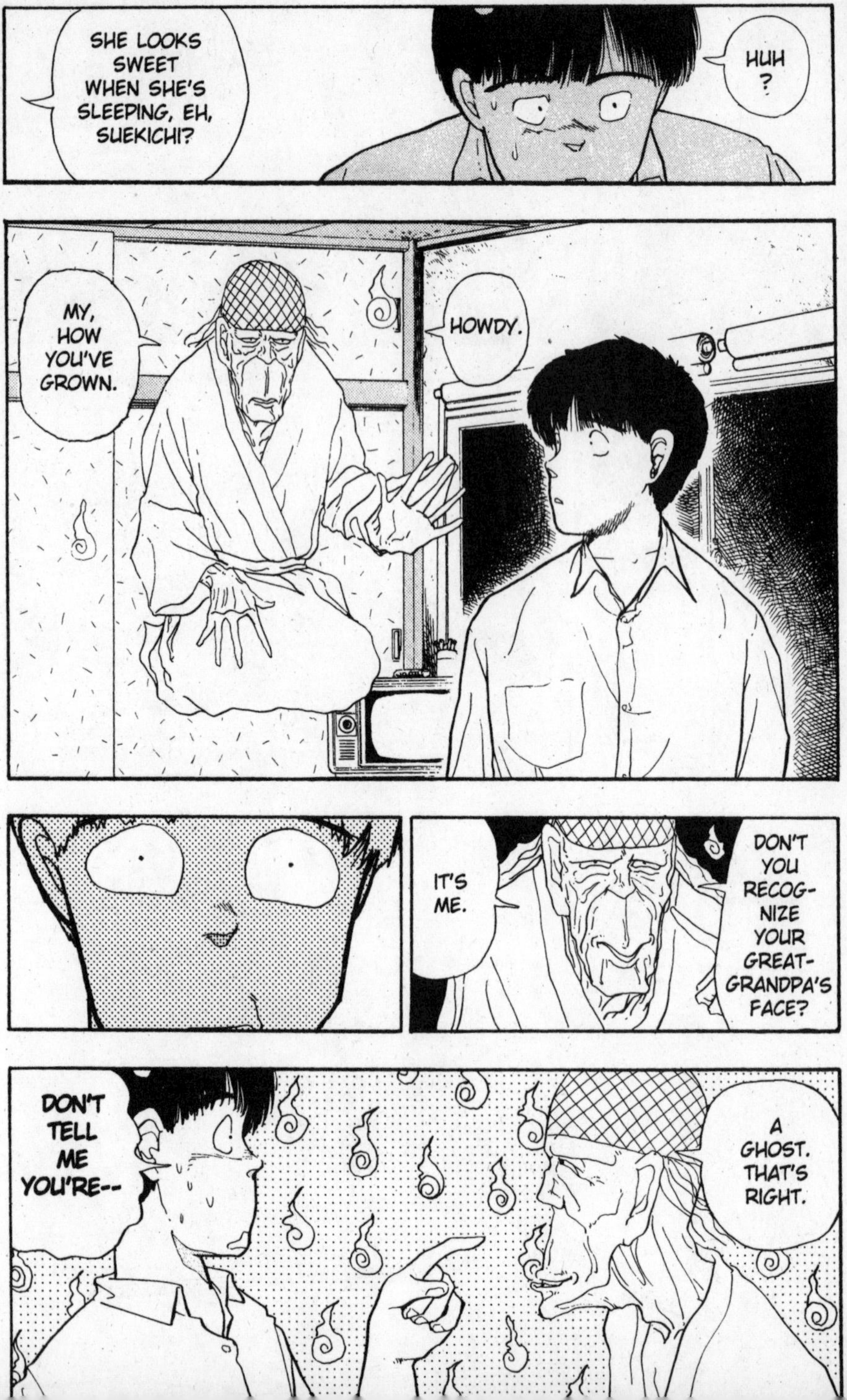
SHE LOOKS SWEET WHEN SHE'S SLEEPING, EH, SUEKICHI?
HUH ?
MY, HOW YOU'VE GROWN.
HOWDY.
IT'S ME.
DON'T YOU RECOG-NIZE YOUR GREAT-GRANDPA'S FACE?
DON'T TELL ME YOU'RE--
A GHOST. THAT'S RIGHT.

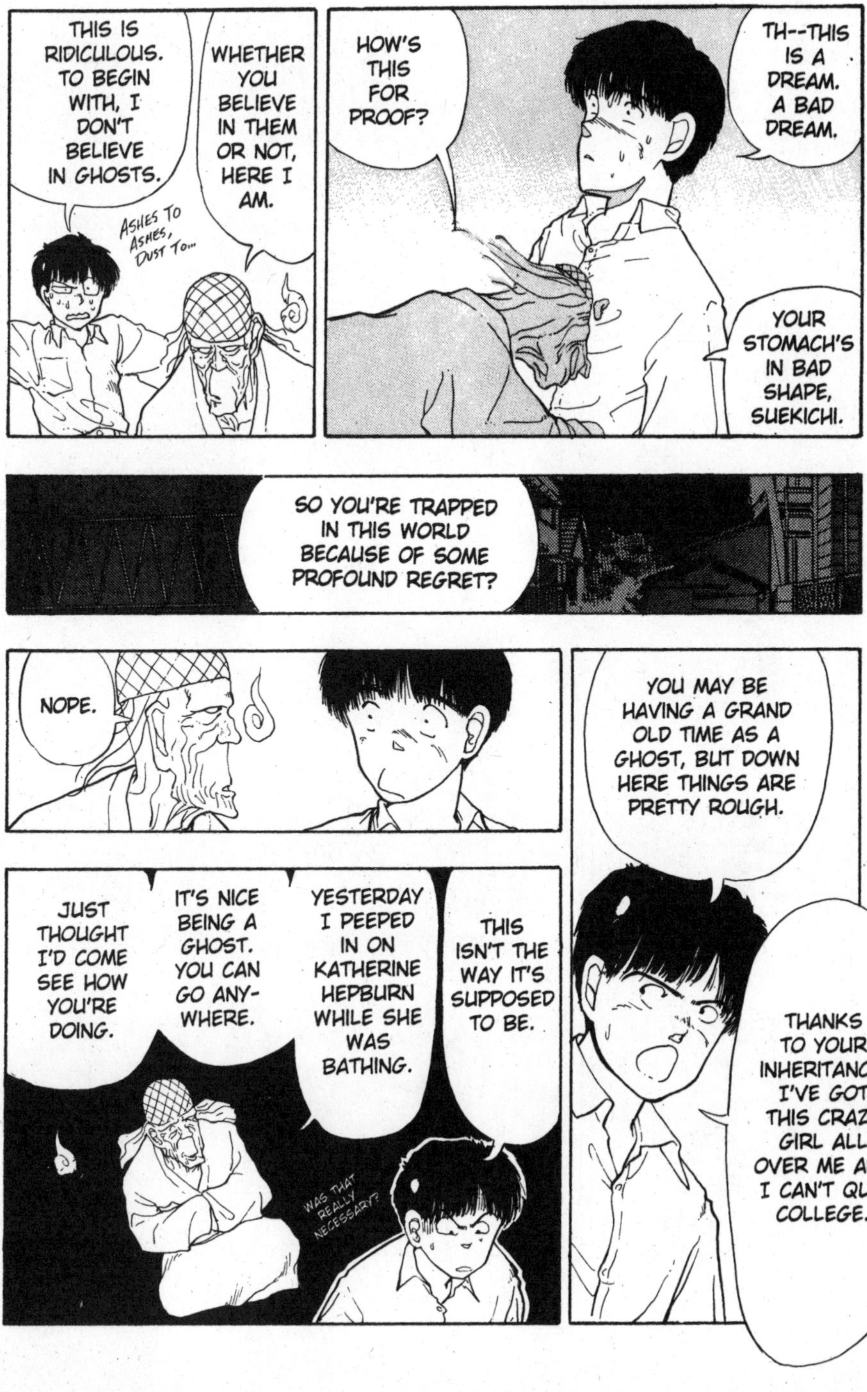
THIS IS RIDICULOUS. TO BEGIN WITH, I DON'T BELIEVE IN GHOSTS.
WHETHER YOU BELIEVE IN THEM OR NOT, HERE I AM.
ASHES TO ASHES, DUST TO...
HOW'S THIS FOR PROOF?
TH--THIS IS A DREAM. A BAD DREAM.
YOUR STOMACH'S IN BAD SHAPE, SUEKICHI.
SO YOU'RE TRAPPED IN THIS WORLD BECAUSE OF SOME PROFOUND REGRET?
NOPE.
JUST THOUGHT I'D COME SEE HOW YOU'RE DOING.
IT'S NICE BEING A GHOST. YOU CAN GO ANY-WHERE.
YESTERDAY I PEEPED IN ON KATHERINE HEPBURN WHILE SHE WAS BATHING.
THIS ISN'T THE WAY IT'S SUPPOSED TO BE.
WAS THAT REALLY NECESSARY?
YOU MAY BE HAVING A GRAND OLD TIME AS A GHOST, BUT DOWN HERE THINGS ARE PRETTY ROUGH.
THANKS TO YOUR INHERITANCE, I'VE GOT THIS CRAZY GIRL ALL OVER ME AND I CAN'T QUIT COLLEGE.

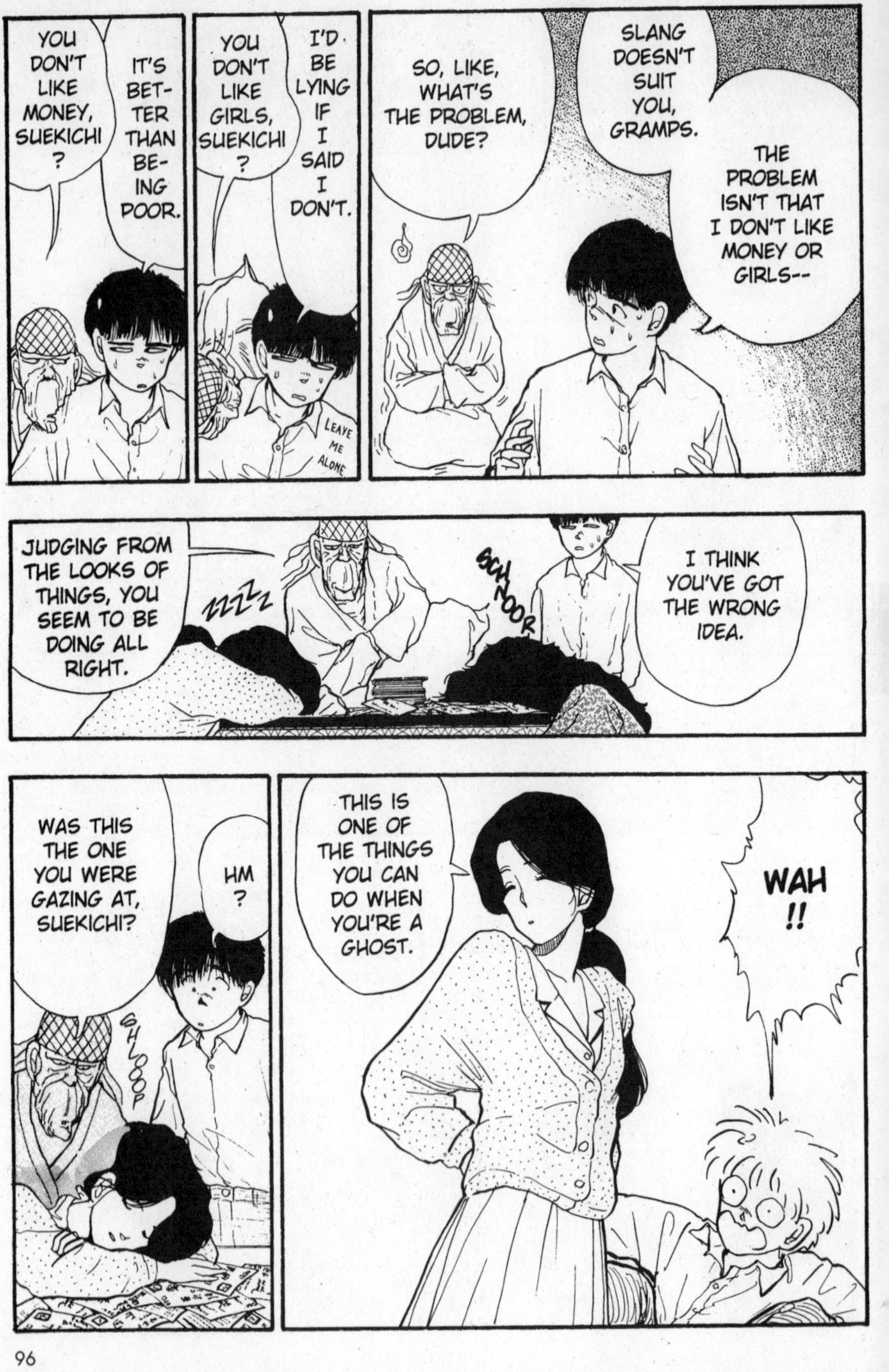

YOU DON'T LIKE MONEY, SUEKICHI?
IT'S BET-TER THAN BE-ING POOR.
YOU DON'T LIKE GIRLS, SUEKICHI?
I'D BE LYING IF I SAID I DON'T.
LEAVE ME ALONE
SO, LIKE, WHAT'S THE PROBLEM, DUDE?
SLANG DOESN'T SUIT YOU, GRAMPS.
THE PROBLEM ISN'T THAT I DON'T LIKE MONEY OR GIRLS--
JUDGING FROM THE LOOKS OF THINGS, YOU SEEM TO BE DOING ALL RIGHT.
ZZZZZ
SCHNOOR
I THINK YOU'VE GOT THE WRONG IDEA.
WAS THIS THE ONE YOU WERE GAZING AT, SUEKICHI?
HM?
SHLOOOP
THIS IS ONE OF THE THINGS YOU CAN DO WHEN YOU'RE A GHOST.
WAH!!

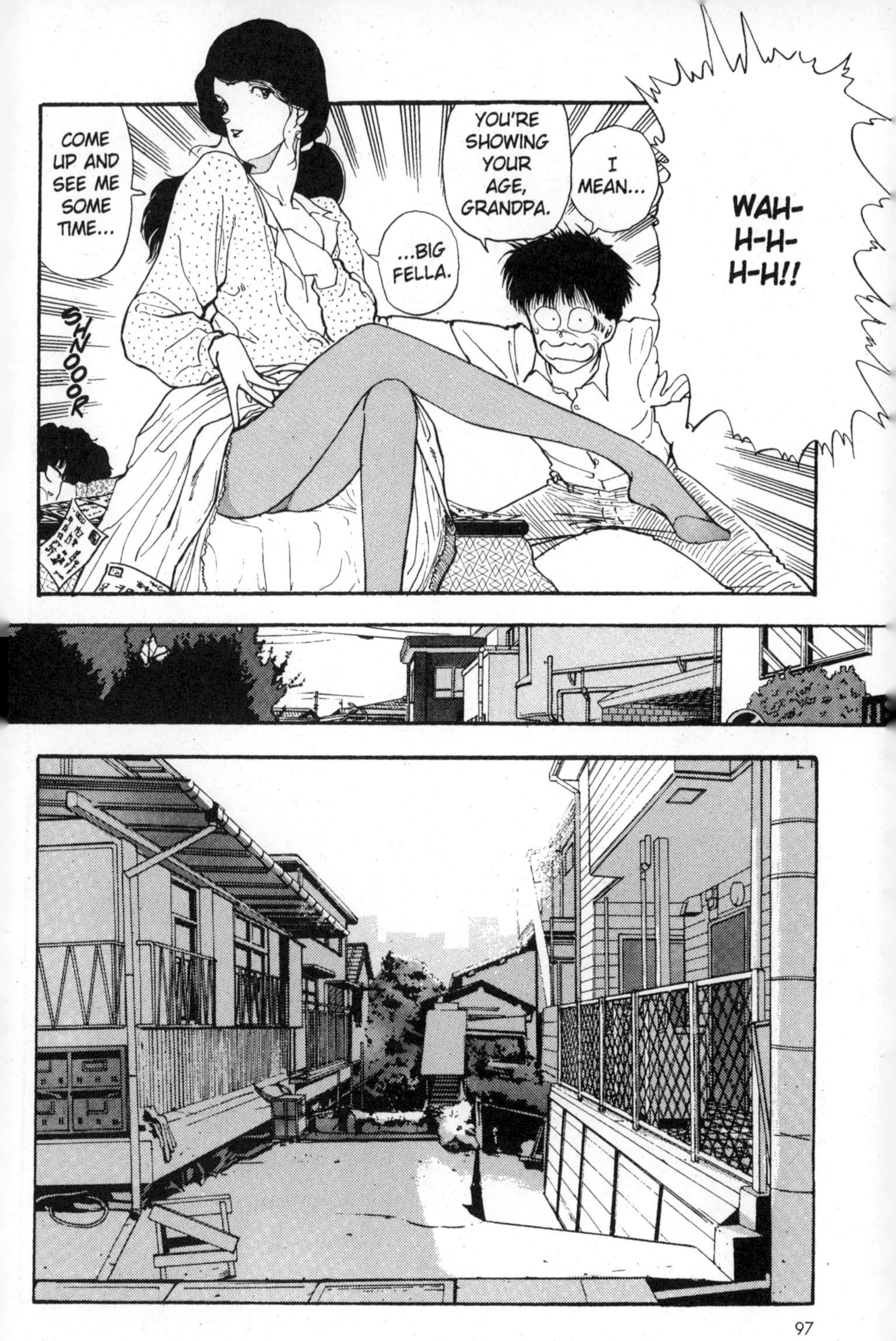
COME UP AND SEE ME SOME TIME...
...BIG FELLA.
SHNOOOR
YOU'RE SHOWING YOUR AGE, GRANDPA.
I MEAN...
WAH-H-H-H-H!!

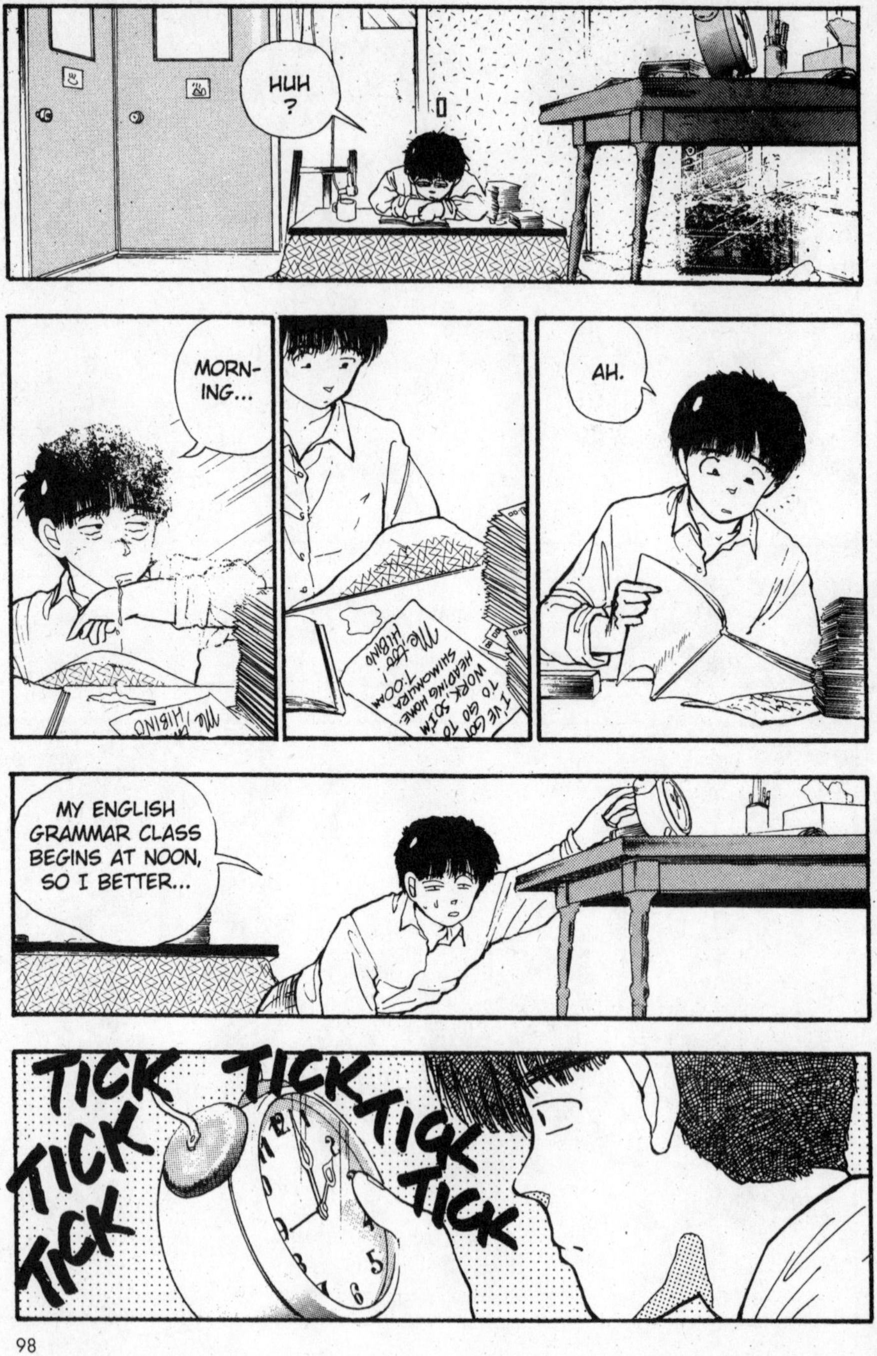
HUH ?
MORNING...
I'VE GOT TO GO TO WORK, SO I'M HEADING HOME. SHIMOMURA 7:00am
Me too! HIBINO
AH.
MY ENGLISH GRAMMAR CLASS BEGINS AT NOON, SO I BETTER...
TICK TICK TICK TICK TICK TICK

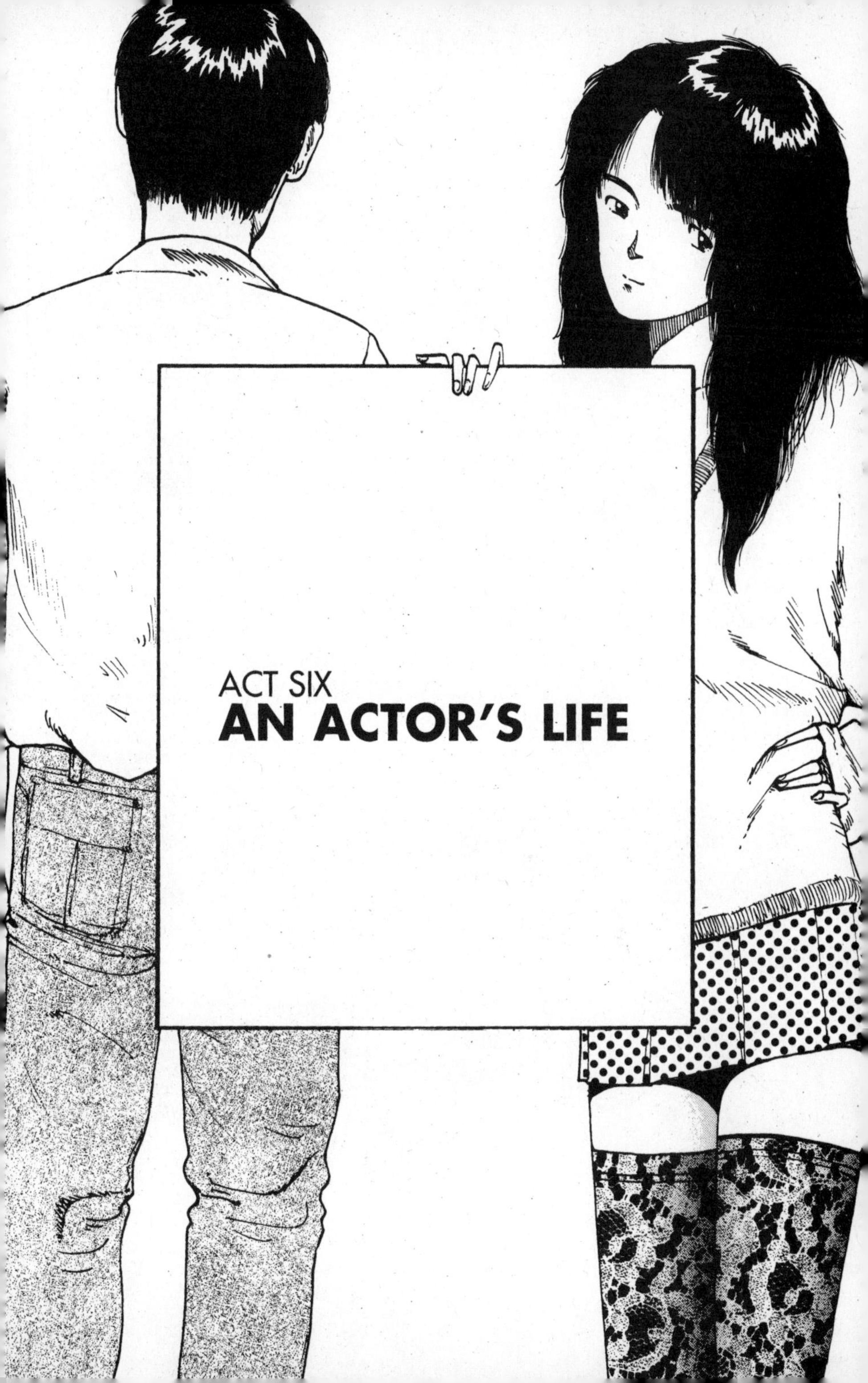
ACT SIX
AN ACTOR'S LIFE

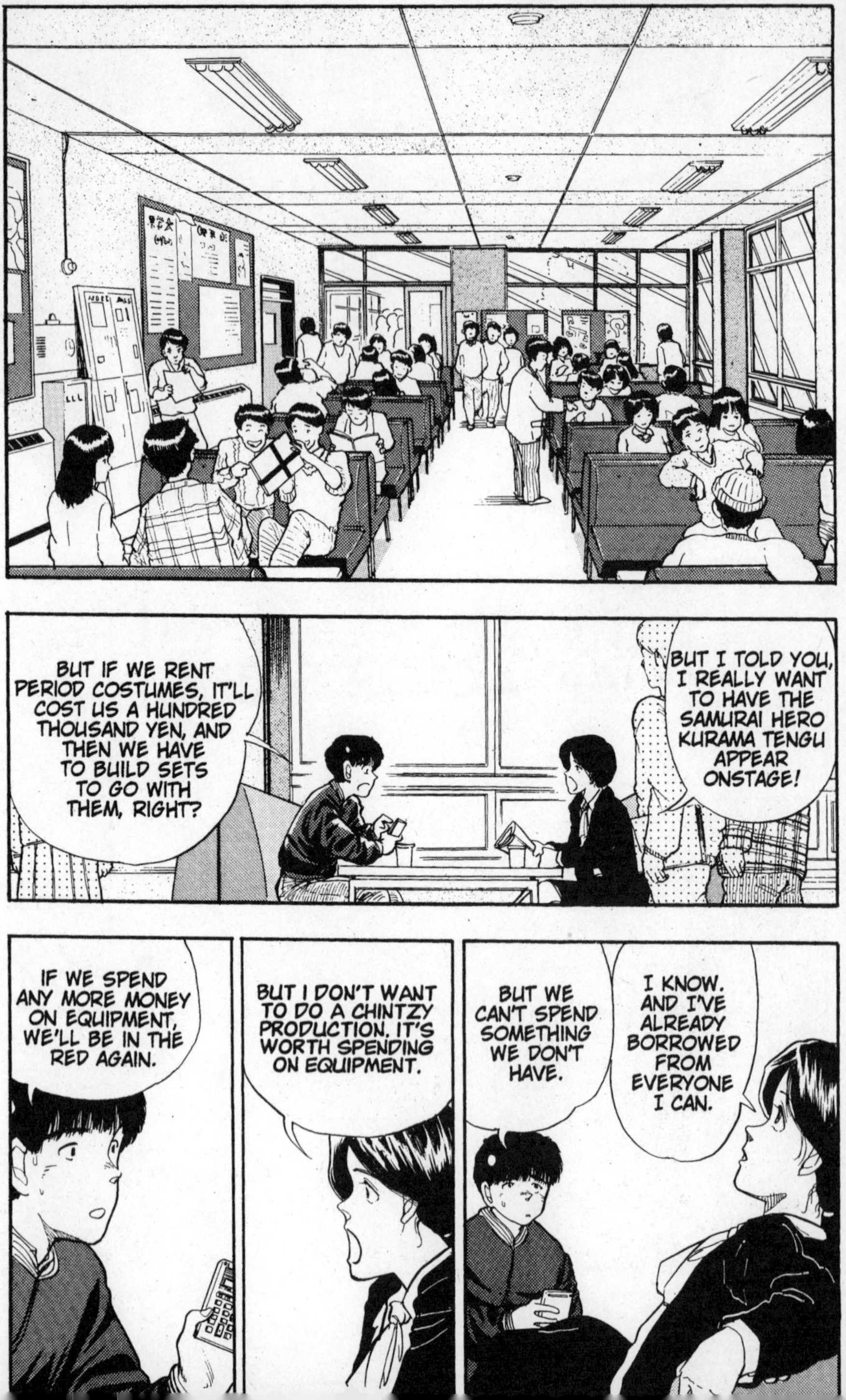
BUT IF WE RENT PERIOD COSTUMES, IT'LL COST US A HUNDRED THOUSAND YEN, AND THEN WE HAVE TO BUILD SETS TO GO WITH THEM, RIGHT?
BUT I TOLD YOU, I REALLY WANT TO HAVE THE SAMURAI HERO KURAMA TENGU APPEAR ONSTAGE!
IF WE SPEND ANY MORE MONEY ON EQUIPMENT, WE'LL BE IN THE RED AGAIN.
BUT I DON'T WANT TO DO A CHINTZY PRODUCTION. IT'S WORTH SPENDING ON EQUIPMENT.
BUT WE CAN'T SPEND SOMETHING WE DON'T HAVE.
I KNOW. AND I'VE ALREADY BORROWED FROM EVERYONE I CAN.

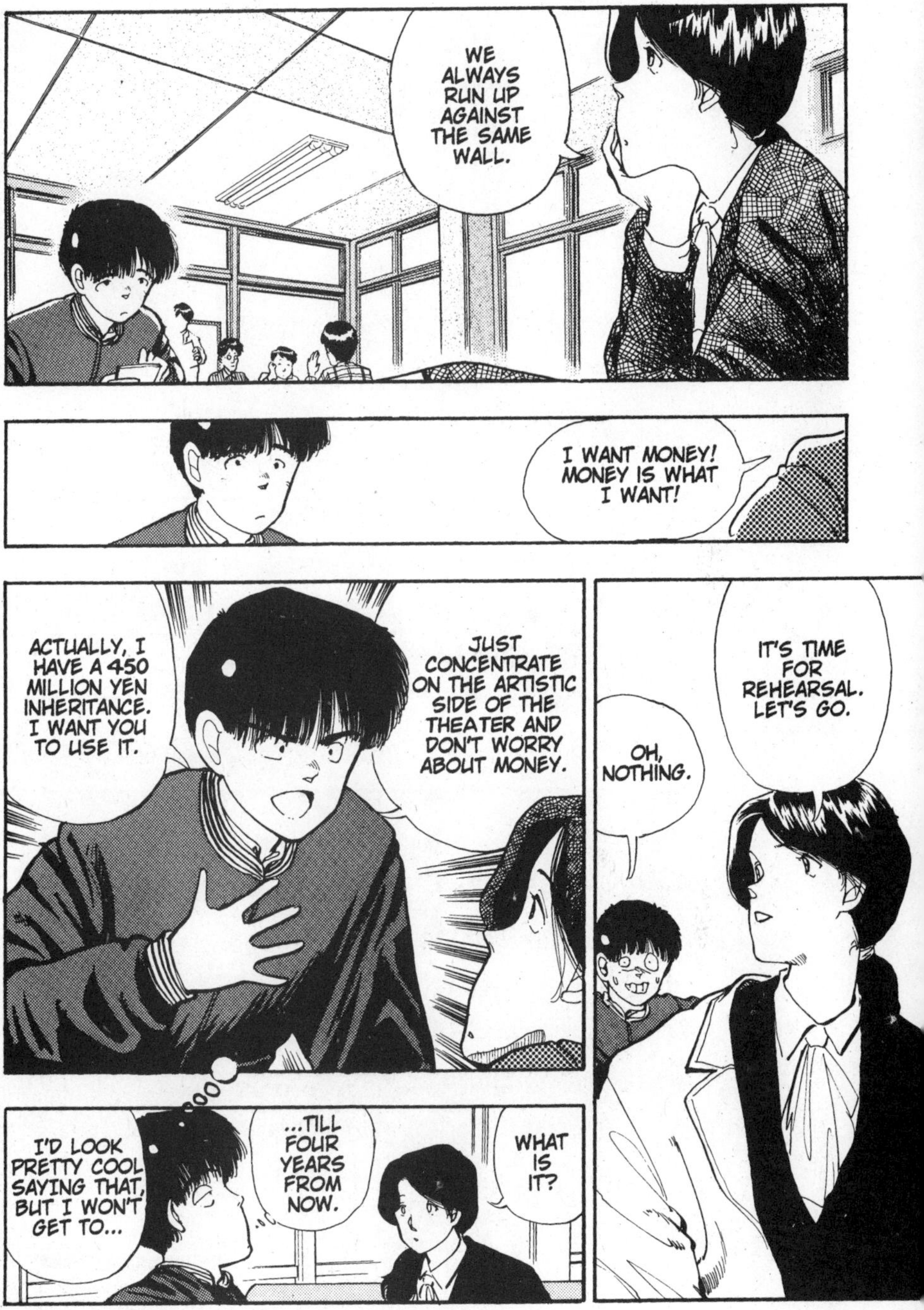
WE ALWAYS RUN UP AGAINST THE SAME WALL.
I WANT MONEY! MONEY IS WHAT I WANT!
ACTUALLY, I HAVE A 450 MILLION YEN INHERITANCE. I WANT YOU TO USE IT.
JUST CONCENTRATE ON THE ARTISTIC SIDE OF THE THEATER AND DON'T WORRY ABOUT MONEY.
I'D LOOK PRETTY COOL SAYING THAT, BUT I WON'T GET TO...
...TILL FOUR YEARS FROM NOW.
WHAT IS IT?
OH, NOTHING.
IT'S TIME FOR REHEARSAL. LET'S GO.

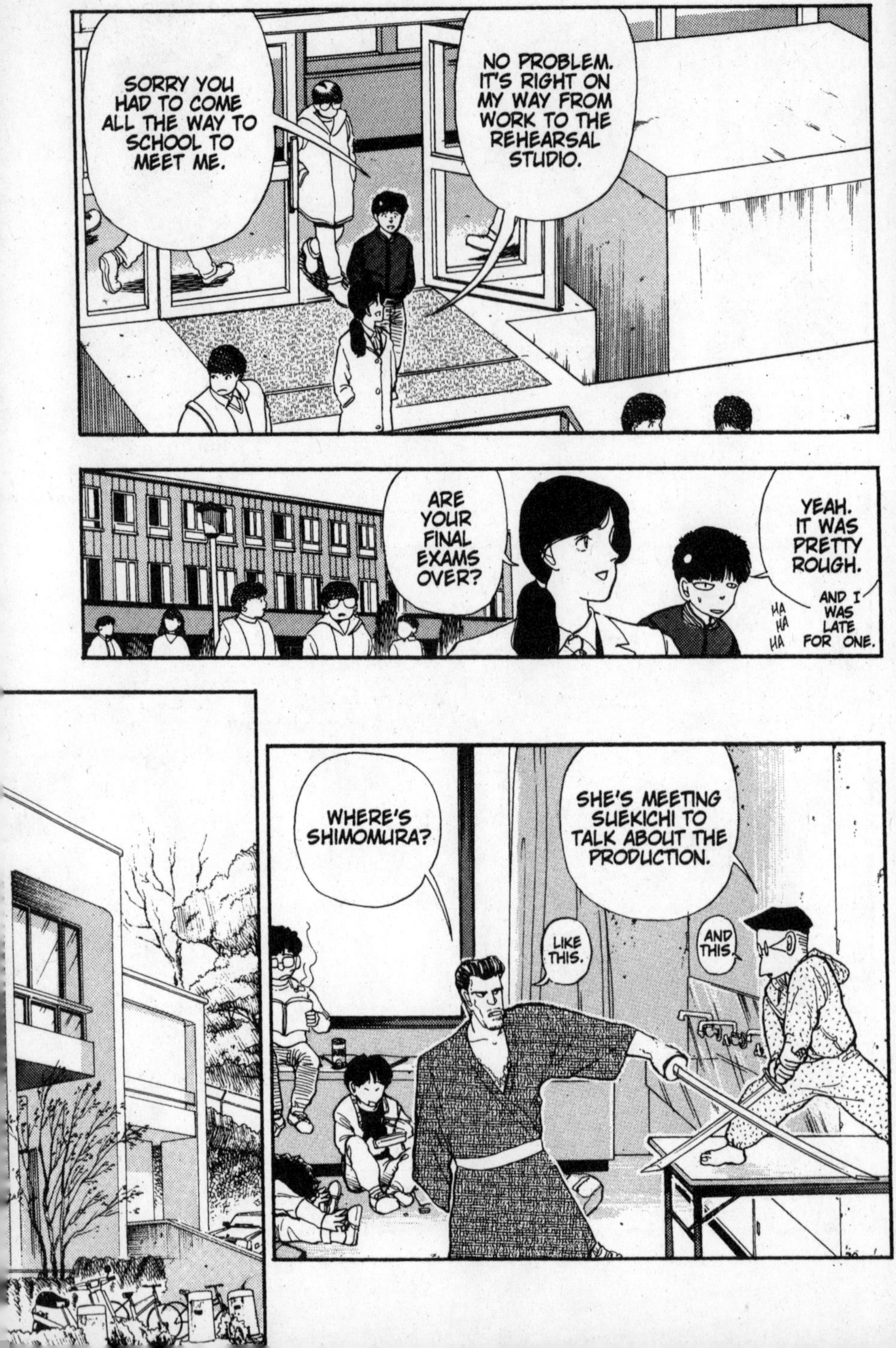
SORRY YOU HAD TO COME ALL THE WAY TO SCHOOL TO MEET ME.
NO PROBLEM. IT'S RIGHT ON MY WAY FROM WORK TO THE REHEARSAL STUDIO.
ARE YOUR FINAL EXAMS OVER?
YEAH. IT WAS PRETTY ROUGH.
HA HA HA
AND I WAS LATE FOR ONE.
WHERE'S SHIMOMURA?
SHE'S MEETING SUEKICHI TO TALK ABOUT THE PRODUCTION.
LIKE THIS.
AND THIS.

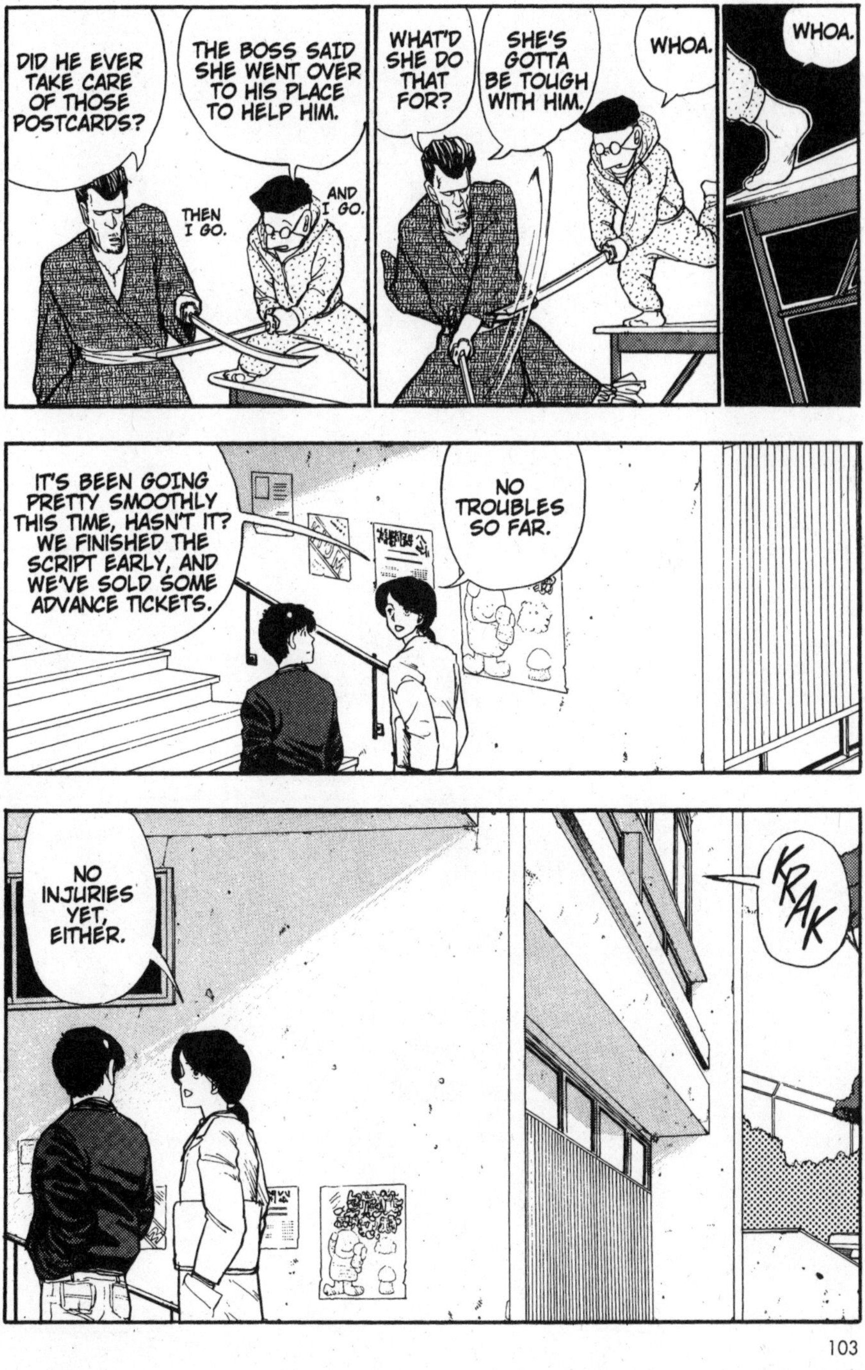
DID HE EVER TAKE CARE OF THOSE POSTCARDS?
THE BOSS SAID SHE WENT OVER TO HIS PLACE TO HELP HIM.
THEN I GO.
AND I GO.
WHAT'D SHE DO THAT FOR?
SHE'S GOTTA BE TOUGH WITH HIM.
WHOA.
WHOA.
IT'S BEEN GOING PRETTY SMOOTHLY THIS TIME, HASN'T IT? WE FINISHED THE SCRIPT EARLY, AND WE'VE SOLD SOME ADVANCE TICKETS.
NO TROUBLES SO FAR.
NO INJURIES YET, EITHER.
KRAK

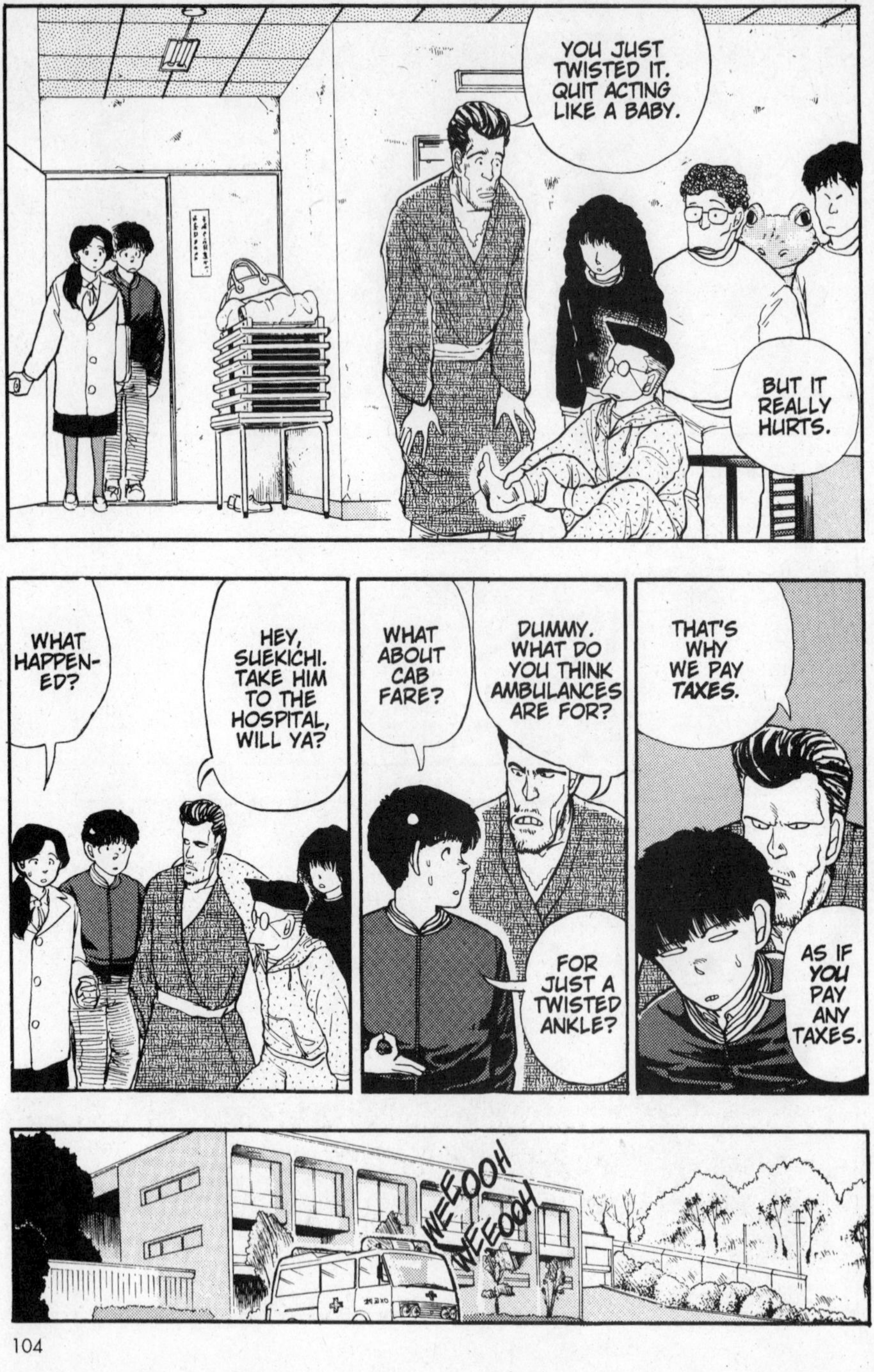
YOU JUST TWISTED IT. QUIT ACTING LIKE A BABY.
BUT IT REALLY HURTS.
WHAT HAPPEN-ED?
HEY, SUEKICHI. TAKE HIM TO THE HOSPITAL, WILL YA?
WHAT ABOUT CAB FARE?
DUMMY. WHAT DO YOU THINK AMBULANCES ARE FOR?
FOR JUST A TWISTED ANKLE?
THAT'S WHY WE PAY TAXES.
AS IF YOU PAY ANY TAXES.
WEEOOH WEEOOH

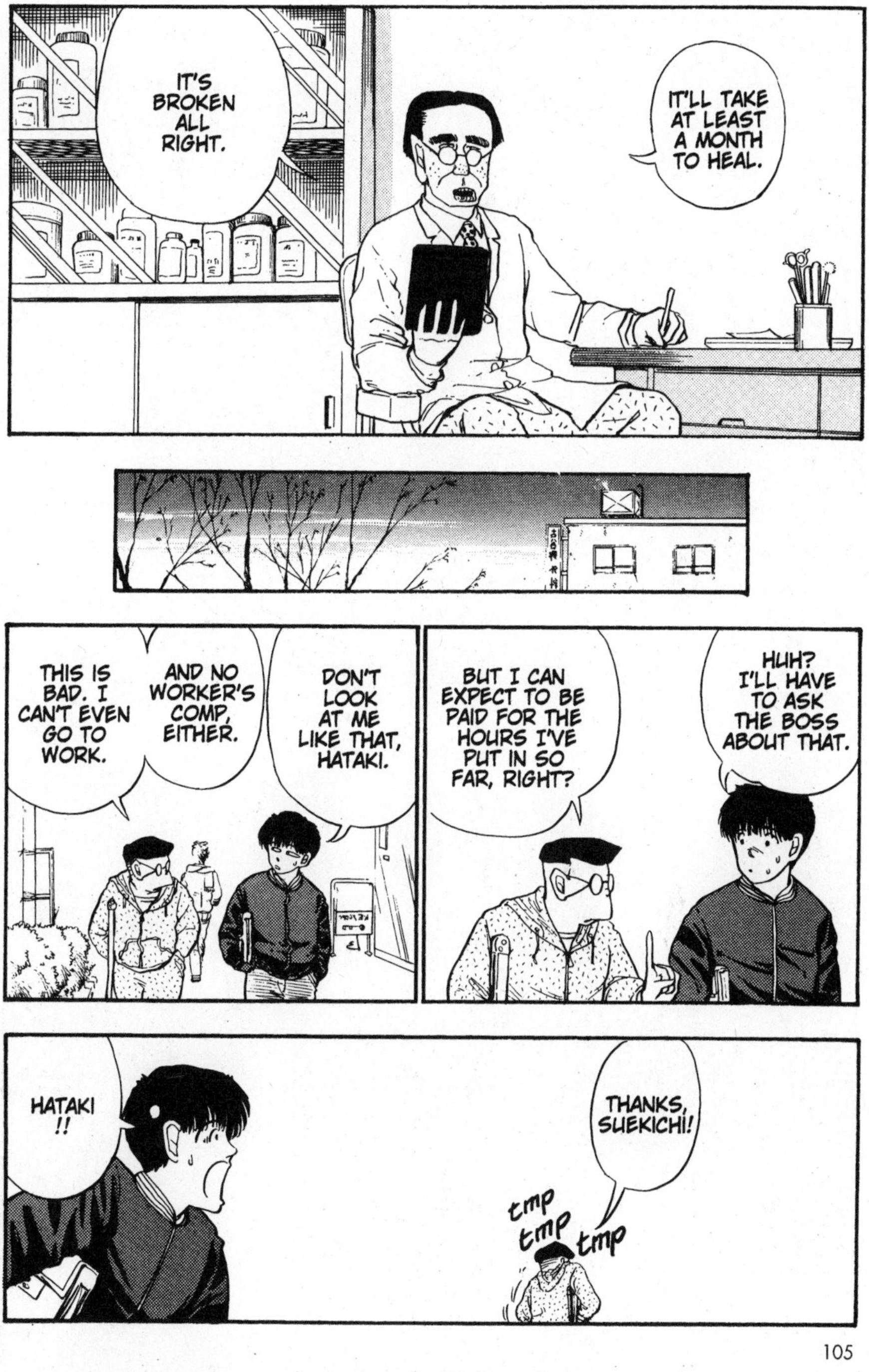
IT'S BROKEN ALL RIGHT.
IT'LL TAKE AT LEAST A MONTH TO HEAL.
THIS IS BAD. I CAN'T EVEN GO TO WORK.
AND NO WORKER'S COMP, EITHER.
DON'T LOOK AT ME LIKE THAT, HATAKI.
BUT I CAN EXPECT TO BE PAID FOR THE HOURS I'VE PUT IN SO FAR, RIGHT?
HUH? I'LL HAVE TO ASK THE BOSS ABOUT THAT.
HATAKI !!
THANKS, SUEKICHI!
tmp
tmp
tmp

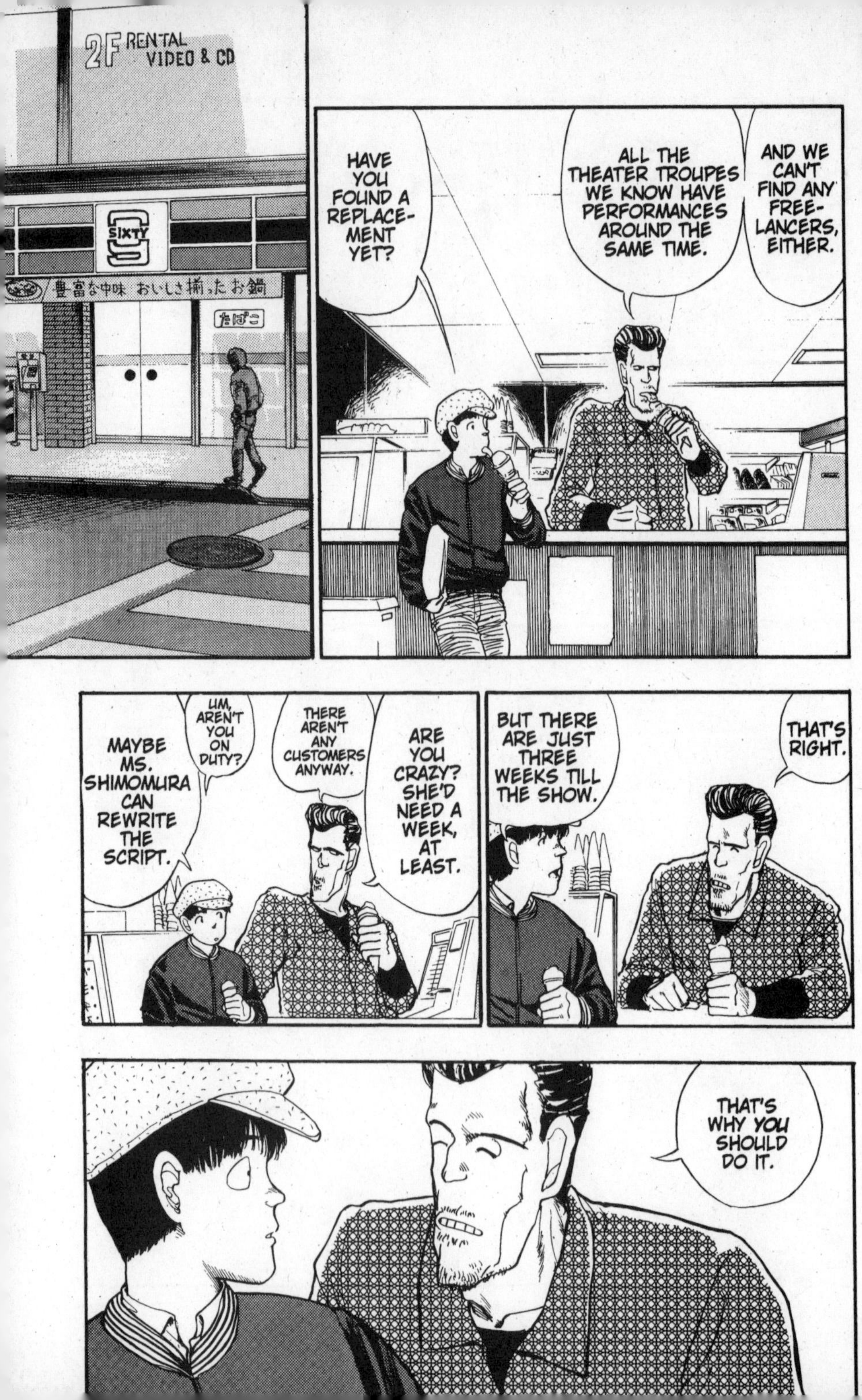
2F RENTAL VIDEO & CD
SIXTY
豊富な中味 おいしさ揃ったお鍋
たばこ
HAVE YOU FOUND A REPLACEMENT YET?
ALL THE THEATER TROUPES WE KNOW HAVE PERFORMANCES AROUND THE SAME TIME.
AND WE CAN'T FIND ANY FREELANCERS, EITHER.
MAYBE MS. SHIMOMURA CAN REWRITE THE SCRIPT.
UM, AREN'T YOU ON DUTY?
THERE AREN'T ANY CUSTOMERS ANYWAY.
ARE YOU CRAZY? SHE'D NEED A WEEK, AT LEAST.
BUT THERE ARE JUST THREE WEEKS TILL THE SHOW.
THAT'S RIGHT.
THAT'S WHY YOU SHOULD DO IT.

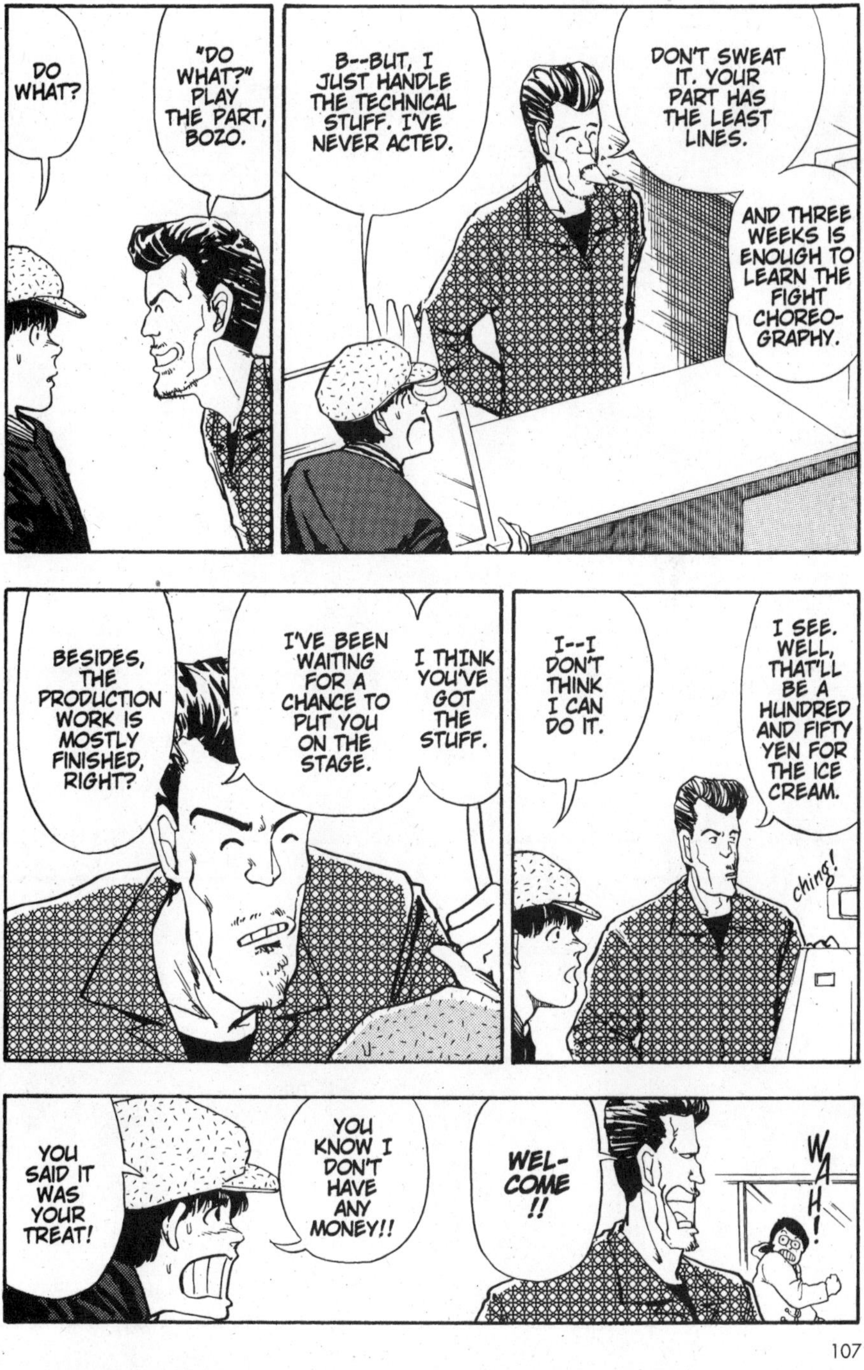
DO WHAT?
"DO WHAT?" PLAY THE PART, BOZO.
B--BUT, I JUST HANDLE THE TECHNICAL STUFF. I'VE NEVER ACTED.
DON'T SWEAT IT. YOUR PART HAS THE LEAST LINES.
AND THREE WEEKS IS ENOUGH TO LEARN THE FIGHT CHOREOGRAPHY.
BESIDES, THE PRODUCTION WORK IS MOSTLY FINISHED, RIGHT?
I'VE BEEN WAITING FOR A CHANCE TO PUT YOU ON THE STAGE.
I THINK YOU'VE GOT THE STUFF.
I--I DON'T THINK I CAN DO IT.
I SEE. WELL, THAT'LL BE A HUNDRED AND FIFTY YEN FOR THE ICE CREAM.
ching!
YOU SAID IT WAS YOUR TREAT!
YOU KNOW I DON'T HAVE ANY MONEY!!
WEL-COME!!
WAH!

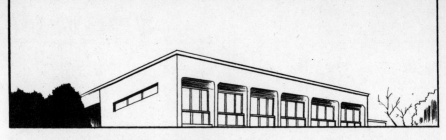

S--STOP, PLEASE. I HAVE A WIFE AND CHILDREN...

...AND A SEVENTY-YEAR-OLD --OOPS.

UM ...

I--I'M SORRY. THIS ISN'T WORKING, IS IT? I'M JUST MAKING TROUBLE FOR EVERYONE ELSE.

IT'S NOT BAD FOR A FIRST TRY.

YEAH. JUST BE CAREFUL NOT TO MISS YOUR CUES.

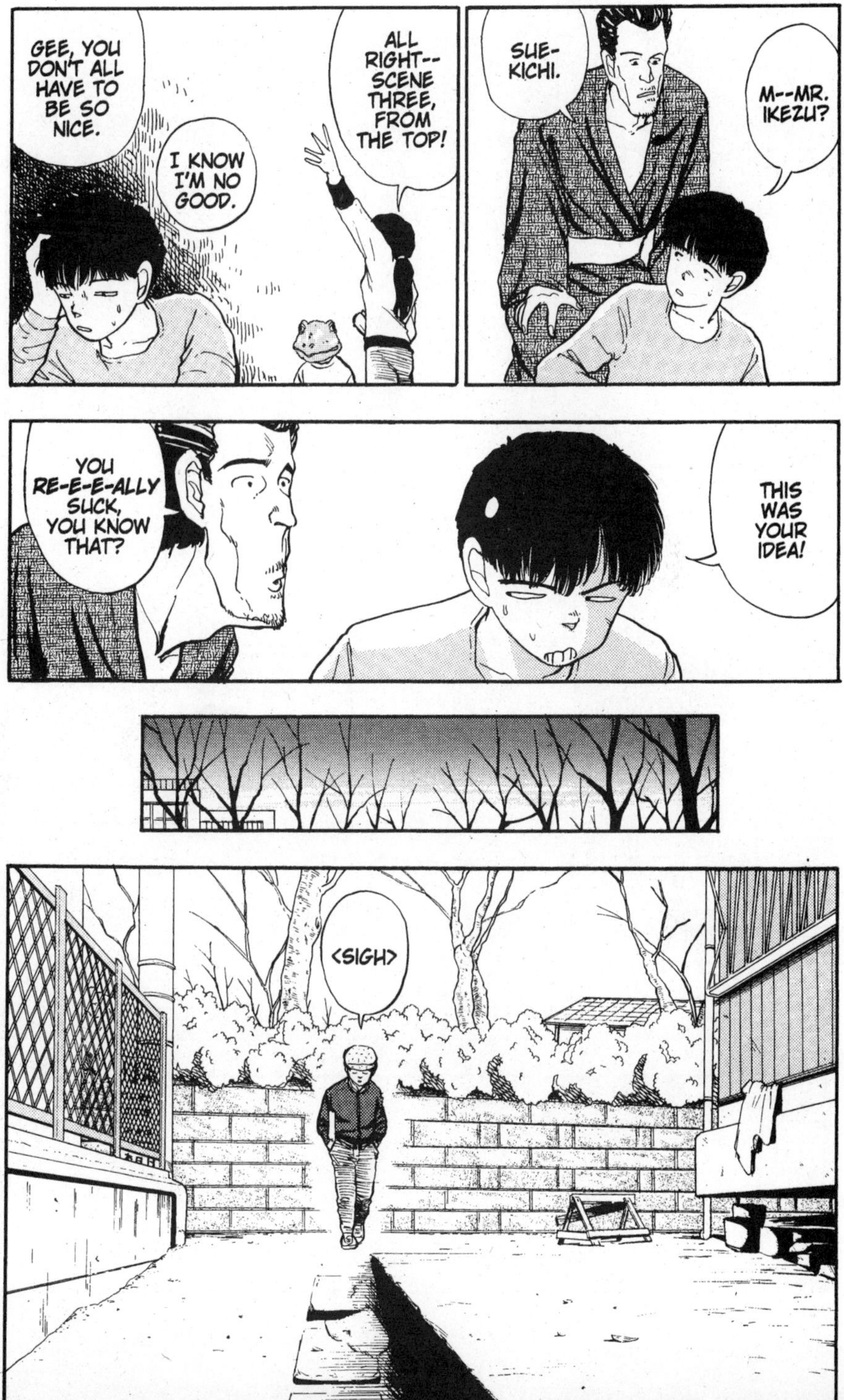
GEE, YOU DON'T ALL HAVE TO BE SO NICE.
I KNOW I'M NO GOOD.
ALL RIGHT-- SCENE THREE, FROM THE TOP!
SUE-KICHI.
M--MR. IKEZU?
YOU RE-E-E-ALLY SUCK, YOU KNOW THAT?
THIS WAS YOUR IDEA!
<SIGH>

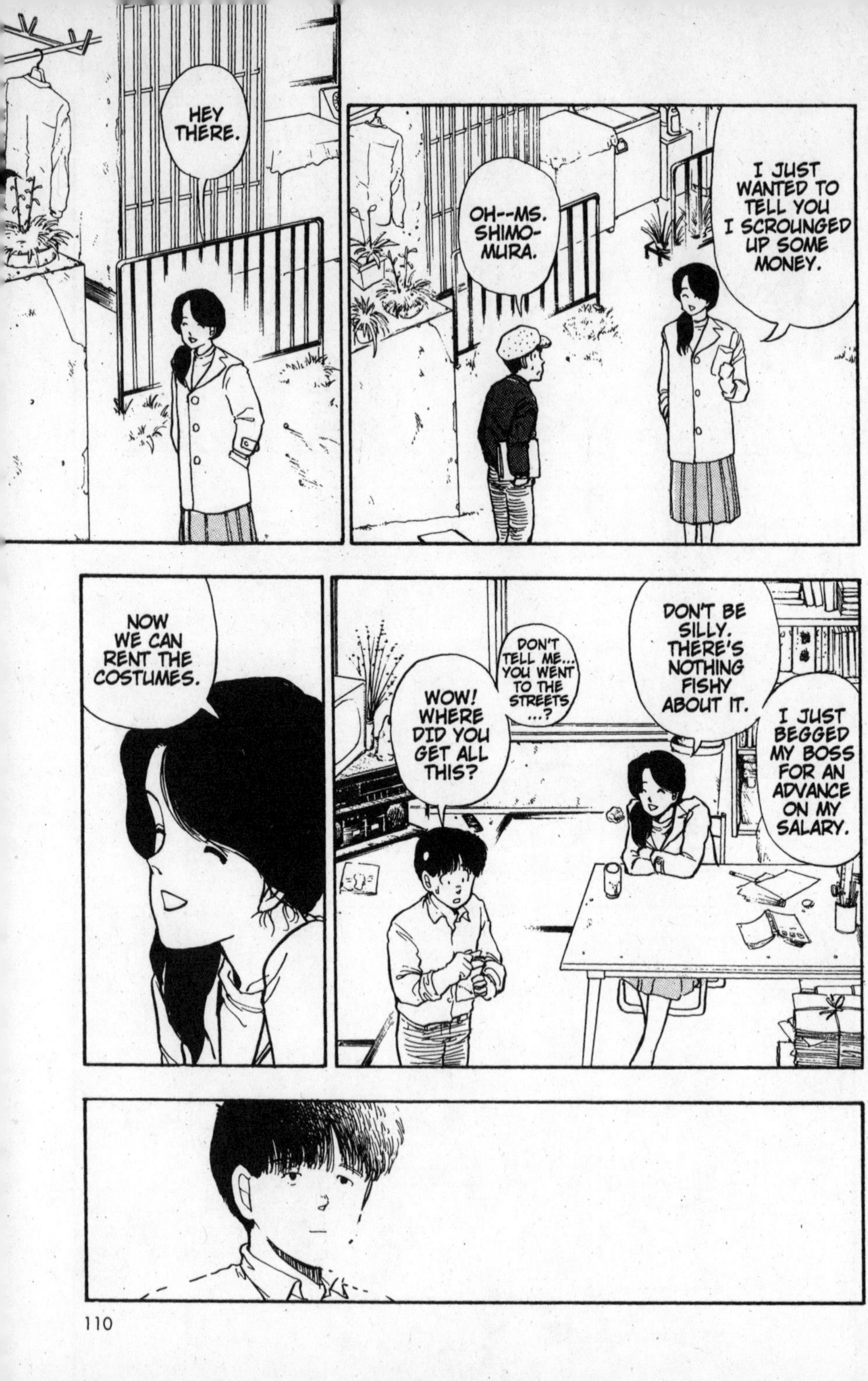
HEY THERE.
OH--MS. SHIMOMURA.
I JUST WANTED TO TELL YOU I SCROUNGED UP SOME MONEY.
NOW WE CAN RENT THE COSTUMES.
WOW! WHERE DID YOU GET ALL THIS?
DON'T TELL ME... YOU WENT TO THE STREETS ...?
DON'T BE SILLY. THERE'S NOTHING FISHY ABOUT IT.
I JUST BEGGED MY BOSS FOR AN ADVANCE ON MY SALARY.

YOU REALLY LOVE THE THEATER, DON'T YOU?

DON'T WE ALL?

NO ONE MAKES ANY MONEY, SO THEY MUST DO IT FOR LOVE.

YOU'RE NO DIFFERENT, RIGHT?

I--I GUESS NOT.

DON'T YOU WANT TO PLAY THE ROLE, SUEKICHI?

N--NO, IT'S NOT THAT, IT'S JUST THAT ...

IT'S JUST THAT I DON'T THINK I HAVE WHAT IT TAKES.

YOU'RE GOING?

WE'LL BE PRACTICING DAY AND NIGHT NEXT WEEK, RIGHT? I'VE GOT TO EARN SOME MONEY WHILE I CAN.

NOT TO MENTION THE ADVANCE.

I THINK PLAYING THIS ROLE WILL BE A GOOD EXPERIENCE FOR YOU AS PRODUCER.

GIVE IT YOUR BEST. I WILL, TOO.

111

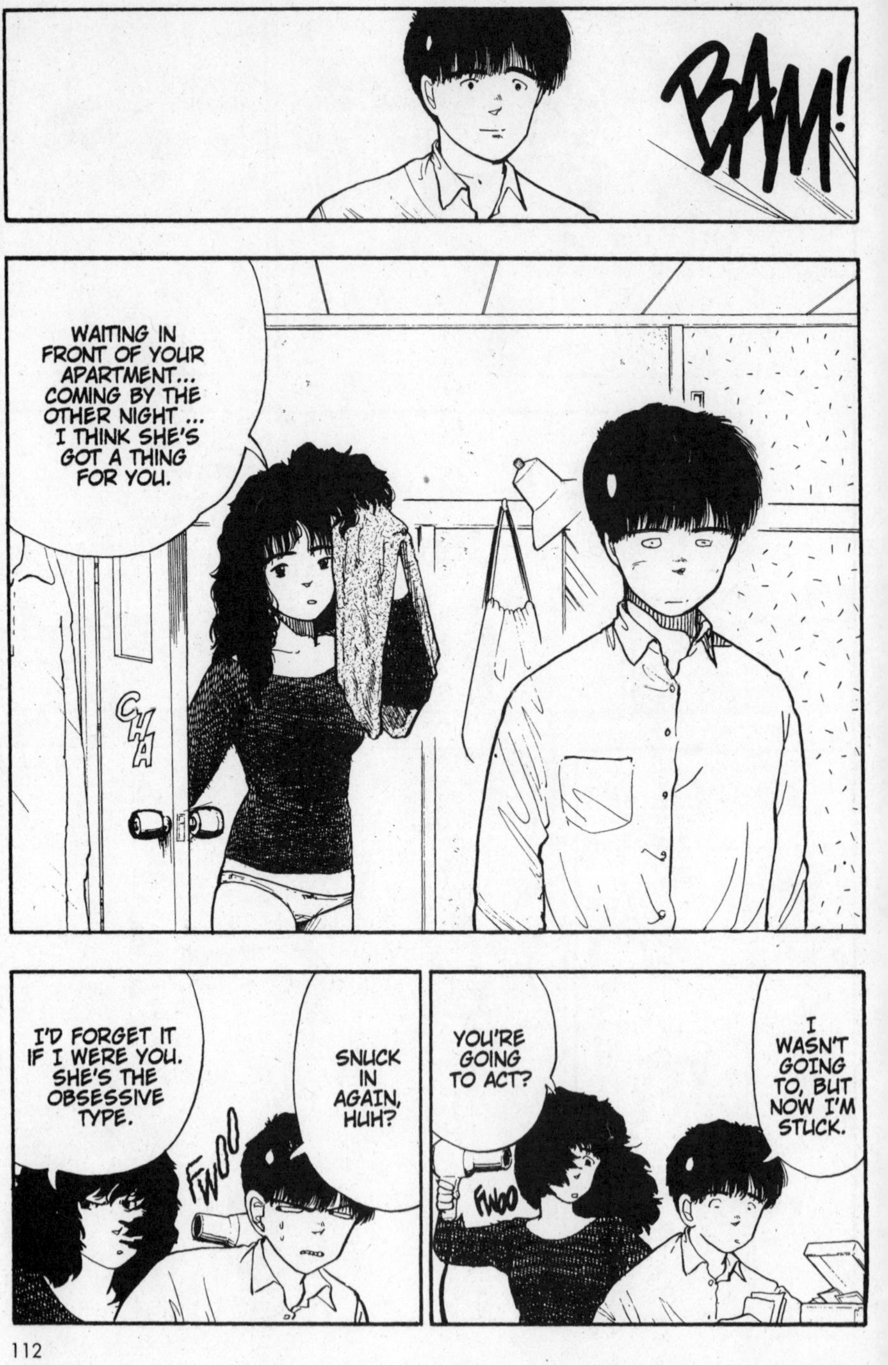
BAM!
WAITING IN FRONT OF YOUR APARTMENT... COMING BY THE OTHER NIGHT ... I THINK SHE'S GOT A THING FOR YOU.
CHA
I'D FORGET IT IF I WERE YOU. SHE'S THE OBSESSIVE TYPE.
FWOO
SNUCK IN AGAIN, HUH?
YOU'RE GOING TO ACT?
FWOO
I WASN'T GOING TO, BUT NOW I'M STUCK.

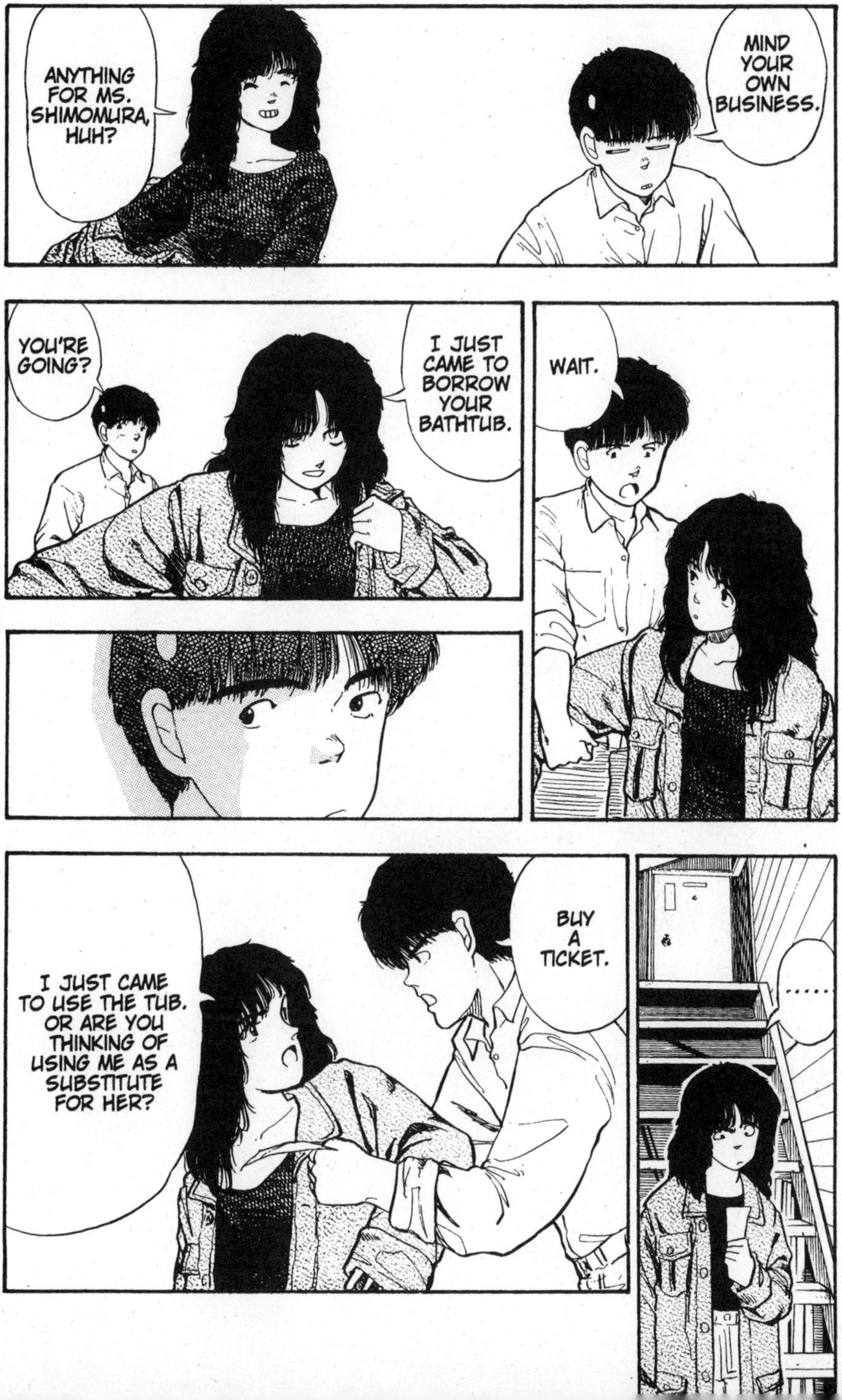
ANYTHING FOR MS. SHIMOMURA, HUH?
MIND YOUR OWN BUSINESS.
YOU'RE GOING?
I JUST CAME TO BORROW YOUR BATHTUB.
WAIT.
I JUST CAME TO USE THE TUB. OR ARE YOU THINKING OF USING ME AS A SUBSTITUTE FOR HER?
BUY A TICKET.
......

THIS MUST BE THE PLACE.

PLEASE, PLEASE. I HAVE A WIFE AND CHILDREN AND A SIXTY-YEAR-OLD MOTHER.

HEH, HEH, HEH. YOUR MOUTH SAYS STOP, BUT YOUR BODY ...

HOLD IT RIGHT THERE.

AND NOW YOU TAKE THE STAGE.

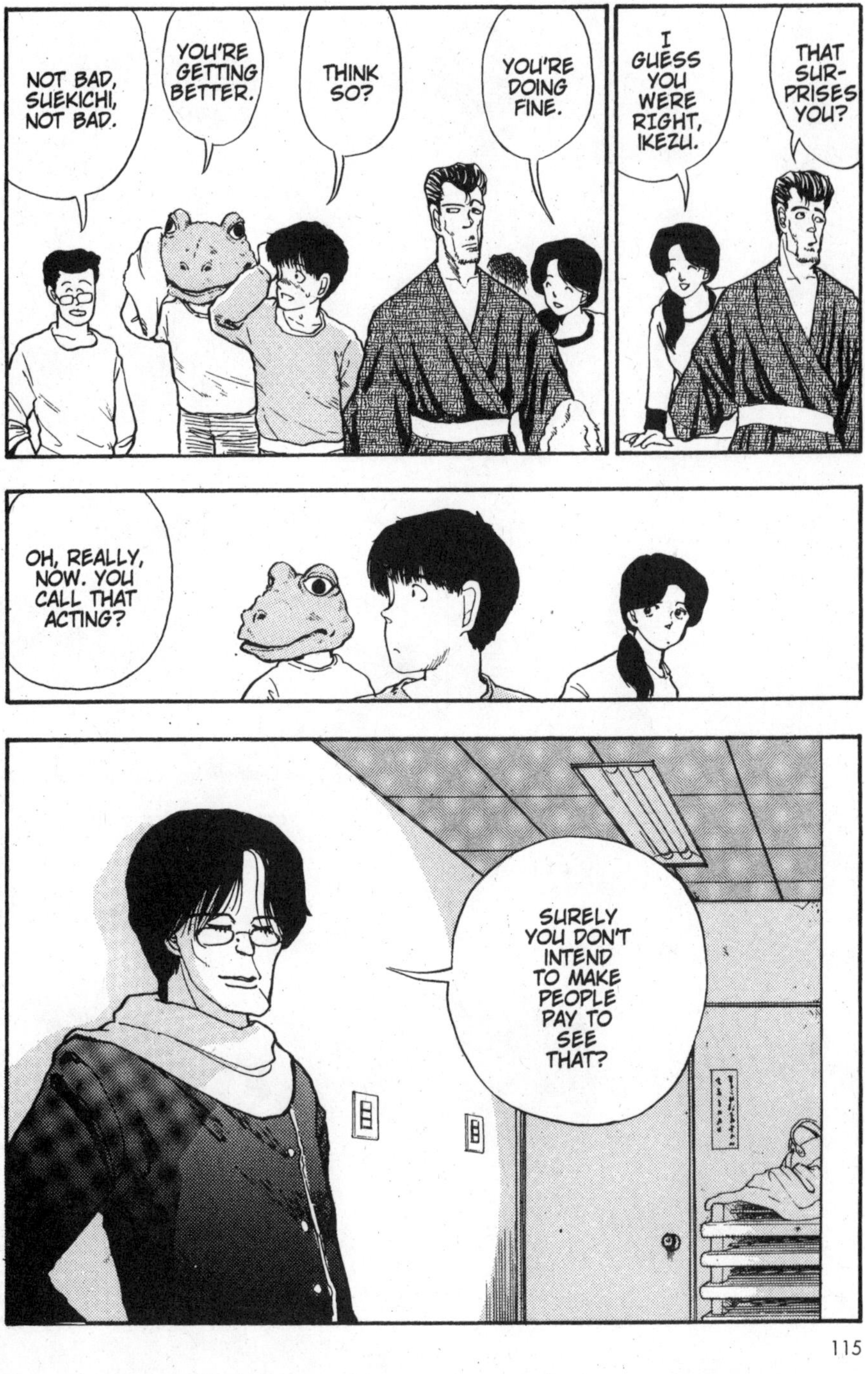
NOT BAD, SUEKICHI, NOT BAD.
YOU'RE GETTING BETTER.
THINK SO?
YOU'RE DOING FINE.
I GUESS YOU WERE RIGHT, IKEZU.
THAT SUR-PRISES YOU?
OH, REALLY, NOW. YOU CALL THAT ACTING?
SURELY YOU DON'T INTEND TO MAKE PEOPLE PAY TO SEE THAT?

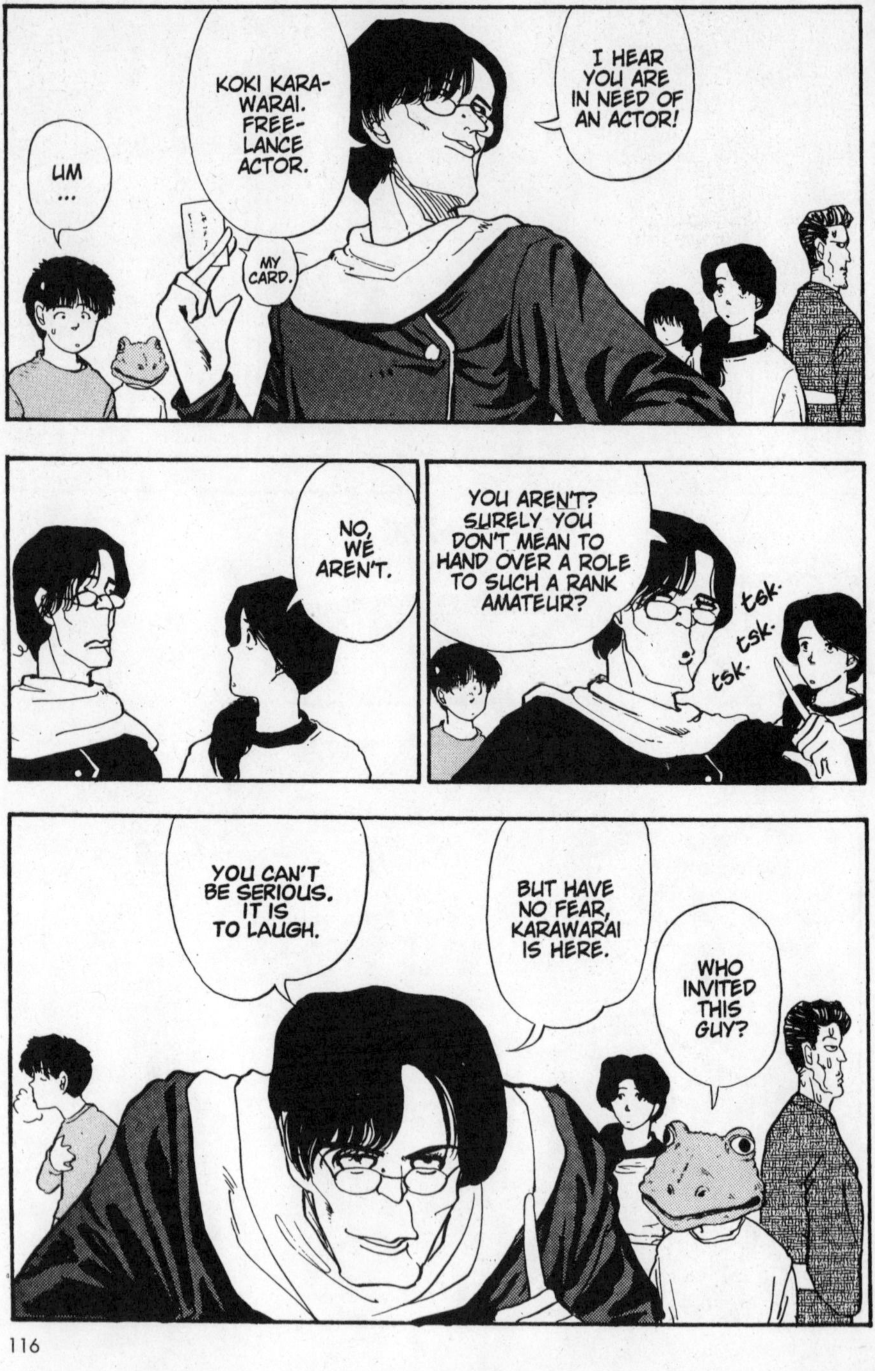
UM ...
KOKI KARA-WARAI. FREE-LANCE ACTOR.
MY CARD.
I HEAR YOU ARE IN NEED OF AN ACTOR!
NO, WE AREN'T.
YOU AREN'T? SURELY YOU DON'T MEAN TO HAND OVER A ROLE TO SUCH A RANK AMATEUR?
tsk. tsk. tsk.
YOU CAN'T BE SERIOUS. IT IS TO LAUGH.
BUT HAVE NO FEAR, KARAWARAI IS HERE.
WHO INVITED THIS GUY?

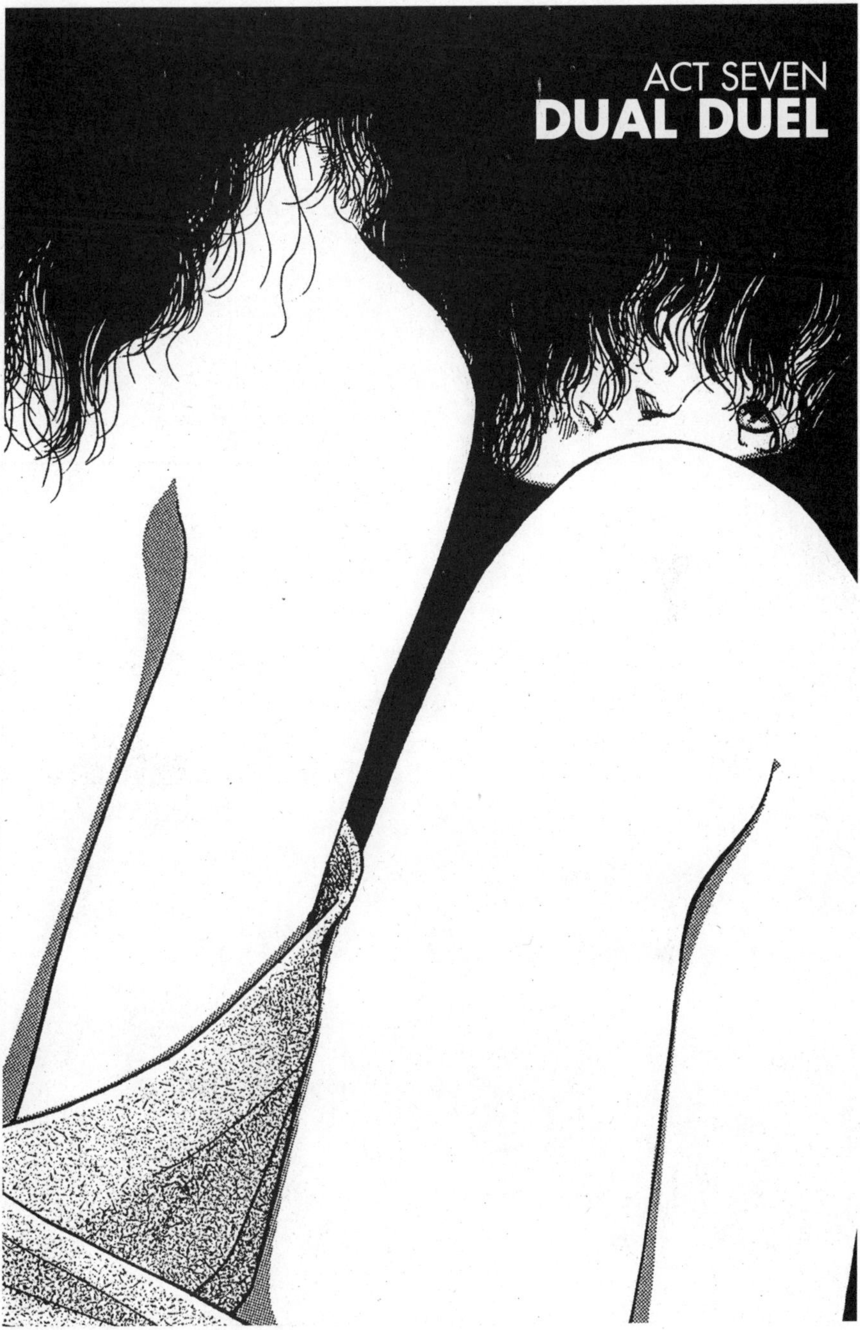
ACT SEVEN
DUAL DUEL

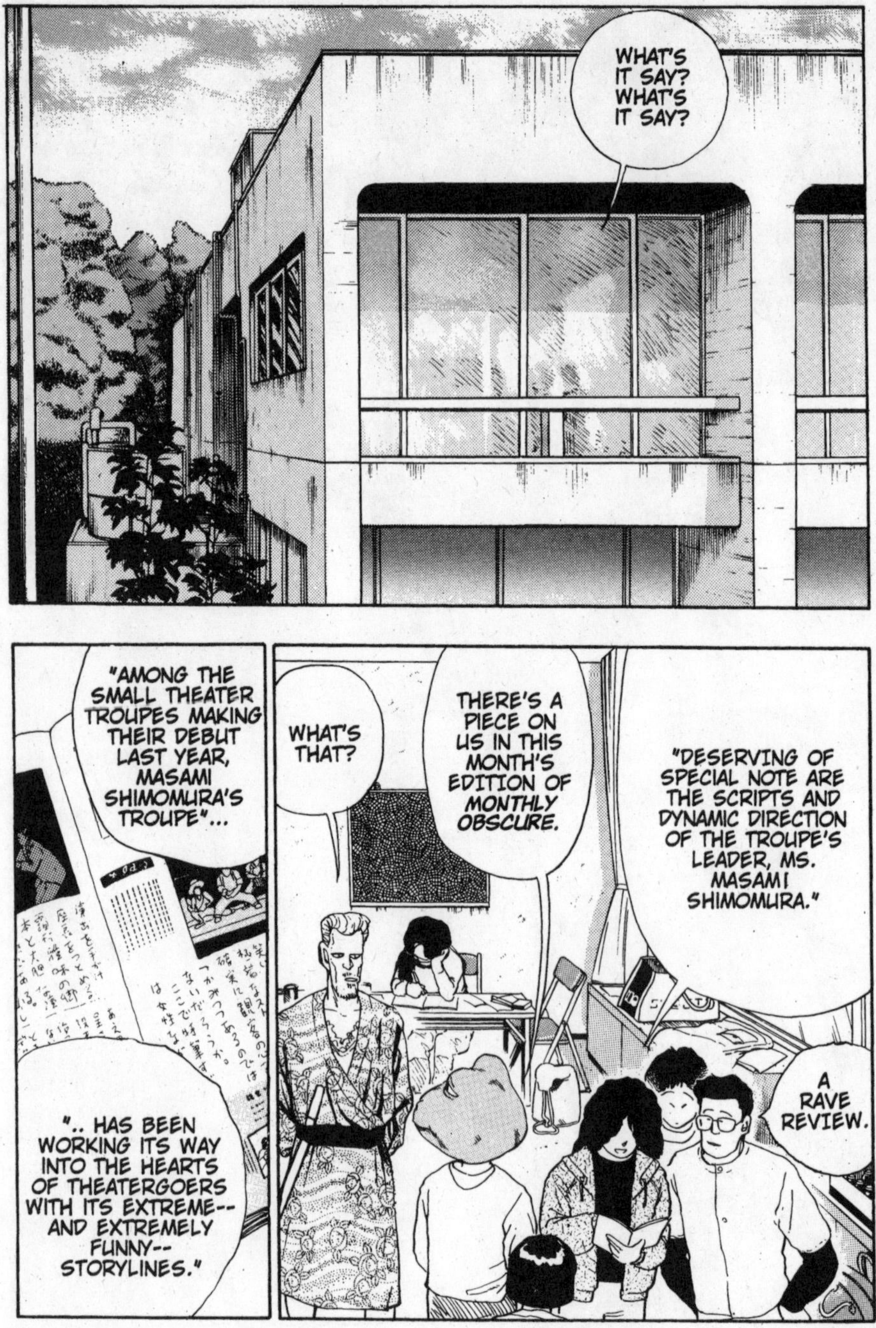
WHAT'S IT SAY? WHAT'S IT SAY?
"AMONG THE SMALL THEATER TROUPES MAKING THEIR DEBUT LAST YEAR, MASAMI SHIMOMURA'S TROUPE"...
".. HAS BEEN WORKING ITS WAY INTO THE HEARTS OF THEATERGOERS WITH ITS EXTREME-- AND EXTREMELY FUNNY-- STORYLINES."
WHAT'S THAT?
THERE'S A PIECE ON US IN THIS MONTH'S EDITION OF *MONTHLY OBSCURE*.
"DESERVING OF SPECIAL NOTE ARE THE SCRIPTS AND DYNAMIC DIRECTION OF THE TROUPE'S LEADER, MS. MASAMI SHIMOMURA."
A RAVE REVIEW.

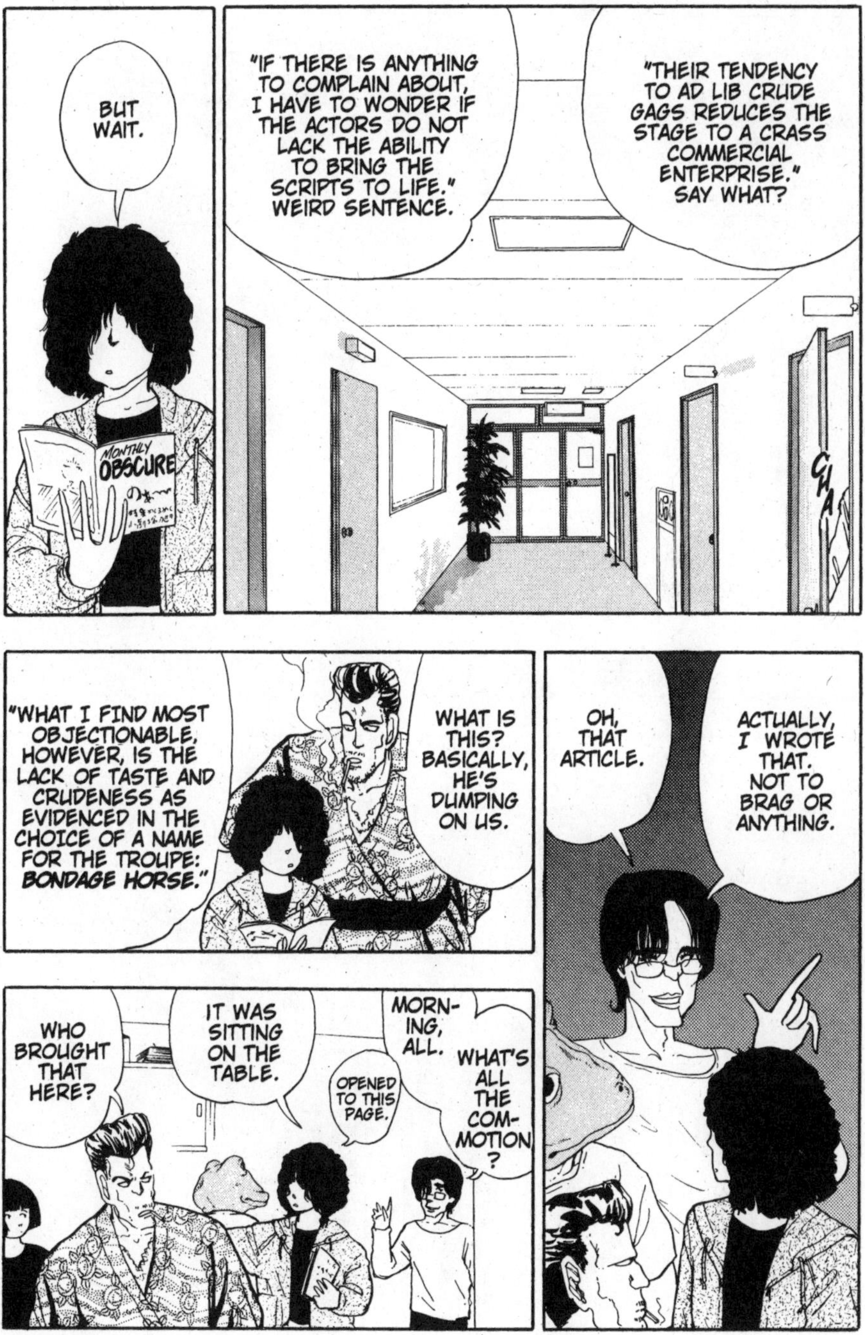
BUT WAIT.
MONTHLY OBSCURE
"IF THERE IS ANYTHING TO COMPLAIN ABOUT, I HAVE TO WONDER IF THE ACTORS DO NOT LACK THE ABILITY TO BRING THE SCRIPTS TO LIFE." WEIRD SENTENCE.
"THEIR TENDENCY TO AD LIB CRUDE GAGS REDUCES THE STAGE TO A CRASS COMMERCIAL ENTERPRISE." SAY WHAT?
CHA
"WHAT I FIND MOST OBJECTIONABLE, HOWEVER, IS THE LACK OF TASTE AND CRUDENESS AS EVIDENCED IN THE CHOICE OF A NAME FOR THE TROUPE: BONDAGE HORSE."
WHAT IS THIS? BASICALLY, HE'S DUMPING ON US.
WHO BROUGHT THAT HERE?
IT WAS SITTING ON THE TABLE.
OPENED TO THIS PAGE.
MORN-ING, ALL.
WHAT'S ALL THE COM-MOTION?
OH, THAT ARTICLE.
ACTUALLY, I WROTE THAT. NOT TO BRAG OR ANYTHING.

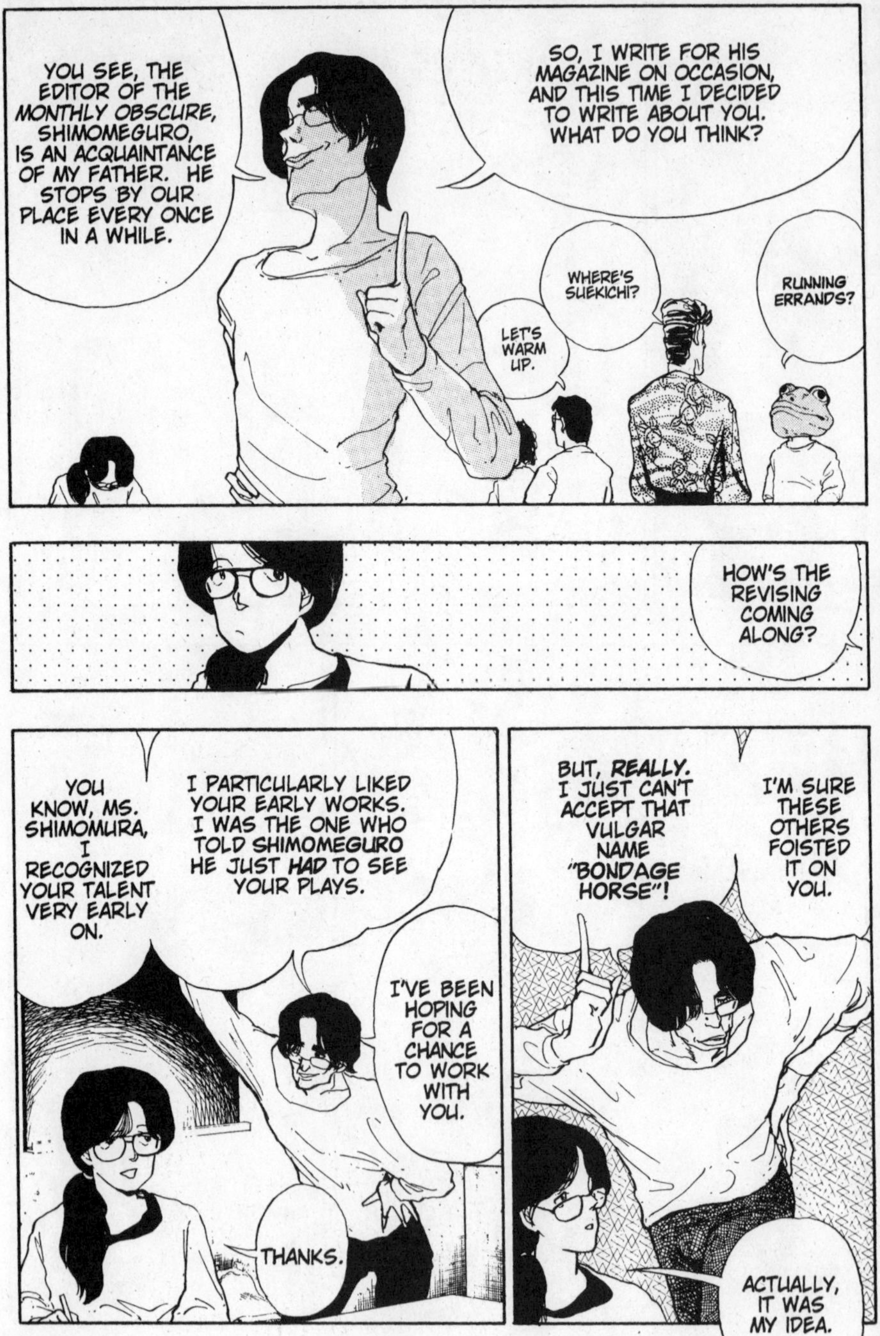
YOU SEE, THE EDITOR OF THE MONTHLY OBSCURE, SHIMOMEGURO, IS AN ACQUAINTANCE OF MY FATHER. HE STOPS BY OUR PLACE EVERY ONCE IN A WHILE.
SO, I WRITE FOR HIS MAGAZINE ON OCCASION, AND THIS TIME I DECIDED TO WRITE ABOUT YOU. WHAT DO YOU THINK?
LET'S WARM UP.
WHERE'S SUEKICHI?
RUNNING ERRANDS?
HOW'S THE REVISING COMING ALONG?
YOU KNOW, MS. SHIMOMURA, I RECOGNIZED YOUR TALENT VERY EARLY ON.
I PARTICULARLY LIKED YOUR EARLY WORKS. I WAS THE ONE WHO TOLD SHIMOMEGURO HE JUST HAD TO SEE YOUR PLAYS.
I'VE BEEN HOPING FOR A CHANCE TO WORK WITH YOU.
THANKS.
BUT, REALLY. I JUST CAN'T ACCEPT THAT VULGAR NAME "BONDAGE HORSE"!
I'M SURE THESE OTHERS FOISTED IT ON YOU.
ACTUALLY, IT WAS MY IDEA.

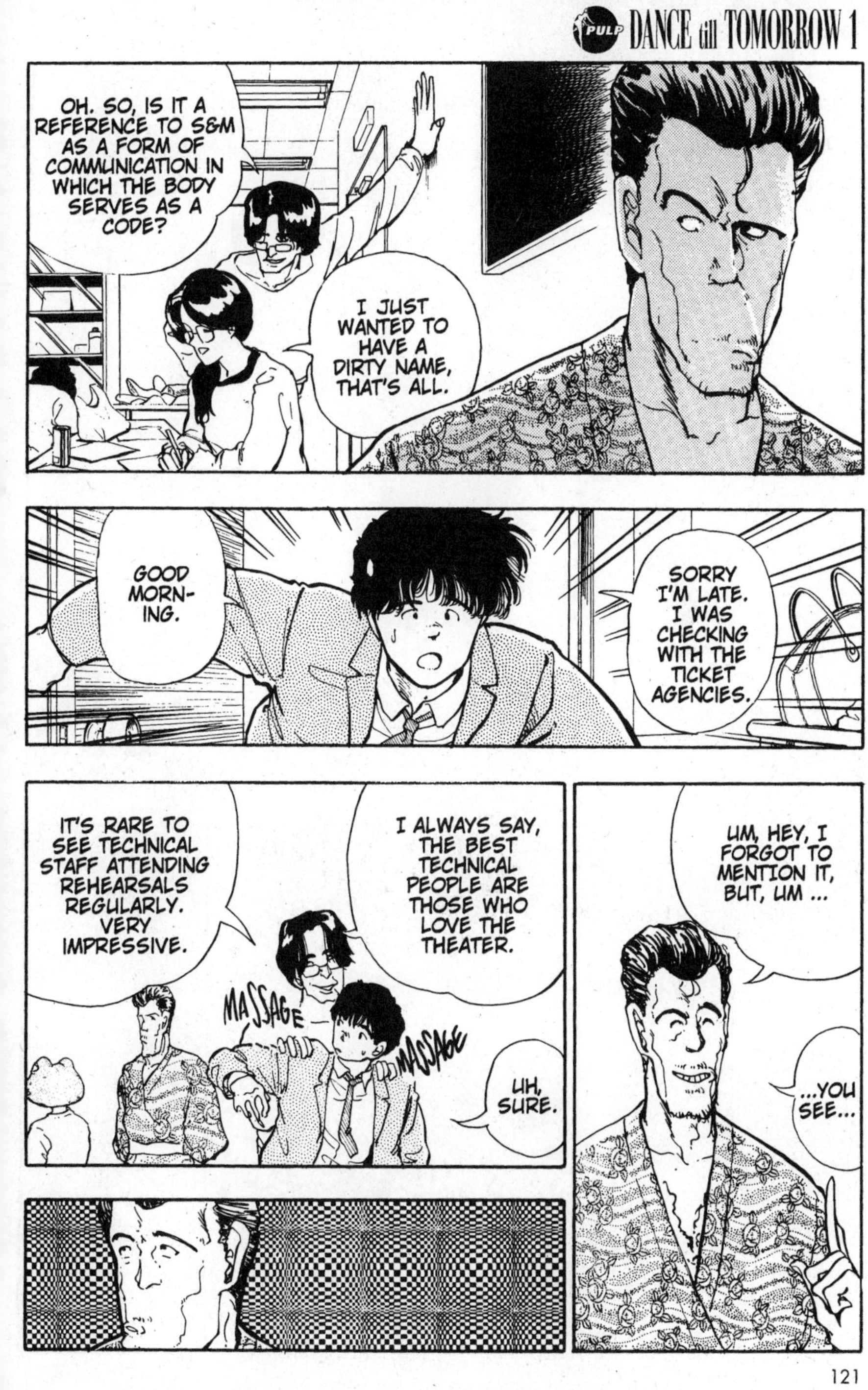
OH. SO, IS IT A REFERENCE TO S&M AS A FORM OF COMMUNICATION IN WHICH THE BODY SERVES AS A CODE?
I JUST WANTED TO HAVE A DIRTY NAME, THAT'S ALL.
GOOD MORNING.
SORRY I'M LATE. I WAS CHECKING WITH THE TICKET AGENCIES.
IT'S RARE TO SEE TECHNICAL STAFF ATTENDING REHEARSALS REGULARLY. VERY IMPRESSIVE.
I ALWAYS SAY, THE BEST TECHNICAL PEOPLE ARE THOSE WHO LOVE THE THEATER.
MASSAGE
MASSAGE
UH, SURE.
UM, HEY, I FORGOT TO MENTION IT, BUT, UM ...
...YOU SEE...

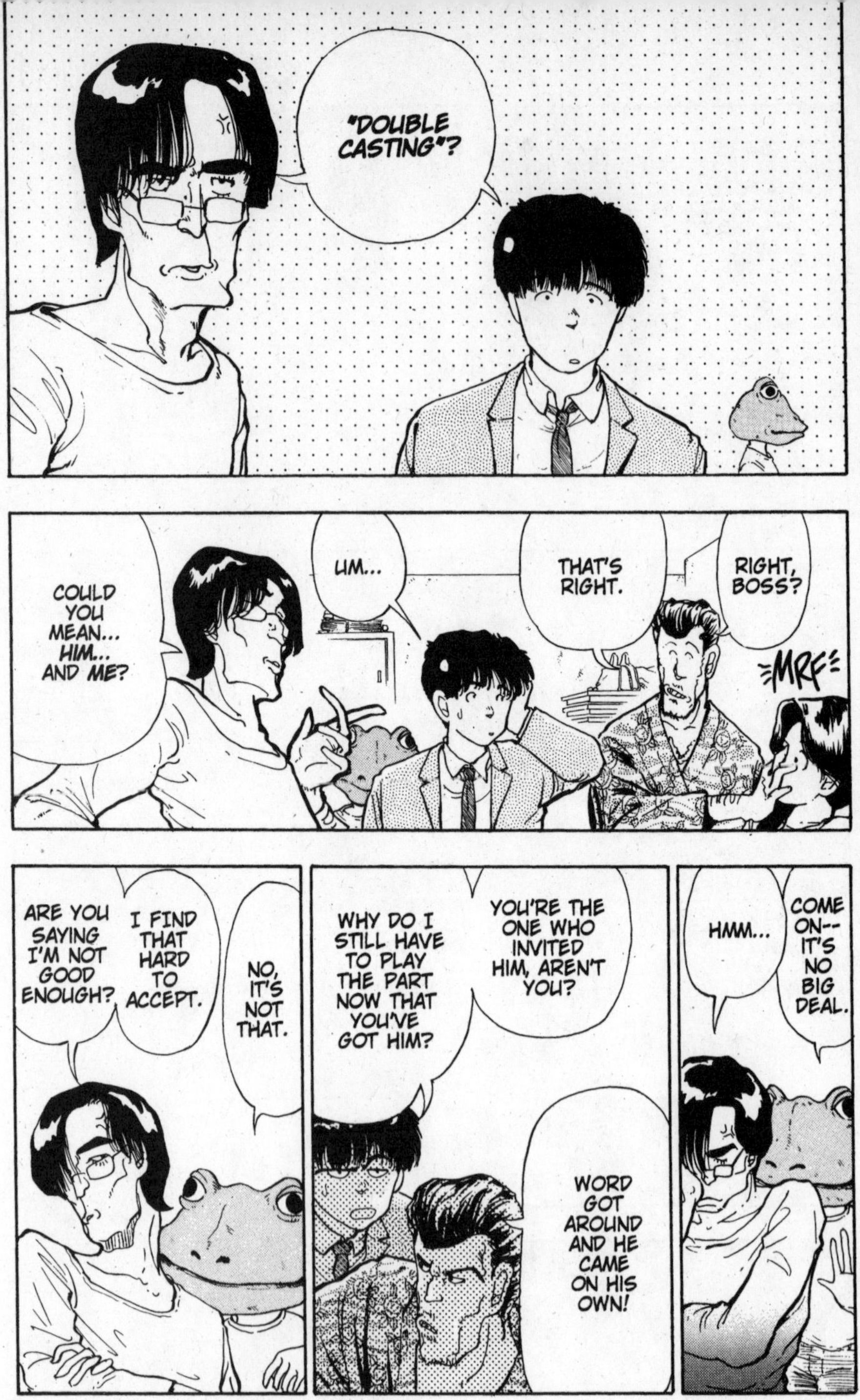
"DOUBLE CASTING"?
COULD YOU MEAN... HIM... AND ME?
UM...
THAT'S RIGHT.
RIGHT, BOSS?
MRF
ARE YOU SAYING I'M NOT GOOD ENOUGH?
I FIND THAT HARD TO ACCEPT.
NO, IT'S NOT THAT.
WHY DO I STILL HAVE TO PLAY THE PART NOW THAT YOU'VE GOT HIM?
YOU'RE THE ONE WHO INVITED HIM, AREN'T YOU?
WORD GOT AROUND AND HE CAME ON HIS OWN!
HMM...
COME ON-- IT'S NO BIG DEAL.

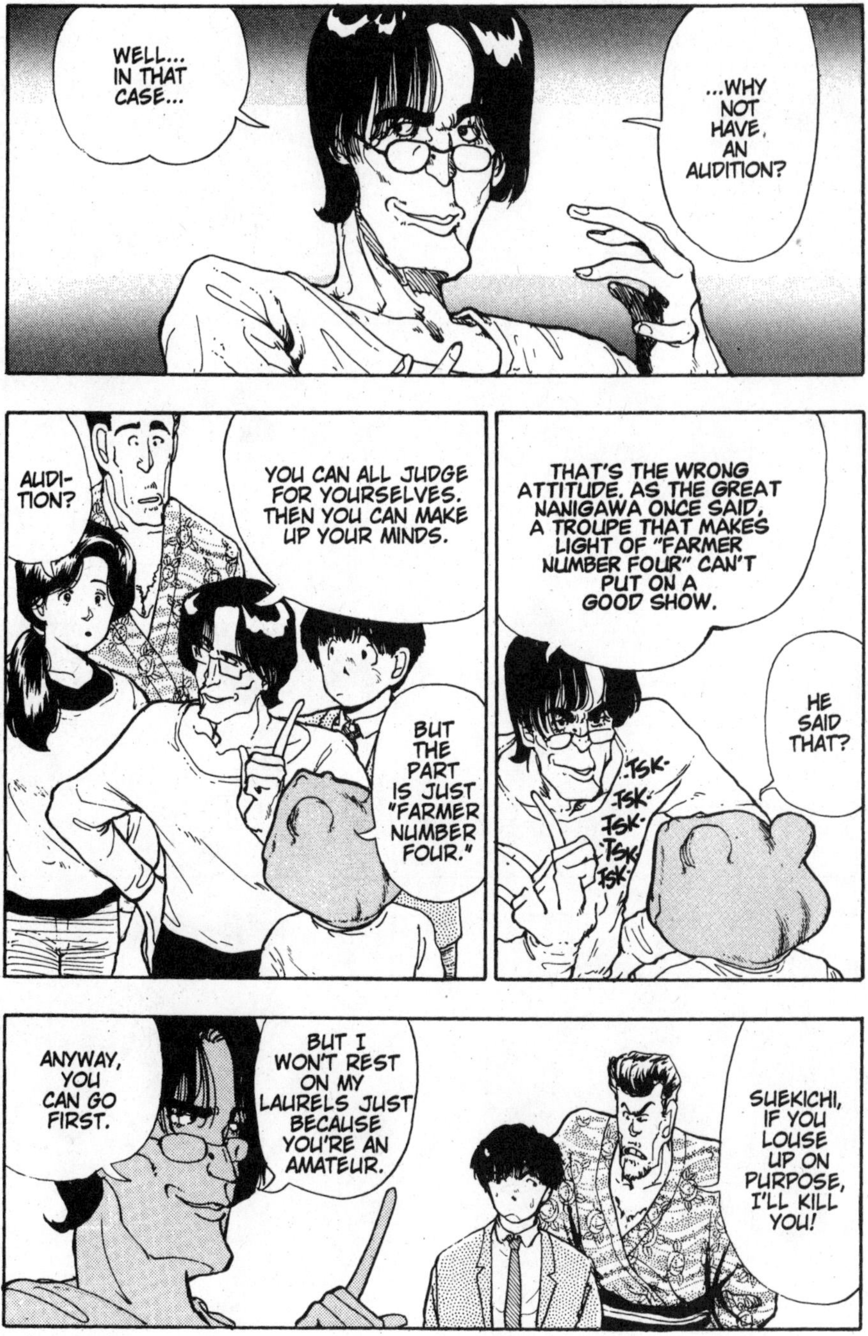
WELL... IN THAT CASE...
...WHY NOT HAVE, AN AUDITION?
AUDI-TION?
YOU CAN ALL JUDGE FOR YOURSELVES. THEN YOU CAN MAKE UP YOUR MINDS.
BUT THE PART IS JUST "FARMER NUMBER FOUR."
THAT'S THE WRONG ATTITUDE. AS THE GREAT NANIGAWA ONCE SAID, A TROUPE THAT MAKES LIGHT OF "FARMER NUMBER FOUR" CAN'T PUT ON A GOOD SHOW.
TSK TSK TSK TSK TSK
HE SAID THAT?
ANYWAY, YOU CAN GO FIRST.
BUT I WON'T REST ON MY LAURELS JUST BECAUSE YOU'RE AN AMATEUR.
SUEKICHI, IF YOU LOUSE UP ON PURPOSE, I'LL KILL YOU!

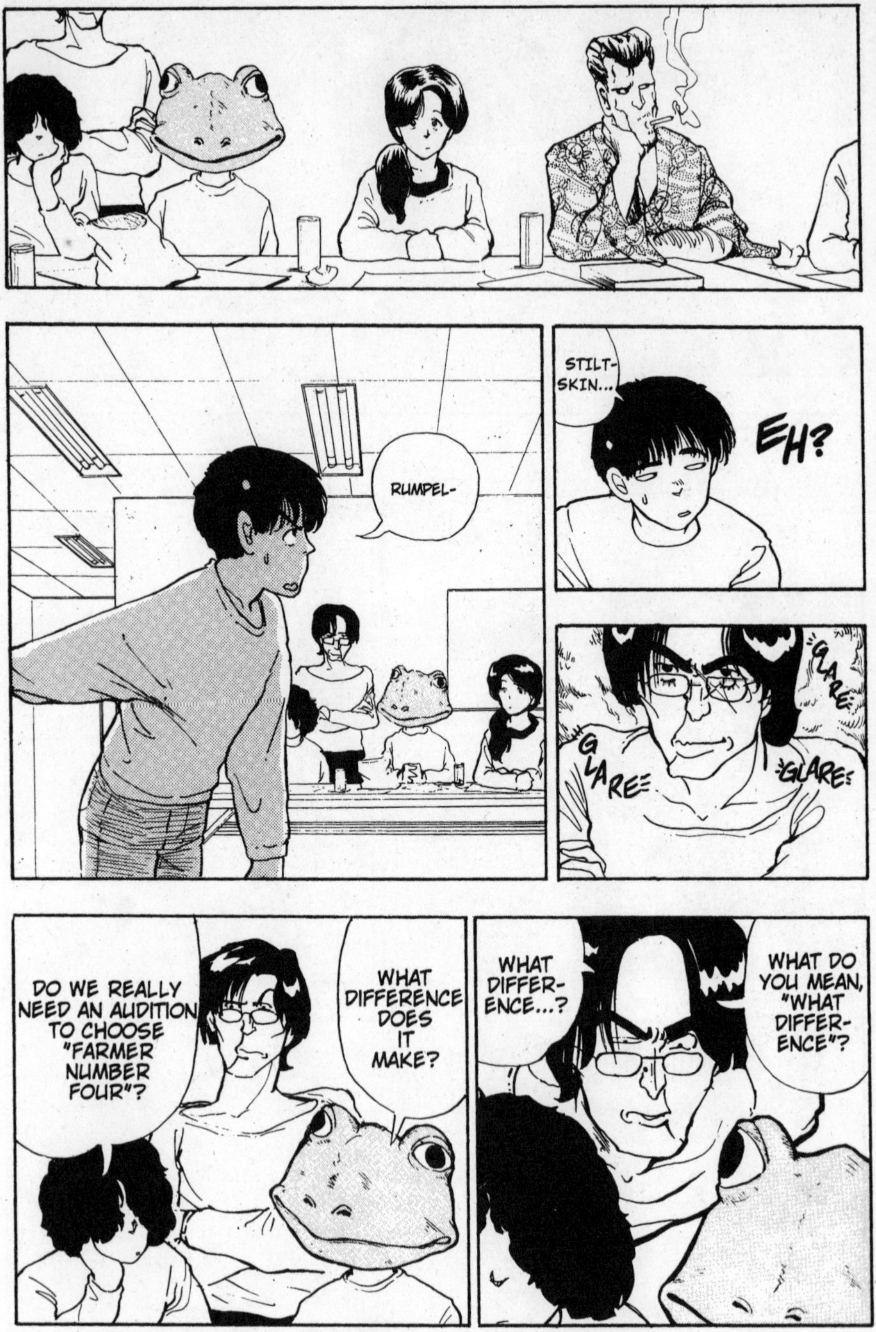
RUMPEL-
STILT-SKIN...
EH?
GLARE GLARE GLARE
DO WE REALLY NEED AN AUDITION TO CHOOSE "FARMER NUMBER FOUR"?
WHAT DIFFERENCE DOES IT MAKE?
WHAT DIFFER-ENCE...?
WHAT DO YOU MEAN, "WHAT DIFFER-ENCE"?

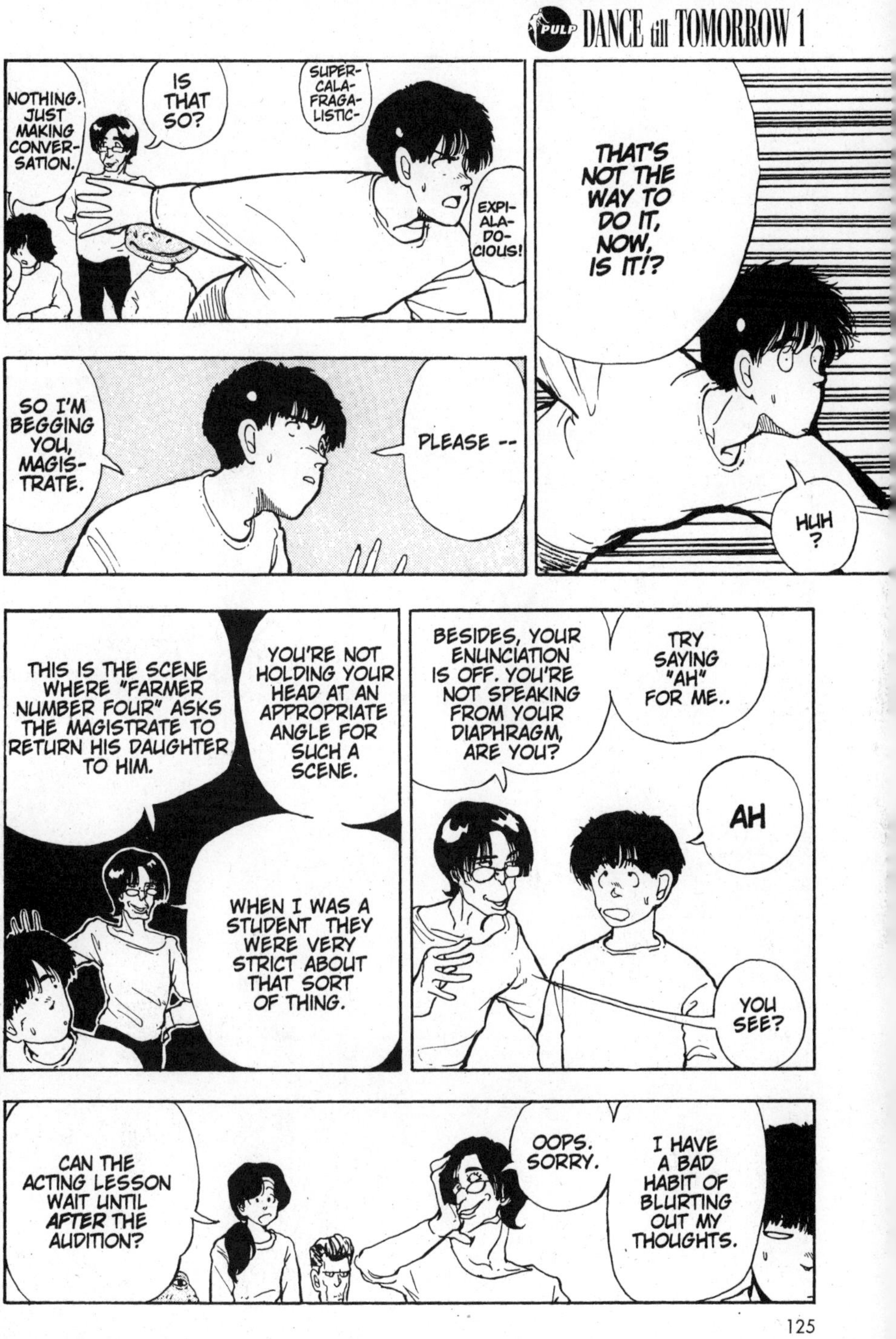
NOTHING. JUST MAKING CONVERSATION.
IS THAT SO?
SUPER-CALA-FRAGA-LISTIC-
EXPI-ALA-DO-CIOUS!
SO I'M BEGGING YOU, MAGISTRATE.
PLEASE --
THAT'S NOT THE WAY TO DO IT, NOW, IS IT!?
HUH?
THIS IS THE SCENE WHERE "FARMER NUMBER FOUR" ASKS THE MAGISTRATE TO RETURN HIS DAUGHTER TO HIM.
YOU'RE NOT HOLDING YOUR HEAD AT AN APPROPRIATE ANGLE FOR SUCH A SCENE.
WHEN I WAS A STUDENT THEY WERE VERY STRICT ABOUT THAT SORT OF THING.
BESIDES, YOUR ENUNCIATION IS OFF. YOU'RE NOT SPEAKING FROM YOUR DIAPHRAGM, ARE YOU?
TRY SAYING "AH" FOR ME..
AH
YOU SEE?
CAN THE ACTING LESSON WAIT UNTIL AFTER THE AUDITION?
OOPS. SORRY.
I HAVE A BAD HABIT OF BLURTING OUT MY THOUGHTS.

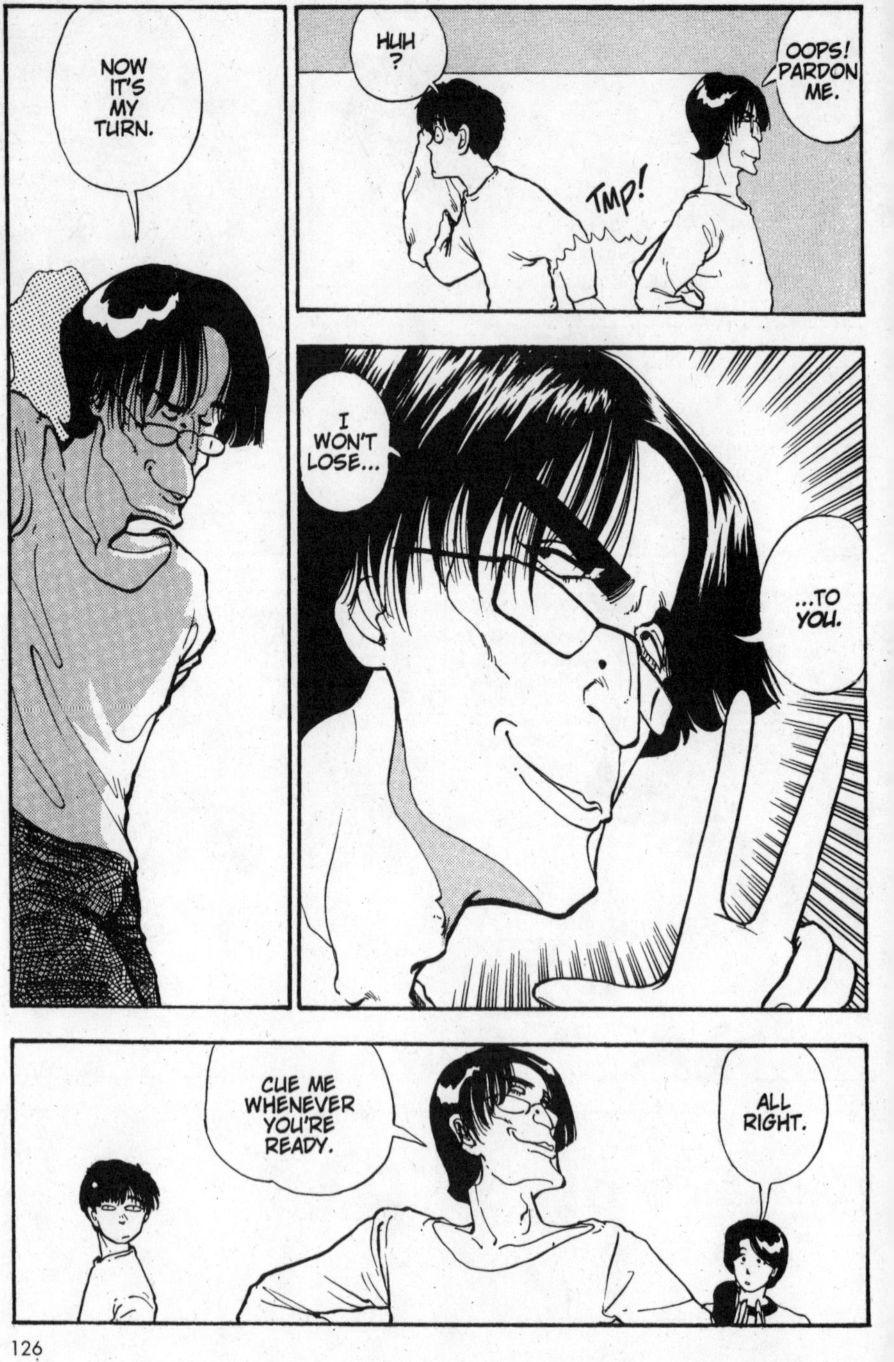
NOW IT'S MY TURN.
HUH?
TMP!
OOPS! PARDON ME.
I WON'T LOSE...
...TO YOU.
CUE ME WHENEVER YOU'RE READY.
ALL RIGHT.

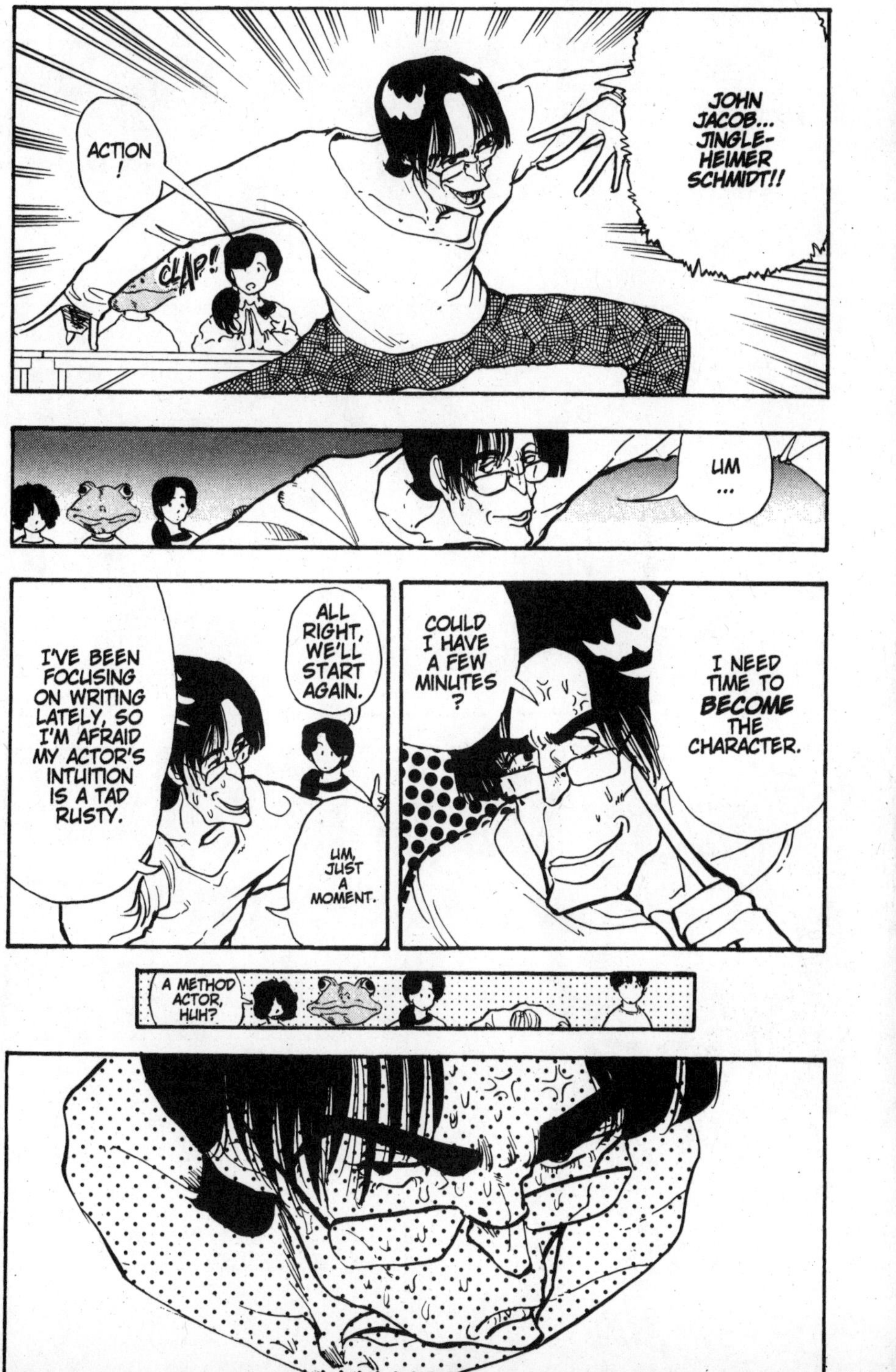
ACTION!
CLAP!
JOHN JACOB... JINGLE-HEIMER SCHMIDT!!
UM ...
I'VE BEEN FOCUSING ON WRITING LATELY, SO I'M AFRAID MY ACTOR'S INTUITION IS A TAD RUSTY.
ALL RIGHT, WE'LL START AGAIN.
UM, JUST A MOMENT.
COULD I HAVE A FEW MINUTES?
I NEED TIME TO BECOME THE CHARACTER.
A METHOD ACTOR, HUH?

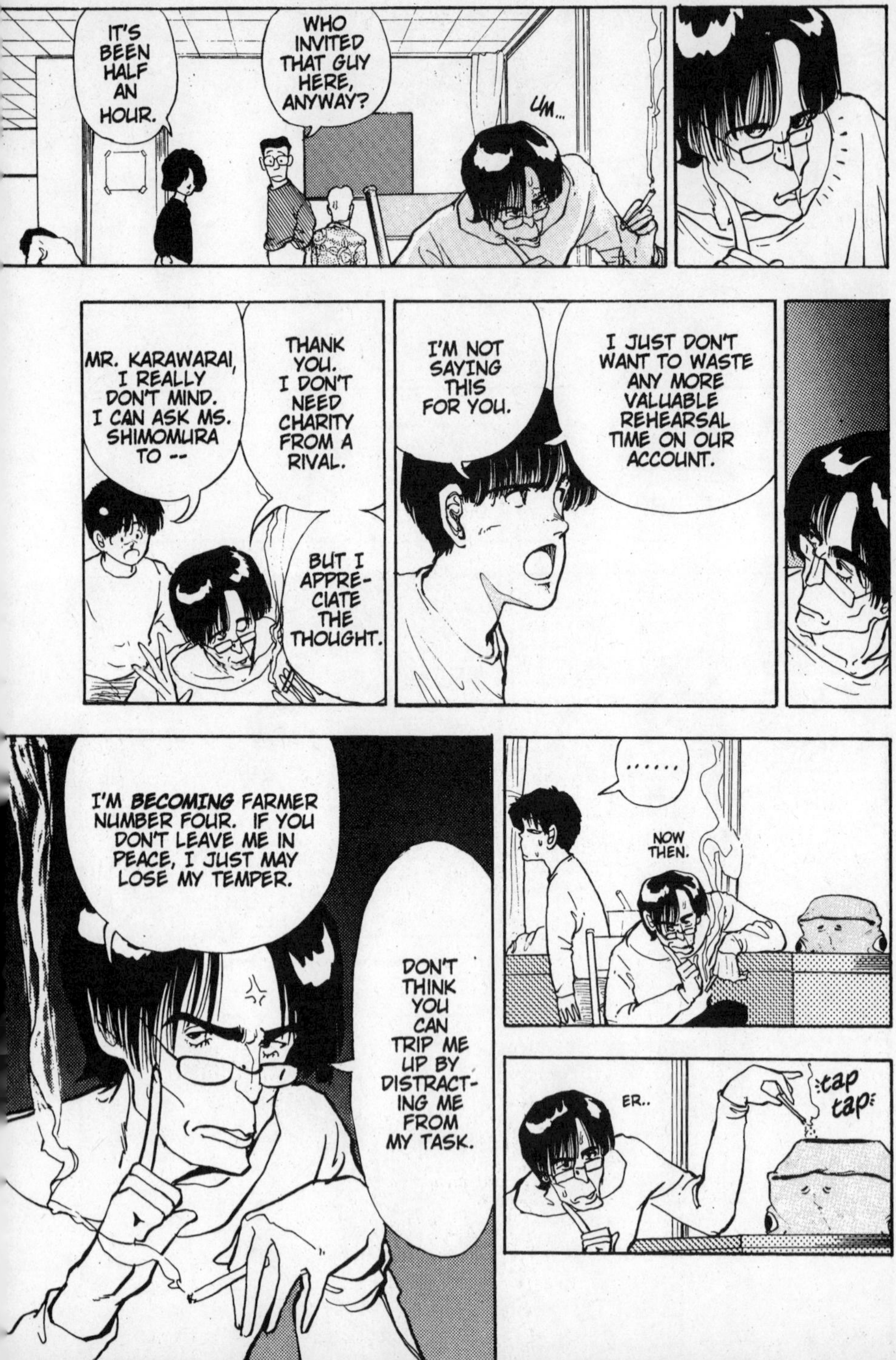
IT'S BEEN HALF AN HOUR.
WHO INVITED THAT GUY HERE, ANYWAY?
UM...
MR. KARAWARAI, I REALLY DON'T MIND. I CAN ASK MS. SHIMOMURA TO --
THANK YOU. I DON'T NEED CHARITY FROM A RIVAL.
BUT I APPRECIATE THE THOUGHT.
I'M NOT SAYING THIS FOR YOU.
I JUST DON'T WANT TO WASTE ANY MORE VALUABLE REHEARSAL TIME ON OUR ACCOUNT.
I'M BECOMING FARMER NUMBER FOUR. IF YOU DON'T LEAVE ME IN PEACE, I JUST MAY LOSE MY TEMPER.
DON'T THINK YOU CAN TRIP ME UP BY DISTRACTING ME FROM MY TASK.
......
NOW THEN.
ER..
tap tap

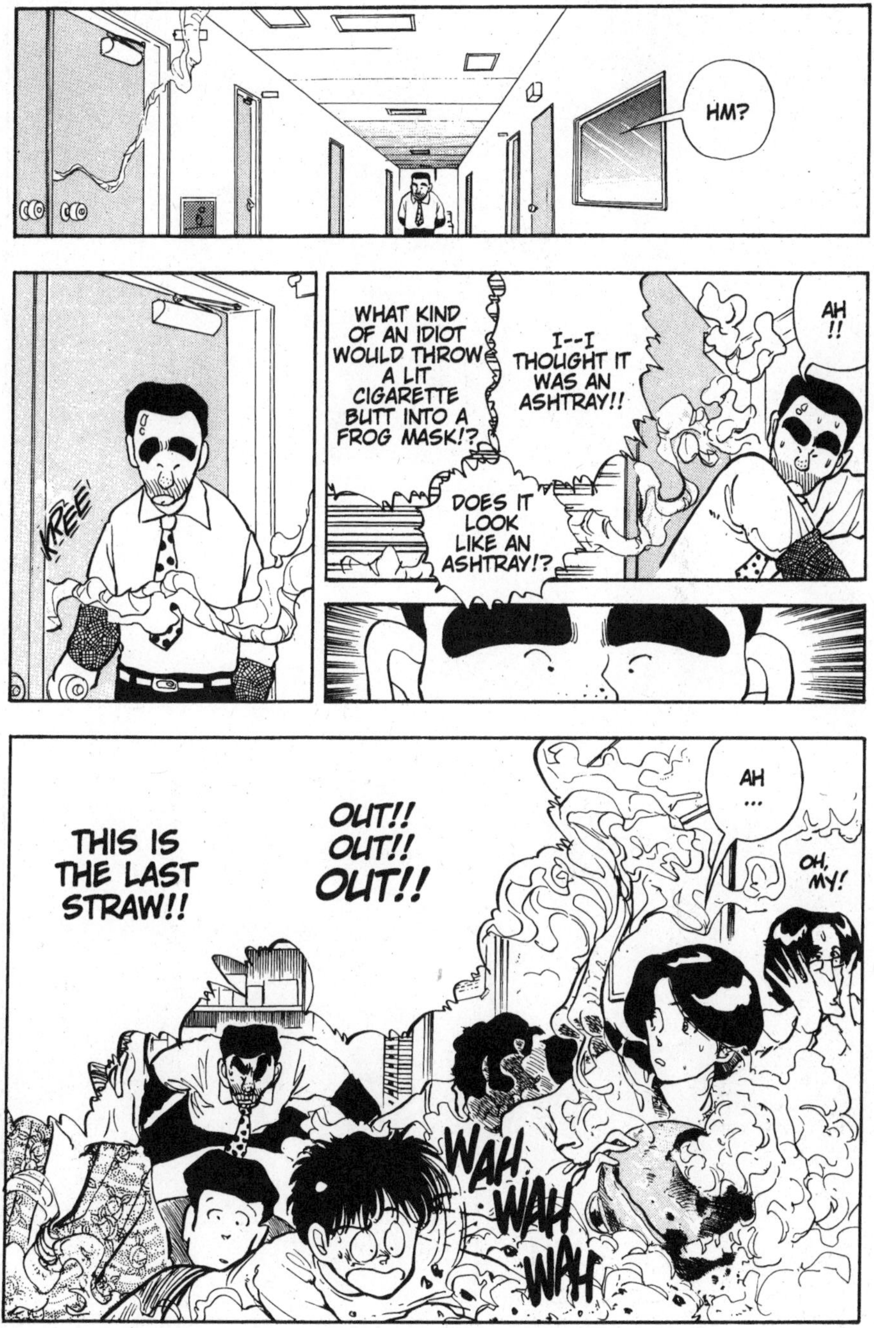
HM?
KREE
WHAT KIND OF AN IDIOT WOULD THROW A LIT CIGARETTE BUTT INTO A FROG MASK!?
I--I THOUGHT IT WAS AN ASHTRAY!!
AH !!
DOES IT LOOK LIKE AN ASHTRAY!?
THIS IS THE LAST STRAW!!
OUT!! OUT!! OUT!!
AH ...
OH, MY!
WAH WAH WAH

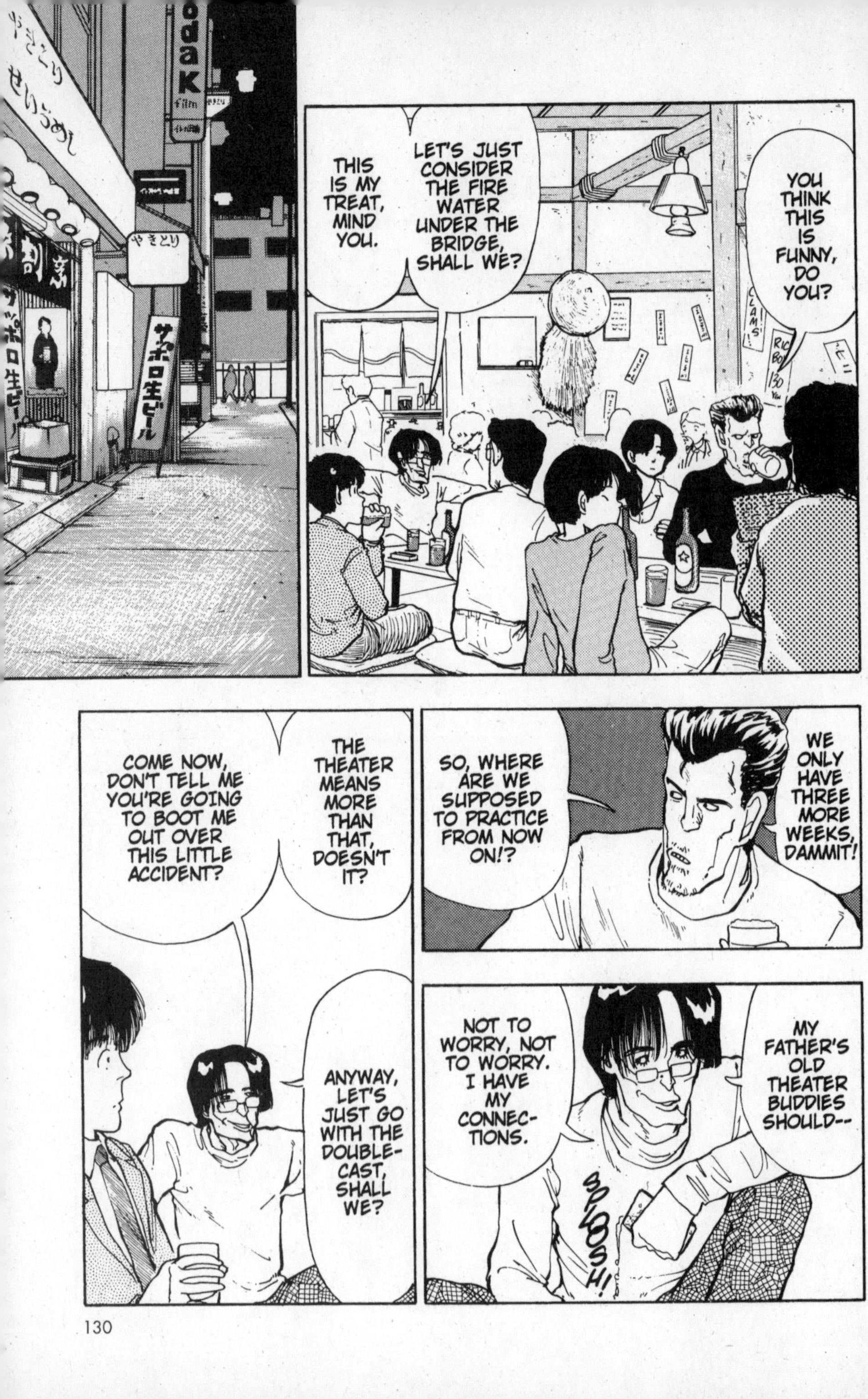

やきとり
サッポロ生ビール
THIS IS MY TREAT, MIND YOU.
LET'S JUST CONSIDER THE FIRE WATER UNDER THE BRIDGE, SHALL WE?
CLAMS!
YOU THINK THIS IS FUNNY, DO YOU?
COME NOW, DON'T TELL ME YOU'RE GOING TO BOOT ME OUT OVER THIS LITTLE ACCIDENT?
THE THEATER MEANS MORE THAN THAT, DOESN'T IT?
ANYWAY, LET'S JUST GO WITH THE DOUBLE-CAST, SHALL WE?
SO, WHERE ARE WE SUPPOSED TO PRACTICE FROM NOW ON!?
WE ONLY HAVE THREE MORE WEEKS, DAMMIT!
NOT TO WORRY, NOT TO WORRY. I HAVE MY CONNEC-TIONS.
MY FATHER'S OLD THEATER BUDDIES SHOULD--
SPLOOSH!

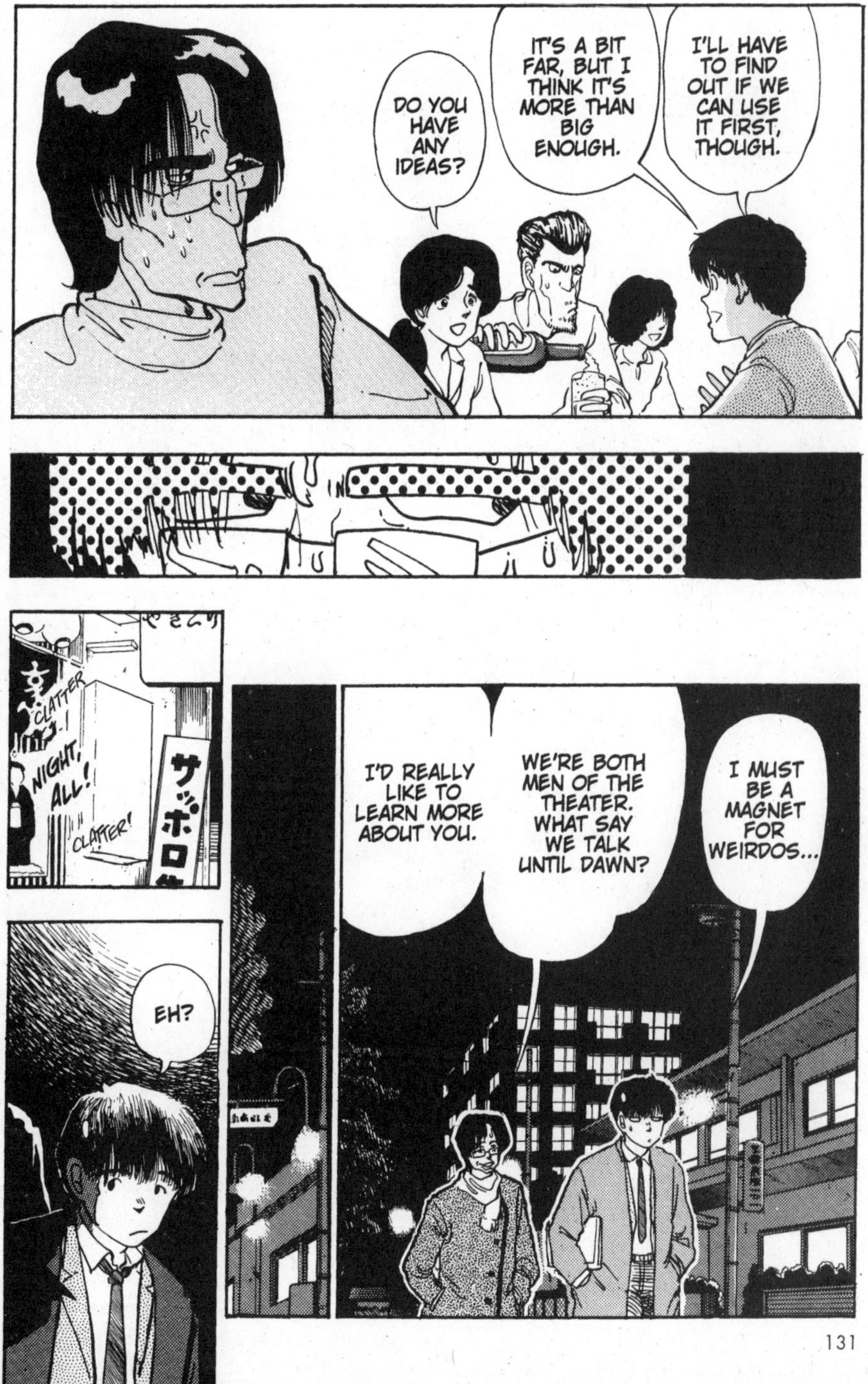
DO YOU HAVE ANY IDEAS?
IT'S A BIT FAR, BUT I THINK IT'S MORE THAN BIG ENOUGH.
I'LL HAVE TO FIND OUT IF WE CAN USE IT FIRST, THOUGH.
CLATTER
NIGHT, ALL!
CLATTER!
EH?
I'D REALLY LIKE TO LEARN MORE ABOUT YOU.
WE'RE BOTH MEN OF THE THEATER. WHAT SAY WE TALK UNTIL DAWN?
I MUST BE A MAGNET FOR WEIRDOS...

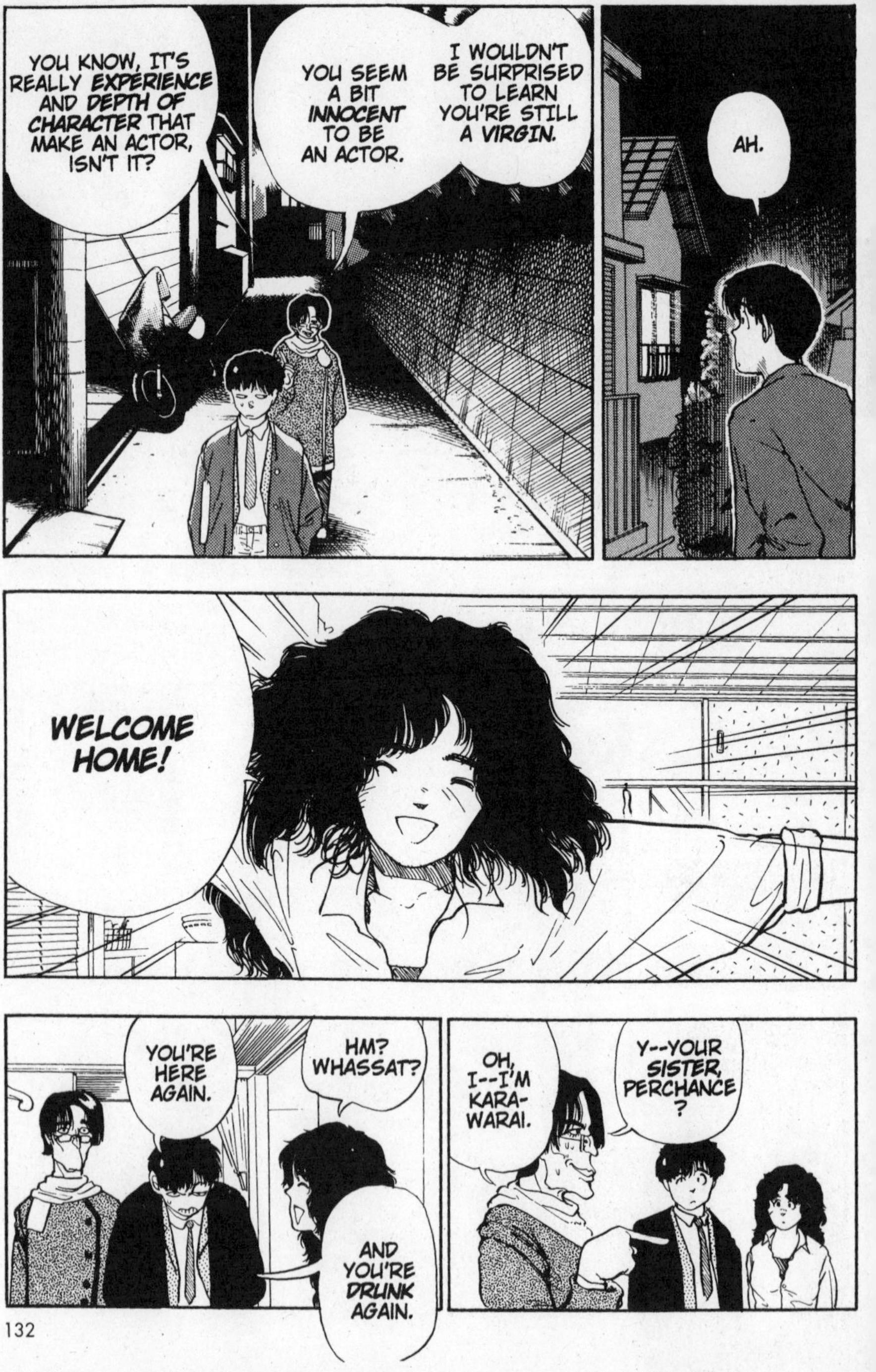
YOU KNOW, IT'S REALLY EXPERIENCE AND DEPTH OF CHARACTER THAT MAKE AN ACTOR, ISN'T IT?
YOU SEEM A BIT INNOCENT TO BE AN ACTOR.
I WOULDN'T BE SURPRISED TO LEARN YOU'RE STILL A VIRGIN.
AH.
WELCOME HOME!
YOU'RE HERE AGAIN.
HM? WHASSAT?
AND YOU'RE DRUNK AGAIN.
OH, I--I'M KARAWARAI.
Y--YOUR SISTER, PERCHANCE?

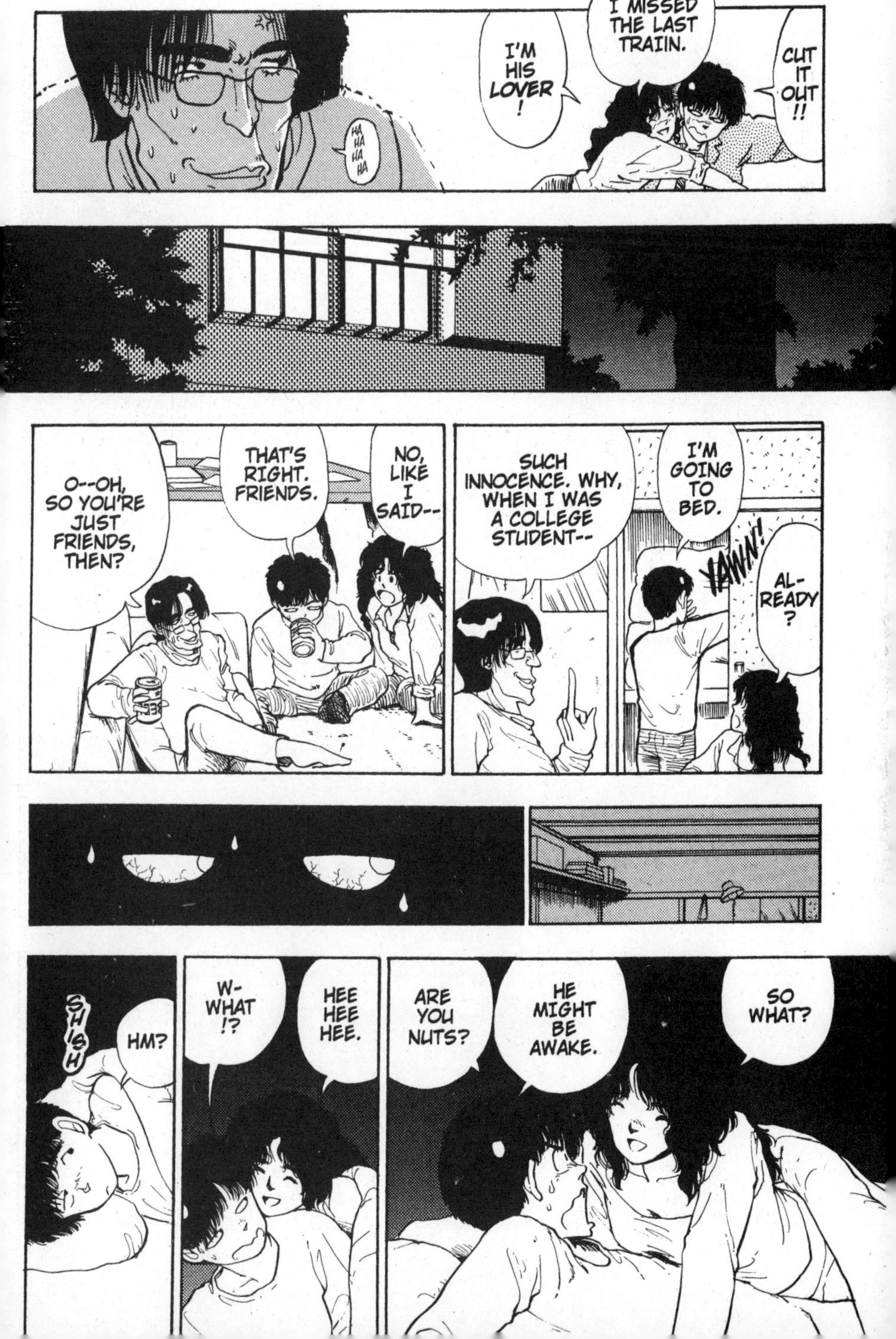
HA HA HA HA
I'M HIS LOVER!
I MISSED THE LAST TRAIN.
CUT IT OUT!!
O--OH, SO YOU'RE JUST FRIENDS, THEN?
THAT'S RIGHT. FRIENDS.
NO, LIKE I SAID--
SUCH INNOCENCE. WHY, WHEN I WAS A COLLEGE STUDENT--
I'M GOING TO BED.
YAWN!
AL-READY?
SHISH
HM?
W-WHAT!?
HEE HEE HEE.
ARE YOU NUTS?
HE MIGHT BE AWAKE.
SO WHAT?

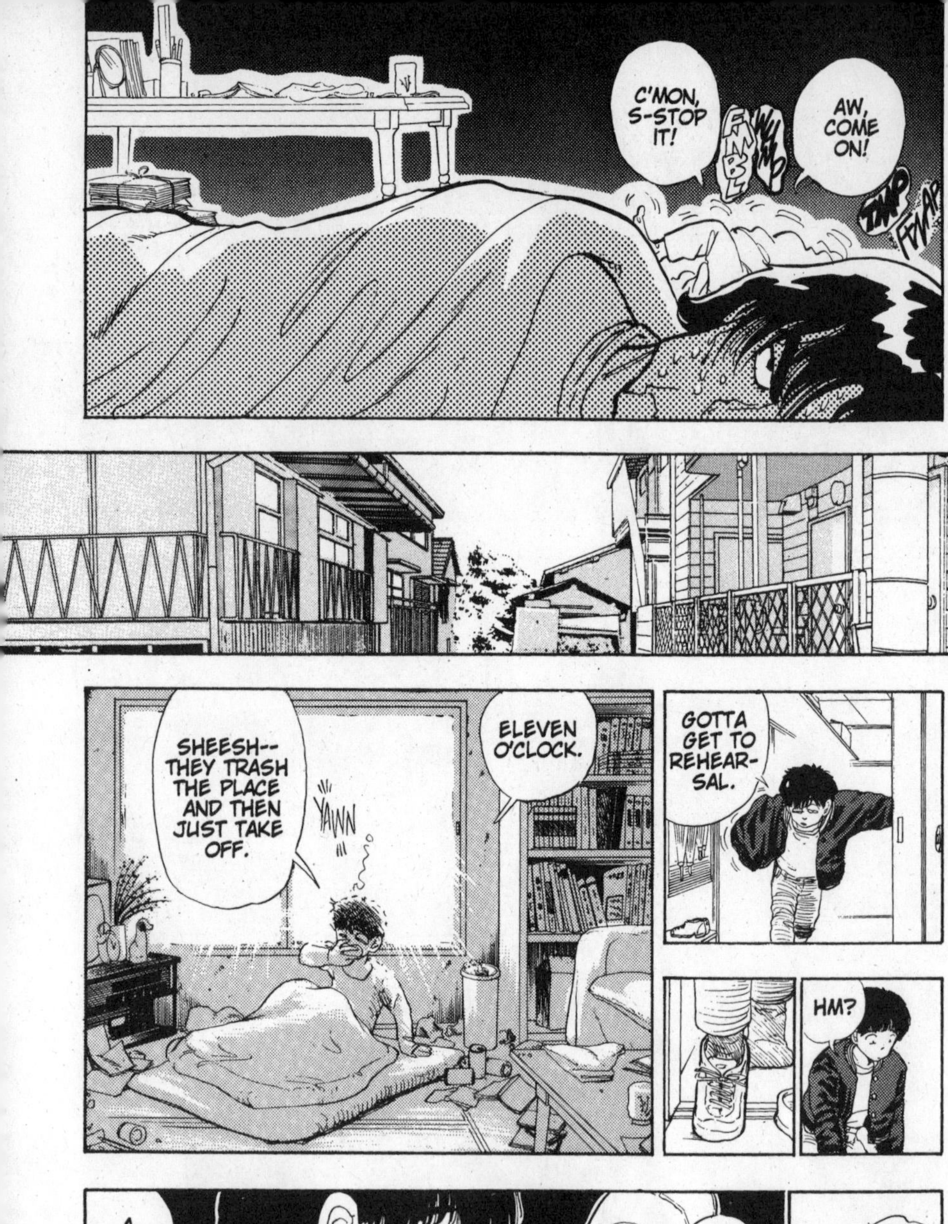
C'MON, S-STOP IT!
WUMP
AW, COME ON!
TMP
FWAP
SHEESH-- THEY TRASH THE PLACE AND THEN JUST TAKE OFF.
YAWN
ELEVEN O'CLOCK.
GOTTA GET TO REHEAR-SAL.
HM?
A TACK...
...IN MY SHOE.
HYOO
HEH HEH HEH.

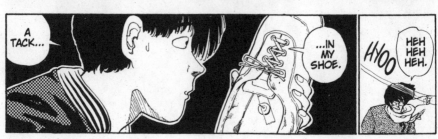

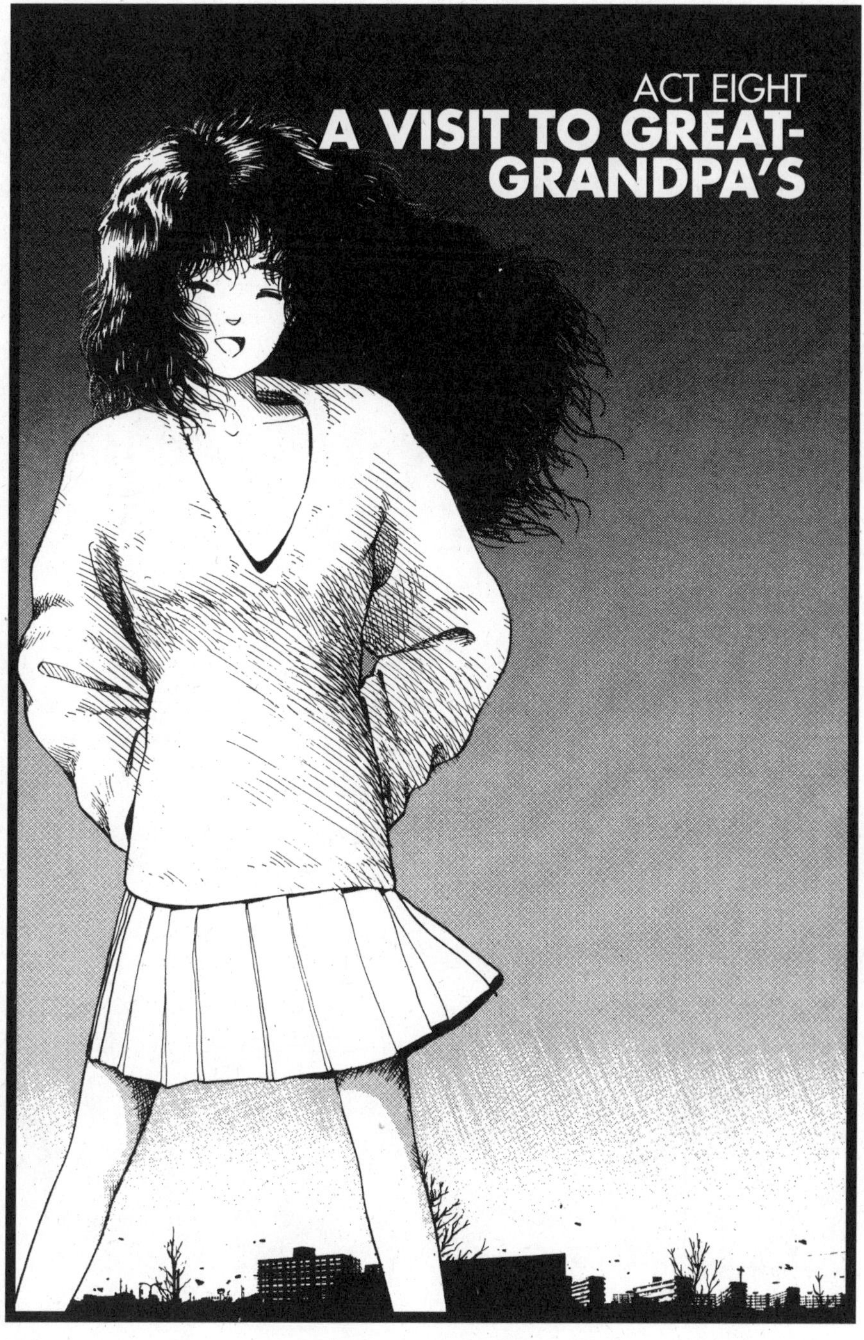
ACT EIGHT
A VISIT TO GREAT-GRANDPA'S

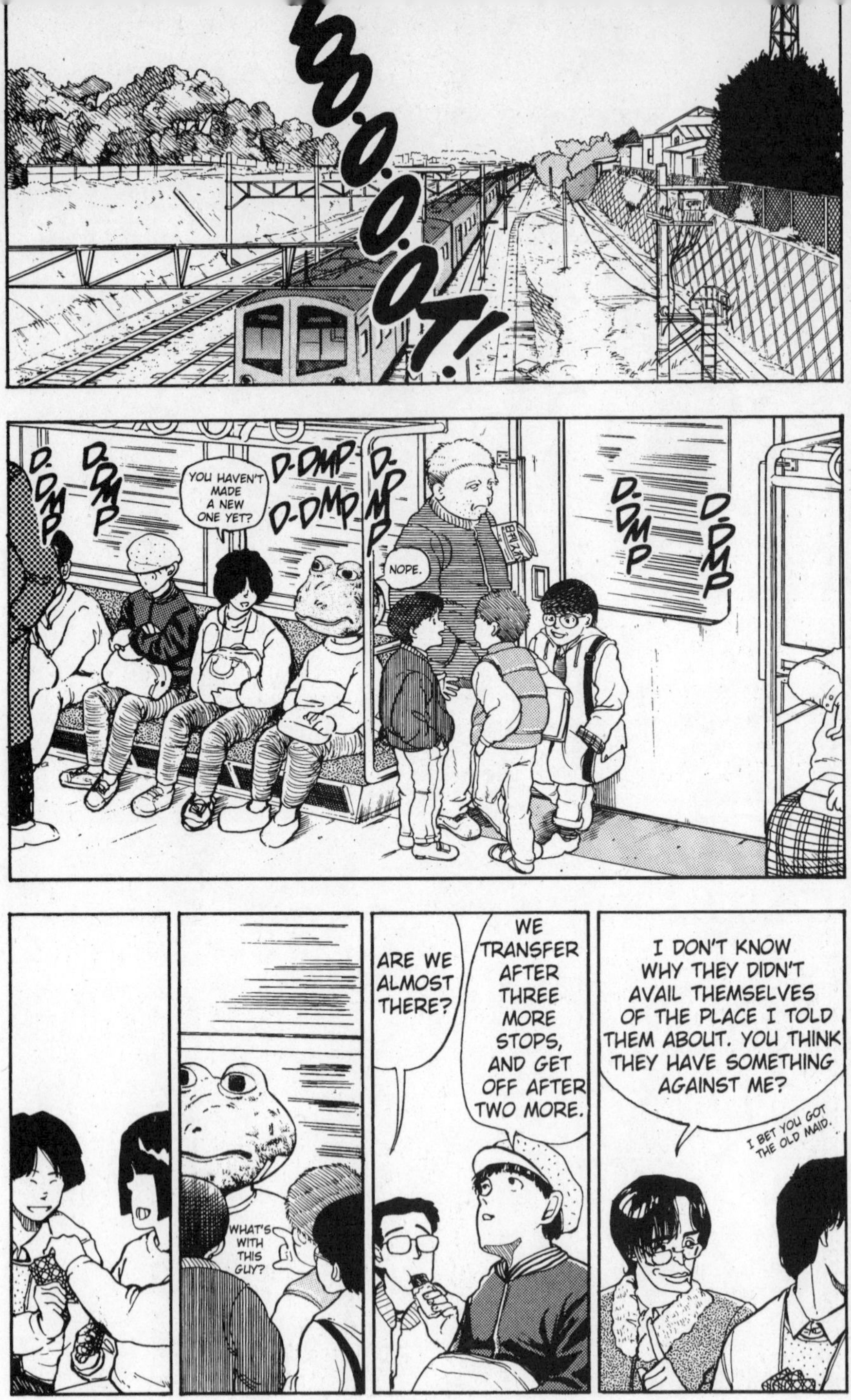
O.O.O.O.T!
D-DMP
D-DMP
YOU HAVEN'T MADE A NEW ONE YET?
D-DMP
D-DMP
D-DMP
NOPE.
D-DMP
D-DMP
WHAT'S WITH THIS GUY?
ARE WE ALMOST THERE?
WE TRANSFER AFTER THREE MORE STOPS, AND GET OFF AFTER TWO MORE.
I DON'T KNOW WHY THEY DIDN'T AVAIL THEMSELVES OF THE PLACE I TOLD THEM ABOUT. YOU THINK THEY HAVE SOMETHING AGAINST ME?
I BET YOU GOT THE OLD MAID.

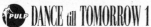

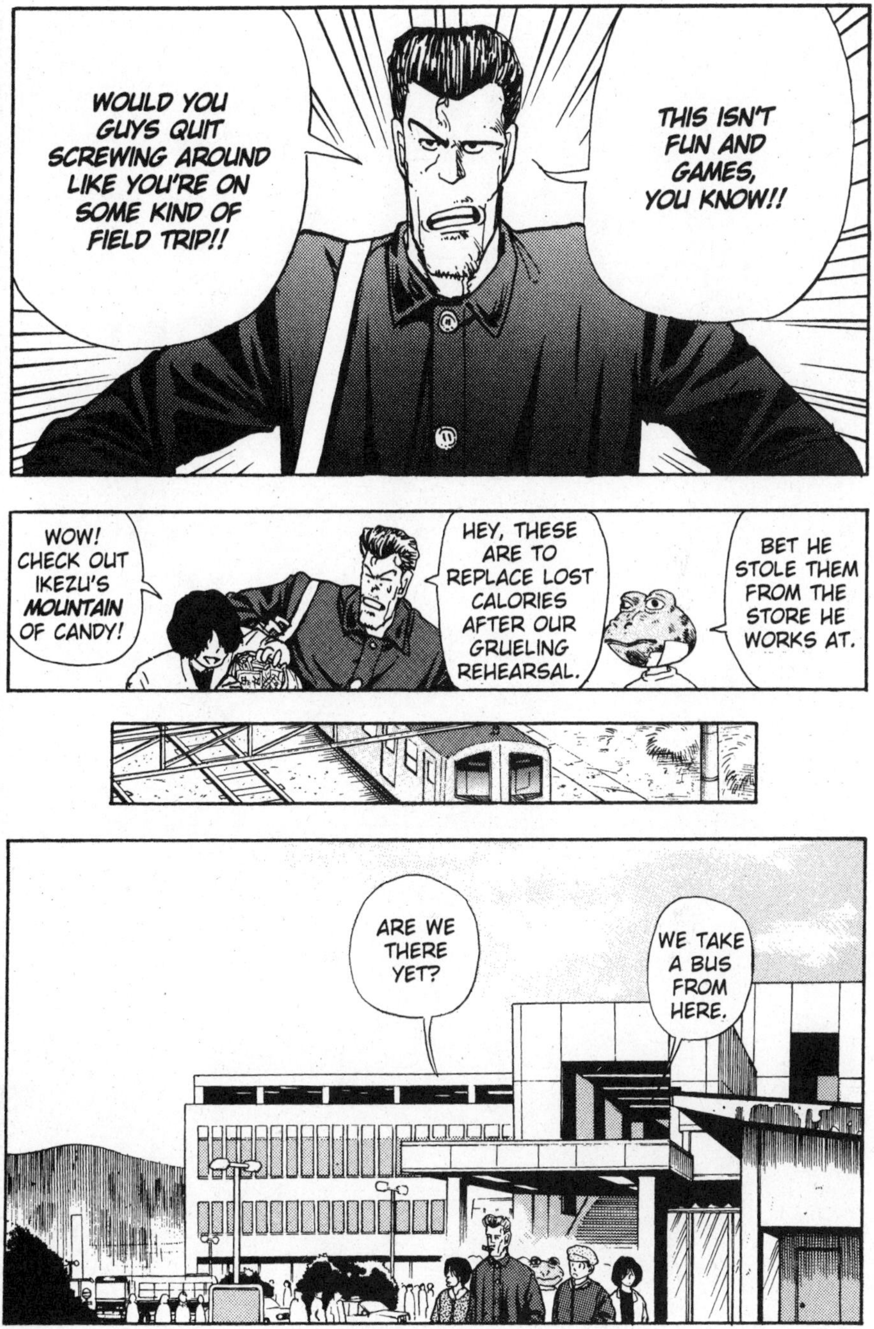
WOULD YOU GUYS QUIT SCREWING AROUND LIKE YOU'RE ON SOME KIND OF FIELD TRIP!!
THIS ISN'T FUN AND GAMES, YOU KNOW!!
WOW! CHECK OUT IKEZU'S *MOUNTAIN* OF CANDY!
HEY, THESE ARE TO REPLACE LOST CALORIES AFTER OUR GRUELING REHEARSAL.
BET HE STOLE THEM FROM THE STORE HE WORKS AT.
ARE WE THERE YET?
WE TAKE A BUS FROM HERE.

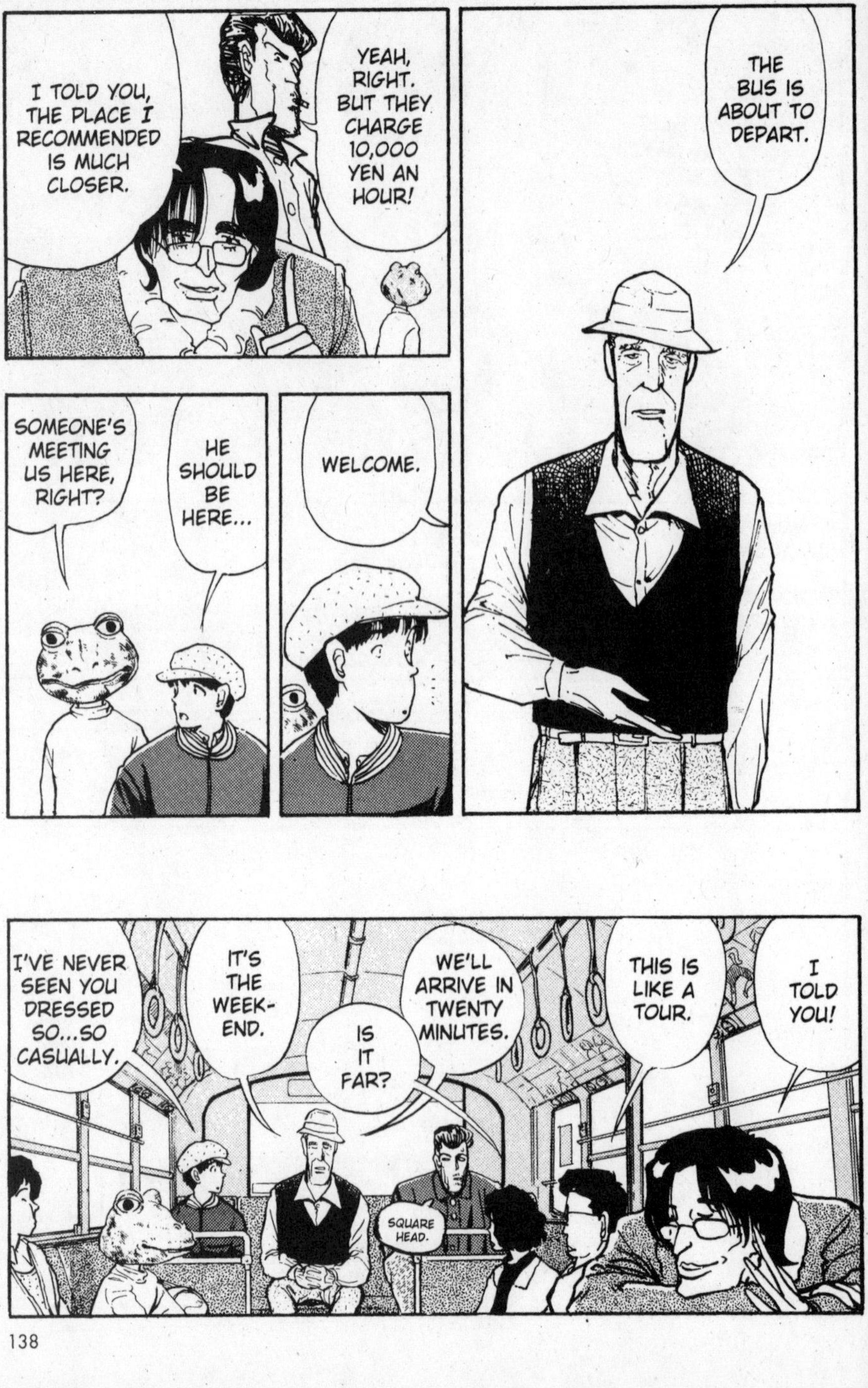
I TOLD YOU, THE PLACE I RECOMMENDED IS MUCH CLOSER.
YEAH, RIGHT. BUT THEY CHARGE 10,000 YEN AN HOUR!
SOMEONE'S MEETING US HERE, RIGHT?
HE SHOULD BE HERE...
WELCOME.
THE BUS IS ABOUT TO DEPART.
I'VE NEVER SEEN YOU DRESSED SO...SO CASUALLY.
IT'S THE WEEK-END.
IS IT FAR?
WE'LL ARRIVE IN TWENTY MINUTES.
SQUARE HEAD.
THIS IS LIKE A TOUR.
I TOLD YOU!

DOES IT BRING BACK MEMORIES?

I HAVEN'T BEEN TO GREAT-GRANDPA'S PLACE IN 10 YEARS.

THANKS FOR THE FAVOR.

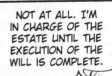

NOT AT ALL. I'M IN CHARGE OF THE ESTATE UNTIL THE EXECUTION OF THE WILL IS COMPLETE.

I DO HOPE, THOUGH, THAT...

DON'T WORRY. NOBODY KNOWS ABOUT THE INHERITANCE.

KAW!

KAW!

WOW.

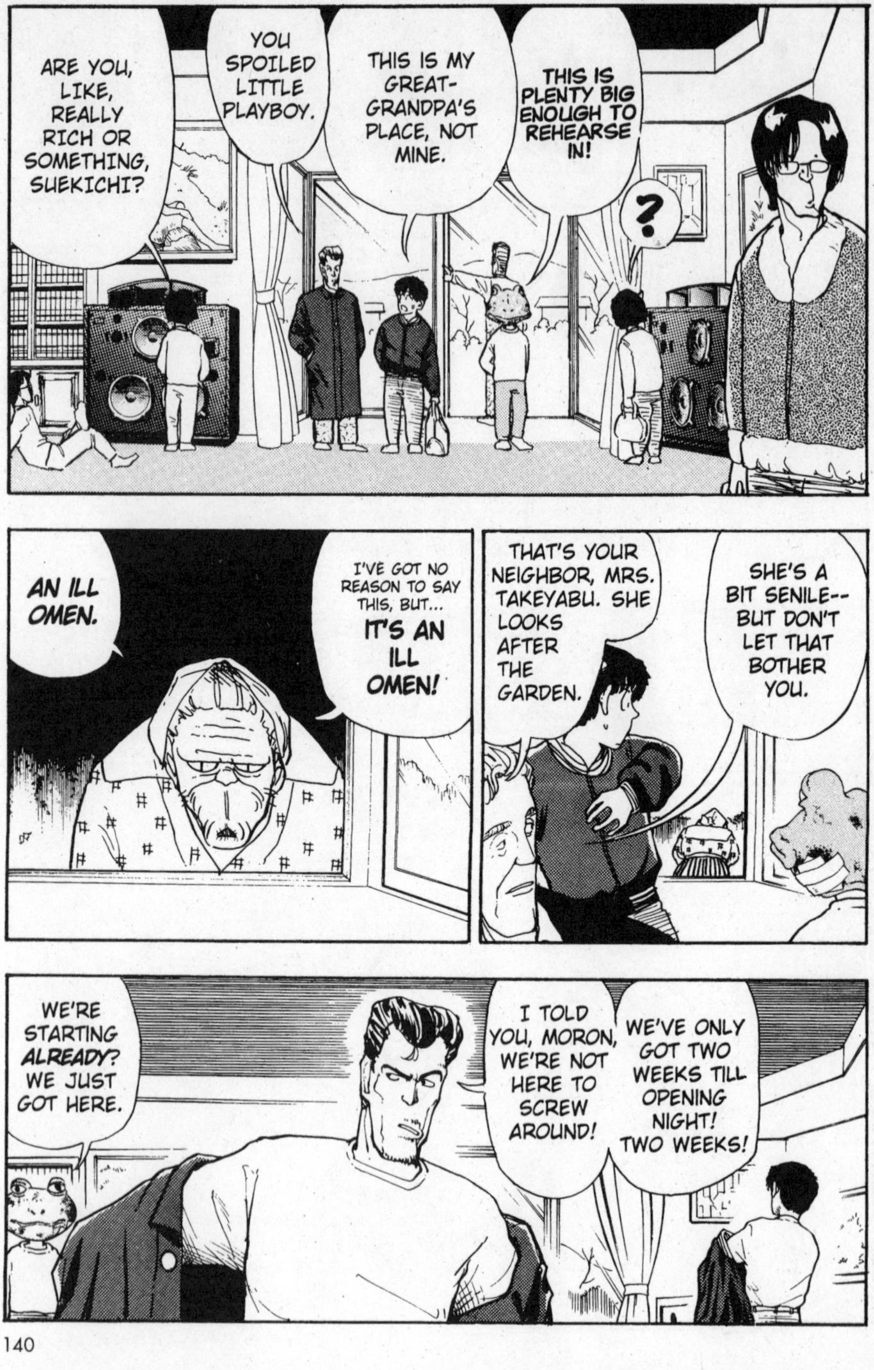
ARE YOU, LIKE, REALLY RICH OR SOMETHING, SUEKICHI?
YOU SPOILED LITTLE PLAYBOY.
THIS IS MY GREAT-GRANDPA'S PLACE, NOT MINE.
THIS IS PLENTY BIG ENOUGH TO REHEARSE IN!
?
AN ILL OMEN.
I'VE GOT NO REASON TO SAY THIS, BUT... IT'S AN ILL OMEN!
THAT'S YOUR NEIGHBOR, MRS. TAKEYABU. SHE LOOKS AFTER THE GARDEN.
SHE'S A BIT SENILE--BUT DON'T LET THAT BOTHER YOU.
WE'RE STARTING ALREADY? WE JUST GOT HERE.
I TOLD YOU, MORON, WE'RE NOT HERE TO SCREW AROUND!
WE'VE ONLY GOT TWO WEEKS TILL OPENING NIGHT! TWO WEEKS!

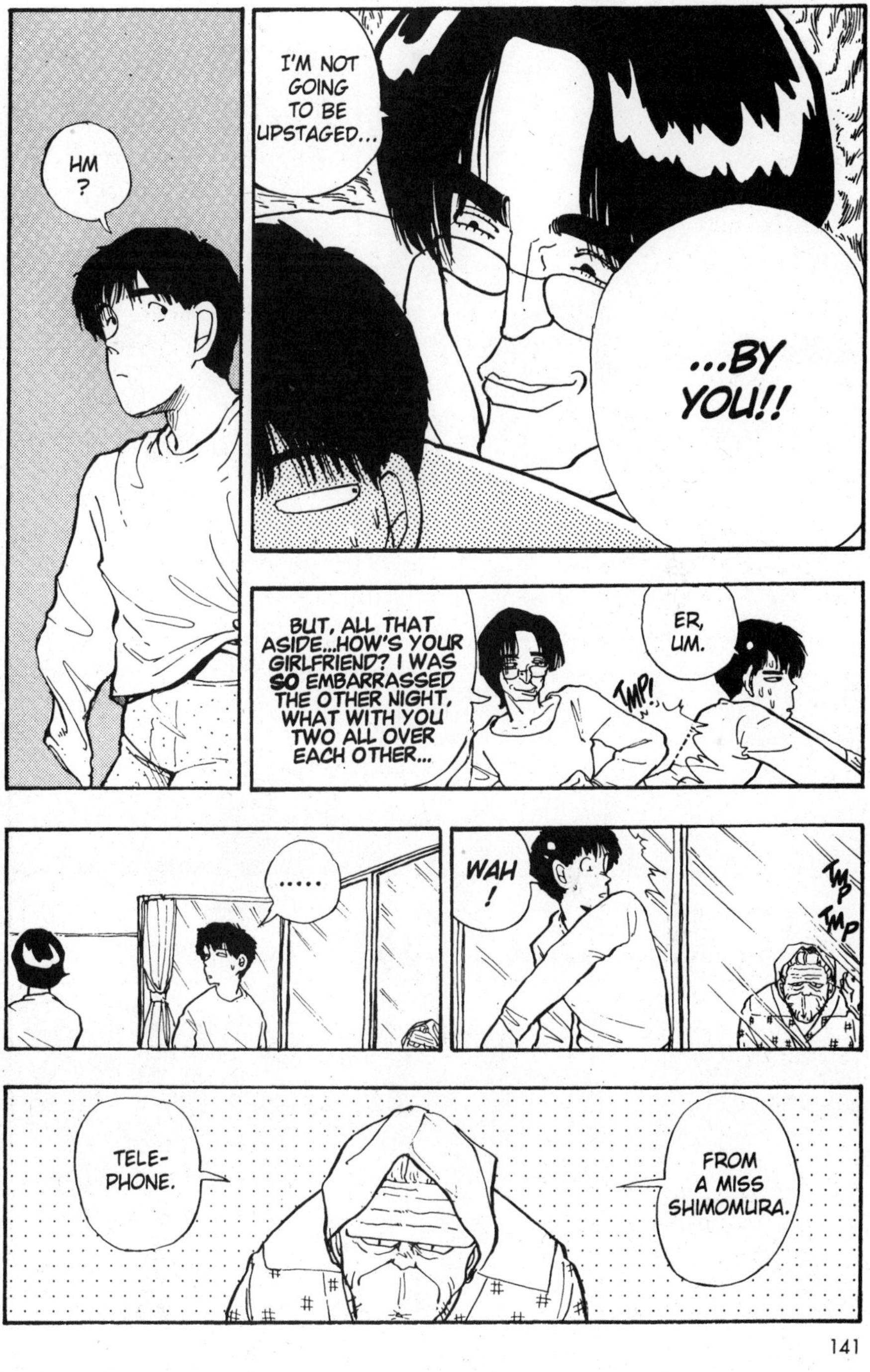
HM ?
I'M NOT GOING TO BE UPSTAGED...
...BY YOU!!
BUT, ALL THAT ASIDE...HOW'S YOUR GIRLFRIEND? I WAS SO EMBARRASSED THE OTHER NIGHT, WHAT WITH YOU TWO ALL OVER EACH OTHER...
TMP!
ER, UM.
......
WAH !
TMP TMP
TELE-PHONE.
FROM A MISS SHIMOMURA.

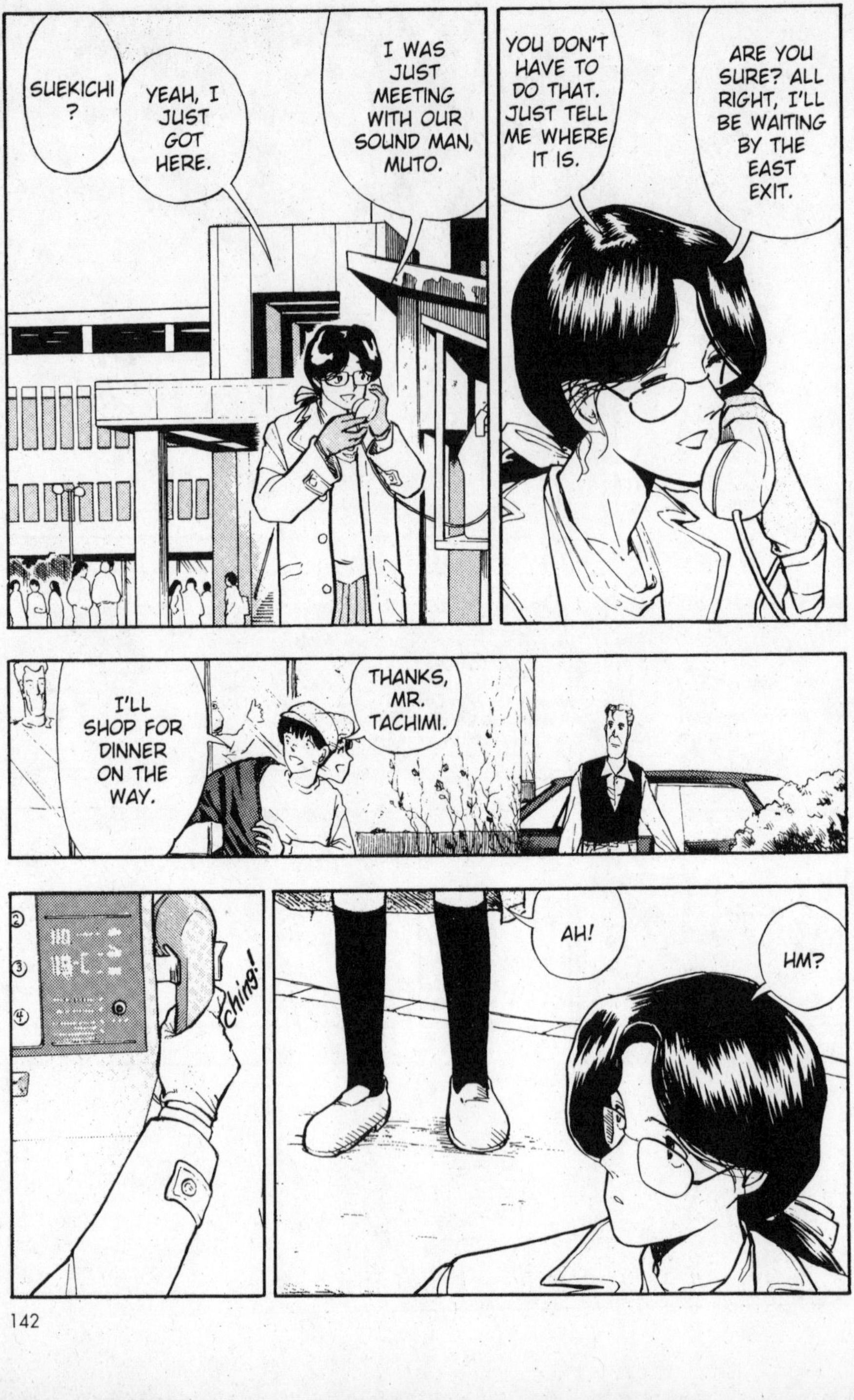
SUEKICHI ?
YEAH, I JUST GOT HERE.
I WAS JUST MEETING WITH OUR SOUND MAN, MUTO.
YOU DON'T HAVE TO DO THAT. JUST TELL ME WHERE IT IS.
ARE YOU SURE? ALL RIGHT, I'LL BE WAITING BY THE EAST EXIT.
I'LL SHOP FOR DINNER ON THE WAY.
THANKS, MR. TACHIMI.
ching!
AH!
HM?

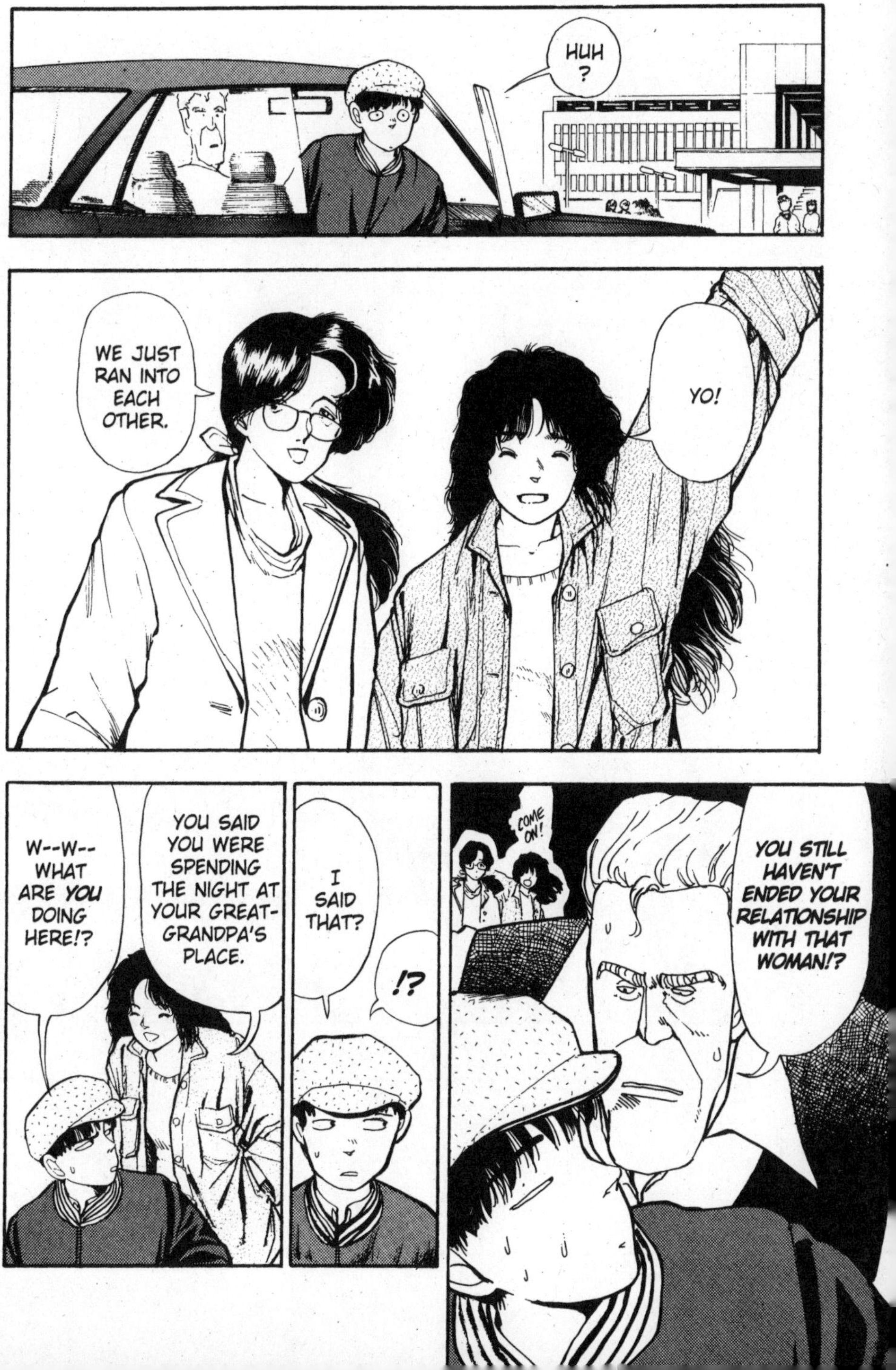
HUH ?
WE JUST RAN INTO EACH OTHER.
YO!
W--W-- WHAT ARE YOU DOING HERE!?
YOU SAID YOU WERE SPENDING THE NIGHT AT YOUR GREAT-GRANDPA'S PLACE.
I SAID THAT?
!?
COME ON!
YOU STILL HAVEN'T ENDED YOUR RELATIONSHIP WITH THAT WOMAN!?

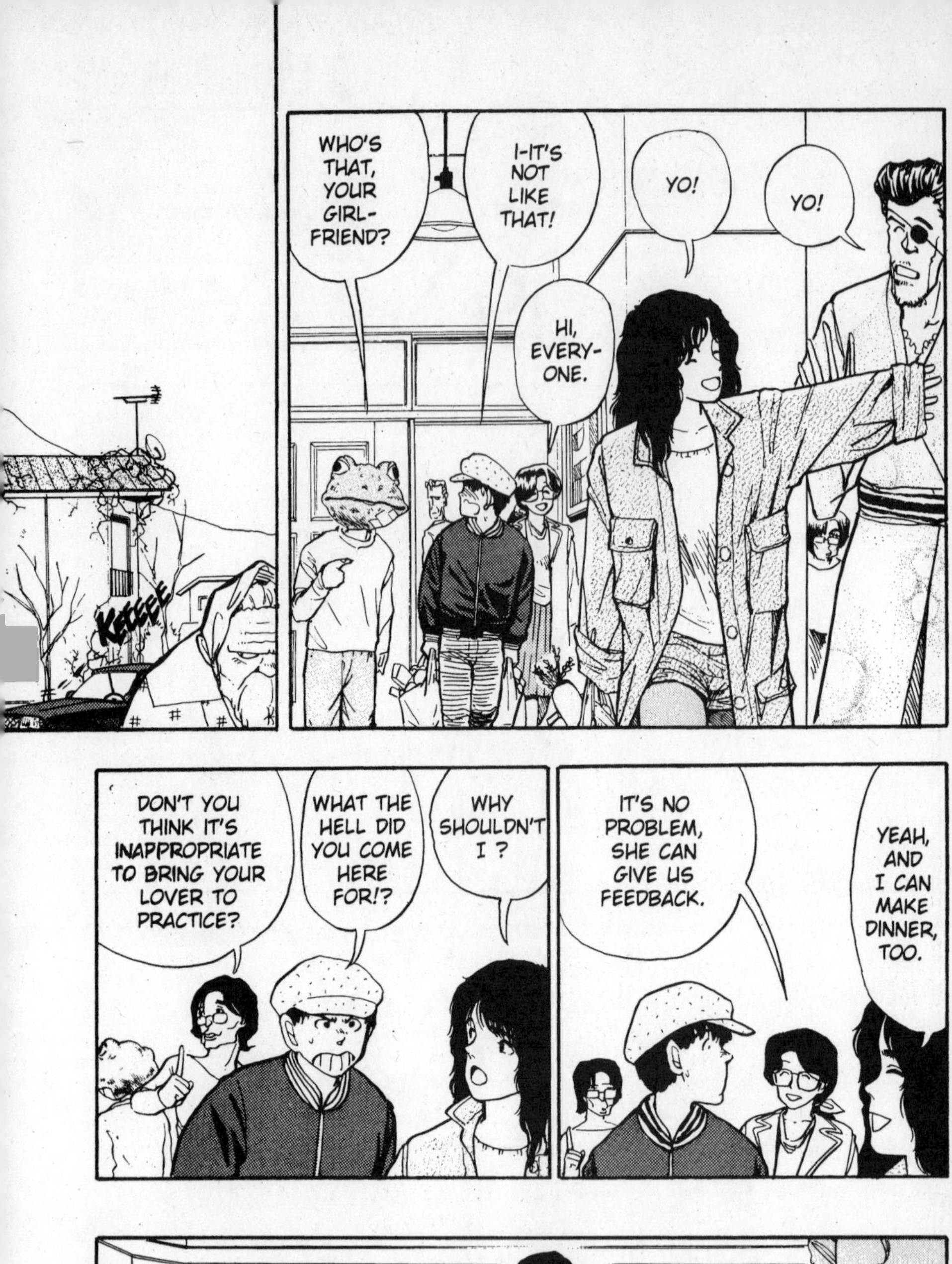
KEEEEE
WHO'S THAT, YOUR GIRL-FRIEND?
I-IT'S NOT LIKE THAT!
YO!
YO!
HI, EVERY-ONE.
DON'T YOU THINK IT'S INAPPROPRIATE TO BRING YOUR LOVER TO PRACTICE?
WHAT THE HELL DID YOU COME HERE FOR!?
WHY SHOULDN'T I ?
IT'S NO PROBLEM, SHE CAN GIVE US FEEDBACK.
YEAH, AND I CAN MAKE DINNER, TOO.

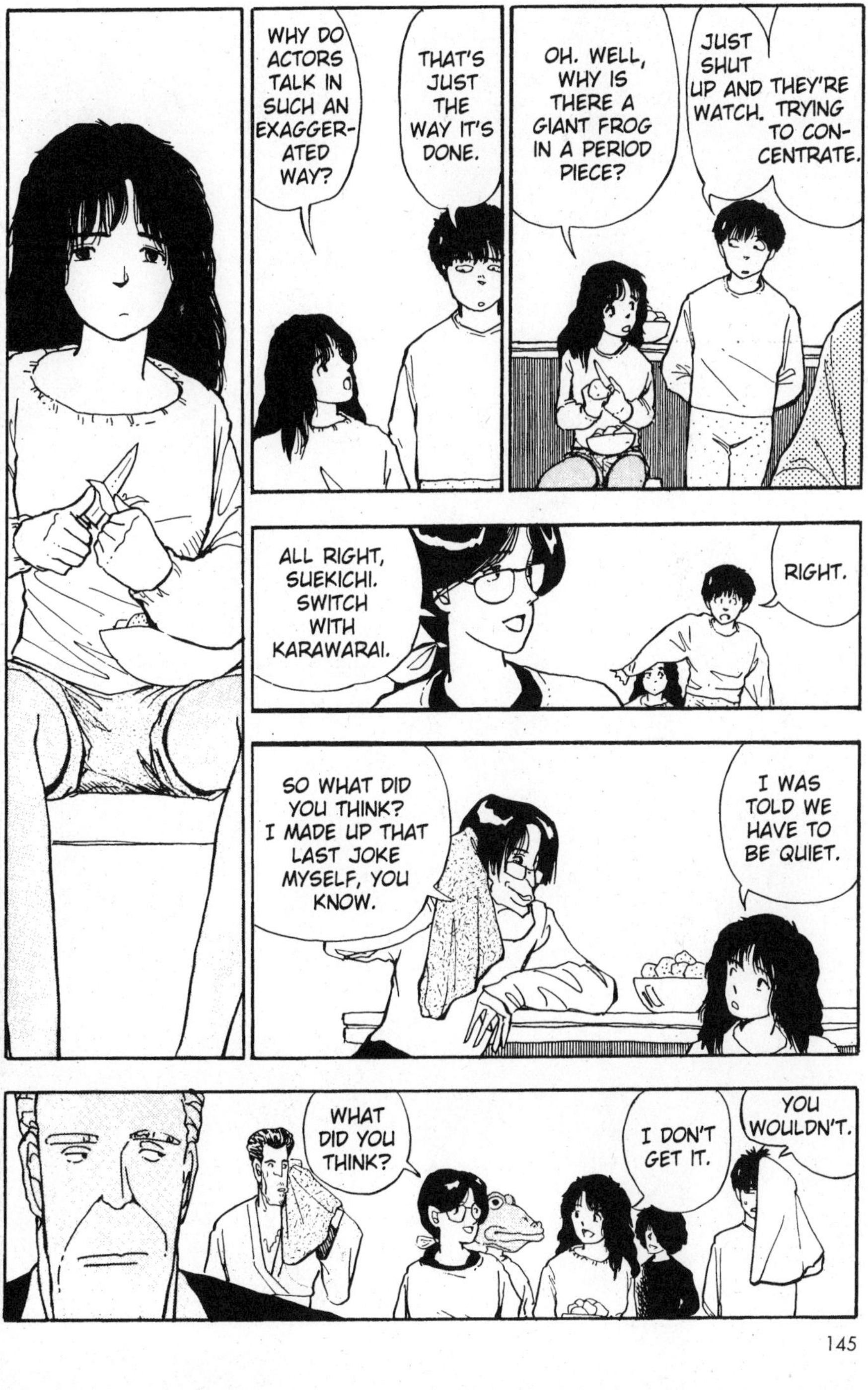
WHY DO ACTORS TALK IN SUCH AN EXAGGER-ATED WAY?
THAT'S JUST THE WAY IT'S DONE.
OH. WELL, WHY IS THERE A GIANT FROG IN A PERIOD PIECE?
JUST SHUT UP AND WATCH.
THEY'RE TRYING TO CON-CENTRATE.
ALL RIGHT, SUEKICHI. SWITCH WITH KARAWARAI.
RIGHT.
SO WHAT DID YOU THINK? I MADE UP THAT LAST JOKE MYSELF, YOU KNOW.
I WAS TOLD WE HAVE TO BE QUIET.
WHAT DID YOU THINK?
I DON'T GET IT.
YOU WOULDN'T.

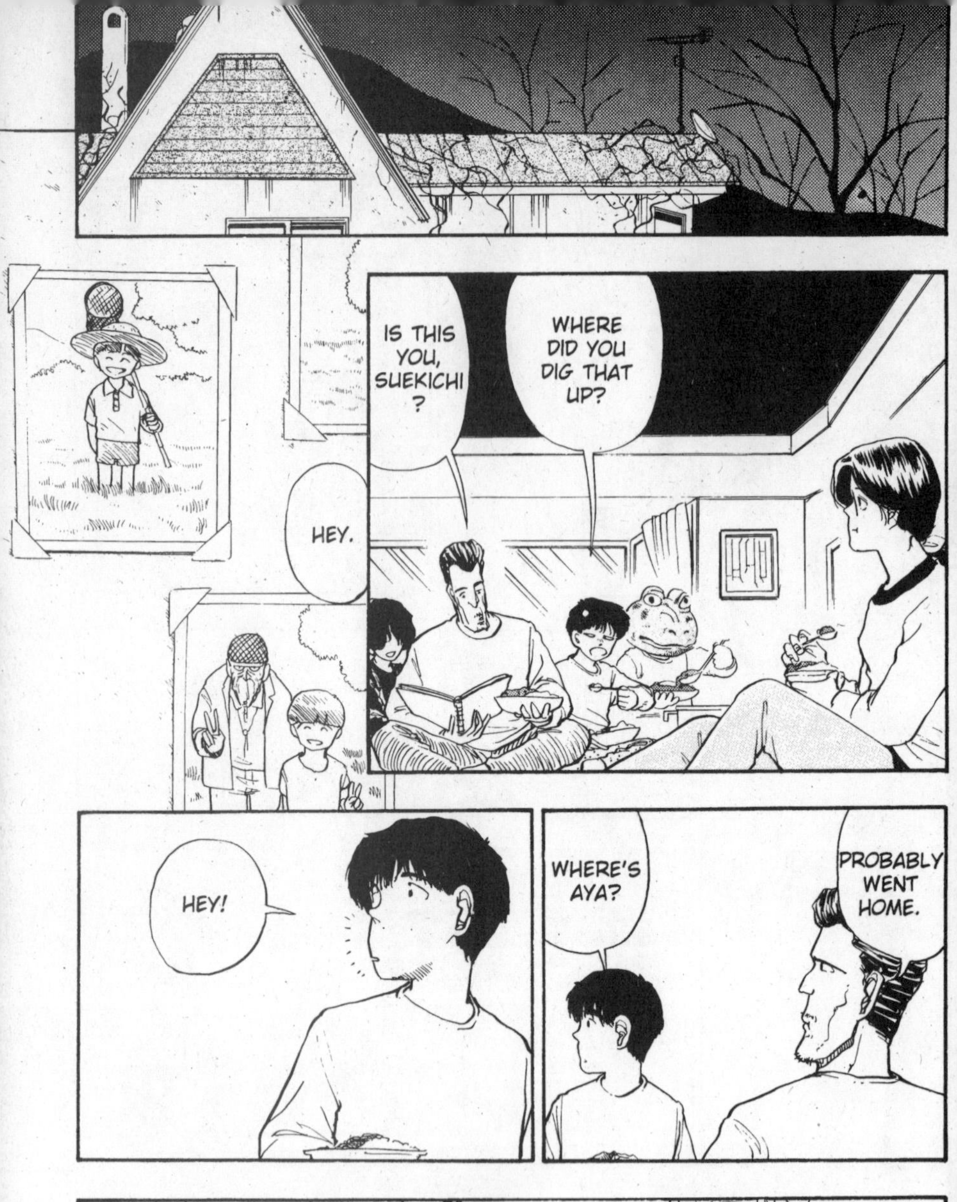
HEY.
IS THIS YOU, SUEKICHI?
WHERE DID YOU DIG THAT UP?
HEY!
WHERE'S AYA?
PROBABLY WENT HOME.
AT THIS HOUR?
DON'T LOOK AT ME.
I SENT HER HOME.

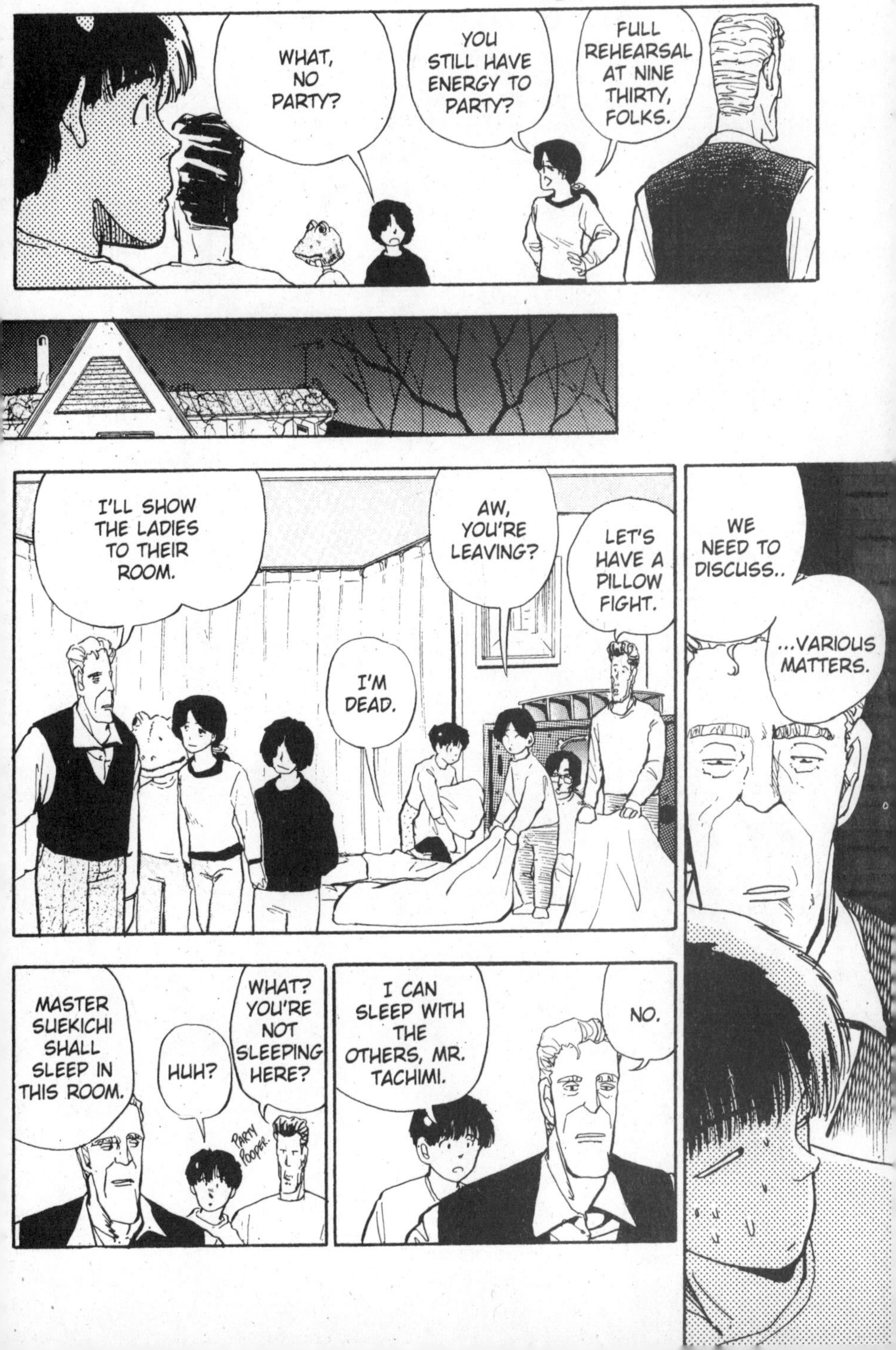
WHAT, NO PARTY?
YOU STILL HAVE ENERGY TO PARTY?
FULL REHEARSAL AT NINE THIRTY, FOLKS.
I'LL SHOW THE LADIES TO THEIR ROOM.
I'M DEAD.
AW, YOU'RE LEAVING?
LET'S HAVE A PILLOW FIGHT.
MASTER SUEKICHI SHALL SLEEP IN THIS ROOM.
HUH?
WHAT? YOU'RE NOT SLEEPING HERE?
PARTY POOPER.
I CAN SLEEP WITH THE OTHERS, MR. TACHIMI.
NO.
WE NEED TO DISCUSS..
...VARIOUS MATTERS.

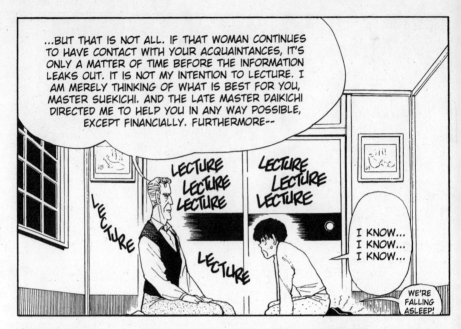

...BUT THAT IS NOT ALL. IF THAT WOMAN CONTINUES TO HAVE CONTACT WITH YOUR ACQUAINTANCES, IT'S ONLY A MATTER OF TIME BEFORE THE INFORMATION LEAKS OUT. IT IS NOT MY INTENTION TO LECTURE. I AM MERELY THINKING OF WHAT IS BEST FOR YOU, MASTER SUEKICHI. AND THE LATE MASTER DAIKICHI DIRECTED ME TO HELP YOU IN ANY WAY POSSIBLE, EXCEPT FINANCIALLY. FURTHERMORE--

LECTURE LECTURE LECTURE

LECTURE LECTURE LECTURE

LECTURE

LECTURE

I KNOW...
I KNOW...
I KNOW...

WE'RE FALLING ASLEEP!

OR IS IT THAT YOU DON'T NEED THE 450 MILLION YEN?

IN THAT CASE, THE WILL INSTRUCTS ME TO DONATE THE ENTIRE SUM TO THE KANGAROO FUND.

YEUK!

I NEED IT! I DO NEED IT! I VERY MUCH DO NEED IT!

HYOOOOO

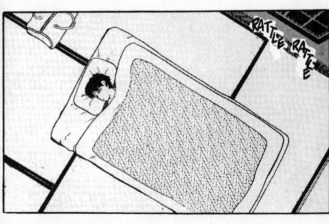

RATTLE RATTLE

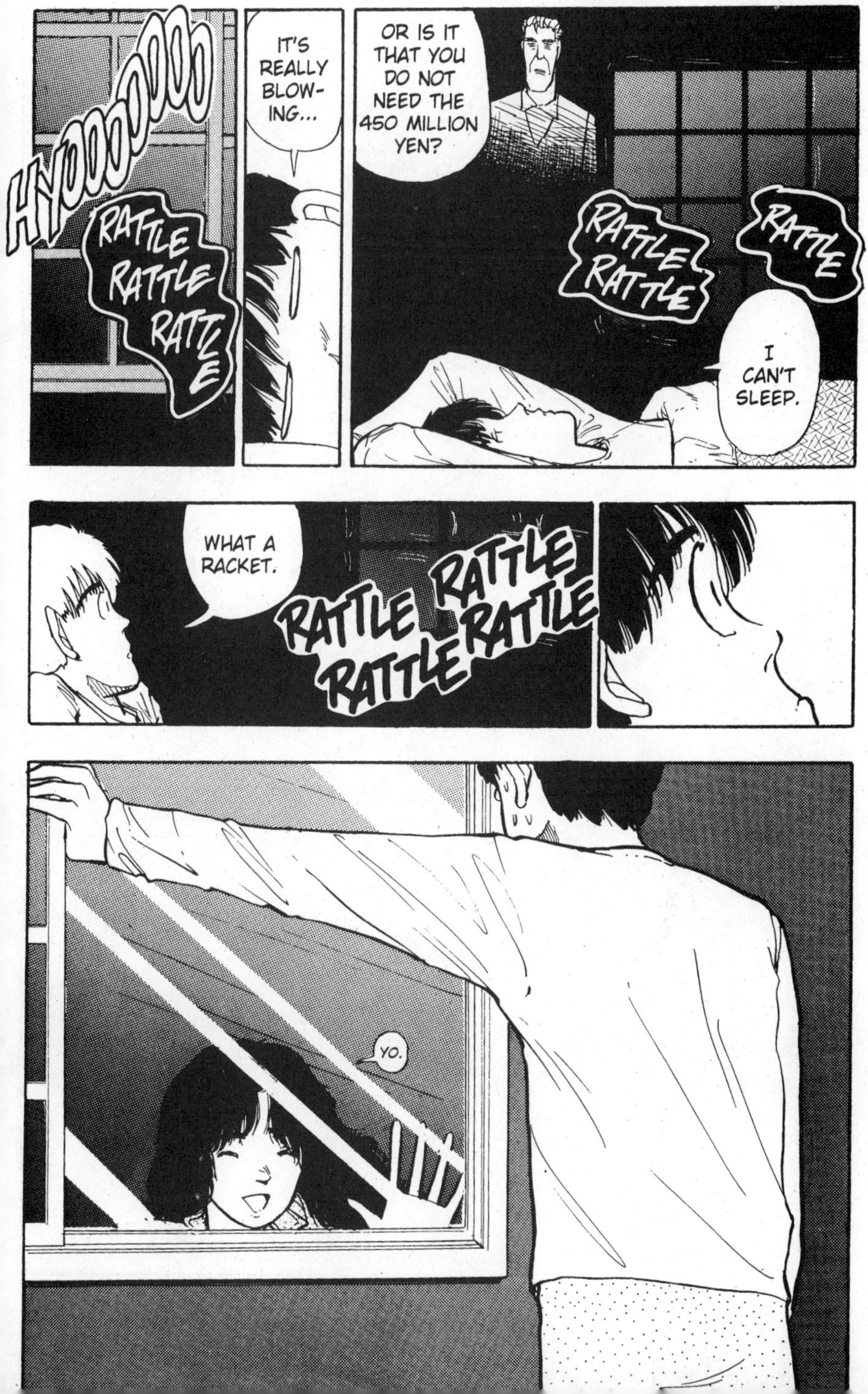
HYOOOOOOO
RATTLE RATTLE RATTLE
IT'S REALLY BLOW-ING...
OR IS IT THAT YOU DO NOT NEED THE 450 MILLION YEN?
RATTLE RATTLE
RATTLE
I CAN'T SLEEP.
WHAT A RACKET.
RATTLE RATTLE RATTLE RATTLE
YO.

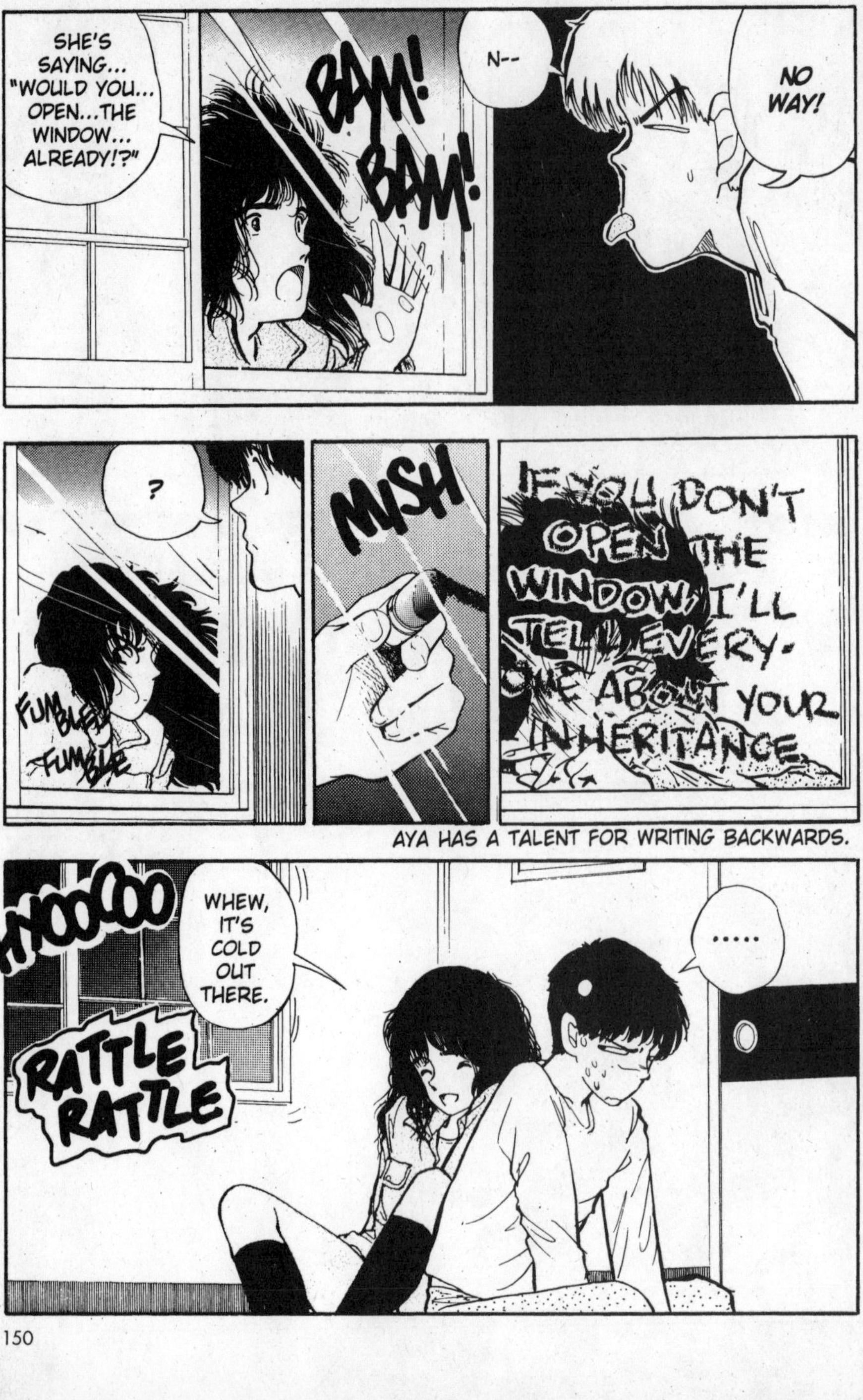
SHE'S SAYING... "WOULD YOU... OPEN...THE WINDOW... ALREADY!?"
BAM! BAM!
N--
NO WAY!
?
FUMBLE FUMBLE
MISH
IF YOU DON'T OPEN THE WINDOW, I'LL TELL EVERY-ONE ABOUT YOUR INHERITANCE.
AYA HAS A TALENT FOR WRITING BACKWARDS.
HYOOOOO
WHEW, IT'S COLD OUT THERE.
RATTLE RATTLE
.....

ACT NINE
HOT AND COLD NIGHTS

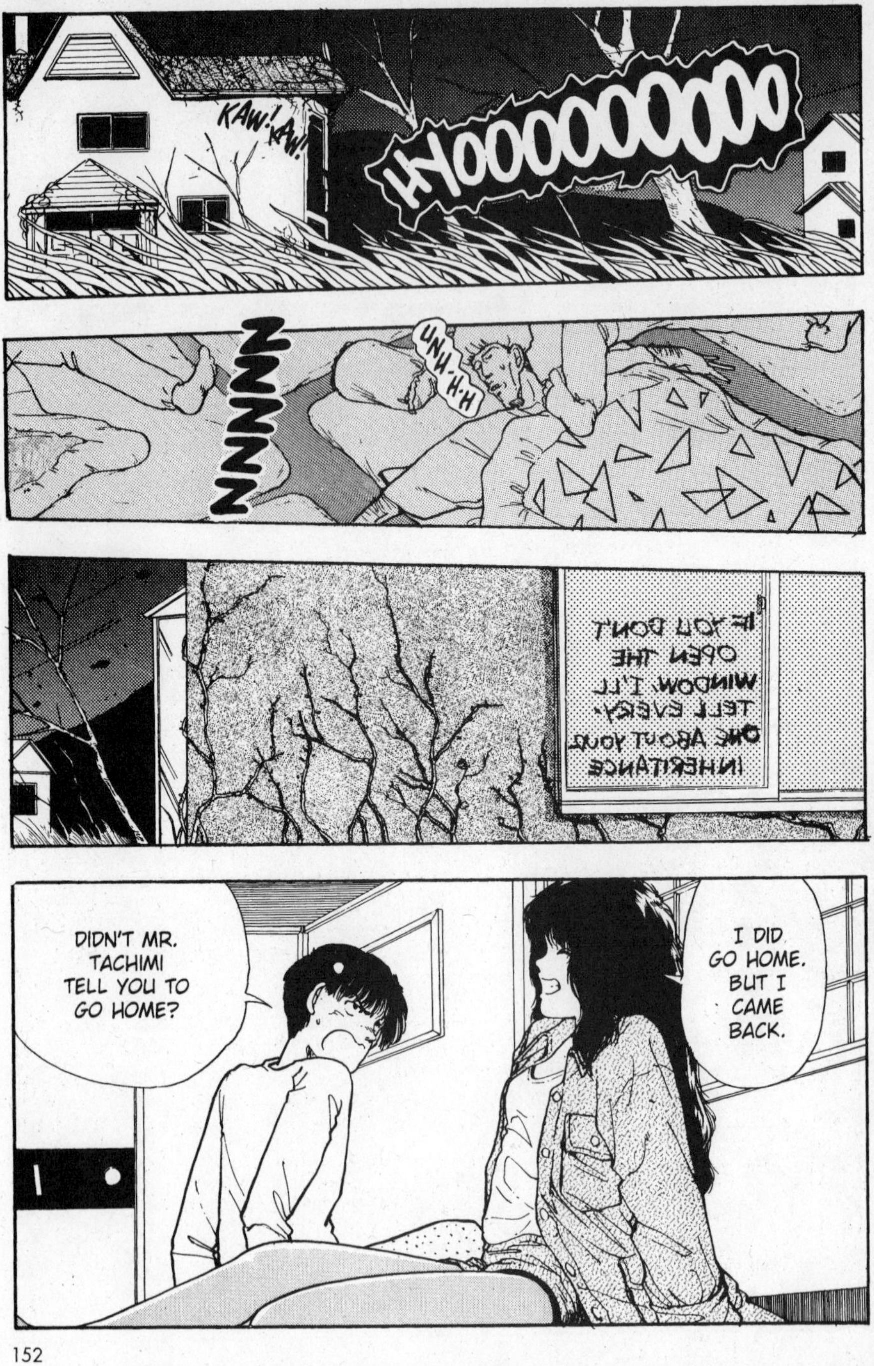
KAW! KAW!
HYOOOOOOOOO
UNH-H-H
ZZZZZ
IF YOU DON'T OPEN THE WINDOW, I'LL TELL EVERY-ONE ABOUT YOUR INHERITANCE
DIDN'T MR. TACHIMI TELL YOU TO GO HOME?
I DID GO HOME. BUT I CAME BACK.

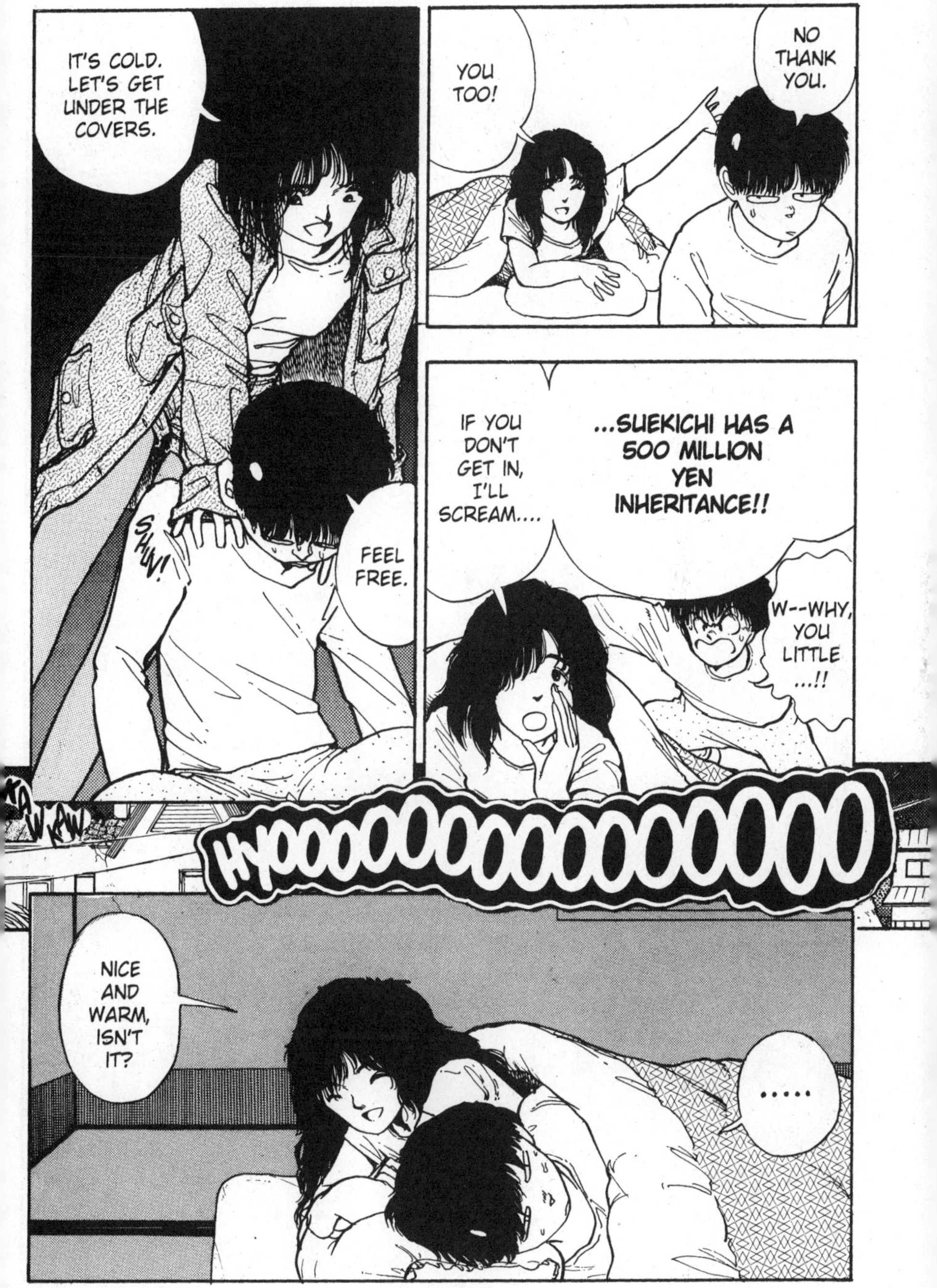
IT'S COLD. LET'S GET UNDER THE COVERS.
SHUN!
FEEL FREE.
YOU TOO!
NO THANK YOU.
IF YOU DON'T GET IN, I'LL SCREAM....
...SUEKICHI HAS A 500 MILLION YEN INHERITANCE!!
W--WHY, YOU LITTLE ...!!
HyOOOOOOOOOOOOOO
NICE AND WARM, ISN'T IT?
.....

YOU KEEP SAYING YOU'LL TELL EVERY-ONE ABOUT THE INHERITANCE, BUT IF YOU DO, YOU WON'T GET ANY OF IT.

HMM.

AFTER THE TAX MEN AND THE RELATIVES GET TO IT THERE WON'T BE A SMIDGEON OF IT LEFT.

AND YOU'RE NOT EVEN A RELATIVE.

ALL I ASK FOR IS TO SLEEP ON THE SAME FUTON AS SUEKICHI.

LIAR.

FUMBLE! FUMBLE!

WHAT ARE YOU DOING?

I TOOK OFF MY UNDIES.

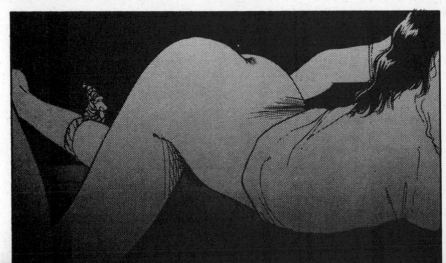

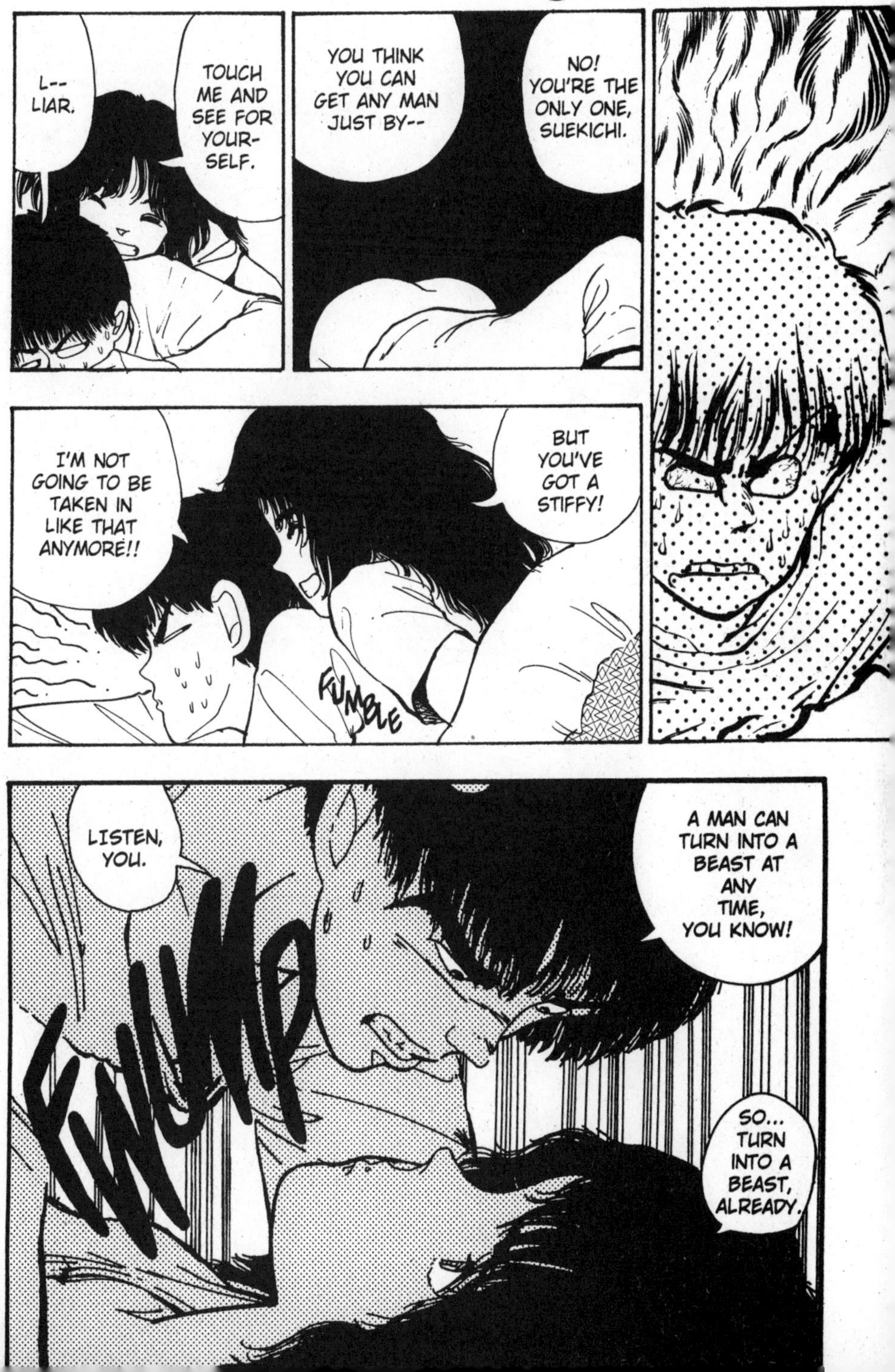
L-- LIAR.
TOUCH ME AND SEE FOR YOUR-SELF.
YOU THINK YOU CAN GET ANY MAN JUST BY--
NO! YOU'RE THE ONLY ONE, SUEKICHI.
I'M NOT GOING TO BE TAKEN IN LIKE THAT ANYMORE!!
BUT YOU'VE GOT A STIFFY!
FUMBLE
LISTEN, YOU.
A MAN CAN TURN INTO A BEAST AT ANY TIME, YOU KNOW!
FWUMP
SO... TURN INTO A BEAST, ALREADY.

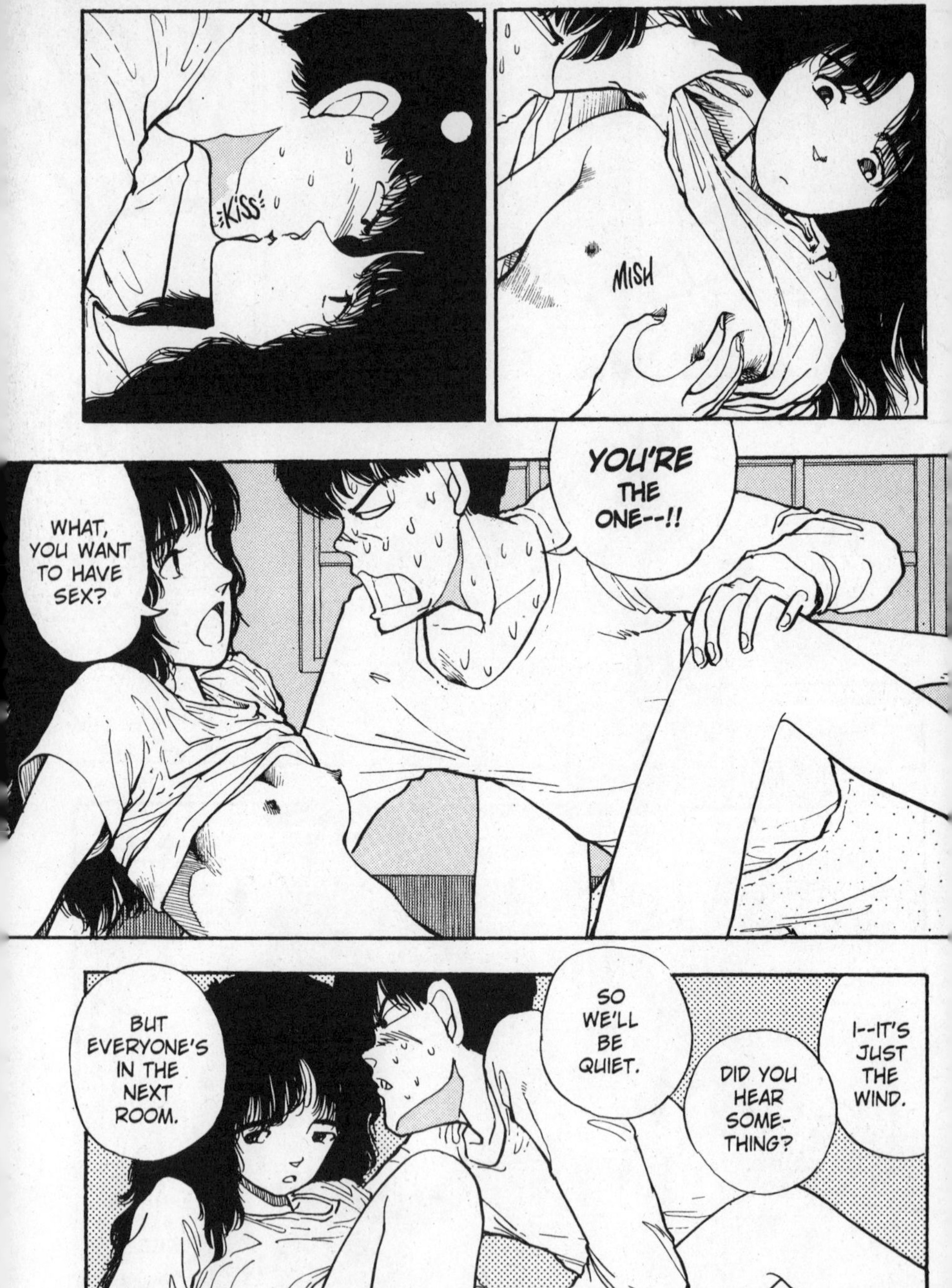
KISS
MISH
WHAT, YOU WANT TO HAVE SEX?
YOU'RE THE ONE--!!
BUT EVERYONE'S IN THE NEXT ROOM.
SO WE'LL BE QUIET.
DID YOU HEAR SOMETHING?
I--IT'S JUST THE WIND.

YOU'RE WET.

YOU DON'T HAVE TO ANNOUNCE IT.

SEX, SEX, SEX. I WONDER IF ALL MEN ARE LIKE THIS.

YOU'RE THE ONE WHO CAME ON TO *ME!*

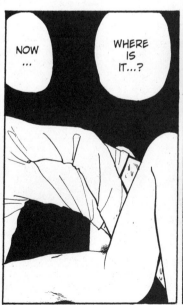

NOW ...

WHERE IS IT...?

RIGHT AROUND HERE, ISN'T IT...?

·····

AH !

NSH

157

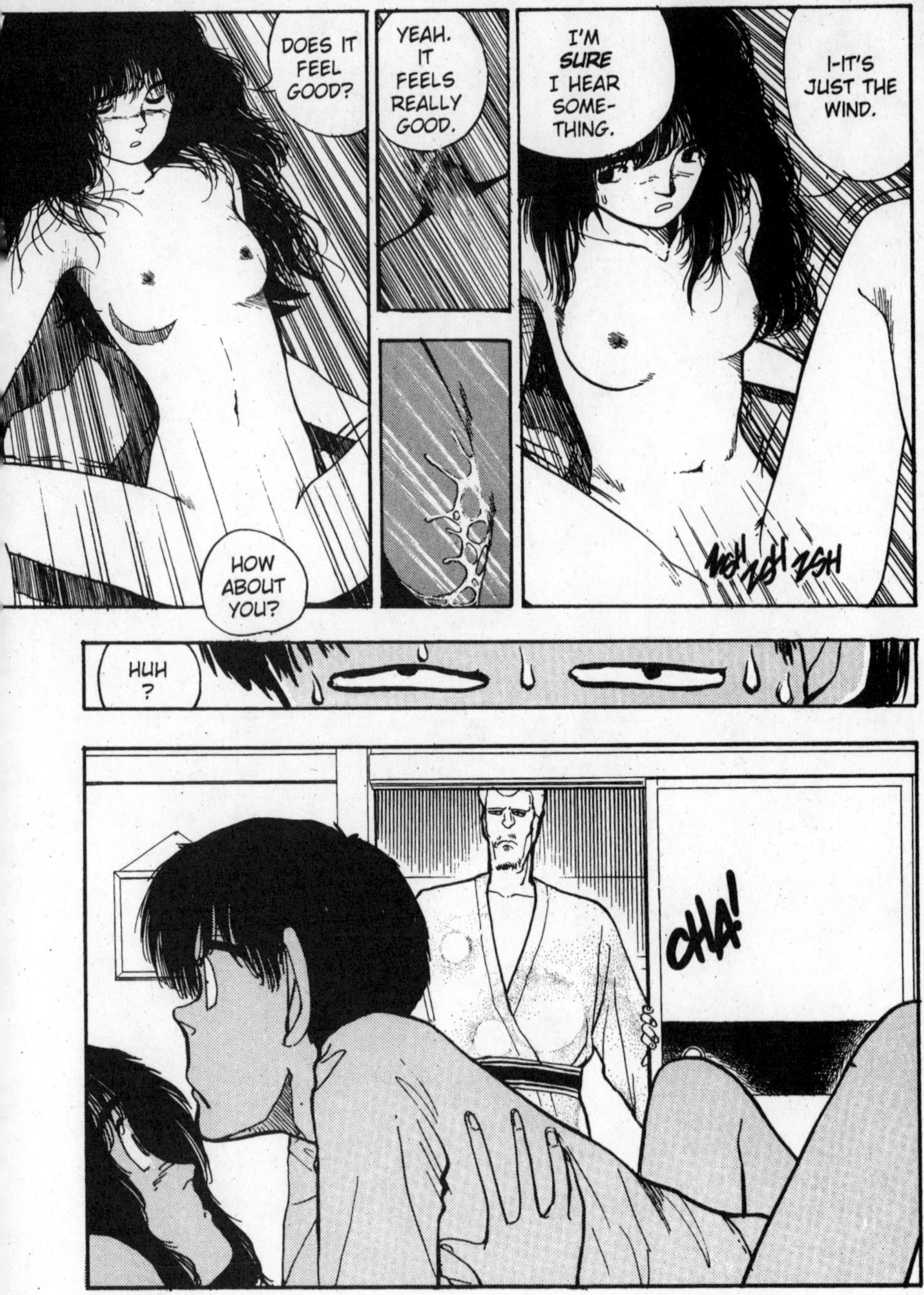
DOES IT FEEL GOOD?
HOW ABOUT YOU?
YEAH. IT FEELS REALLY GOOD.
I'M SURE I HEAR SOME-THING.
I-IT'S JUST THE WIND.
ZSH ZSH ZSH
HUH ?
CHA!

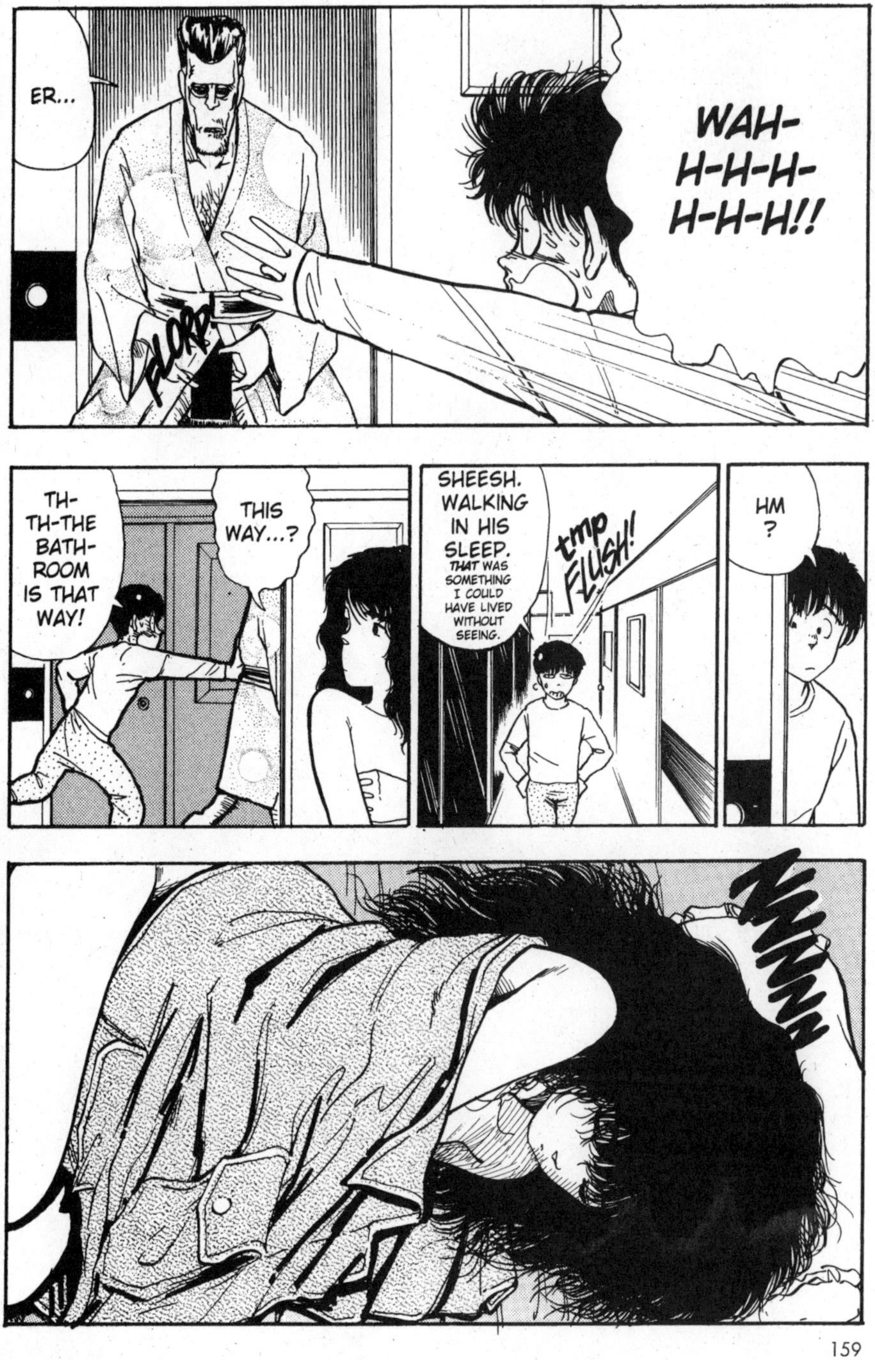
ER...
WAH-H-H-H-H-H-H!!
FLOP!
TH-TH-THE BATH-ROOM IS THAT WAY!
THIS WAY...?
SHEESH. WALKING IN HIS SLEEP. THAT WAS SOMETHING I COULD HAVE LIVED WITHOUT SEEING.
tmp
FLUSH!
HM?
NNNNN

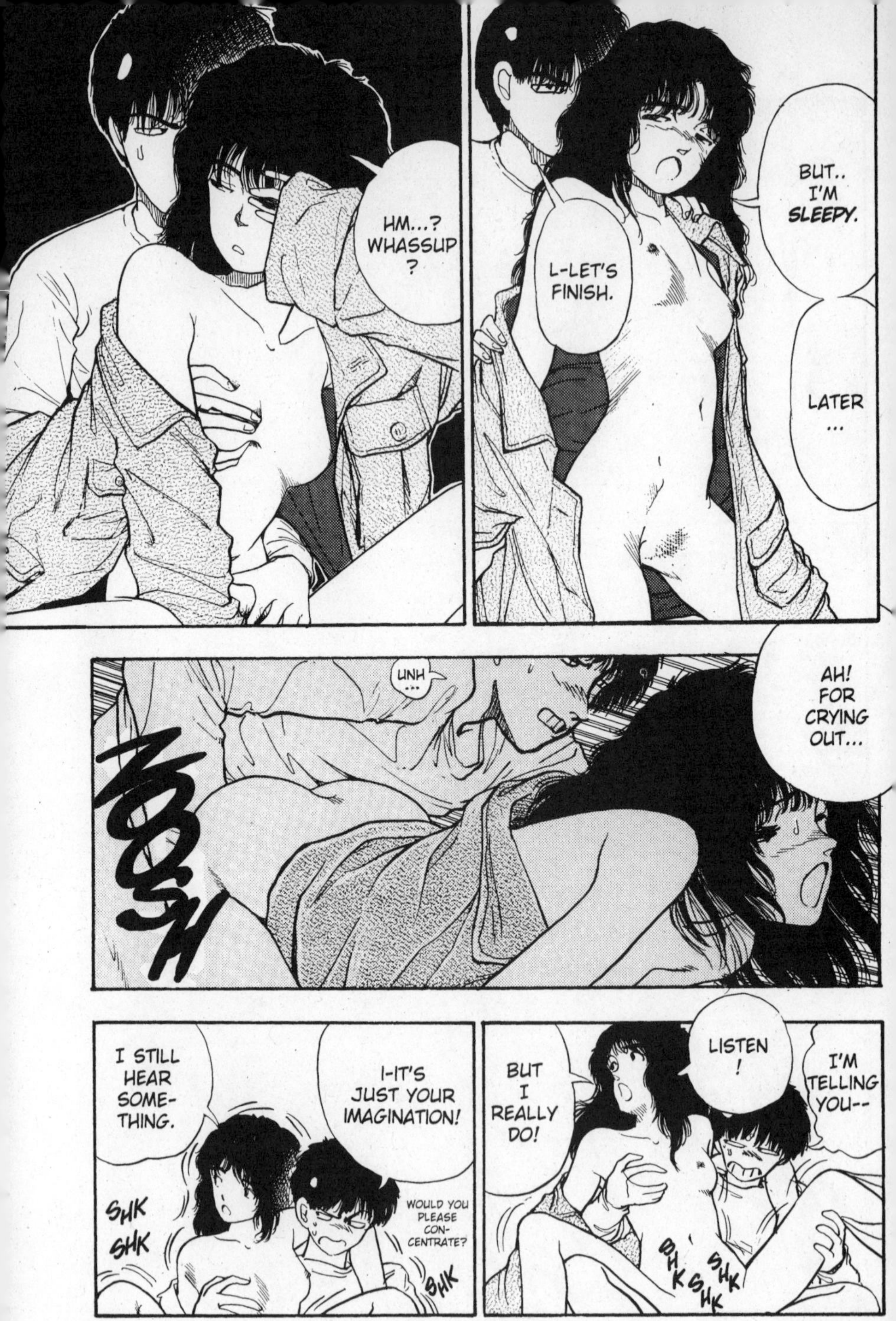
HM...? WHASSUP ?
L-LET'S FINISH.
BUT.. I'M SLEEPY.
LATER ...
UNH ...
WOOSH
AH! FOR CRYING OUT...
I STILL HEAR SOME-THING.
I-IT'S JUST YOUR IMAGINATION!
SHK SHK
WOULD YOU PLEASE CON-CENTRATE?
SHK
BUT I REALLY DO!
LISTEN !
I'M TELLING YOU--
SHK SHK SHK SHK

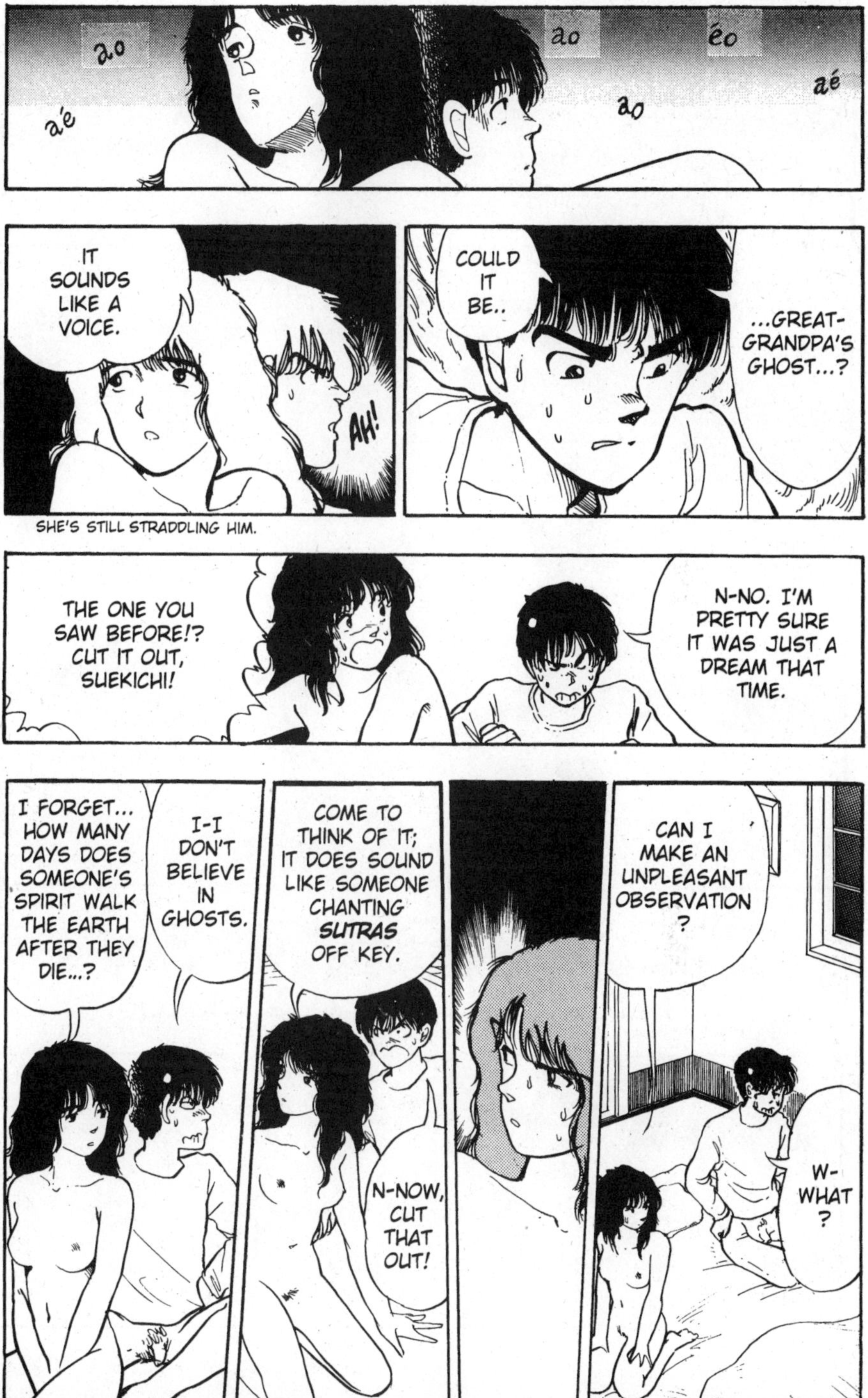
ao
aé
ao
éo
ao
aé
IT SOUNDS LIKE A VOICE.
AH!
COULD IT BE..
...GREAT-GRANDPA'S GHOST...?
SHE'S STILL STRADDLING HIM.
THE ONE YOU SAW BEFORE!? CUT IT OUT, SUEKICHI!
N-NO. I'M PRETTY SURE IT WAS JUST A DREAM THAT TIME.
I FORGET... HOW MANY DAYS DOES SOMEONE'S SPIRIT WALK THE EARTH AFTER THEY DIE...?
I-I DON'T BELIEVE IN GHOSTS.
COME TO THINK OF IT; IT DOES SOUND LIKE SOMEONE CHANTING **SUTRAS** OFF KEY.
N-NOW, CUT THAT OUT!
CAN I MAKE AN UNPLEASANT OBSERVATION?
W-WHAT?

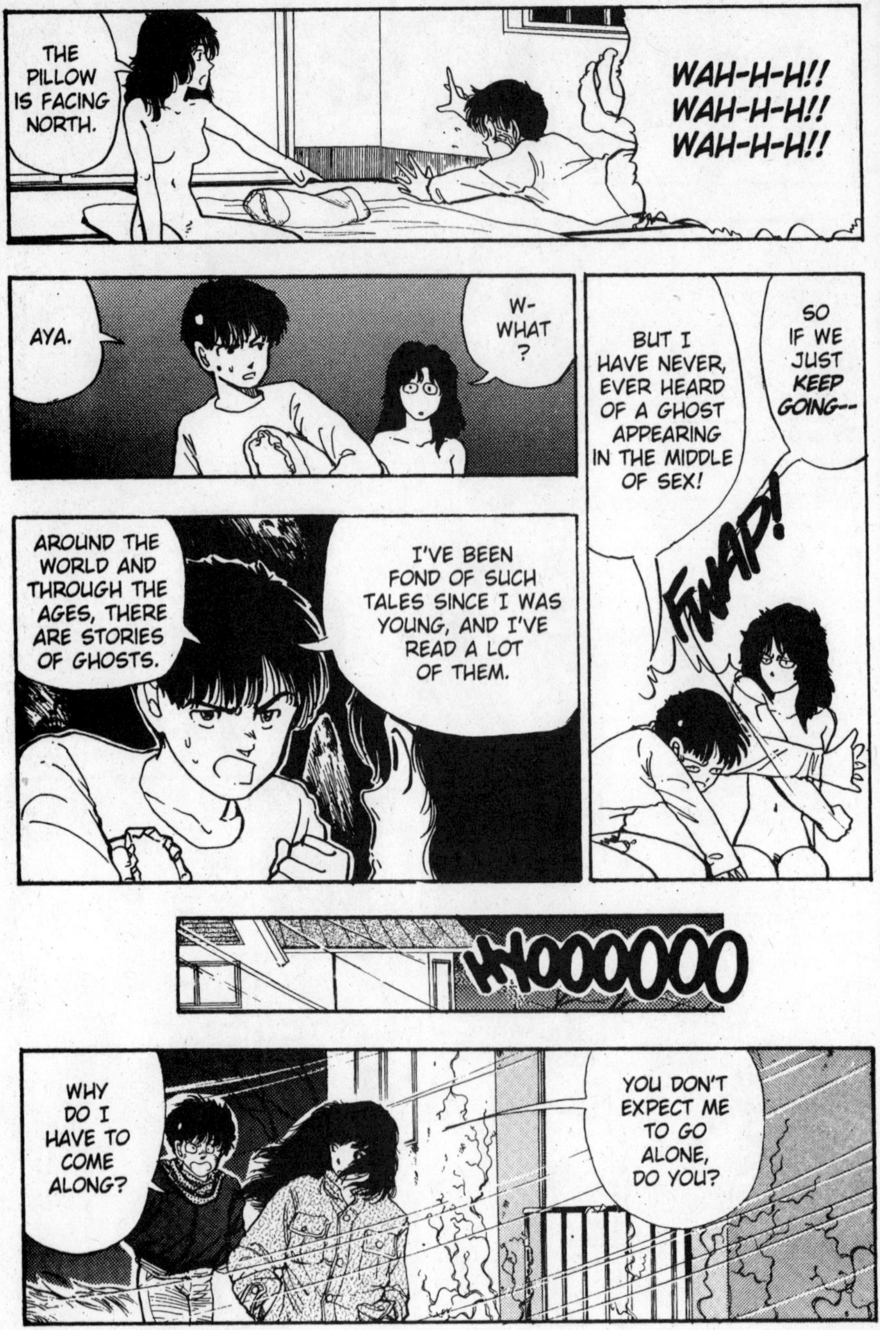
THE PILLOW IS FACING NORTH.
WAH-H-H!! WAH-H-H!! WAH-H-H!!
AYA.
W-WHAT?
AROUND THE WORLD AND THROUGH THE AGES, THERE ARE STORIES OF GHOSTS.
I'VE BEEN FOND OF SUCH TALES SINCE I WAS YOUNG, AND I'VE READ A LOT OF THEM.
BUT I HAVE NEVER, EVER HEARD OF A GHOST APPEARING IN THE MIDDLE OF SEX!
SO IF WE JUST KEEP GOING--
FWAP!
HYOOOOOO
WHY DO I HAVE TO COME ALONG?
YOU DON'T EXPECT ME TO GO ALONE, DO YOU?

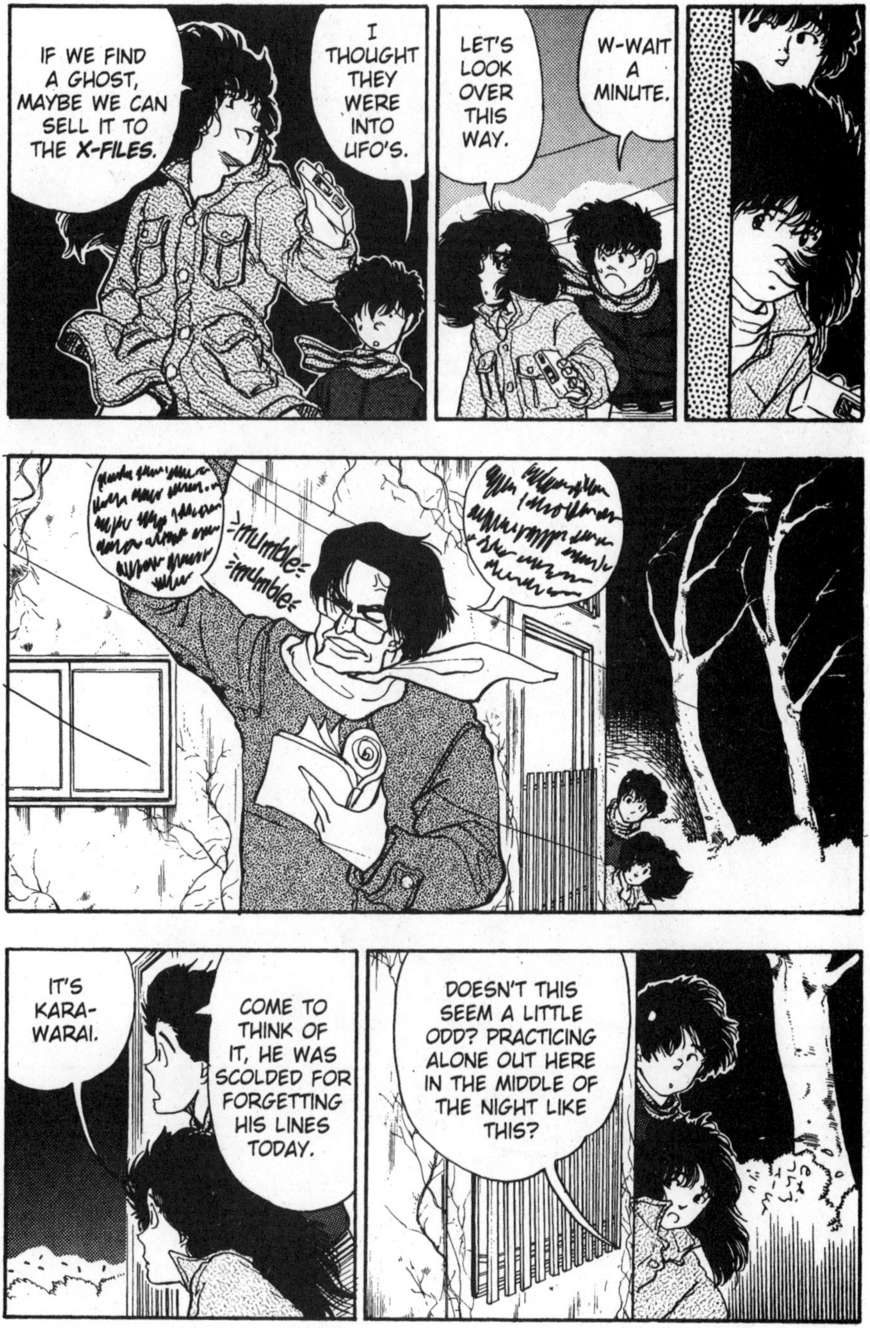
IF WE FIND A GHOST, MAYBE WE CAN SELL IT TO THE X-FILES.
I THOUGHT THEY WERE INTO UFO'S.
LET'S LOOK OVER THIS WAY.
W-WAIT A MINUTE.
=mumble=
=mumble=
IT'S KARA-WARAI.
COME TO THINK OF IT, HE WAS SCOLDED FOR FORGETTING HIS LINES TODAY.
DOESN'T THIS SEEM A LITTLE ODD? PRACTICING ALONE OUT HERE IN THE MIDDLE OF THE NIGHT LIKE THIS?

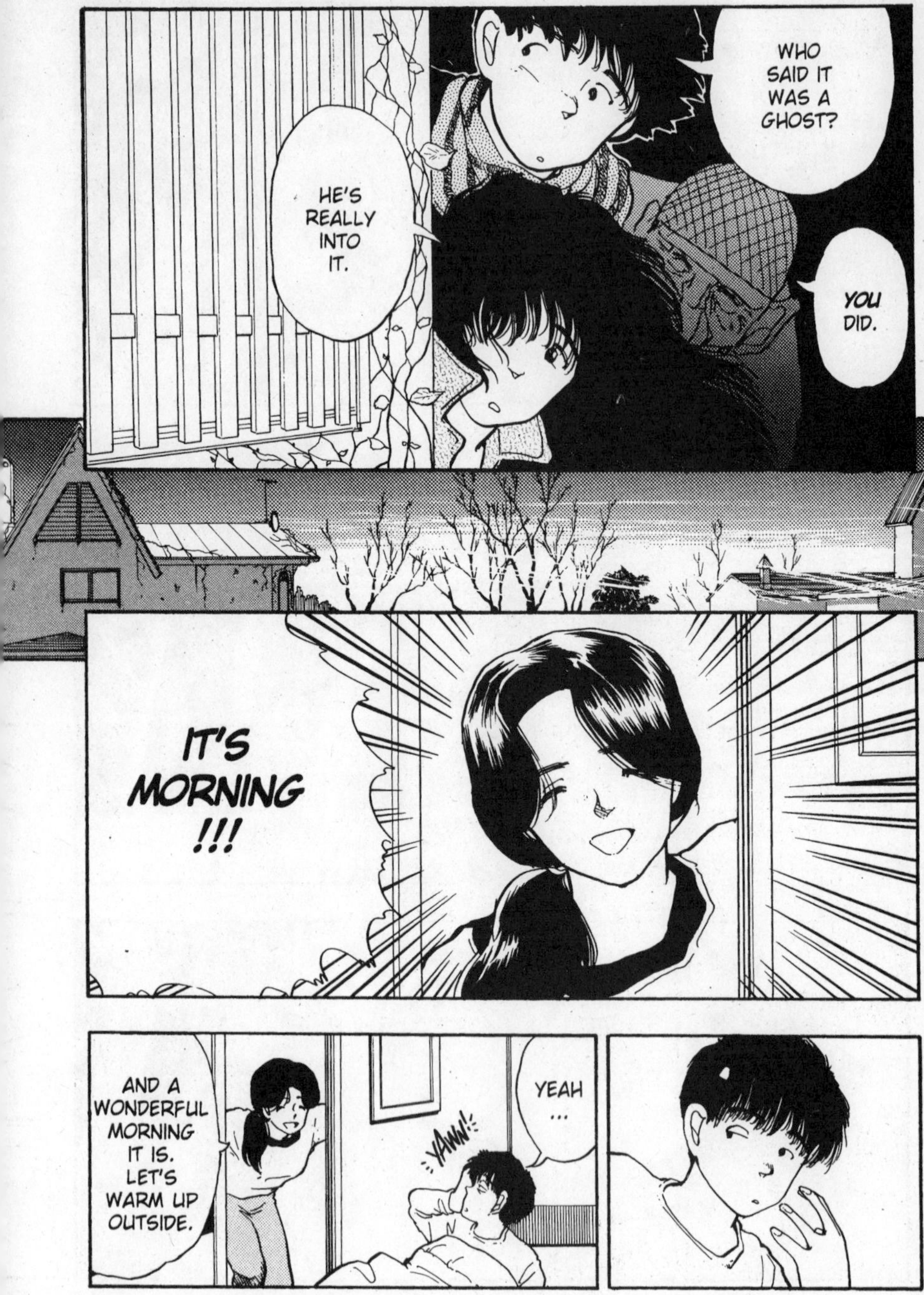
HE'S REALLY INTO IT.
WHO SAID IT WAS A GHOST?
YOU DID.
IT'S MORNING !!!
AND A WONDERFUL MORNING IT IS. LET'S WARM UP OUTSIDE.
YAWN!
YEAH ...

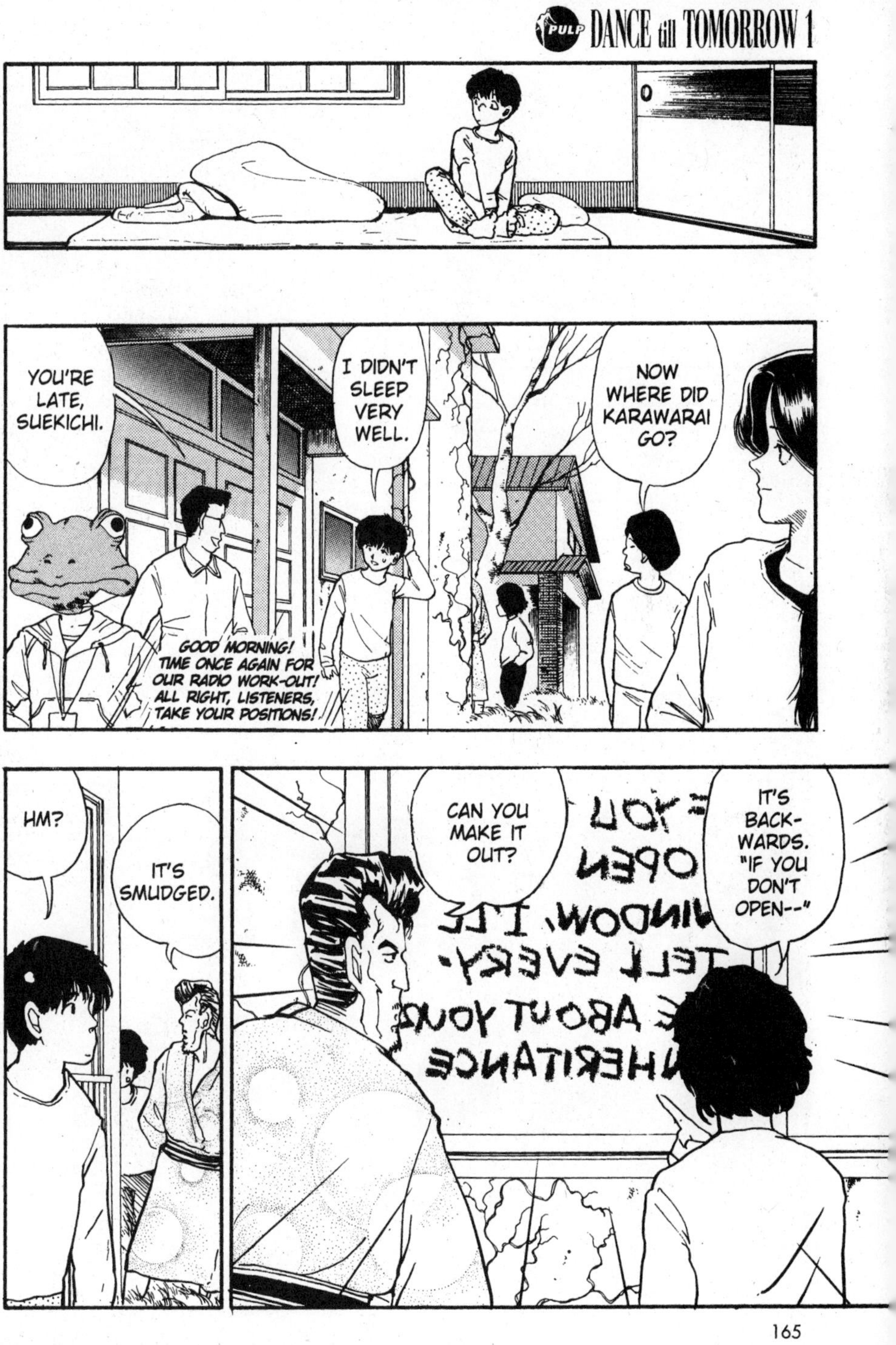
YOU'RE LATE, SUEKICHI.
I DIDN'T SLEEP VERY WELL.
NOW WHERE DID KARAWARAI GO?
GOOD MORNING! TIME ONCE AGAIN FOR OUR RADIO WORK-OUT! ALL RIGHT, LISTENERS, TAKE YOUR POSITIONS!
HM?
IT'S SMUDGED.
CAN YOU MAKE IT OUT?
IT'S BACK-WARDS. "IF YOU DON'T OPEN--"

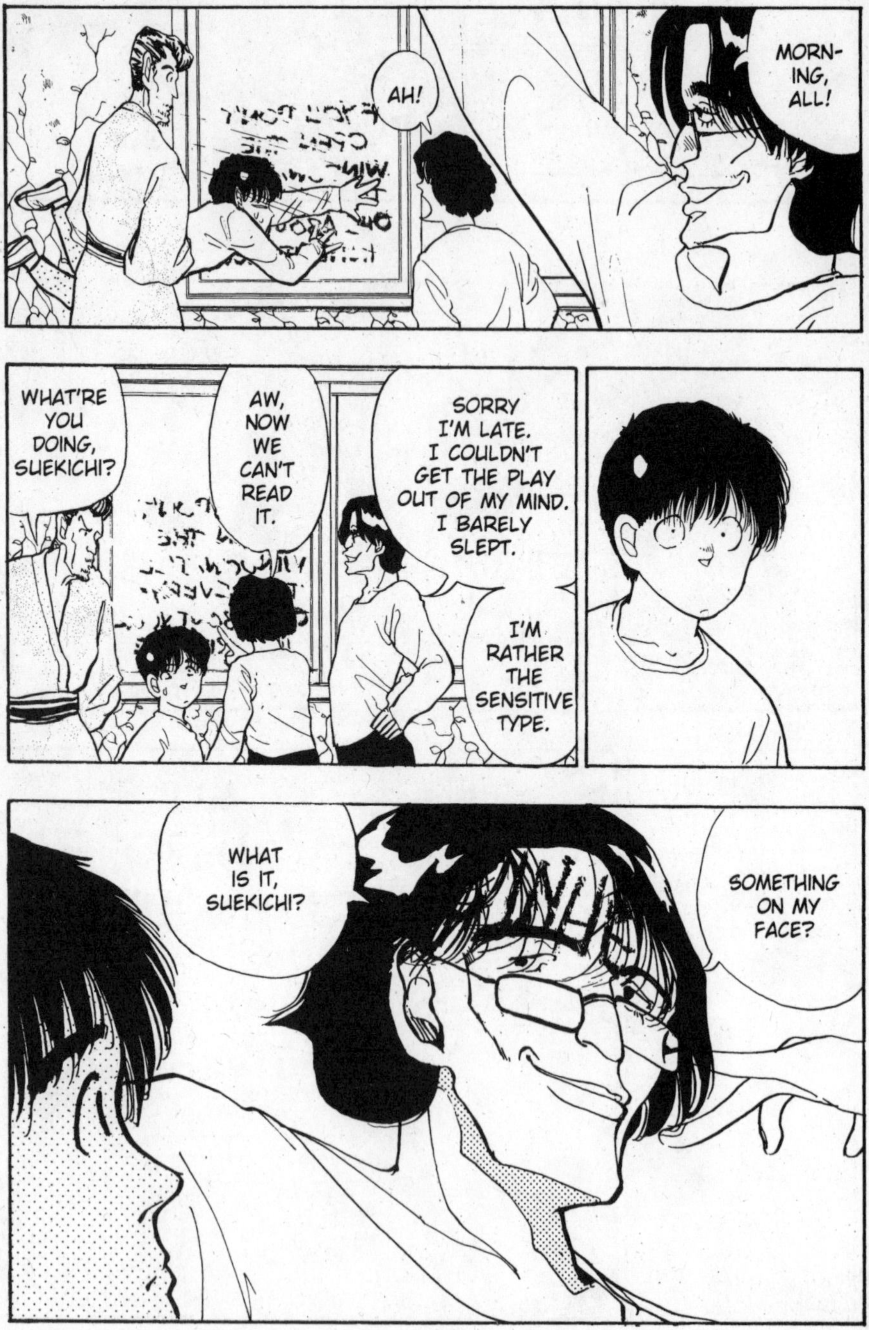
AH!
MORN-ING, ALL!
WHAT'RE YOU DOING, SUEKICHI?
AW, NOW WE CAN'T READ IT.
SORRY I'M LATE. I COULDN'T GET THE PLAY OUT OF MY MIND. I BARELY SLEPT.
I'M RATHER THE SENSITIVE TYPE.
WHAT IS IT, SUEKICHI?
SOMETHING ON MY FACE?

ACT TEN

JUST BEFORE OPENING NIGHT

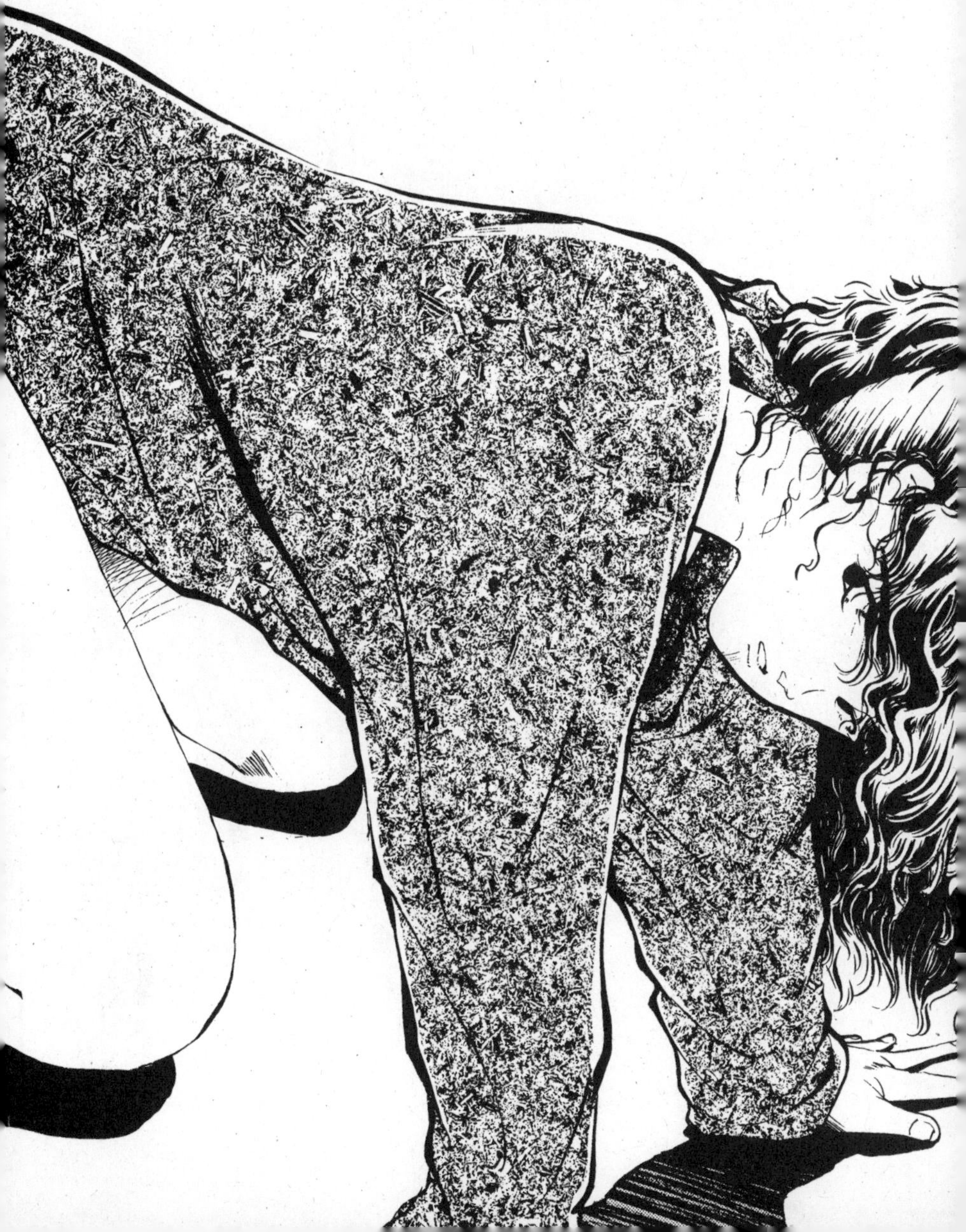

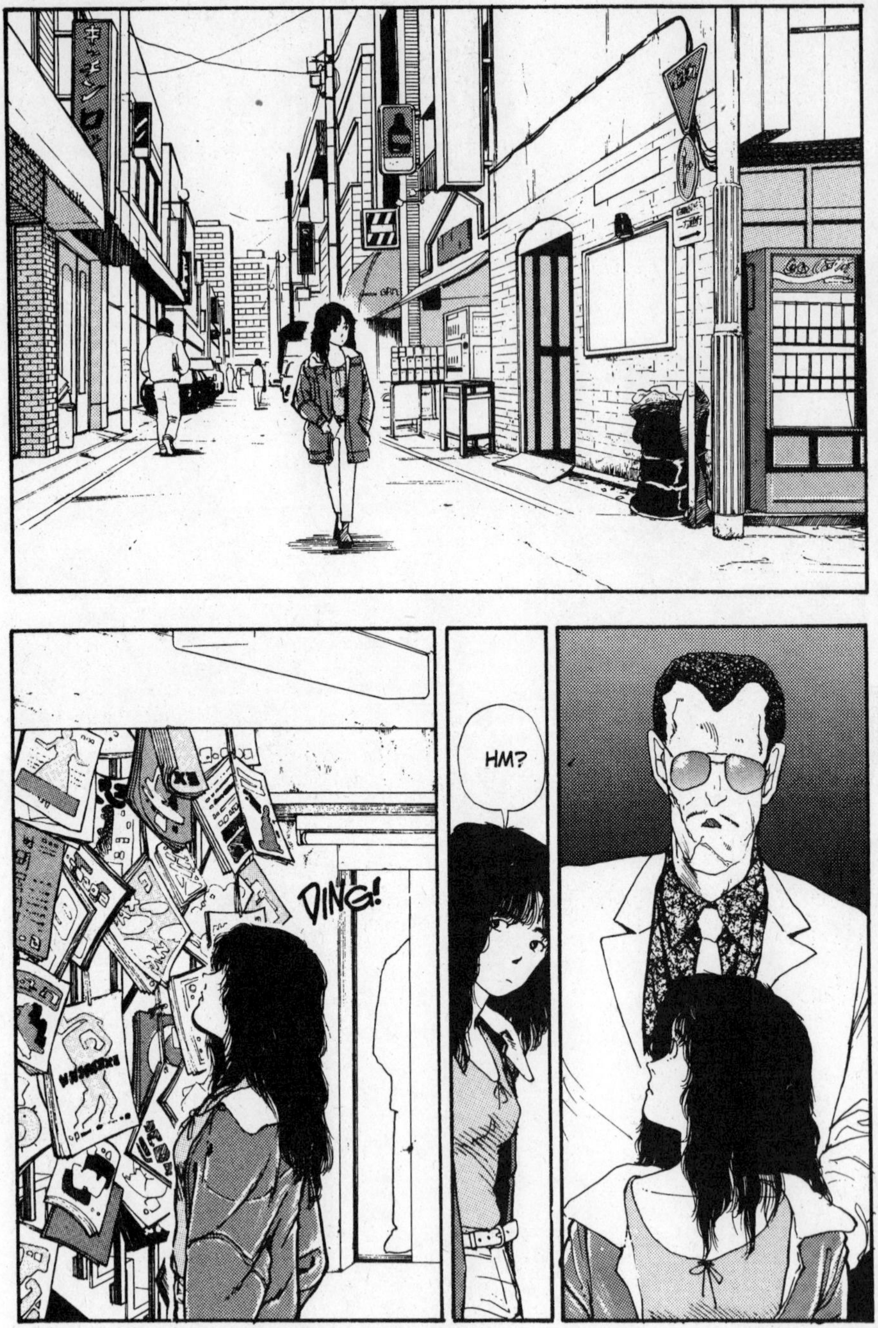
DING!
HM?

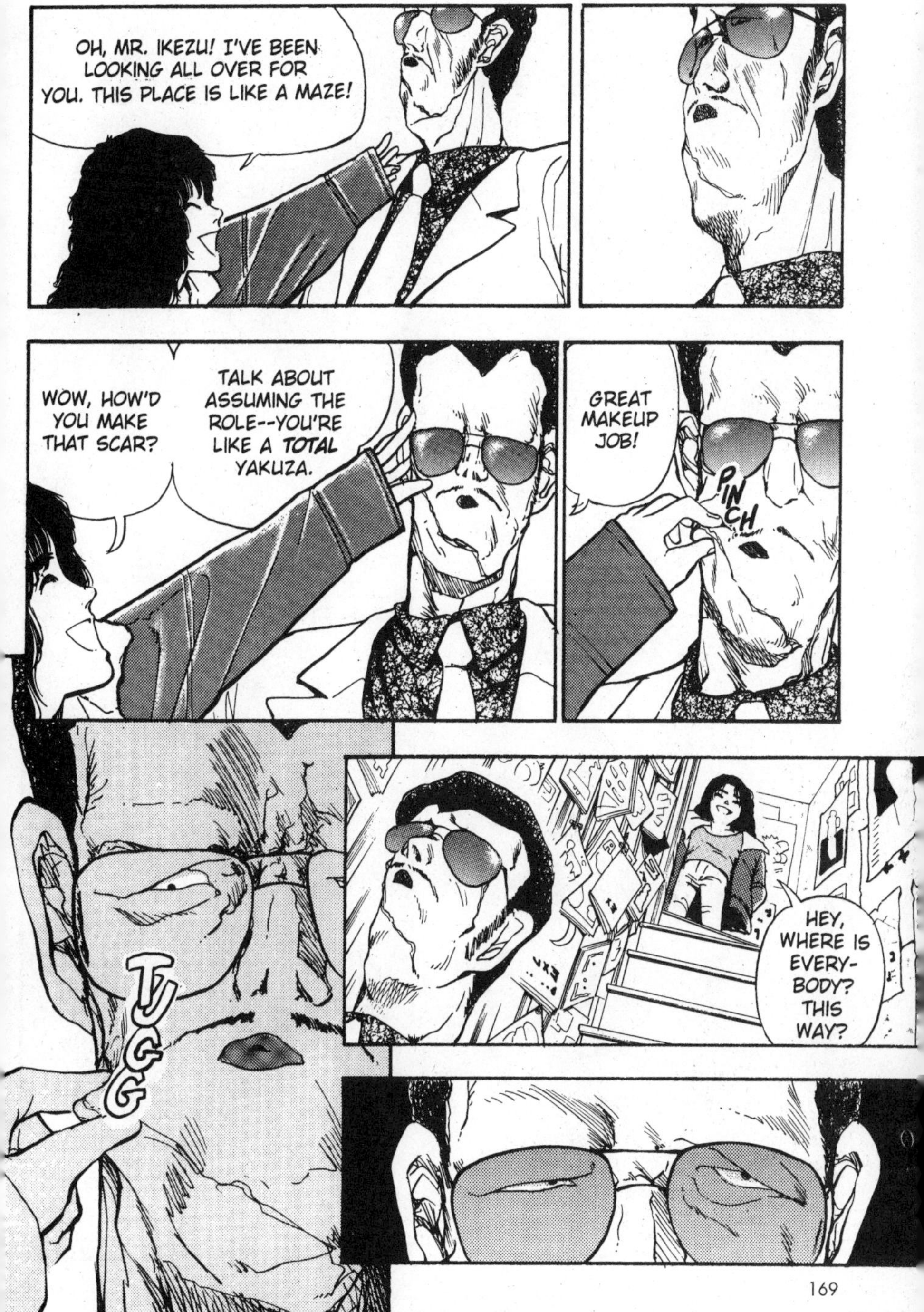
OH, MR. IKEZU! I'VE BEEN LOOKING ALL OVER FOR YOU. THIS PLACE IS LIKE A MAZE!
WOW, HOW'D YOU MAKE THAT SCAR?
TALK ABOUT ASSUMING THE ROLE--YOU'RE LIKE A TOTAL YAKUZA.
GREAT MAKEUP JOB!
PINCH
TUGG
HEY, WHERE IS EVERY-BODY? THIS WAY?

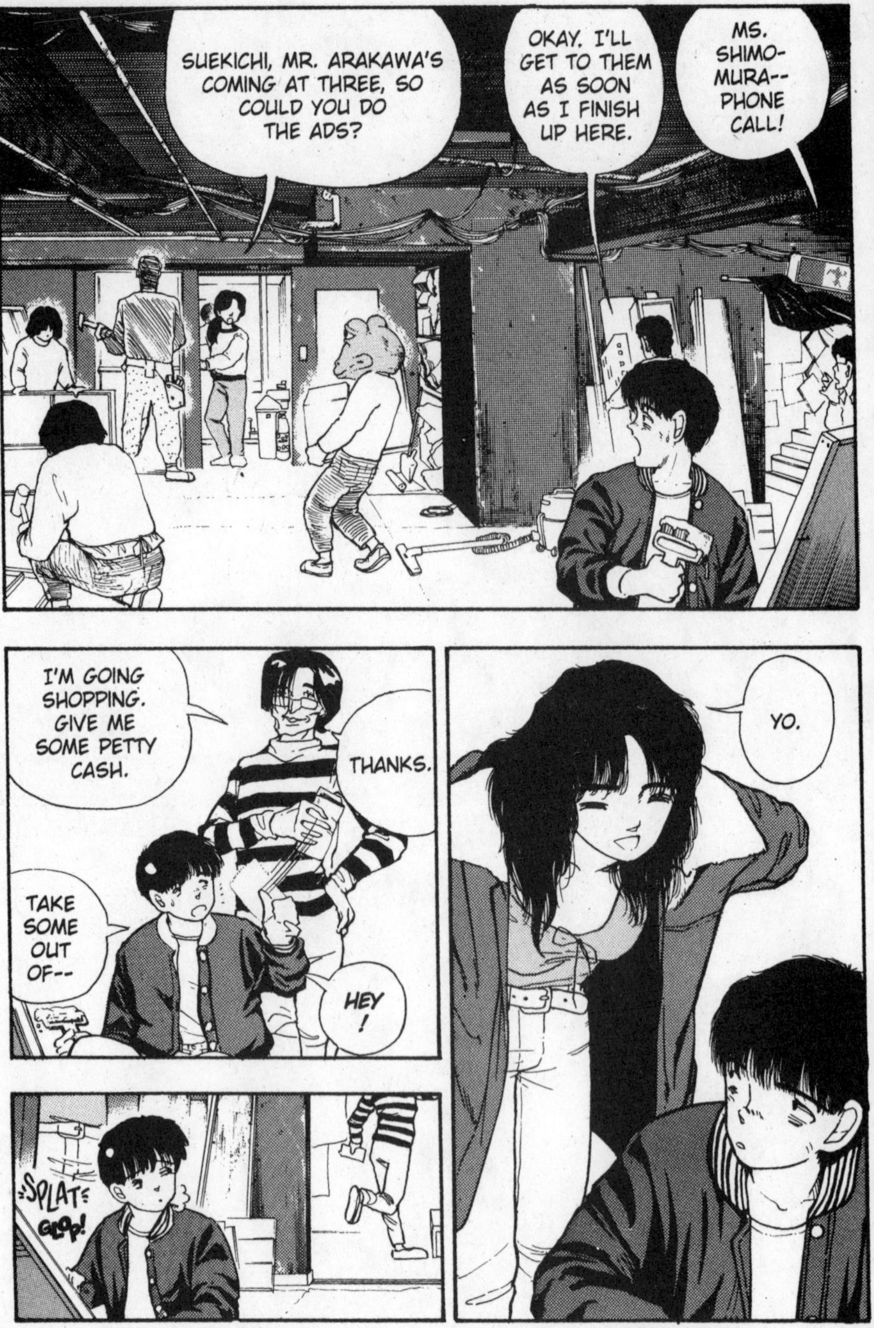
SUEKICHI, MR. ARAKAWA'S COMING AT THREE, SO COULD YOU DO THE ADS?
OKAY. I'LL GET TO THEM AS SOON AS I FINISH UP HERE.
MS. SHIMOMURA-- PHONE CALL!
I'M GOING SHOPPING. GIVE ME SOME PETTY CASH.
THANKS.
TAKE SOME OUT OF--
HEY!
SPLAT
GLOP!
YO.

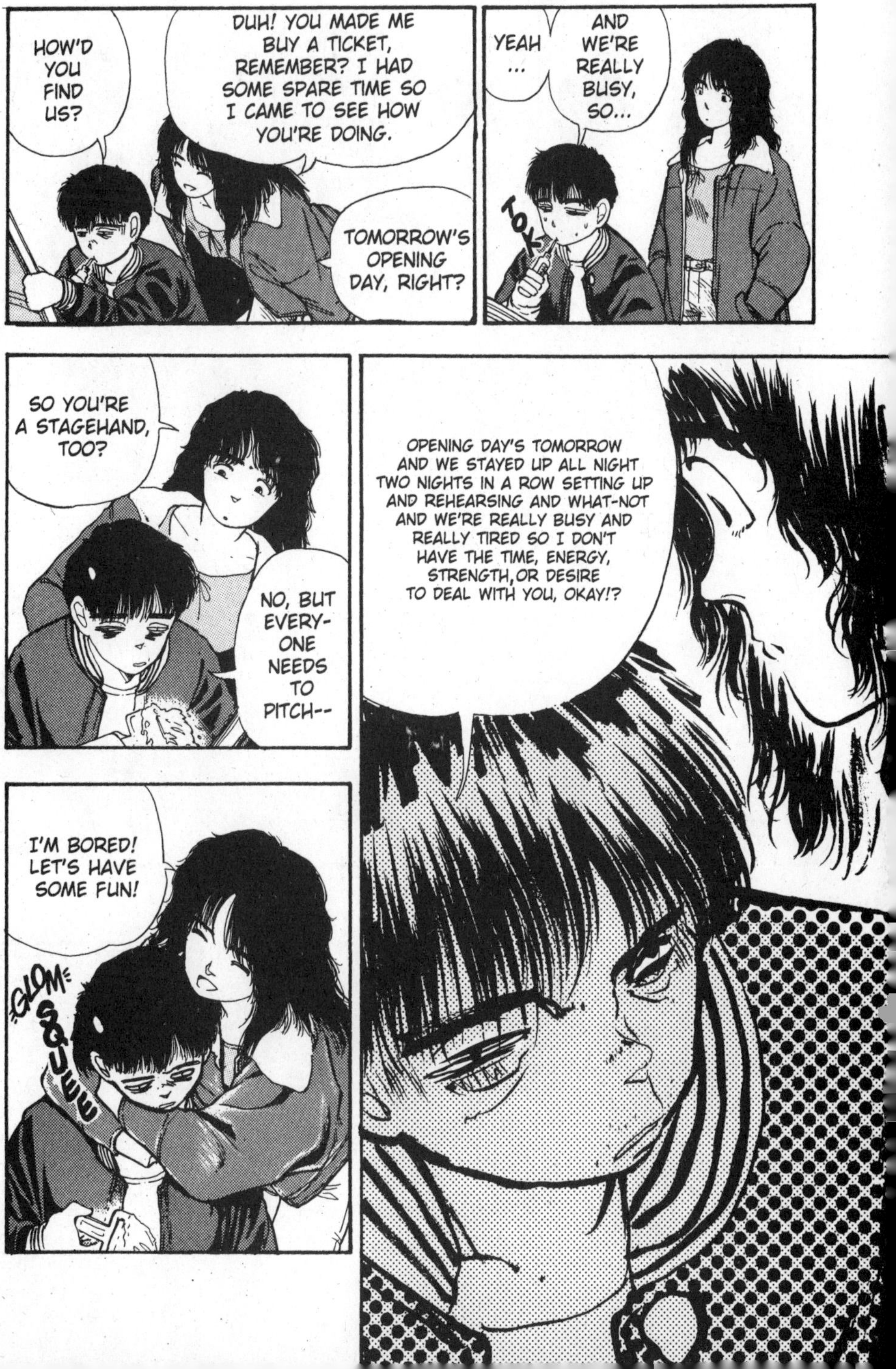
HOW'D YOU FIND US?
DUH! YOU MADE ME BUY A TICKET, REMEMBER? I HAD SOME SPARE TIME SO I CAME TO SEE HOW YOU'RE DOING.
TOMORROW'S OPENING DAY, RIGHT?
YEAH ...
AND WE'RE REALLY BUSY, SO...
TOK
SO YOU'RE A STAGEHAND, TOO?
NO, BUT EVERY-ONE NEEDS TO PITCH--
I'M BORED! LET'S HAVE SOME FUN!
GLOM
SQUEEE
OPENING DAY'S TOMORROW AND WE STAYED UP ALL NIGHT TWO NIGHTS IN A ROW SETTING UP AND REHEARSING AND WHAT-NOT AND WE'RE REALLY BUSY AND REALLY TIRED SO I DON'T HAVE THE TIME, ENERGY, STRENGTH,OR DESIRE TO DEAL WITH YOU, OKAY!?

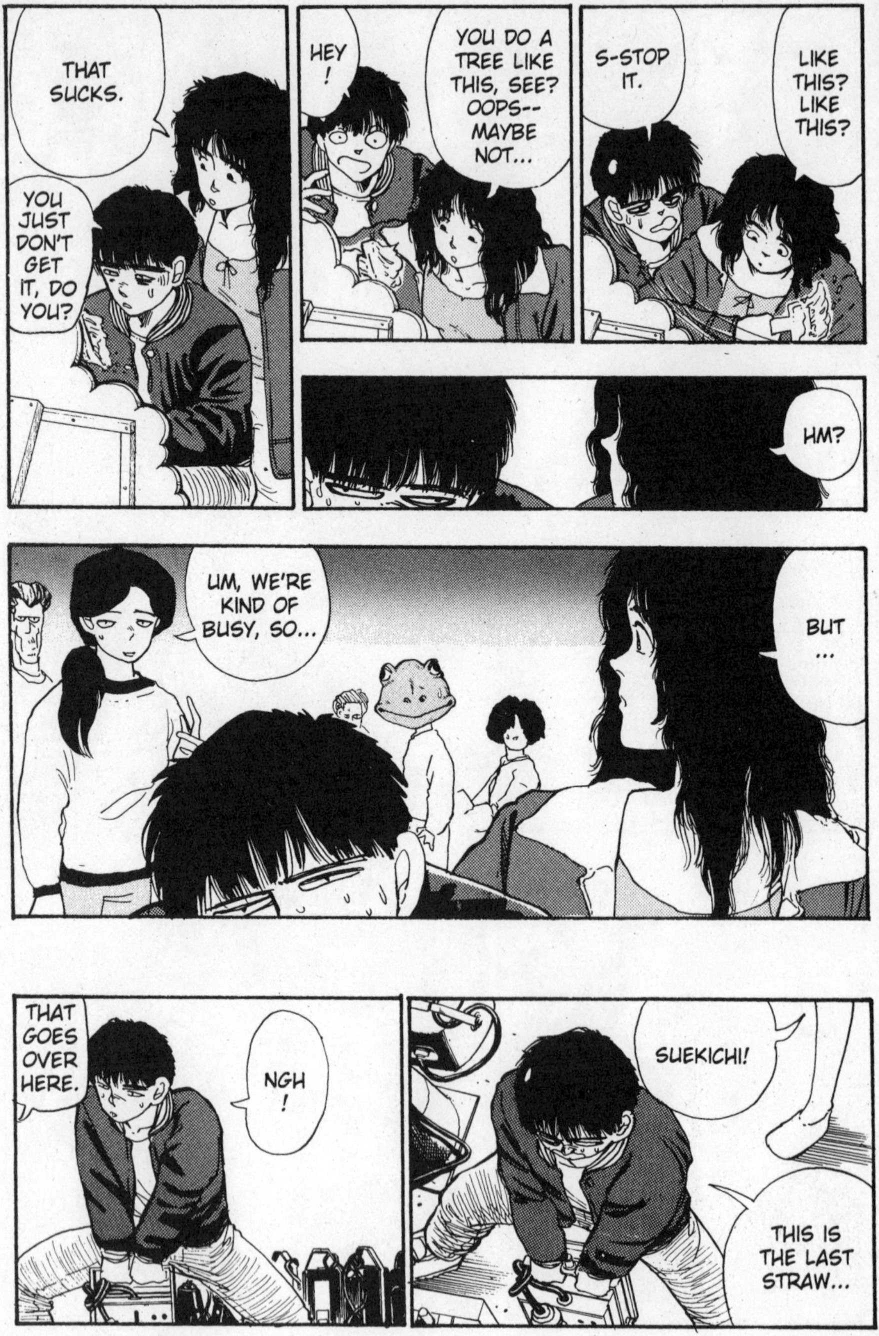
THAT SUCKS.
YOU JUST DON'T GET IT, DO YOU?
HEY!
YOU DO A TREE LIKE THIS, SEE? OOPS-- MAYBE NOT...
S-STOP IT.
LIKE THIS? LIKE THIS?
HM?
UM, WE'RE KIND OF BUSY, SO...
BUT ...
THAT GOES OVER HERE.
NGH!
SUEKICHI!
THIS IS THE LAST STRAW...

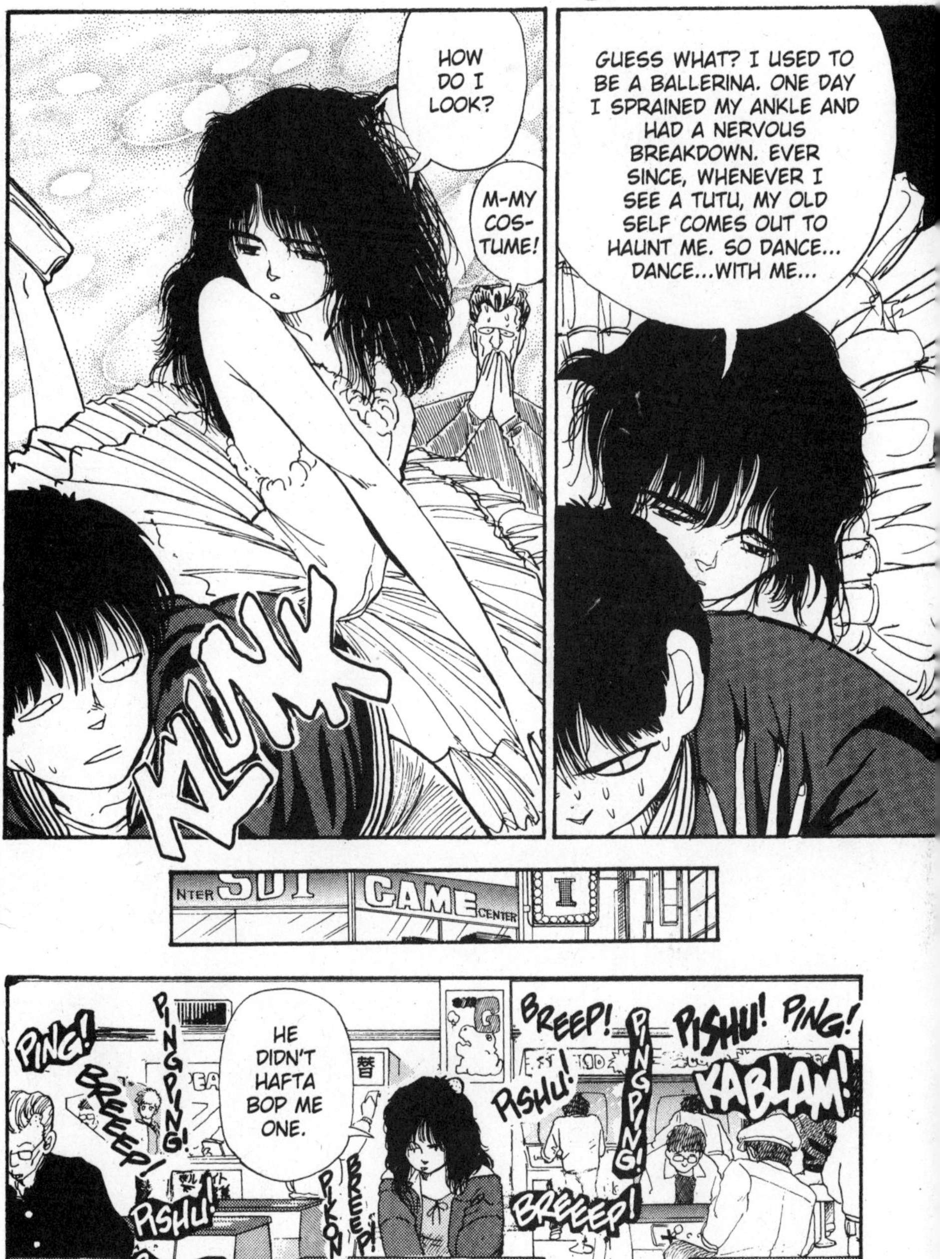
HOW DO I LOOK?
M-MY COS-TUME!
KLUNK
GUESS WHAT? I USED TO BE A BALLERINA. ONE DAY I SPRAINED MY ANKLE AND HAD A NERVOUS BREAKDOWN. EVER SINCE, WHENEVER I SEE A TUTU, MY OLD SELF COMES OUT TO HAUNT ME. SO DANCE... DANCE...WITH ME...
GAME CENTER
PING!
PINGPING!
BREEEP!
PISHU!
BREEP!
HE DIDN'T HAFTA BOP ME ONE.
PIKON
BREEP!
BREEP!
PISHU!
PINGPING!
BREEEP!
PISHU!
PING!
KABLAM!

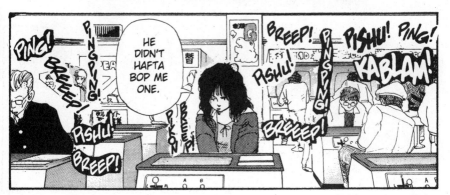

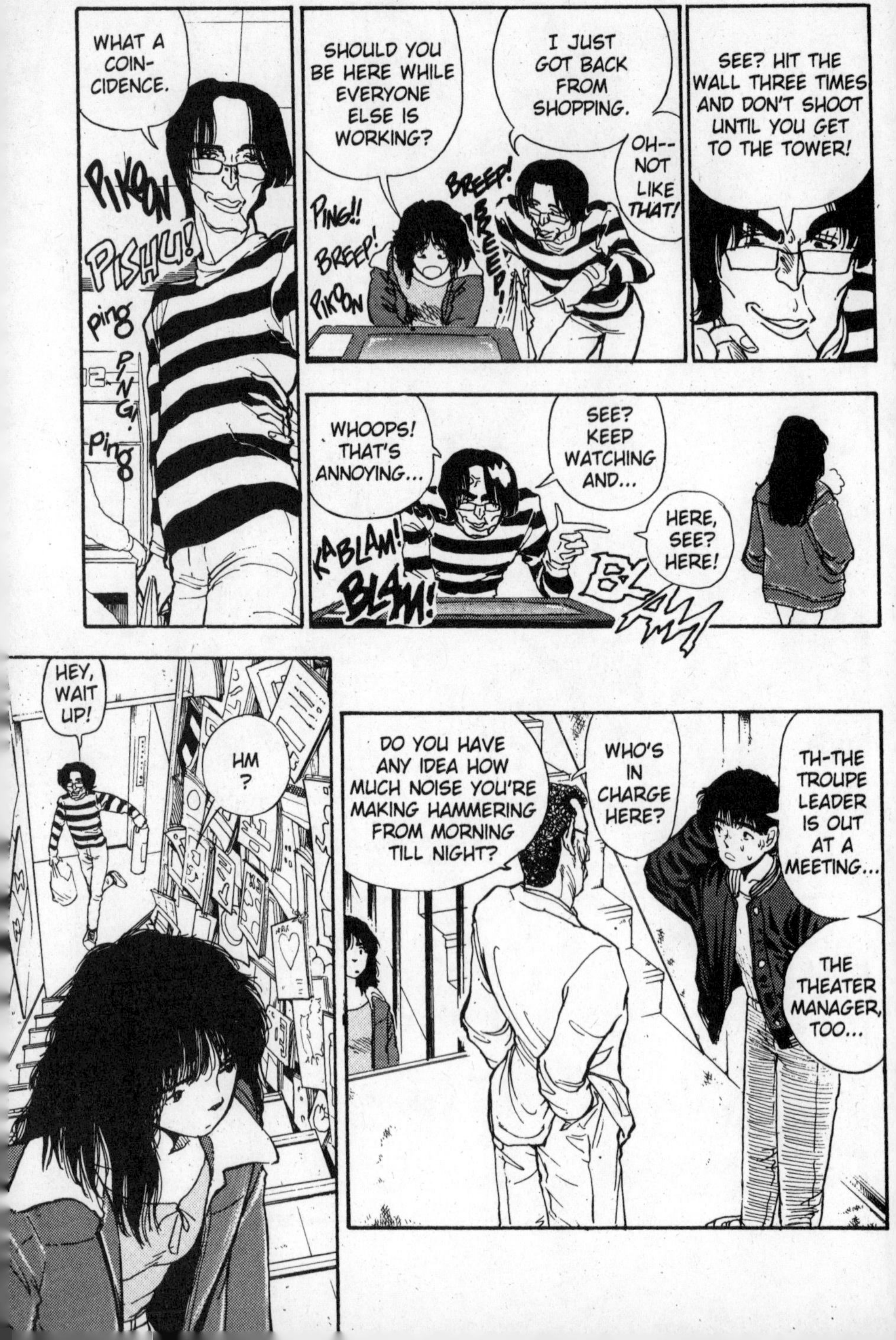
WHAT A COIN-CIDENCE.
PIKOON
PISHU!
ping
PING!
Ping
SHOULD YOU BE HERE WHILE EVERYONE ELSE IS WORKING?
I JUST GOT BACK FROM SHOPPING.
OH-- NOT LIKE THAT!
BREEP!
BREEP!
PING!!
BREEP!
PIKOON
SEE? HIT THE WALL THREE TIMES AND DON'T SHOOT UNTIL YOU GET TO THE TOWER!
WHOOPS! THAT'S ANNOYING...
SEE? KEEP WATCHING AND...
HERE, SEE? HERE!
KABLAM!
BLAM!
BLAM
HEY, WAIT UP!
HM?
DO YOU HAVE ANY IDEA HOW MUCH NOISE YOU'RE MAKING HAMMERING FROM MORNING TILL NIGHT?
WHO'S IN CHARGE HERE?
TH-THE TROUPE LEADER IS OUT AT A MEETING...
THE THEATER MANAGER, TOO...

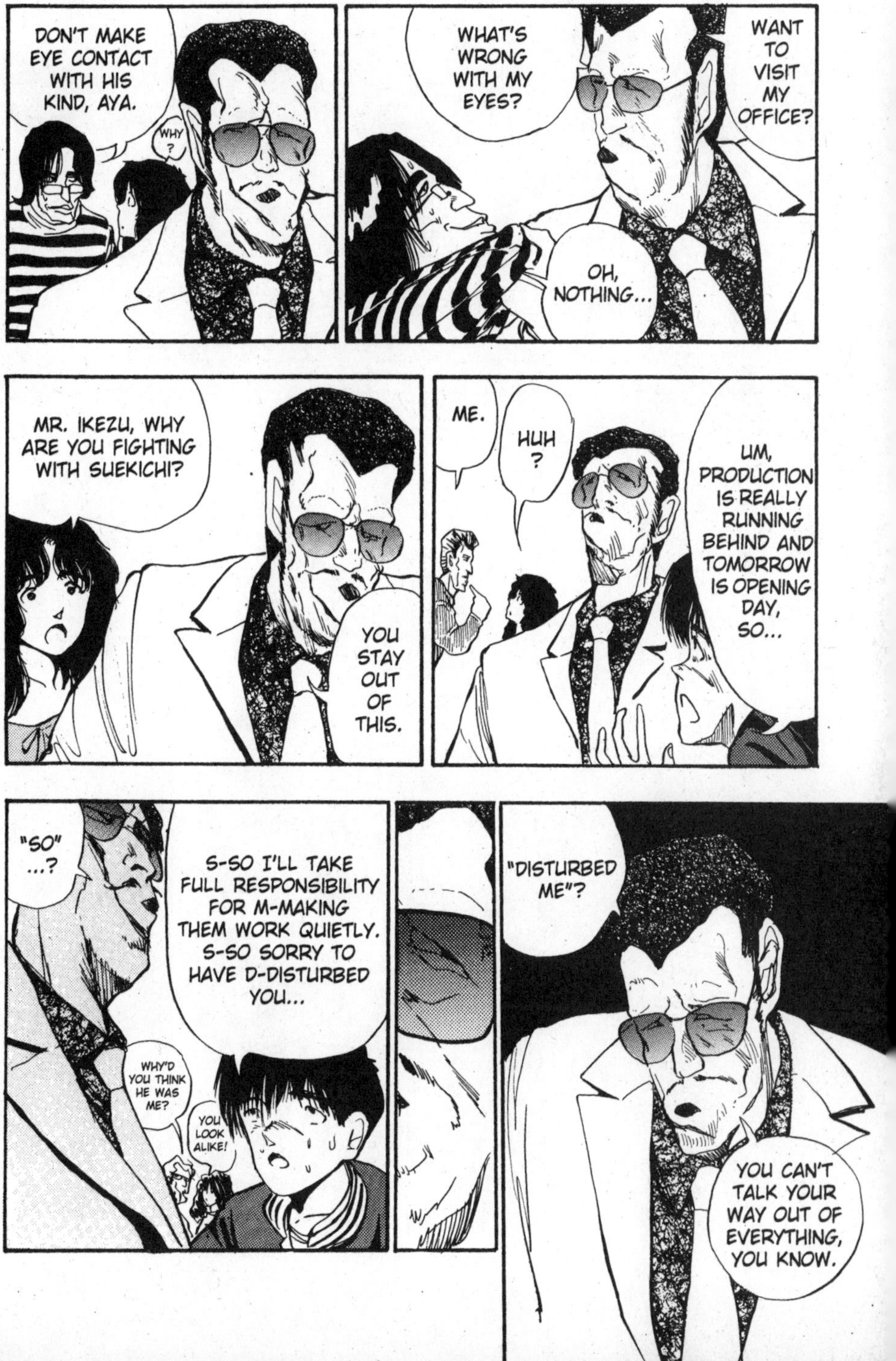
DON'T MAKE EYE CONTACT WITH HIS KIND, AYA.
WHY ?
WHAT'S WRONG WITH MY EYES?
WANT TO VISIT MY OFFICE?
OH, NOTHING...
MR. IKEZU, WHY ARE YOU FIGHTING WITH SUEKICHI?
YOU STAY OUT OF THIS.
ME.
HUH ?
UM, PRODUCTION IS REALLY RUNNING BEHIND AND TOMORROW IS OPENING DAY, SO...
"SO" ...?
S-SO I'LL TAKE FULL RESPONSIBILITY FOR M-MAKING THEM WORK QUIETLY. S-SO SORRY TO HAVE D-DISTURBED YOU...
WHY'D YOU THINK HE WAS ME?
YOU LOOK ALIKE!
"DISTURBED ME"?
YOU CAN'T TALK YOUR WAY OUT OF EVERYTHING, YOU KNOW.

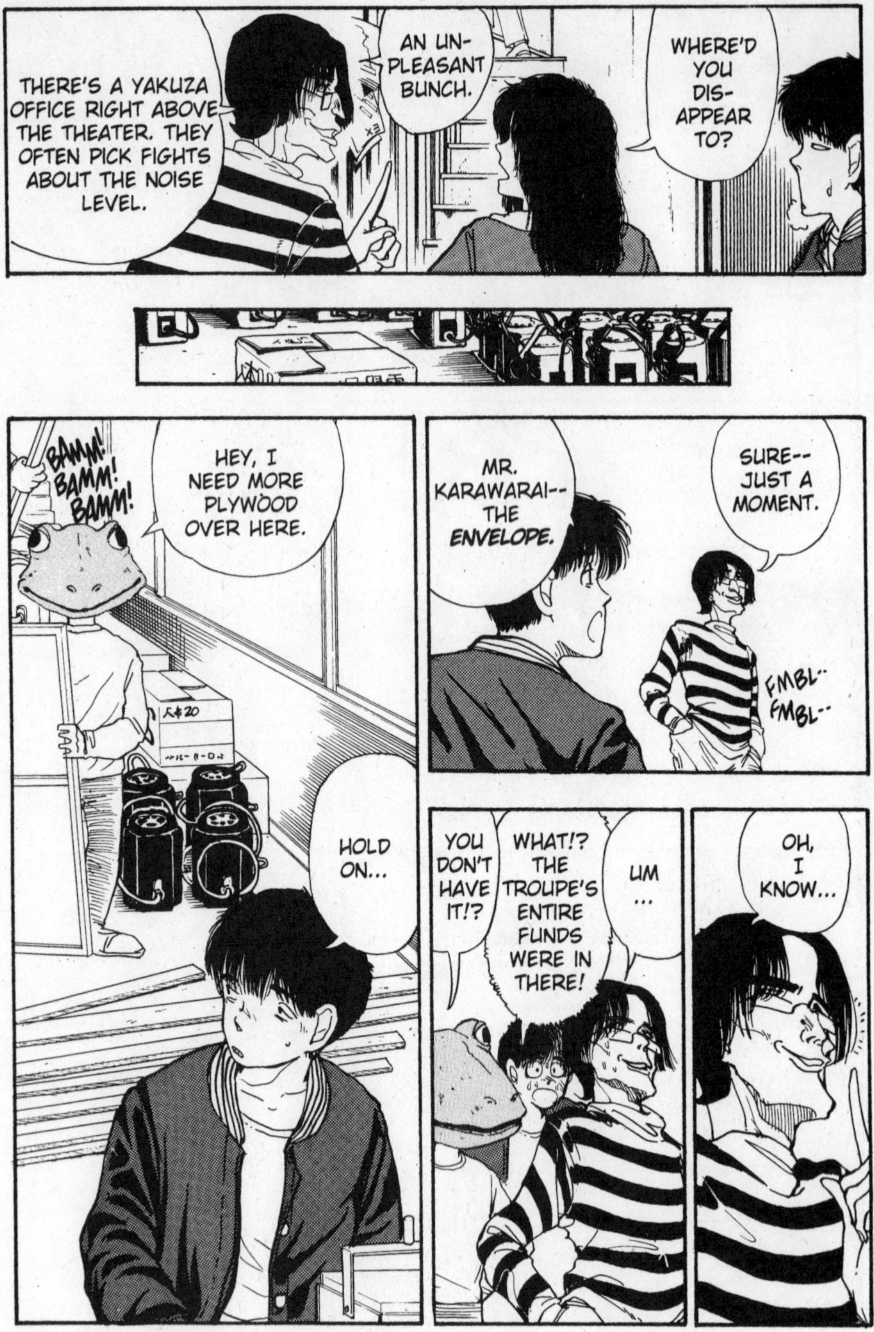

THERE'S A YAKUZA OFFICE RIGHT ABOVE THE THEATER. THEY OFTEN PICK FIGHTS ABOUT THE NOISE LEVEL.
AN UN-PLEASANT BUNCH.
WHERE'D YOU DIS-APPEAR TO?
BAMM! BAMM! BAMM!
HEY, I NEED MORE PLYWOOD OVER HERE.
HOLD ON...
MR. KARAWARAI-- THE *ENVELOPE.*
SURE-- JUST A MOMENT.
FMBL.. FMBL..
YOU DON'T HAVE IT!?
WHAT!? THE TROUPE'S ENTIRE FUNDS WERE IN THERE!
UM ...
OH, I KNOW...

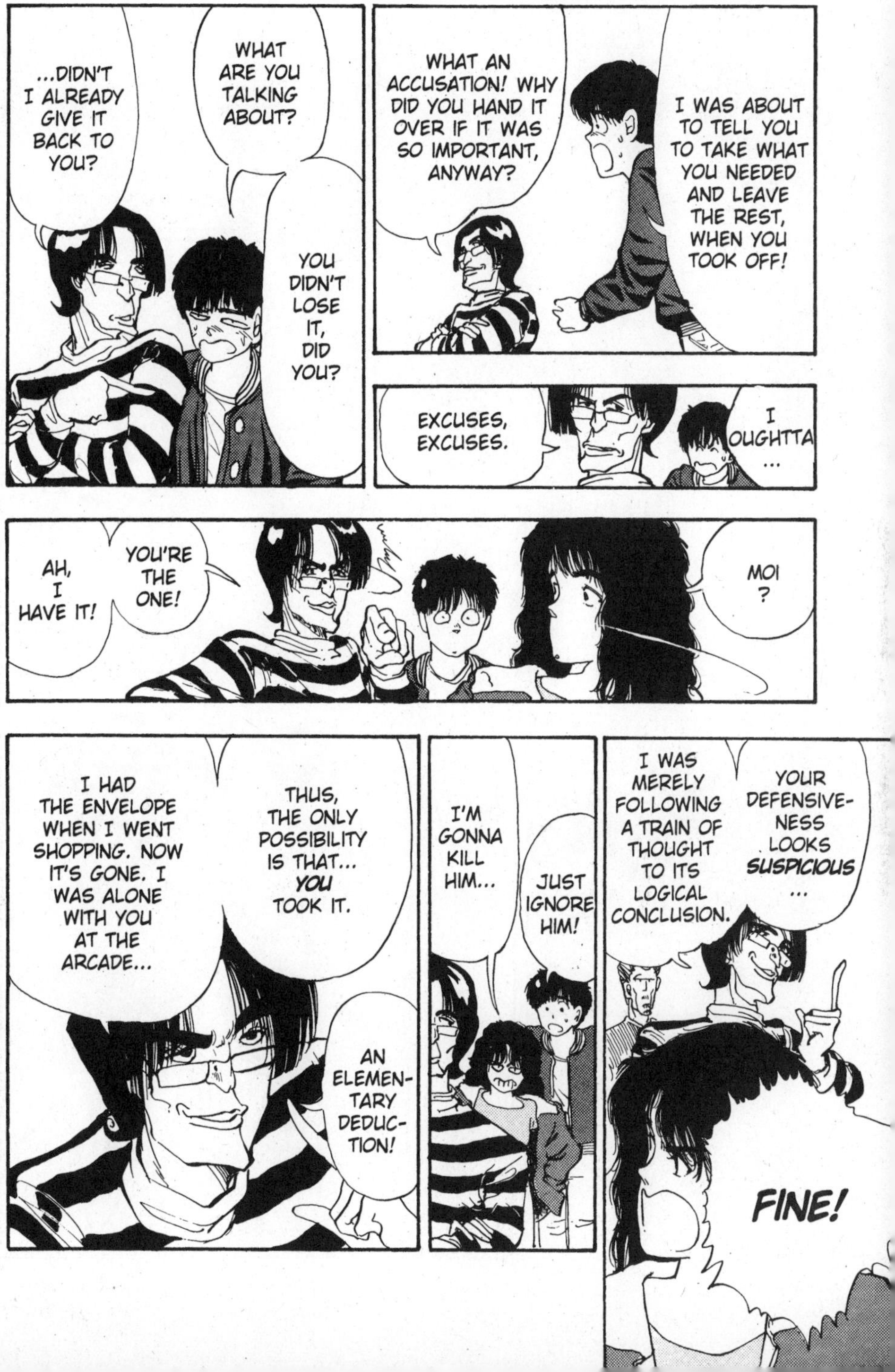
...DIDN'T I ALREADY GIVE IT BACK TO YOU?
WHAT ARE YOU TALKING ABOUT?
YOU DIDN'T LOSE IT, DID YOU?
WHAT AN ACCUSATION! WHY DID YOU HAND IT OVER IF IT WAS SO IMPORTANT, ANYWAY?
I WAS ABOUT TO TELL YOU TO TAKE WHAT YOU NEEDED AND LEAVE THE REST, WHEN YOU TOOK OFF!
EXCUSES, EXCUSES.
I OUGHTTA ...
AH, I HAVE IT!
YOU'RE THE ONE!
MOI ?
I HAD THE ENVELOPE WHEN I WENT SHOPPING. NOW IT'S GONE. I WAS ALONE WITH YOU AT THE ARCADE...
THUS, THE ONLY POSSIBILITY IS THAT... YOU TOOK IT.
AN ELEMENTARY DEDUCTION!
I'M GONNA KILL HIM...
JUST IGNORE HIM!
I WAS MERELY FOLLOWING A TRAIN OF THOUGHT TO ITS LOGICAL CONCLUSION.
YOUR DEFENSIVENESS LOOKS SUSPICIOUS ...
FINE!

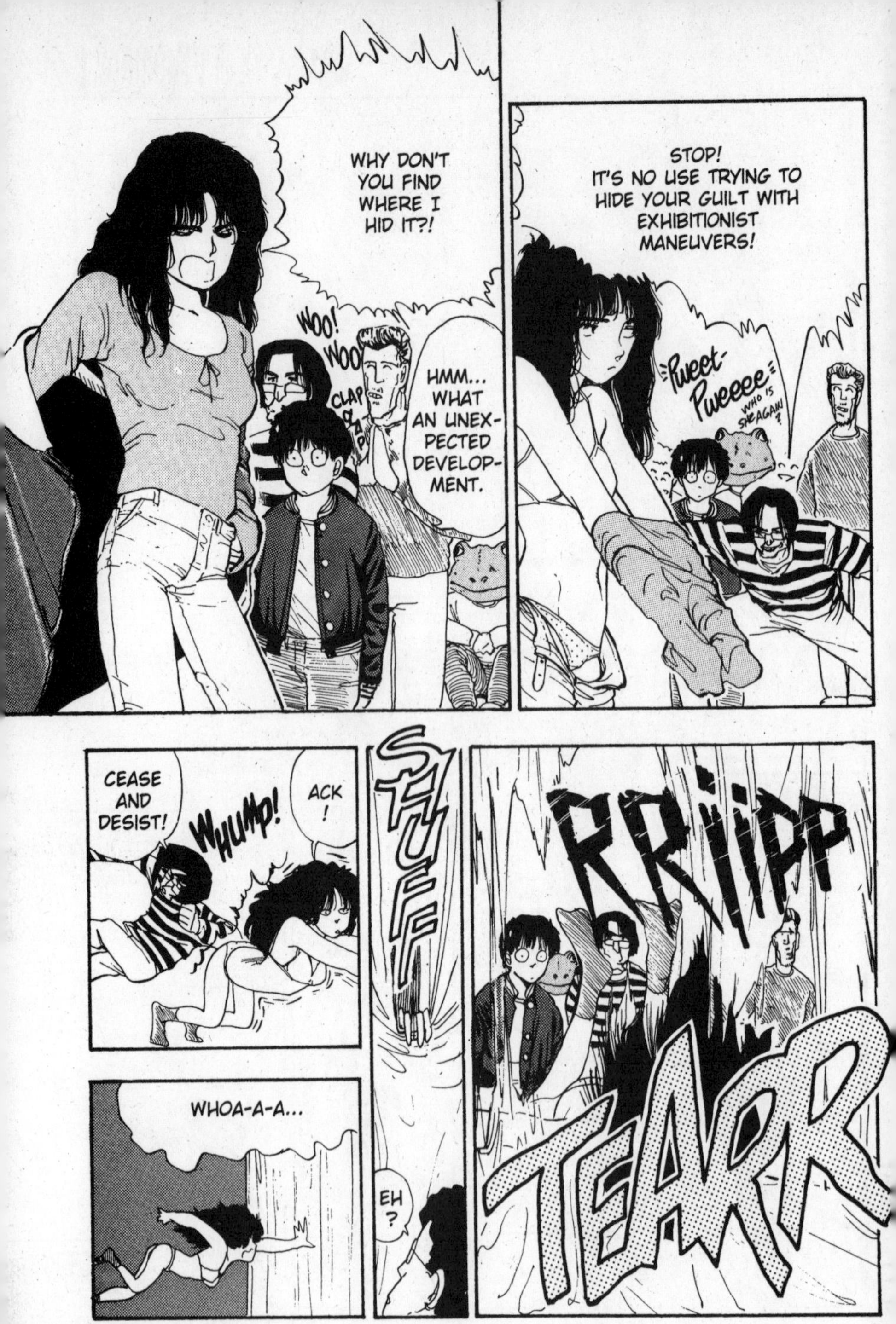
WHY DON'T YOU FIND WHERE I HID IT?!
WOO! WOO!
CLAP CLAP
HMM... WHAT AN UNEXPECTED DEVELOPMENT.
STOP! IT'S NO USE TRYING TO HIDE YOUR GUILT WITH EXHIBITIONIST MANEUVERS!
PWEET-PWEEEE
WHO IS SHE AGAIN?
CEASE AND DESIST!
WHUMP!
ACK!
WHOA-A-A...
STUFF
EH?
RRIIPP
TEARR

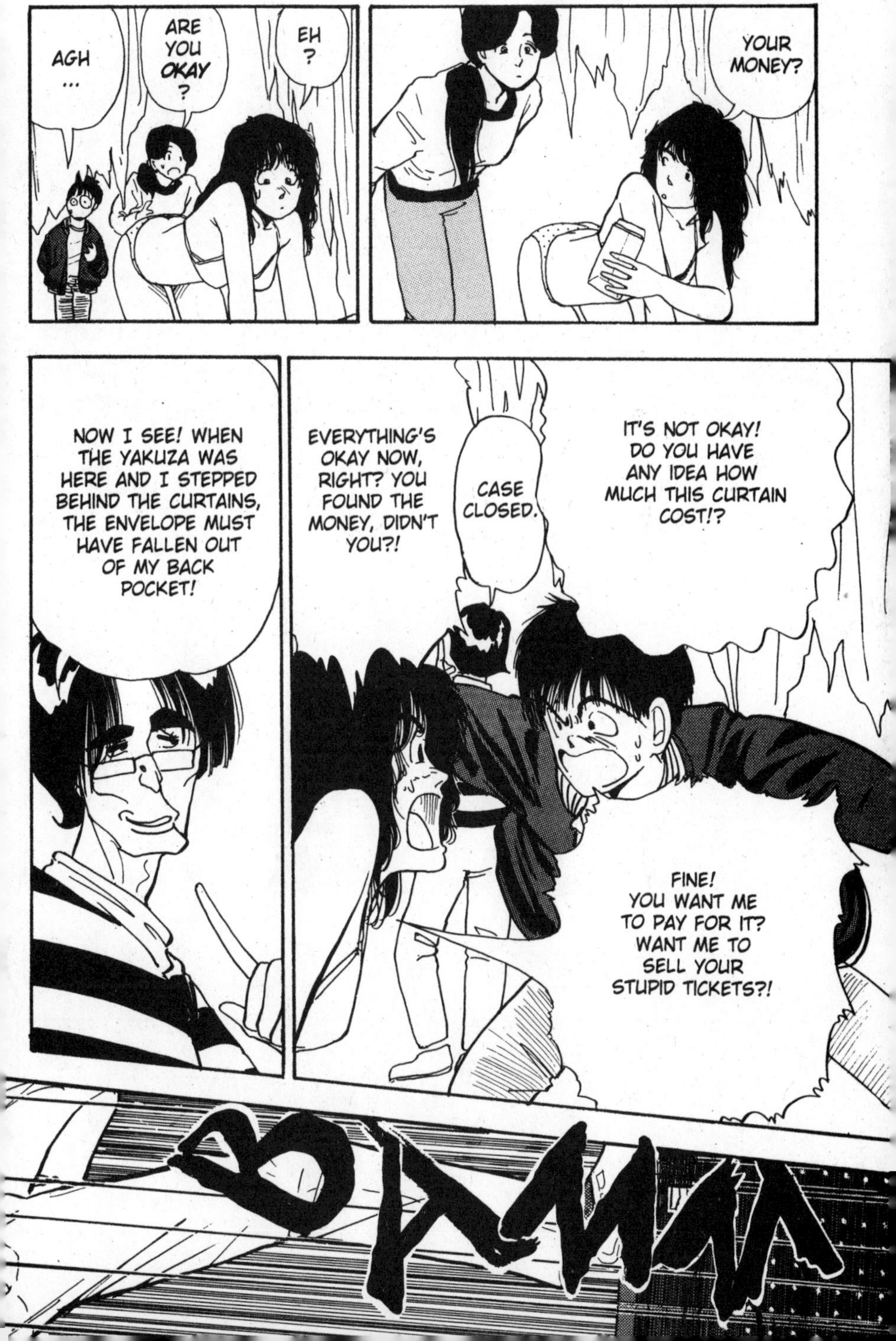
AGH ...
ARE YOU OKAY ?
EH ?
YOUR MONEY?
NOW I SEE! WHEN THE YAKUZA WAS HERE AND I STEPPED BEHIND THE CURTAINS, THE ENVELOPE MUST HAVE FALLEN OUT OF MY BACK POCKET!
EVERYTHING'S OKAY NOW, RIGHT? YOU FOUND THE MONEY, DIDN'T YOU?!
CASE CLOSED.
IT'S NOT OKAY! DO YOU HAVE ANY IDEA HOW MUCH THIS CURTAIN COST!?
FINE! YOU WANT ME TO PAY FOR IT? WANT ME TO SELL YOUR STUPID TICKETS?!
BTMM

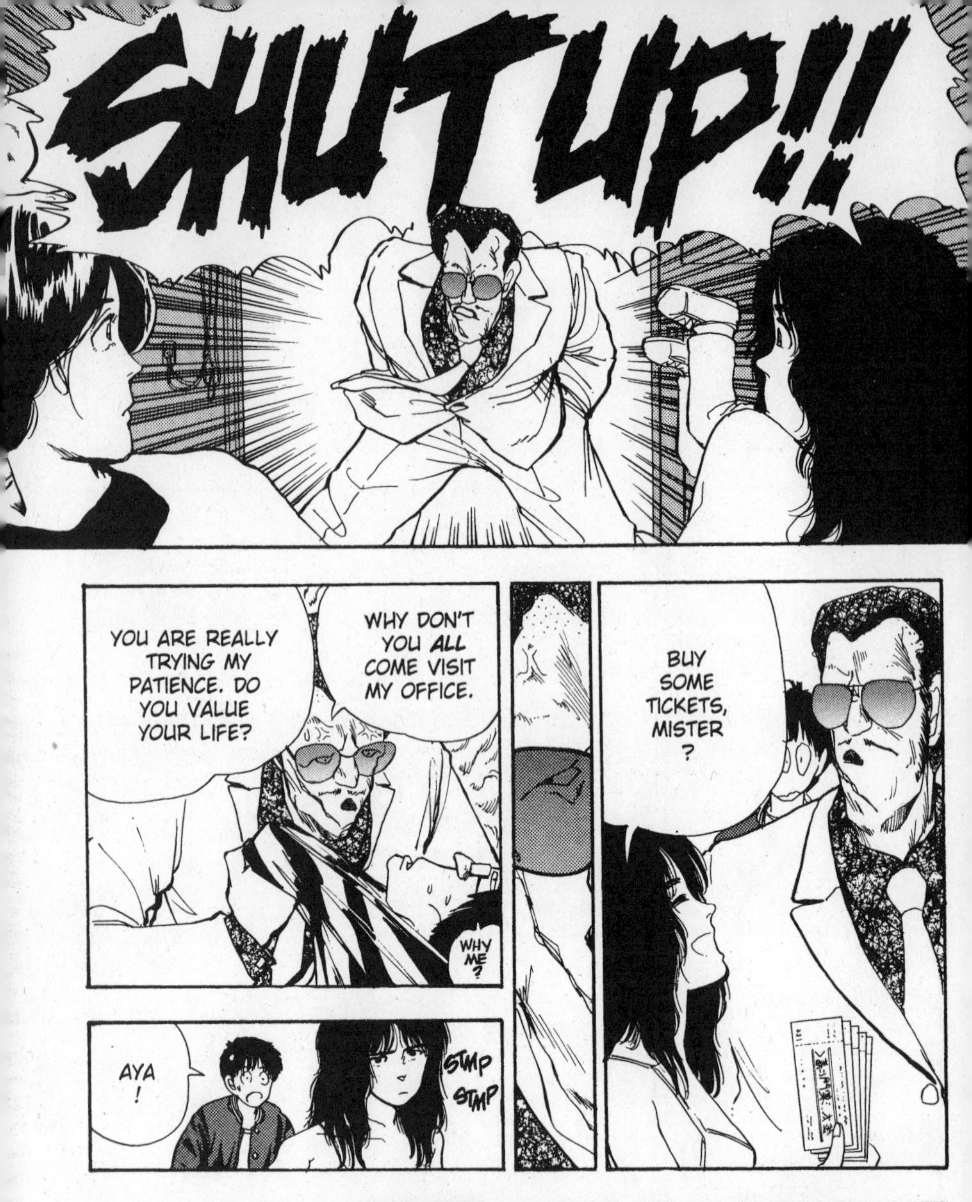

SHUT UP!!
YOU ARE REALLY TRYING MY PATIENCE. DO YOU VALUE YOUR LIFE?
WHY DON'T YOU ALL COME VISIT MY OFFICE.
WHY ME?
AYA!
STMP STMP
BUY SOME TICKETS, MISTER?
WHY SHOULD I BUY THEM?
AGH!
YOU DON'T HAVE TO... BUT I'M GIVING YOU AN OFFER YOU CAN'T REFUSE. THE PLAY'S REALLY FUNNY, AND YOU CAN HAVE THESE FOR HALF PRICE!

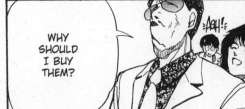

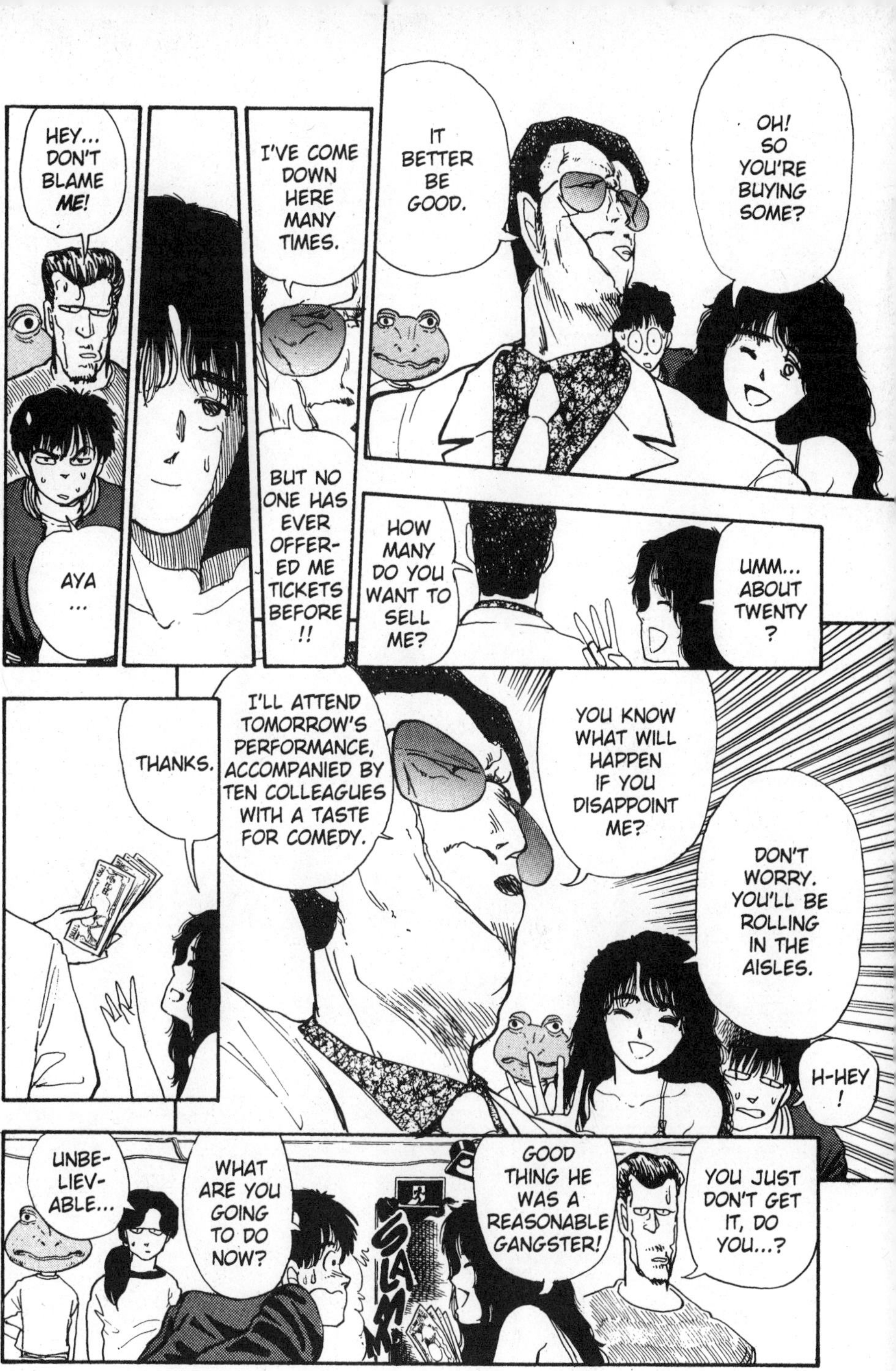
HEY... DON'T BLAME ME!
AYA ...
I'VE COME DOWN HERE MANY TIMES.
BUT NO ONE HAS EVER OFFERED ME TICKETS BEFORE !!
IT BETTER BE GOOD.
OH! SO YOU'RE BUYING SOME?
HOW MANY DO YOU WANT TO SELL ME?
UMM... ABOUT TWENTY ?
THANKS.
I'LL ATTEND TOMORROW'S PERFORMANCE, ACCOMPANIED BY TEN COLLEAGUES WITH A TASTE FOR COMEDY.
YOU KNOW WHAT WILL HAPPEN IF YOU DISAPPOINT ME?
DON'T WORRY. YOU'LL BE ROLLING IN THE AISLES.
H-HEY !
UNBE- LIEV- ABLE...
WHAT ARE YOU GOING TO DO NOW?
SLAM
GOOD THING HE WAS A REASONABLE GANGSTER!
YOU JUST DON'T GET IT, DO YOU...?

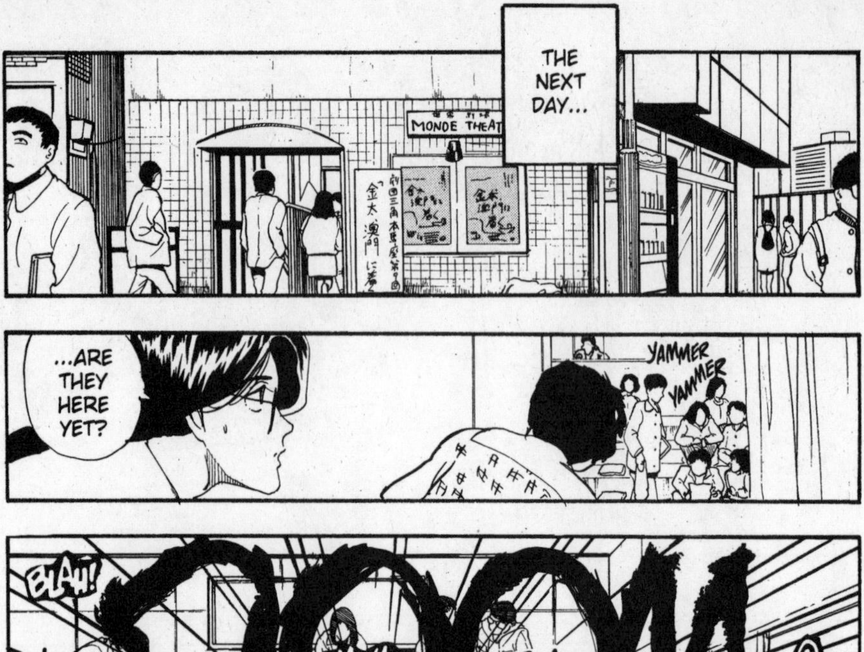
THE NEXT DAY...
MONDE THEAT
...ARE THEY HERE YET?
YAMMER YAMMER
BLAH!
Yammer
YAMMER
BLAH!
BLAH

THIS IS A WORK OF FICTION. ANY SIMILARITY TO ANY PERSON, GROUP, OR THEATER IS PURELY COINCIDENTAL.

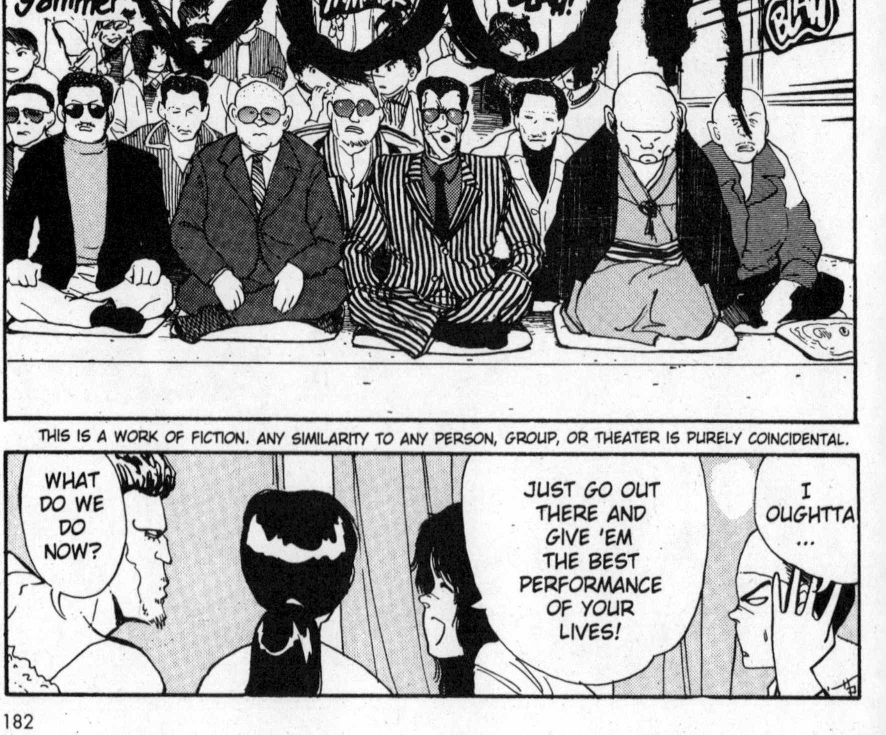
WHAT DO WE DO NOW?
JUST GO OUT THERE AND GIVE 'EM THE BEST PERFORMANCE OF YOUR LIVES!
I OUGHTTA ...

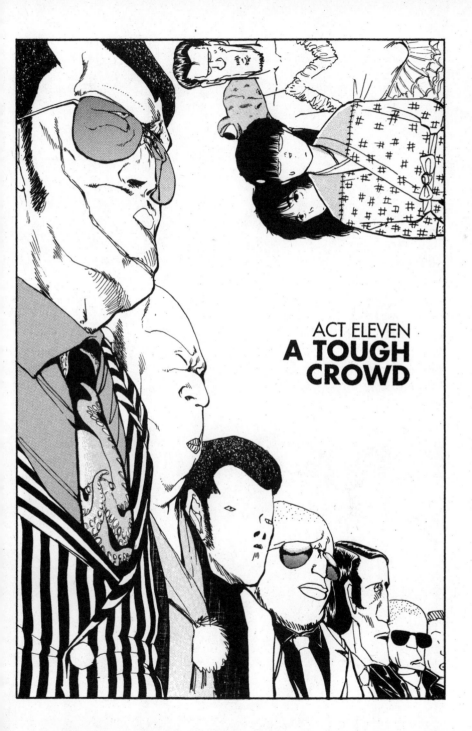

ACT ELEVEN
A TOUGH CROWD

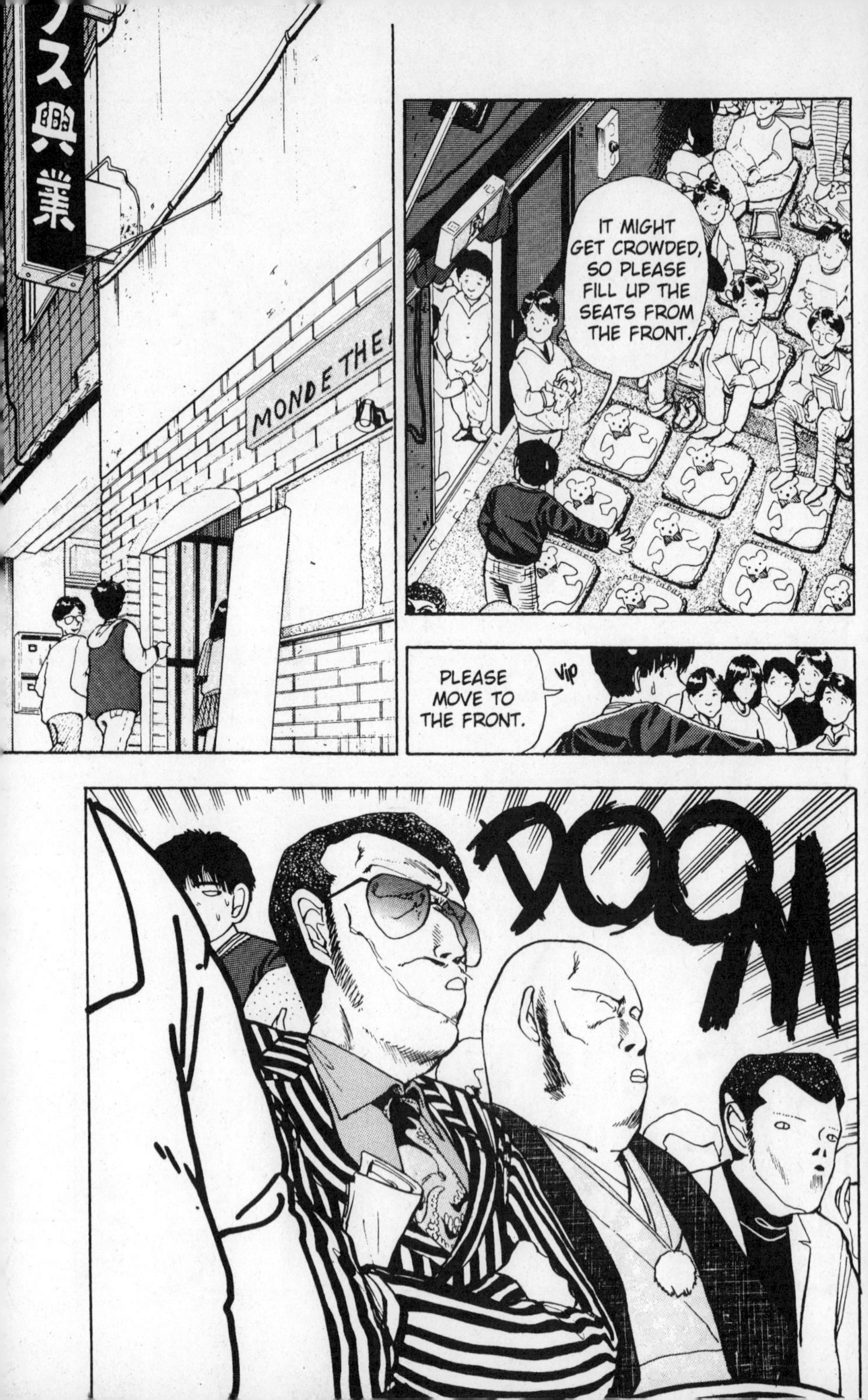
ス興業
MONDE THE
IT MIGHT GET CROWDED, SO PLEASE FILL UP THE SEATS FROM THE FRONT.
PLEASE MOVE TO THE FRONT.
vip
DOOM

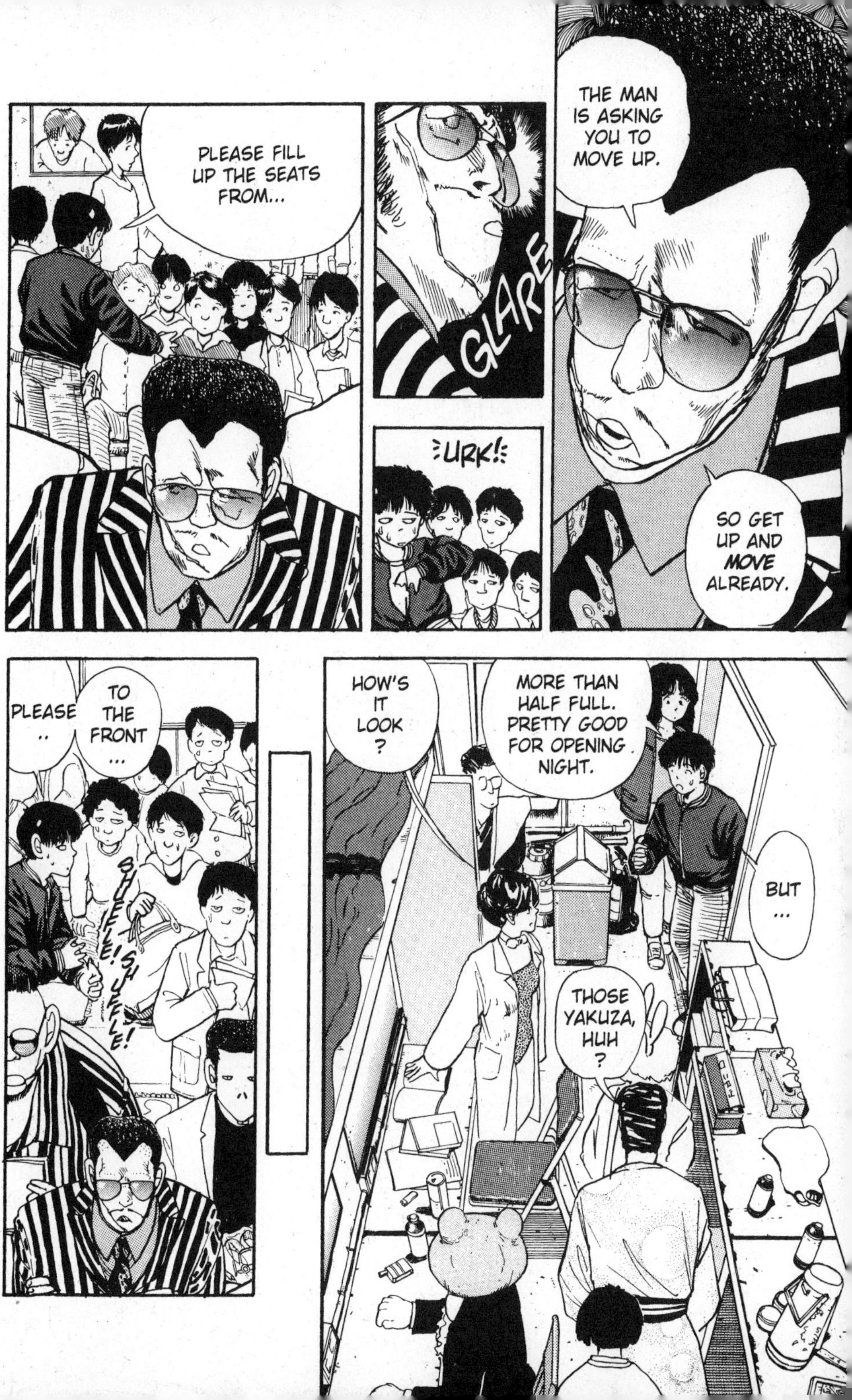
PLEASE FILL UP THE SEATS FROM...
GLARE
THE MAN IS ASKING YOU TO MOVE UP.
URK!
SO GET UP AND MOVE ALREADY.
PLEASE ..
TO THE FRONT ...
SHUFFLE! SHUFFLE!
HOW'S IT LOOK ?
MORE THAN HALF FULL. PRETTY GOOD FOR OPENING NIGHT.
BUT ...
THOSE YAKUZA, HUH ?

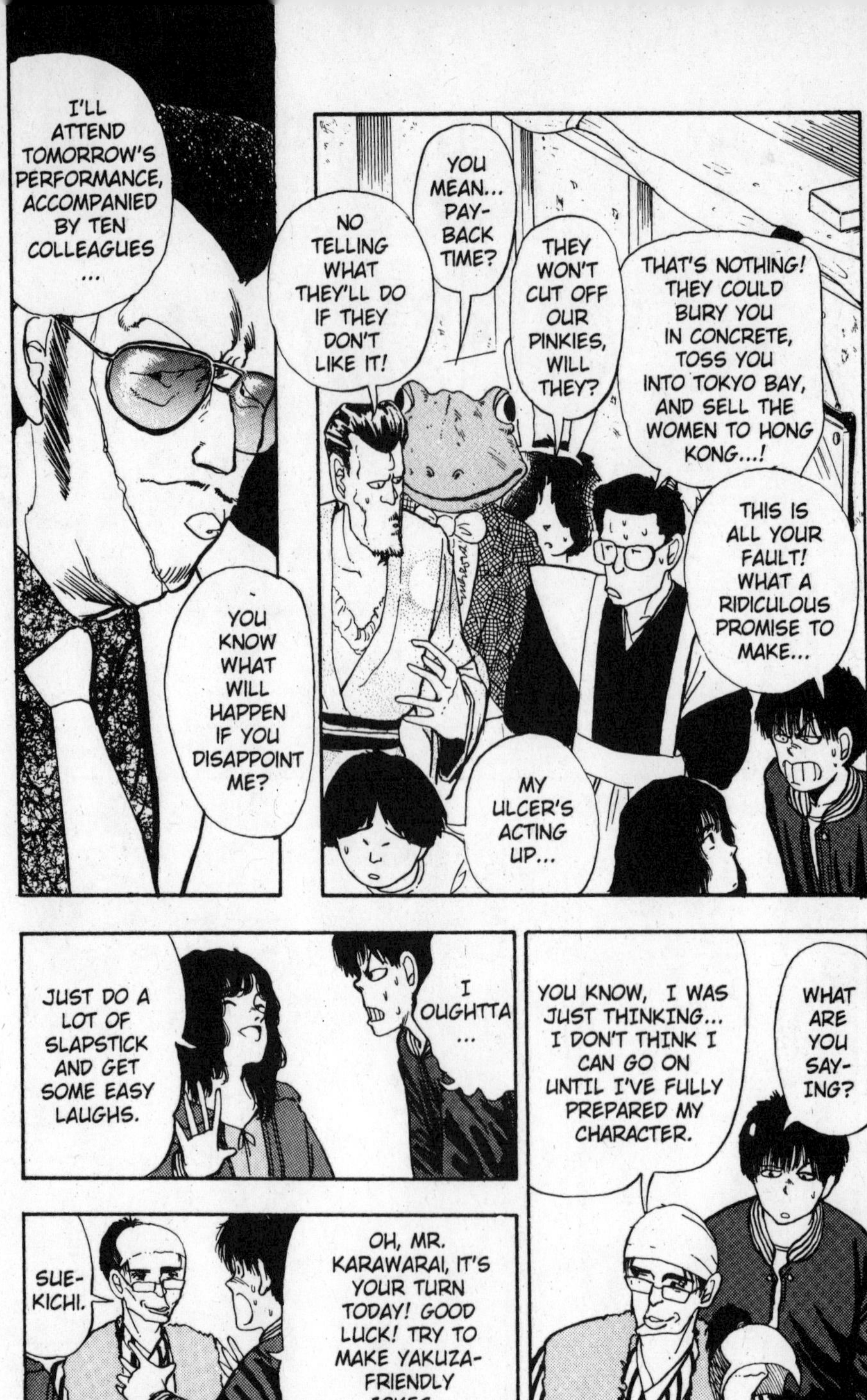
I'LL ATTEND TOMORROW'S PERFORMANCE, ACCOMPANIED BY TEN COLLEAGUES ...
YOU KNOW WHAT WILL HAPPEN IF YOU DISAPPOINT ME?
NO TELLING WHAT THEY'LL DO IF THEY DON'T LIKE IT!
YOU MEAN... PAY-BACK TIME?
THEY WON'T CUT OFF OUR PINKIES, WILL THEY?
THAT'S NOTHING! THEY COULD BURY YOU IN CONCRETE, TOSS YOU INTO TOKYO BAY, AND SELL THE WOMEN TO HONG KONG...!
THIS IS ALL YOUR FAULT! WHAT A RIDICULOUS PROMISE TO MAKE...
MY ULCER'S ACTING UP...
JUST DO A LOT OF SLAPSTICK AND GET SOME EASY LAUGHS.
I OUGHTTA ...
SUE-KICHI.
OH, MR. KARAWARAI, IT'S YOUR TURN TODAY! GOOD LUCK! TRY TO MAKE YAKUZA-FRIENDLY JOKES...
YOU KNOW, I WAS JUST THINKING... I DON'T THINK I CAN GO ON UNTIL I'VE FULLY PREPARED MY CHARACTER.
WHAT ARE YOU SAY-ING?

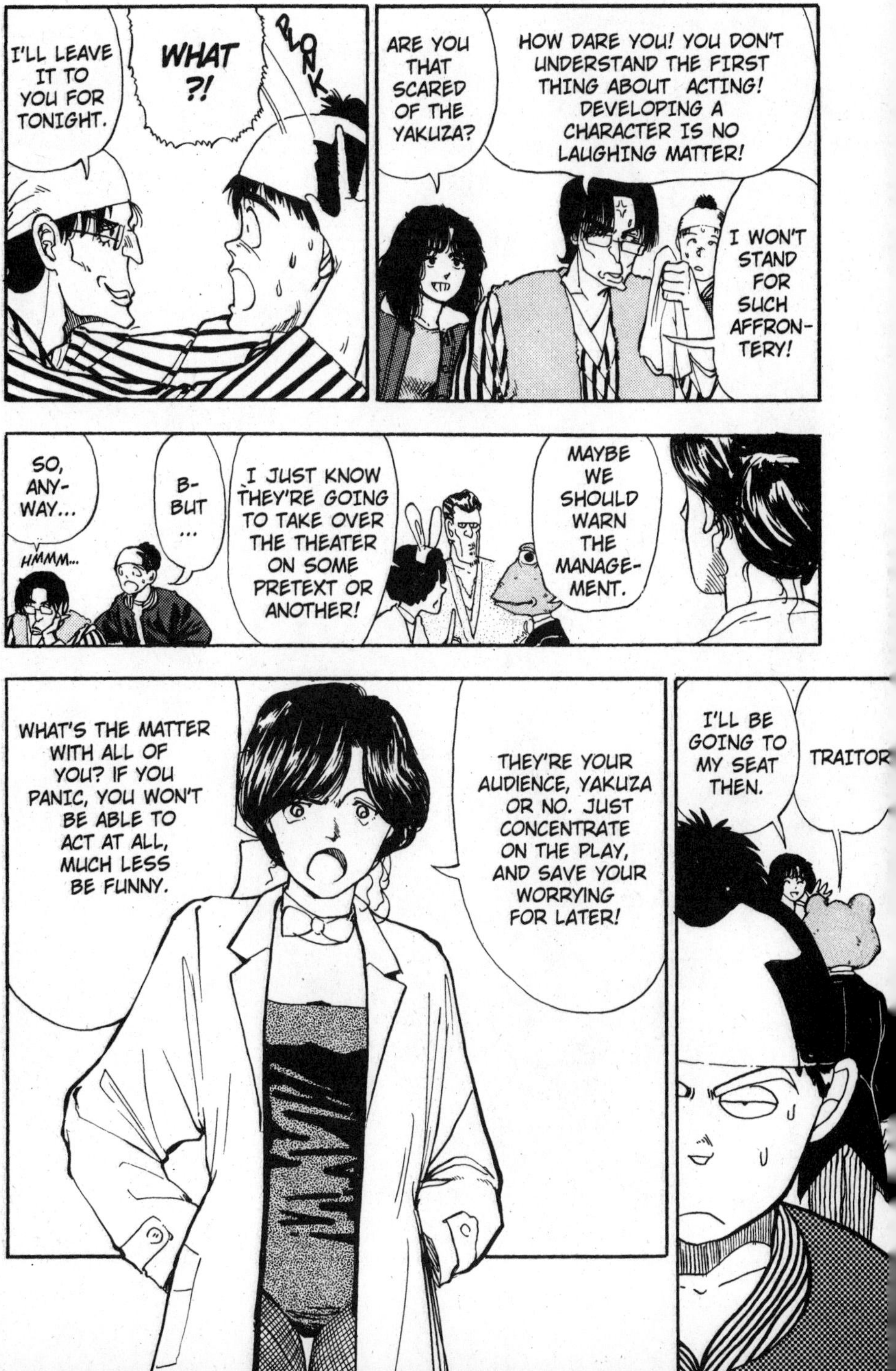
I'LL LEAVE IT TO YOU FOR TONIGHT.
WHAT ?!
BLONK
ARE YOU THAT SCARED OF THE YAKUZA?
HOW DARE YOU! YOU DON'T UNDERSTAND THE FIRST THING ABOUT ACTING! DEVELOPING A CHARACTER IS NO LAUGHING MATTER!
I WON'T STAND FOR SUCH AFFRONTERY!
SO, ANYWAY...
HMMM...
B-BUT ...
I JUST KNOW THEY'RE GOING TO TAKE OVER THE THEATER ON SOME PRETEXT OR ANOTHER!
MAYBE WE SHOULD WARN THE MANAGEMENT.
WHAT'S THE MATTER WITH ALL OF YOU? IF YOU PANIC, YOU WON'T BE ABLE TO ACT AT ALL, MUCH LESS BE FUNNY.
THEY'RE YOUR AUDIENCE, YAKUZA OR NO. JUST CONCENTRATE ON THE PLAY, AND SAVE YOUR WORRYING FOR LATER!
I'LL BE GOING TO MY SEAT THEN.
TRAITOR

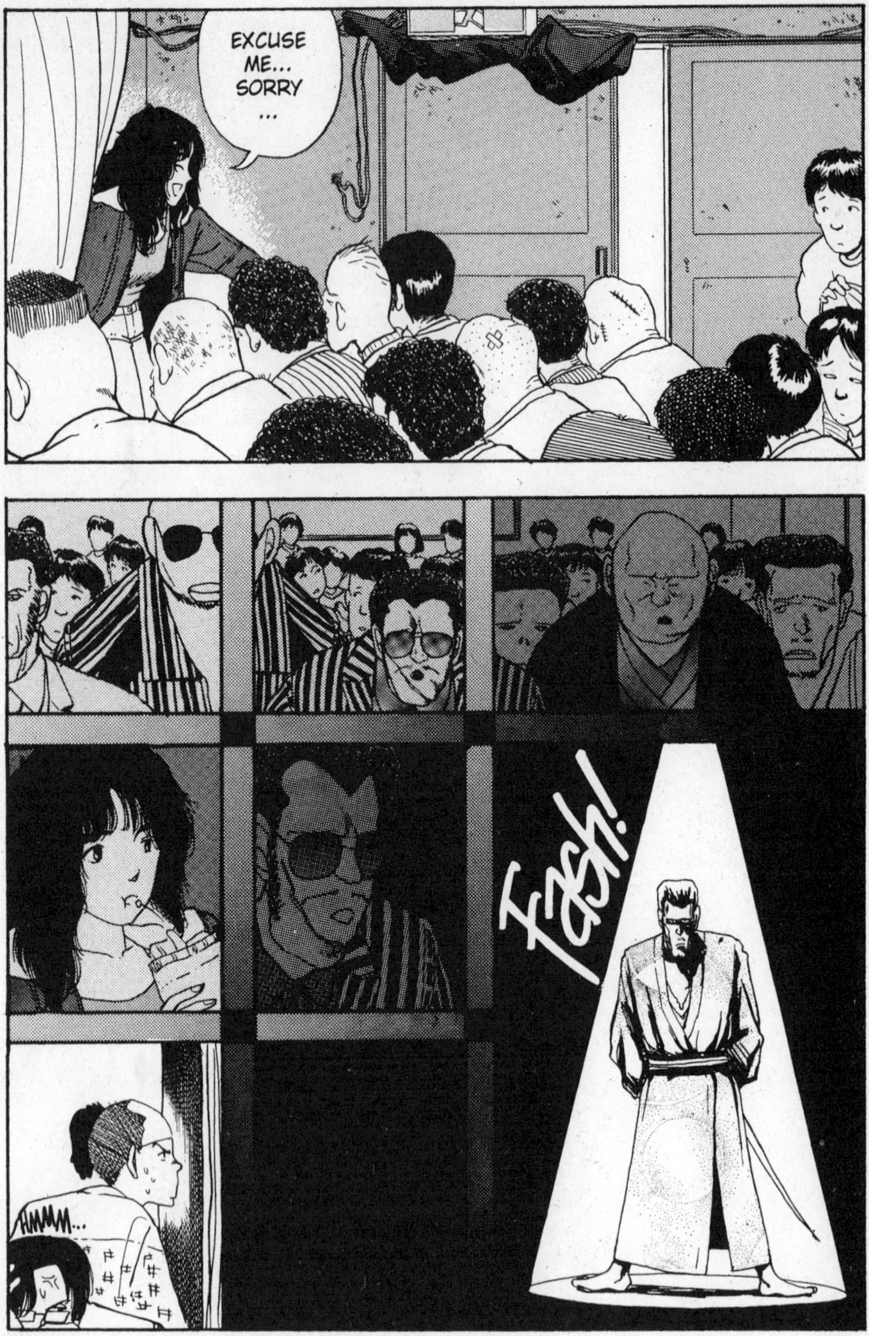
EXCUSE ME... SORRY ...
HMMM...
Fzsh!

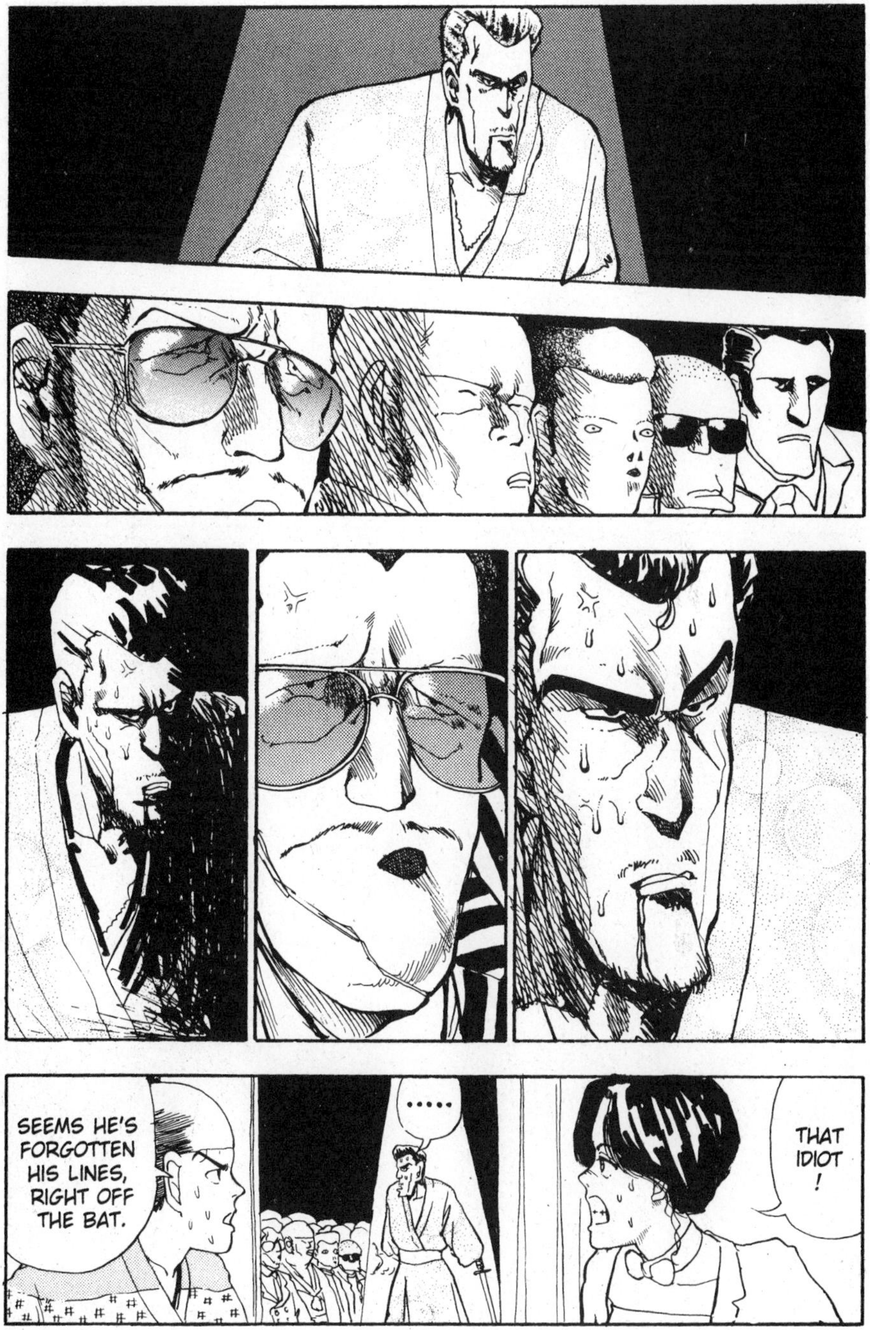
SEEMS HE'S FORGOTTEN HIS LINES, RIGHT OFF THE BAT.
......
THAT IDIOT!

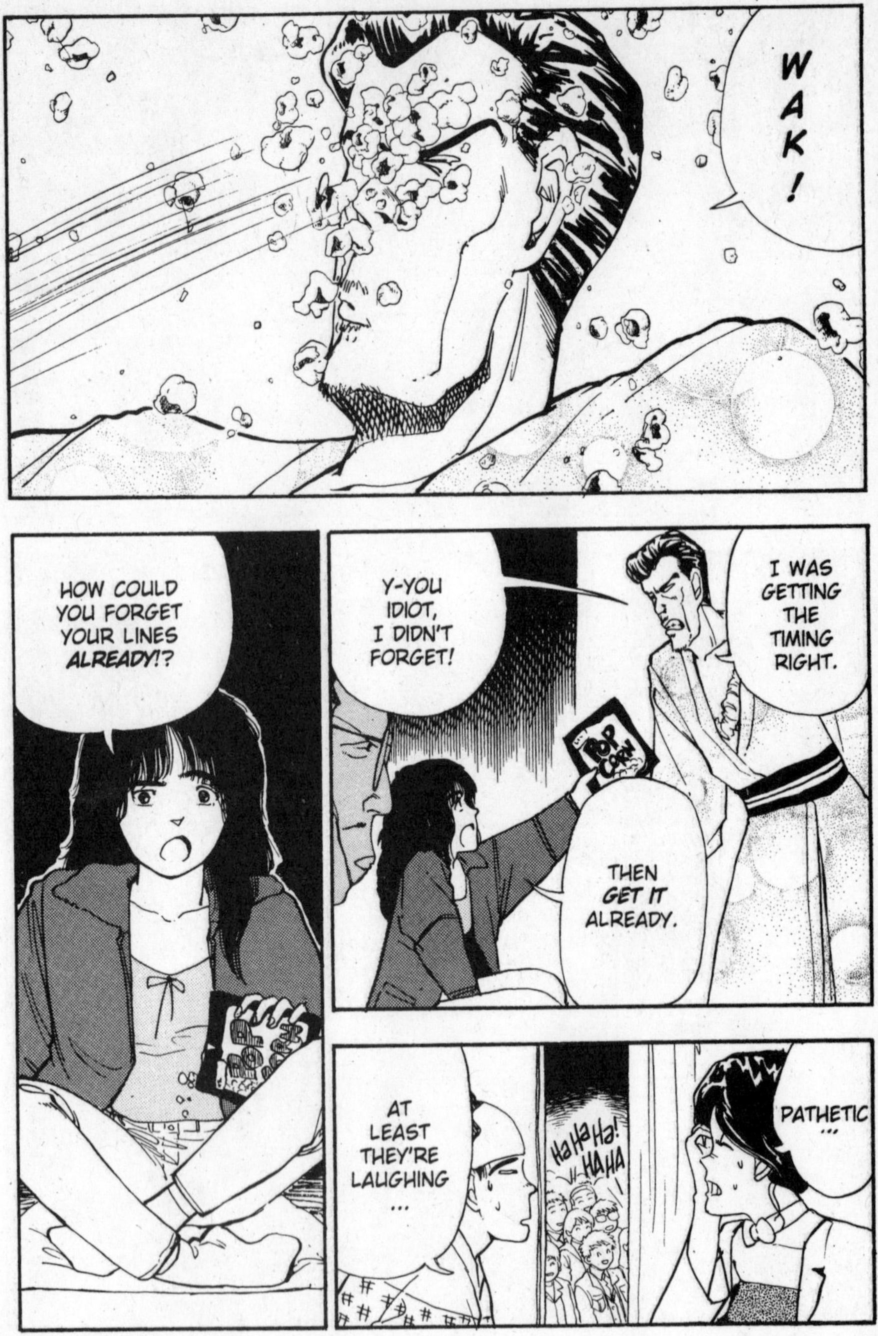
WAK!
HOW COULD YOU FORGET YOUR LINES ALREADY!?
Y-YOU IDIOT, I DIDN'T FORGET!
I WAS GETTING THE TIMING RIGHT.
POP CORN
THEN GET IT ALREADY.
AT LEAST THEY'RE LAUGHING ...
HA HA HA! HA HA
PATHETIC ...

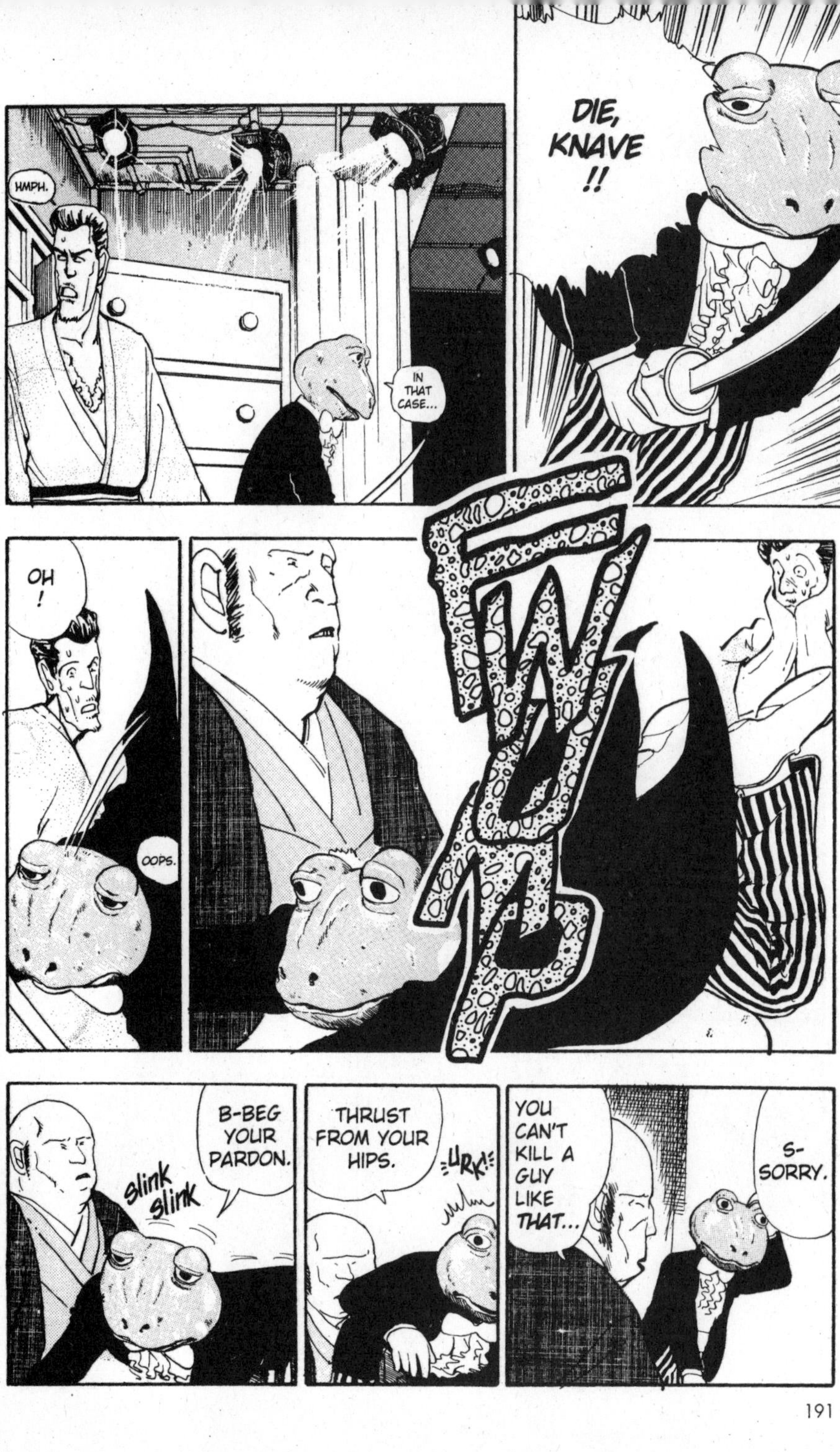
HMPH.
IN THAT CASE...
DIE, KNAVE !!
OH !
OOPS.
B-BEG YOUR PARDON.
slink slink
THRUST FROM YOUR HIPS.
URK!
YOU CAN'T KILL A GUY LIKE THAT...
S-SORRY.

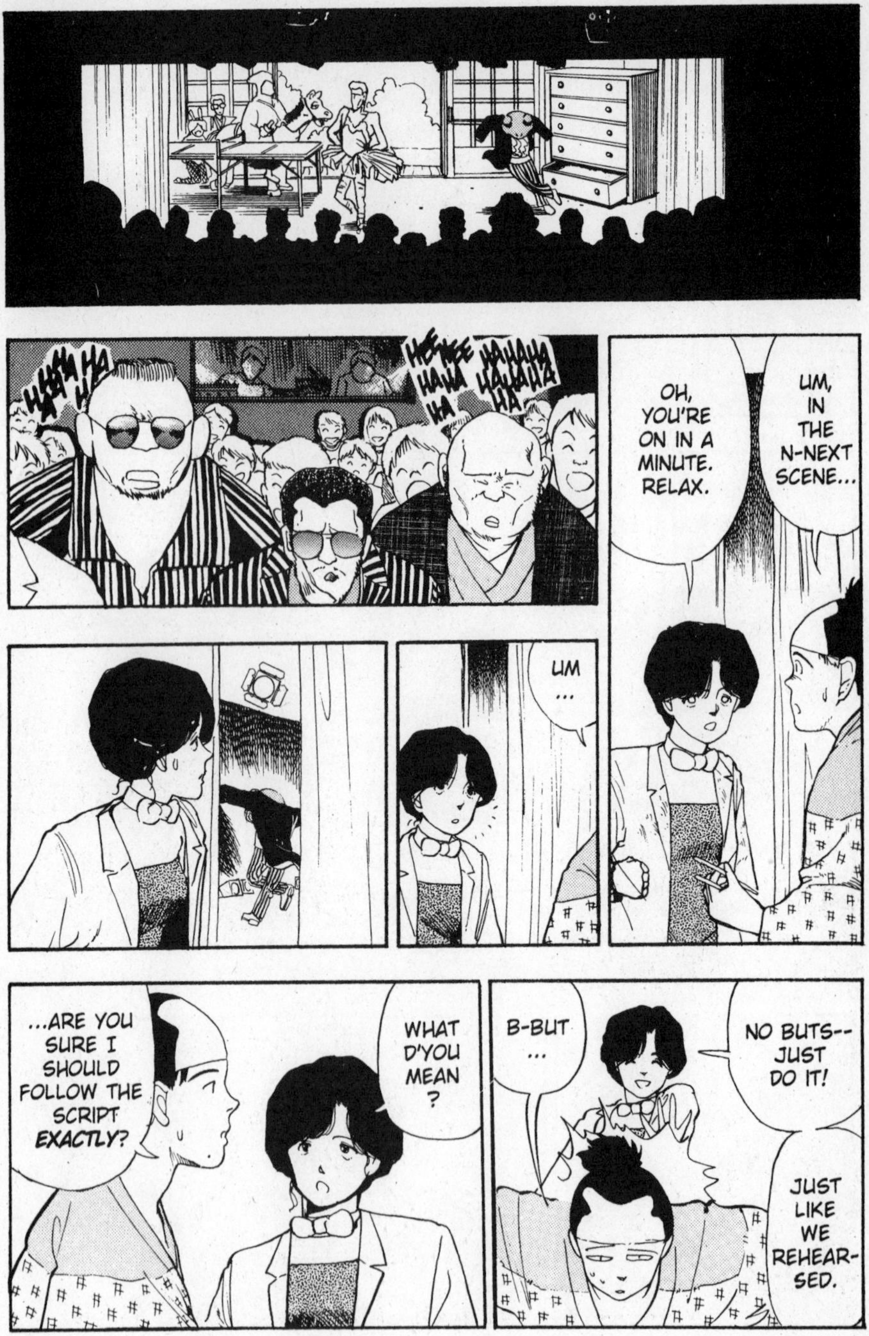
HEE HEE HA HA HA
HAHAHA HAHAHA HA
UM ...
UM, IN THE N-NEXT SCENE...
OH, YOU'RE ON IN A MINUTE. RELAX.
...ARE YOU SURE I SHOULD FOLLOW THE SCRIPT *EXACTLY*?
WHAT D'YOU MEAN ?
B-BUT ...
NO BUTS-- JUST DO IT!
JUST LIKE WE REHEARSED.

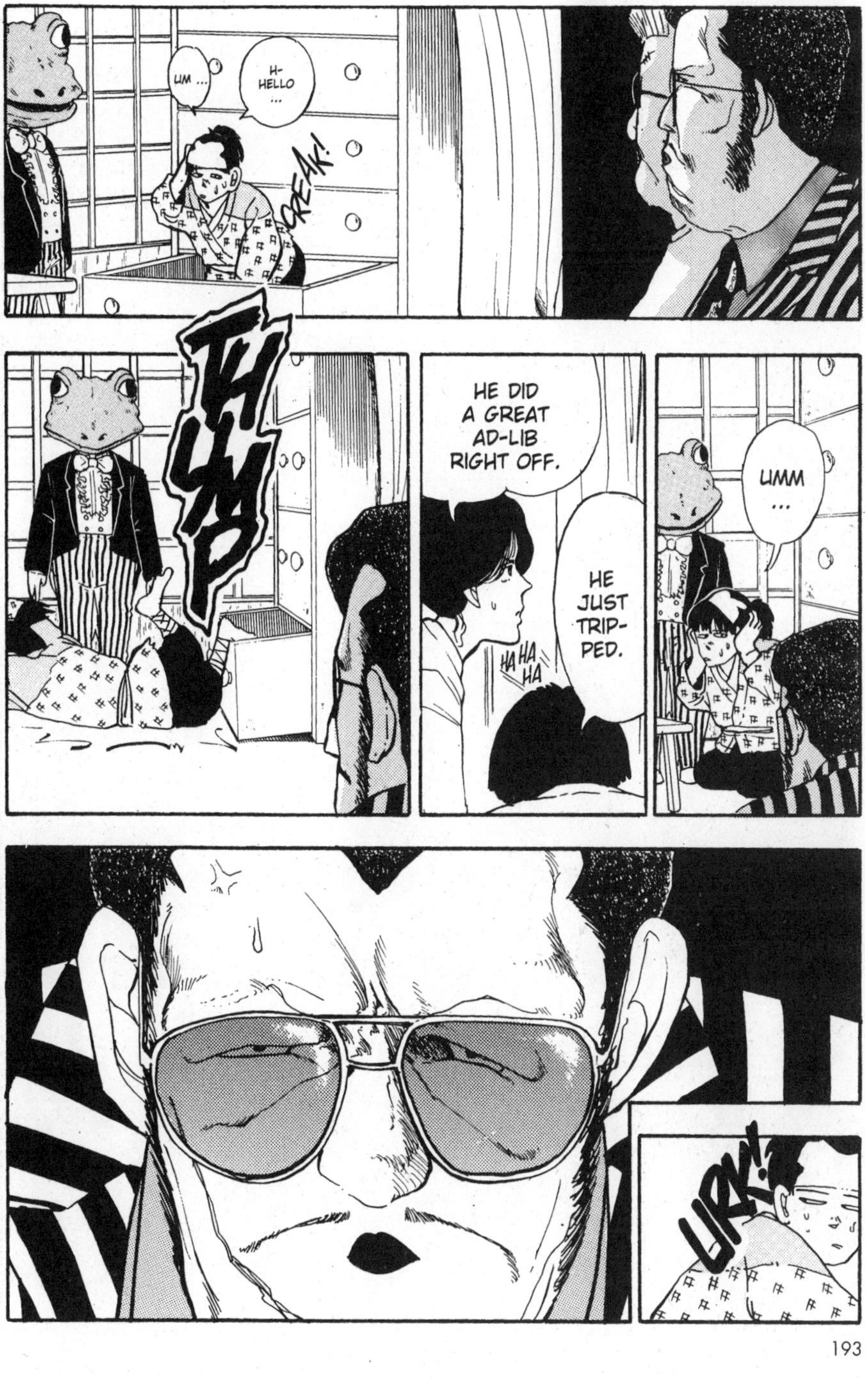
UM ...
H-
HELLO
...
CREAK!
THUMP
HE DID
A GREAT
AD-LIB
RIGHT OFF.
HE
JUST
TRIP-
PED.
HA HA
HA
UMM
...
URK!

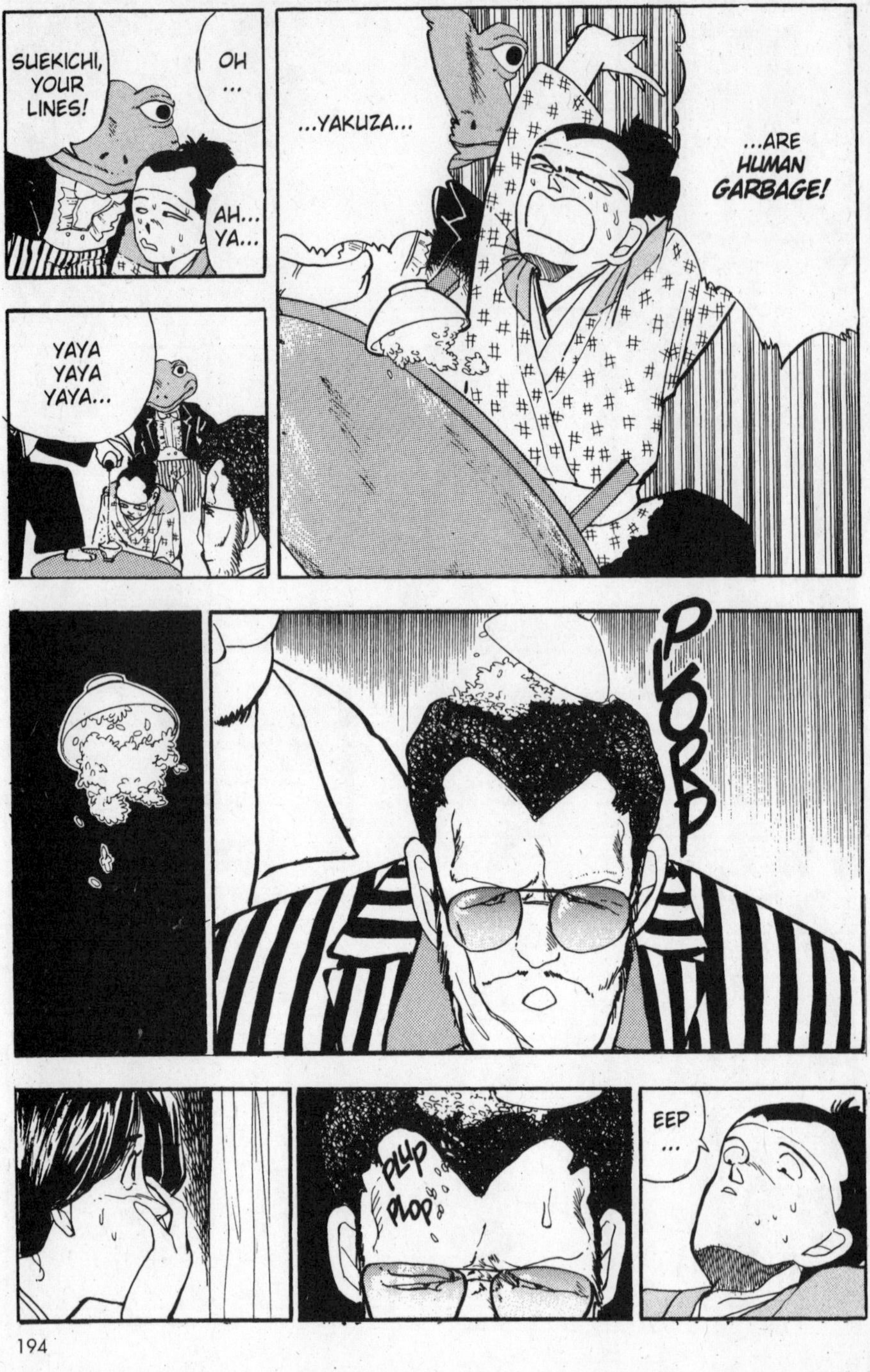
SUEKICHI, YOUR LINES!
OH ...
AH... YA...
YAYA YAYA YAYA...
...YAKUZA...
...ARE HUMAN GARBAGE!
PLOP
PLUP PLOP
EEP ...

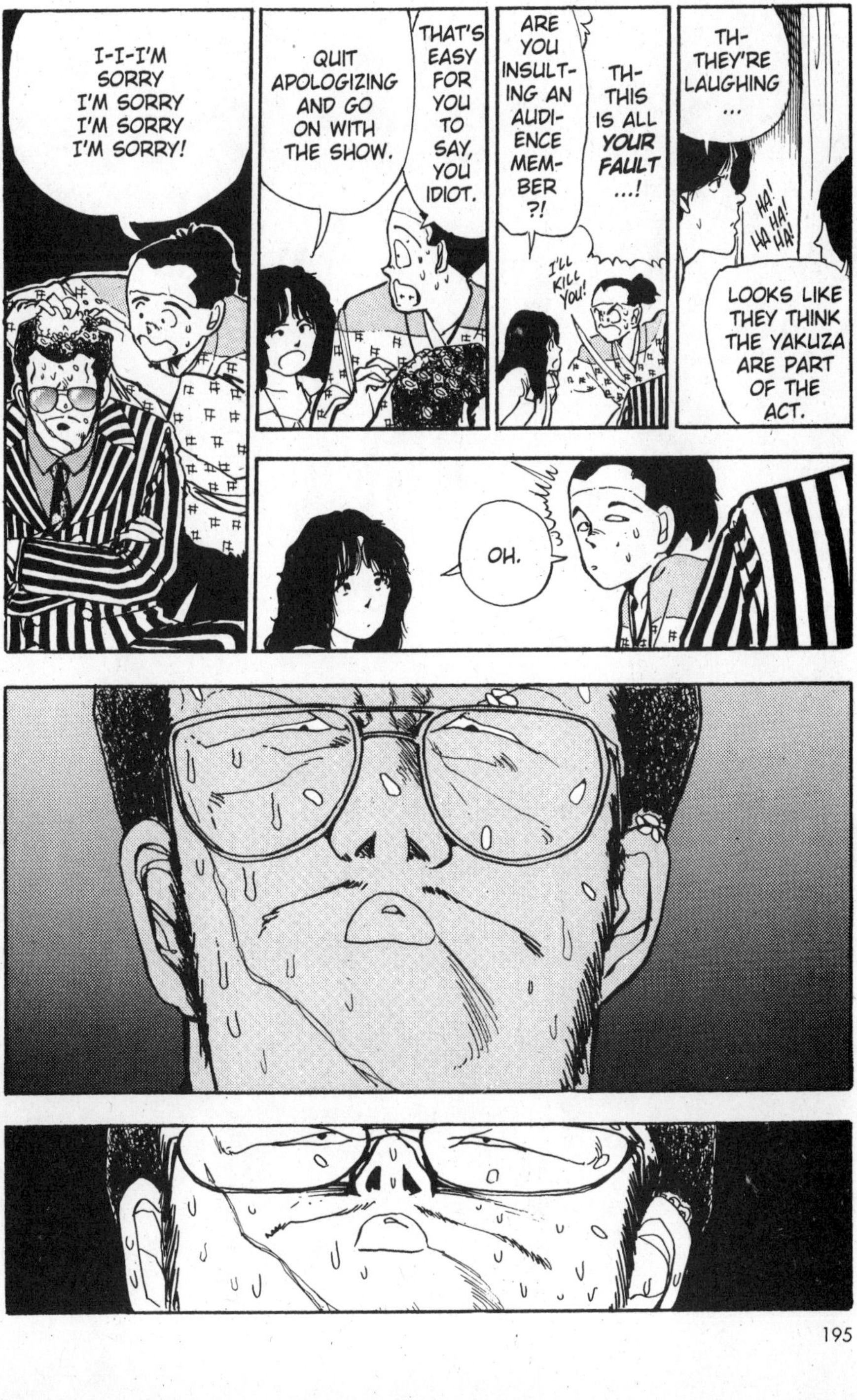
I-I-I'M SORRY I'M SORRY I'M SORRY I'M SORRY!
QUIT APOLOGIZING AND GO ON WITH THE SHOW.
THAT'S EASY FOR YOU TO SAY, YOU IDIOT.
ARE YOU INSULT-ING AN AUDI-ENCE MEM-BER ?!
TH-THIS IS ALL YOUR FAULT ...!
I'LL KILL YOU!
TH-THEY'RE LAUGHING ...
HA! HA! HA! HA!
LOOKS LIKE THEY THINK THE YAKUZA ARE PART OF THE ACT.
OH.

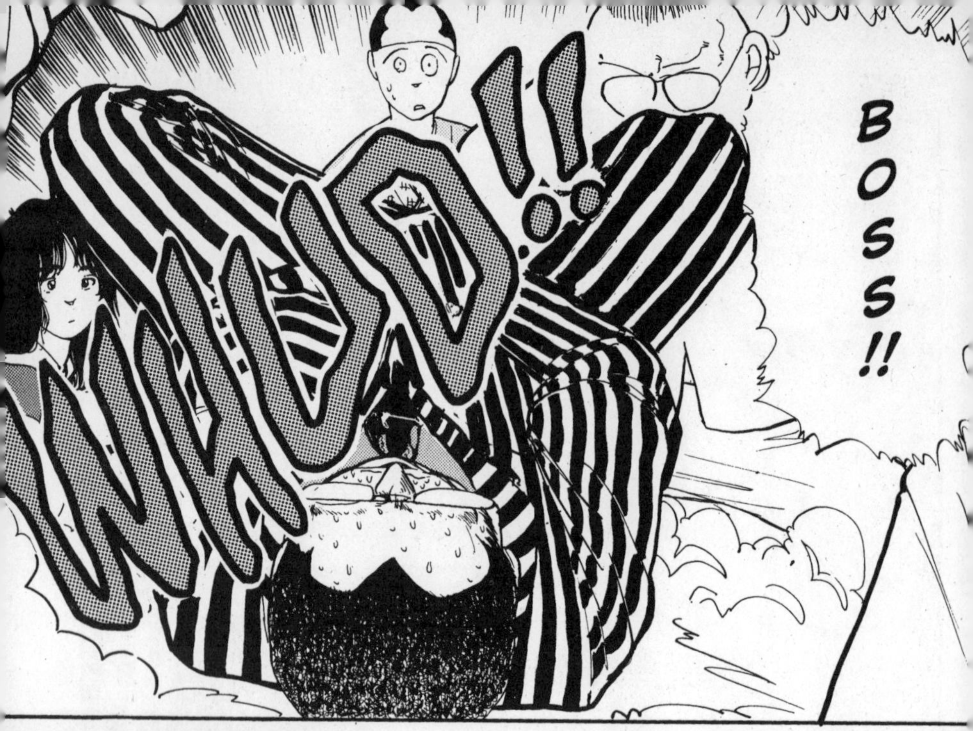
WHUD!!
BOSS!!

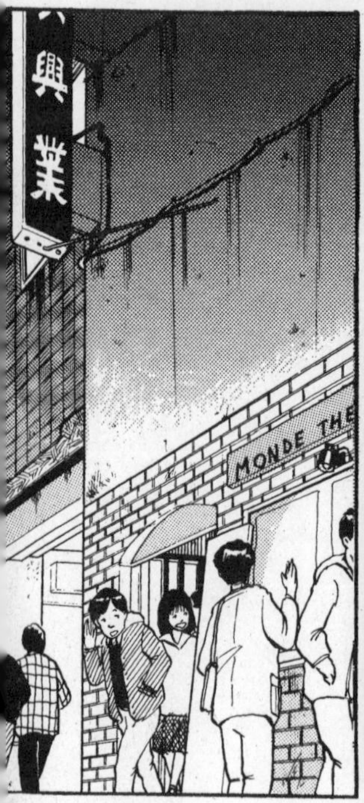
興業
MONDE THE

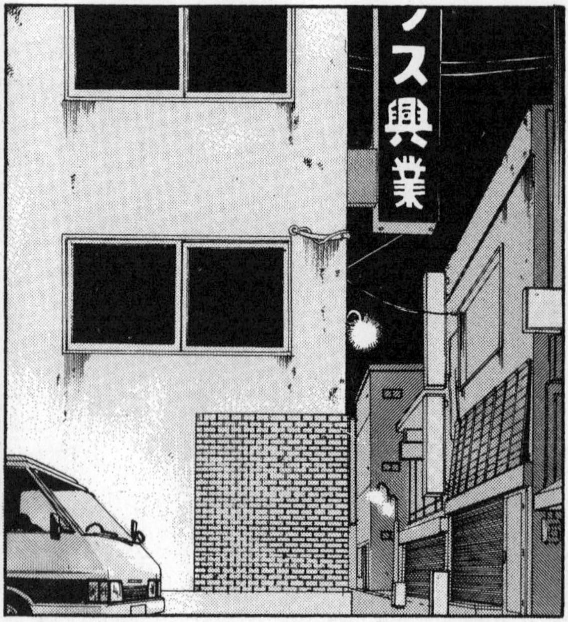
ス興業

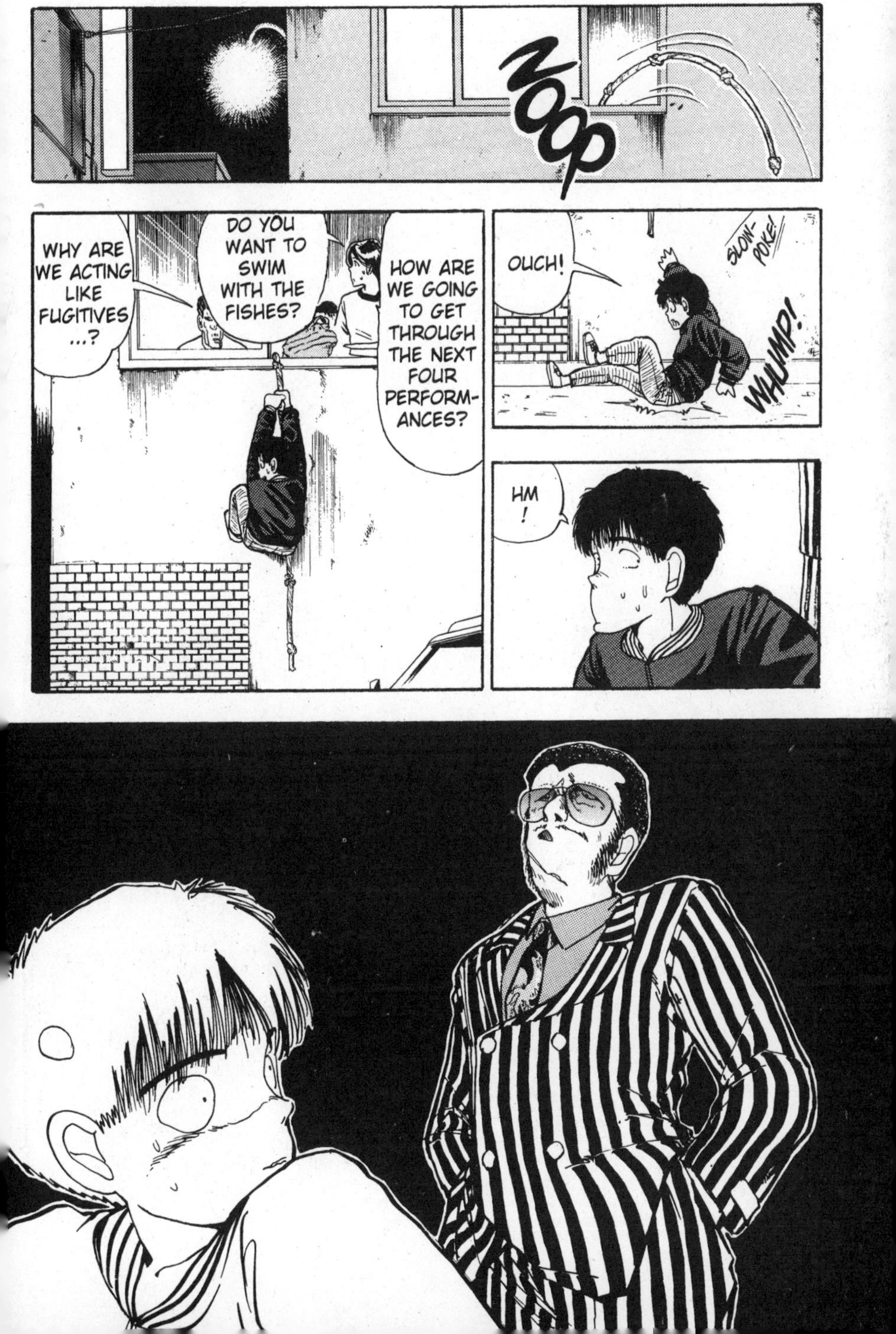
ZOOP
WHY ARE WE ACTING LIKE FUGITIVES ...?
DO YOU WANT TO SWIM WITH THE FISHES?
HOW ARE WE GOING TO GET THROUGH THE NEXT FOUR PERFORM-ANCES?
OUCH!
SLOW-POKE!
WHUMP!
HM!

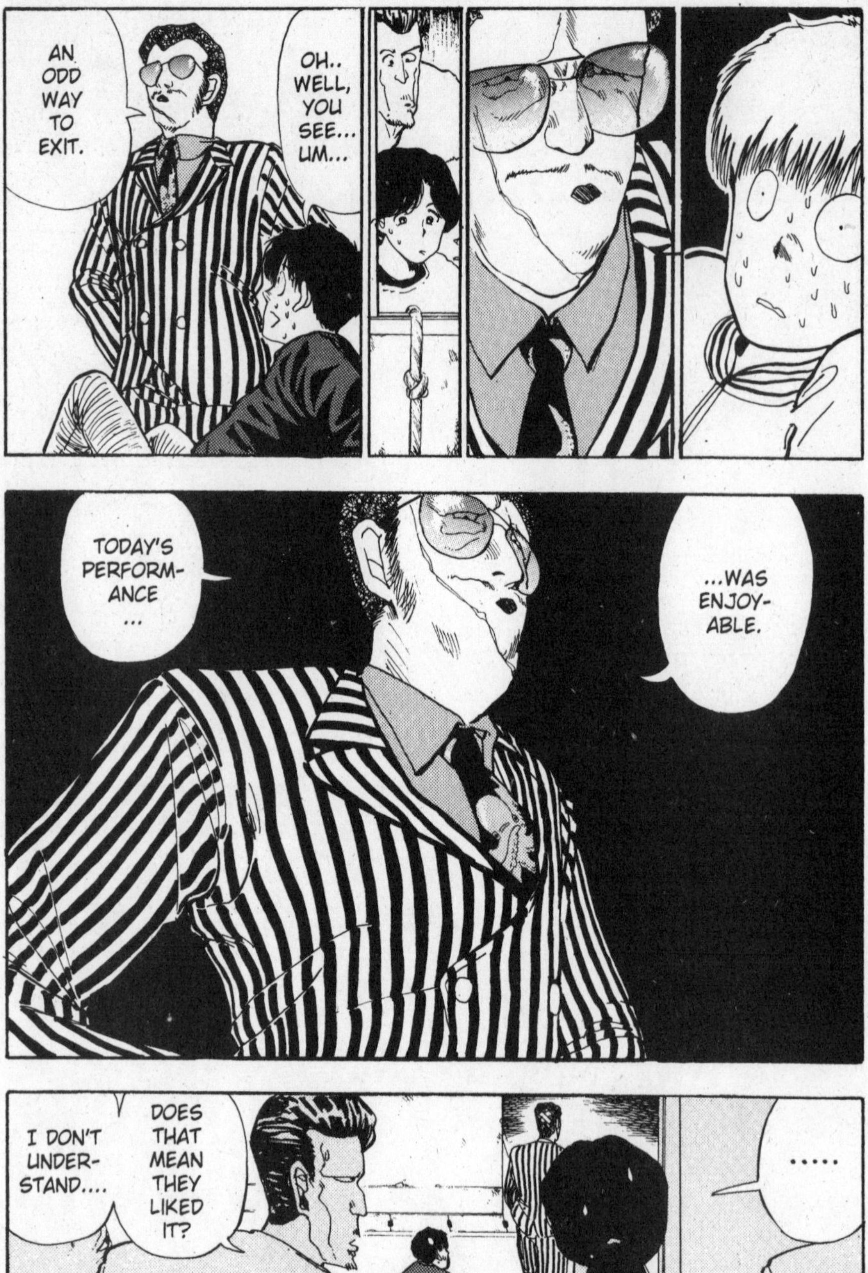
AN ODD WAY TO EXIT.
OH.. WELL, YOU SEE... UM...
TODAY'S PERFORMANCE ...
...WAS ENJOYABLE.
I DON'T UNDERSTAND....
DOES THAT MEAN THEY LIKED IT?
.....

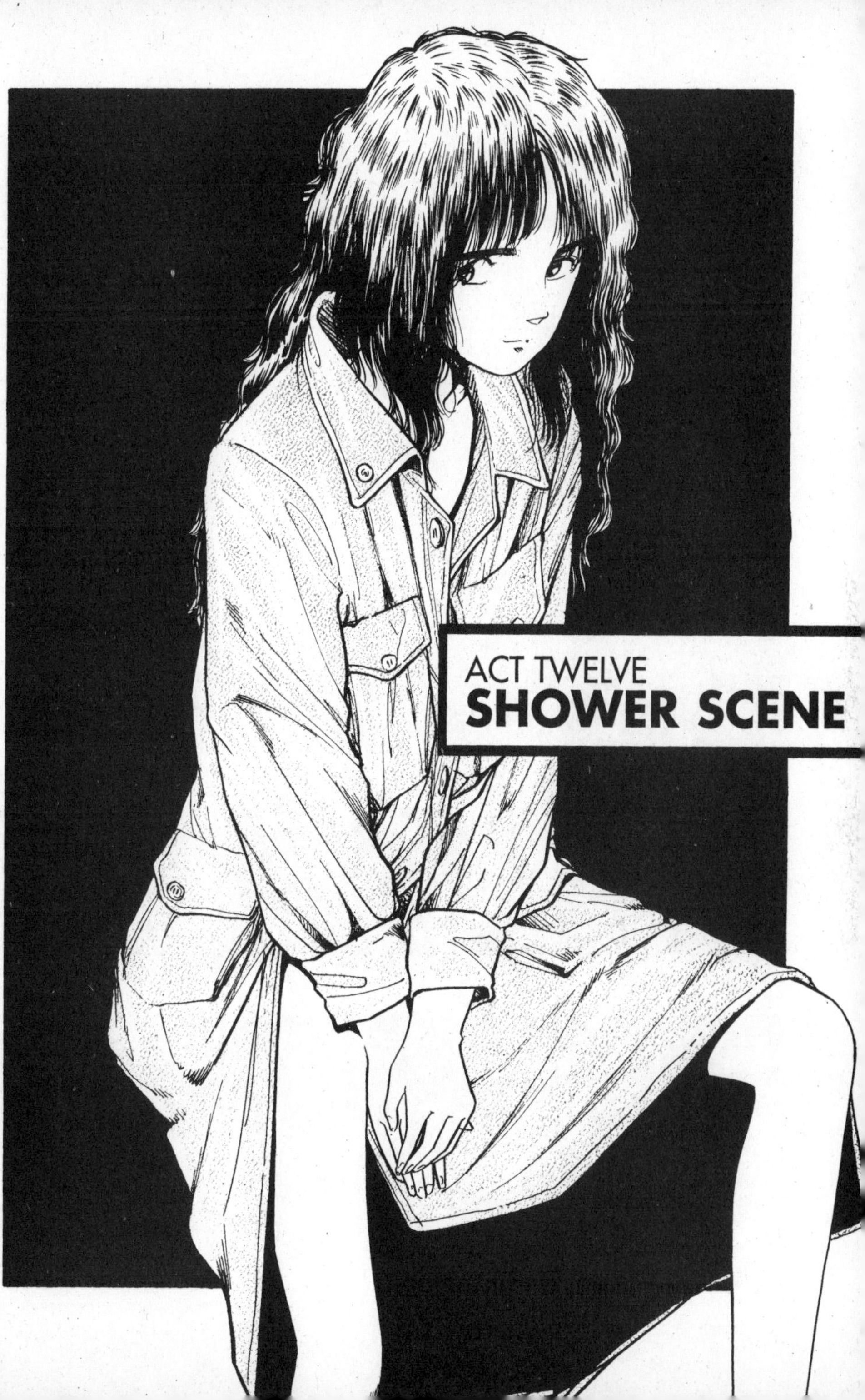

ACT TWELVE
SHOWER SCENE

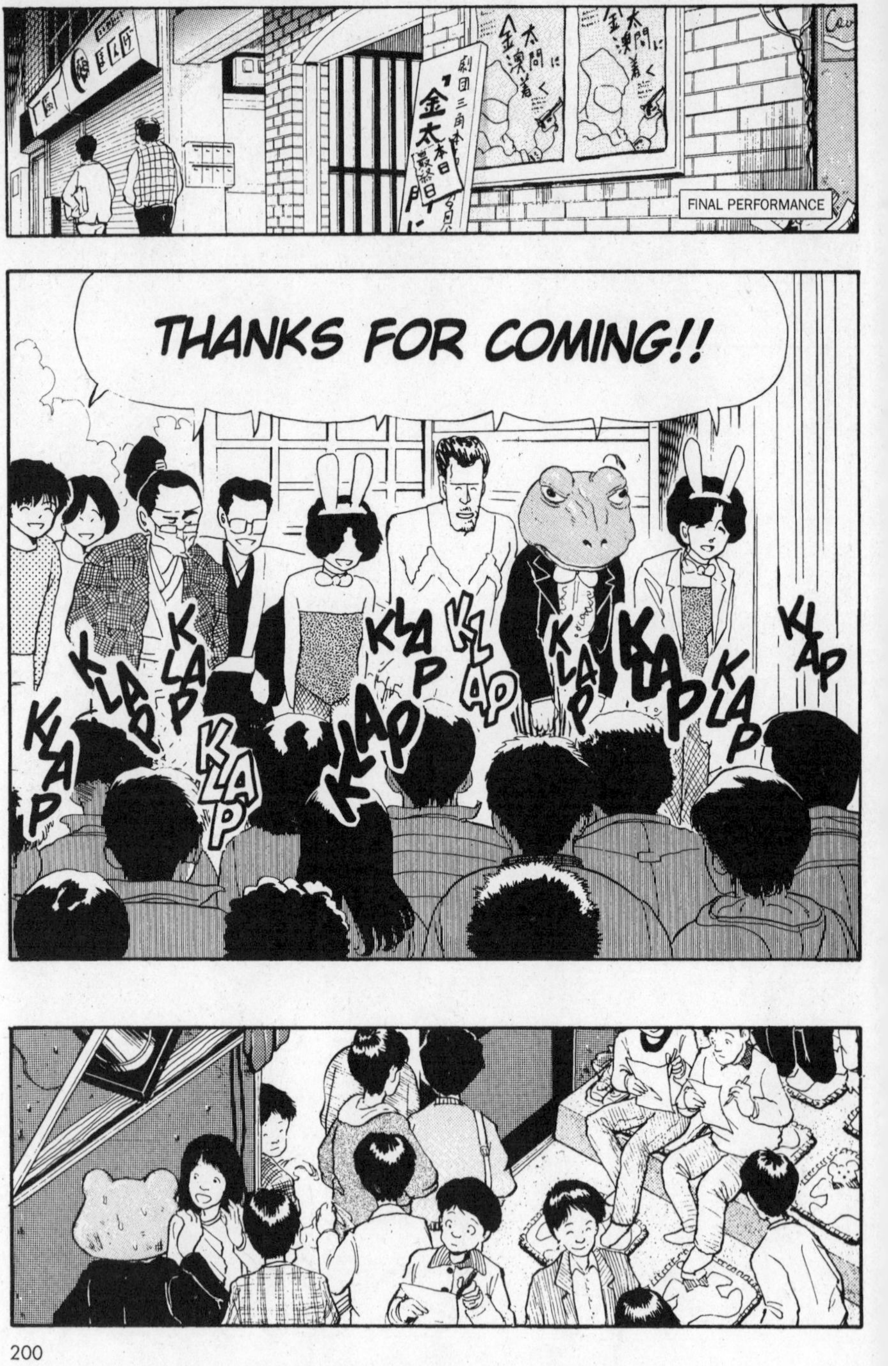
FINAL PERFORMANCE
THANKS FOR COMING!!
KLAP
KLAP
KLAP
KLAP
KLAP
KLAP
KLAP
KLAP
KLAP
KLAP
KLAP
KLAP

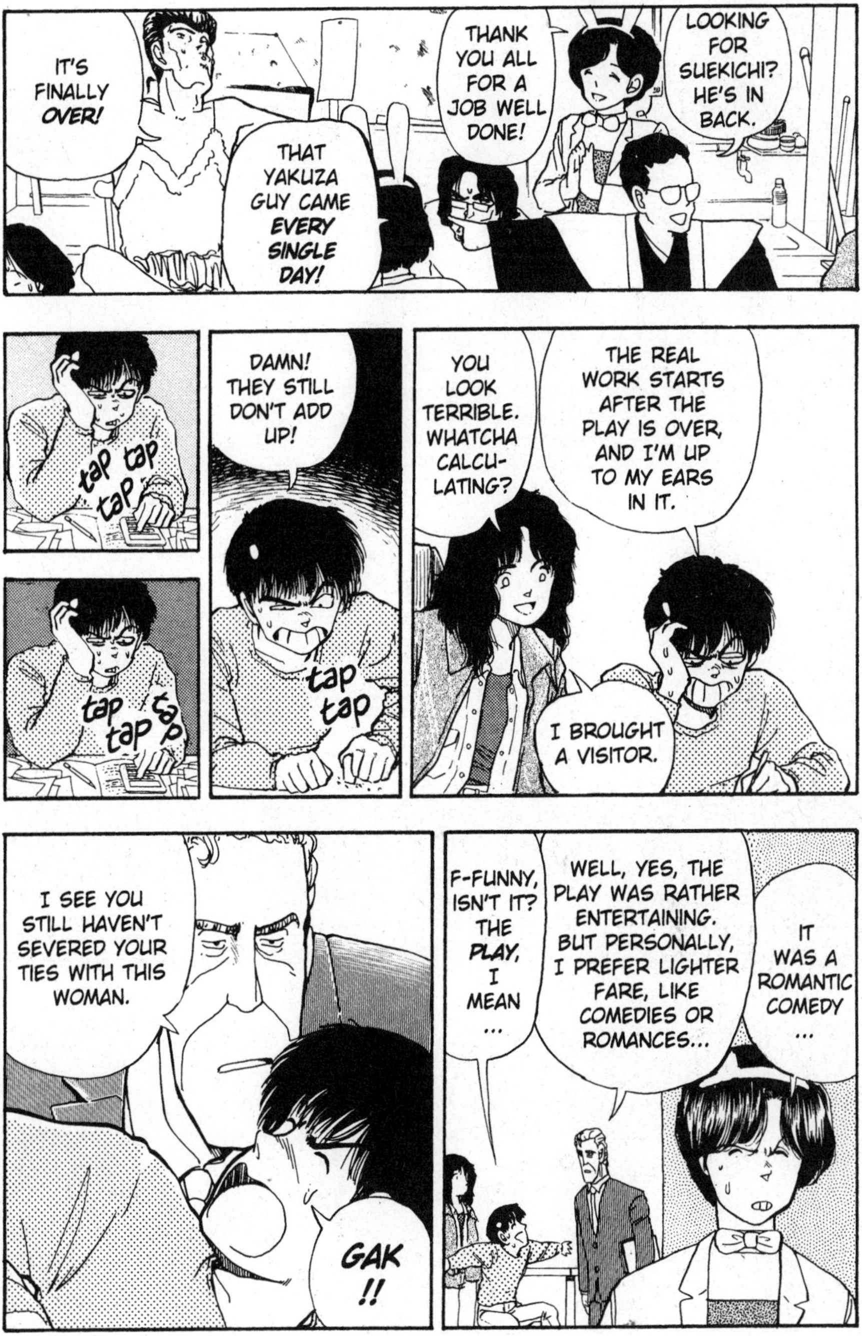
IT'S FINALLY OVER!
THAT YAKUZA GUY CAME EVERY SINGLE DAY!
THANK YOU ALL FOR A JOB WELL DONE!
LOOKING FOR SUEKICHI? HE'S IN BACK.
tap tap tap
tap tap tap
DAMN! THEY STILL DON'T ADD UP!
tap tap
YOU LOOK TERRIBLE. WHATCHA CALCU-LATING?
THE REAL WORK STARTS AFTER THE PLAY IS OVER, AND I'M UP TO MY EARS IN IT.
I BROUGHT A VISITOR.
I SEE YOU STILL HAVEN'T SEVERED YOUR TIES WITH THIS WOMAN.
GAK!!
F-FUNNY, ISN'T IT? THE PLAY, I MEAN...
WELL, YES, THE PLAY WAS RATHER ENTERTAINING. BUT PERSONALLY, I PREFER LIGHTER FARE, LIKE COMEDIES OR ROMANCES...
IT WAS A ROMANTIC COMEDY...

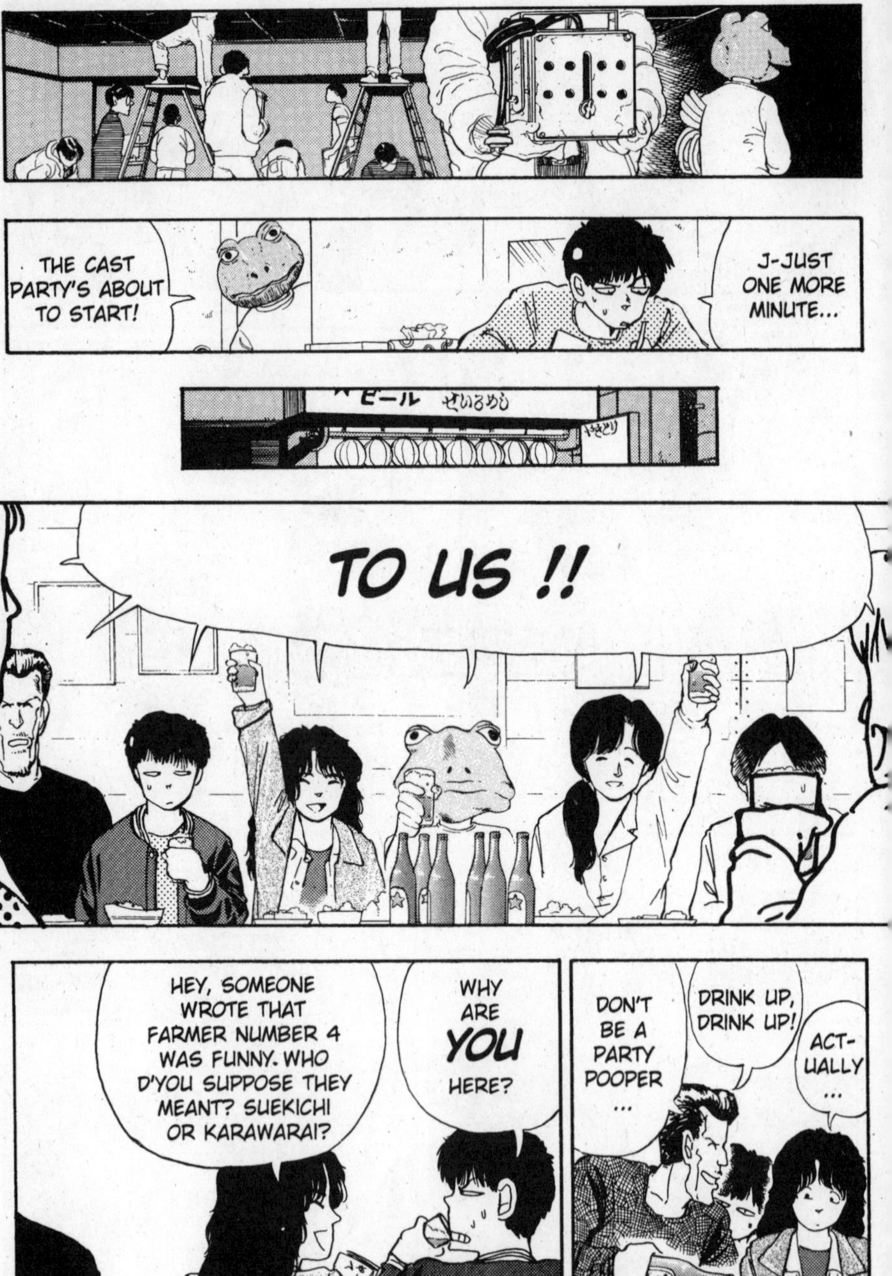
THE CAST PARTY'S ABOUT TO START!
J-JUST ONE MORE MINUTE...
TO US !!
HEY, SOMEONE WROTE THAT FARMER NUMBER 4 WAS FUNNY. WHO D'YOU SUPPOSE THEY MEANT? SUEKICHI OR KARAWARAI?
WHY ARE YOU HERE?
DON'T BE A PARTY POOPER ...
DRINK UP, DRINK UP!
ACT-UALLY ...

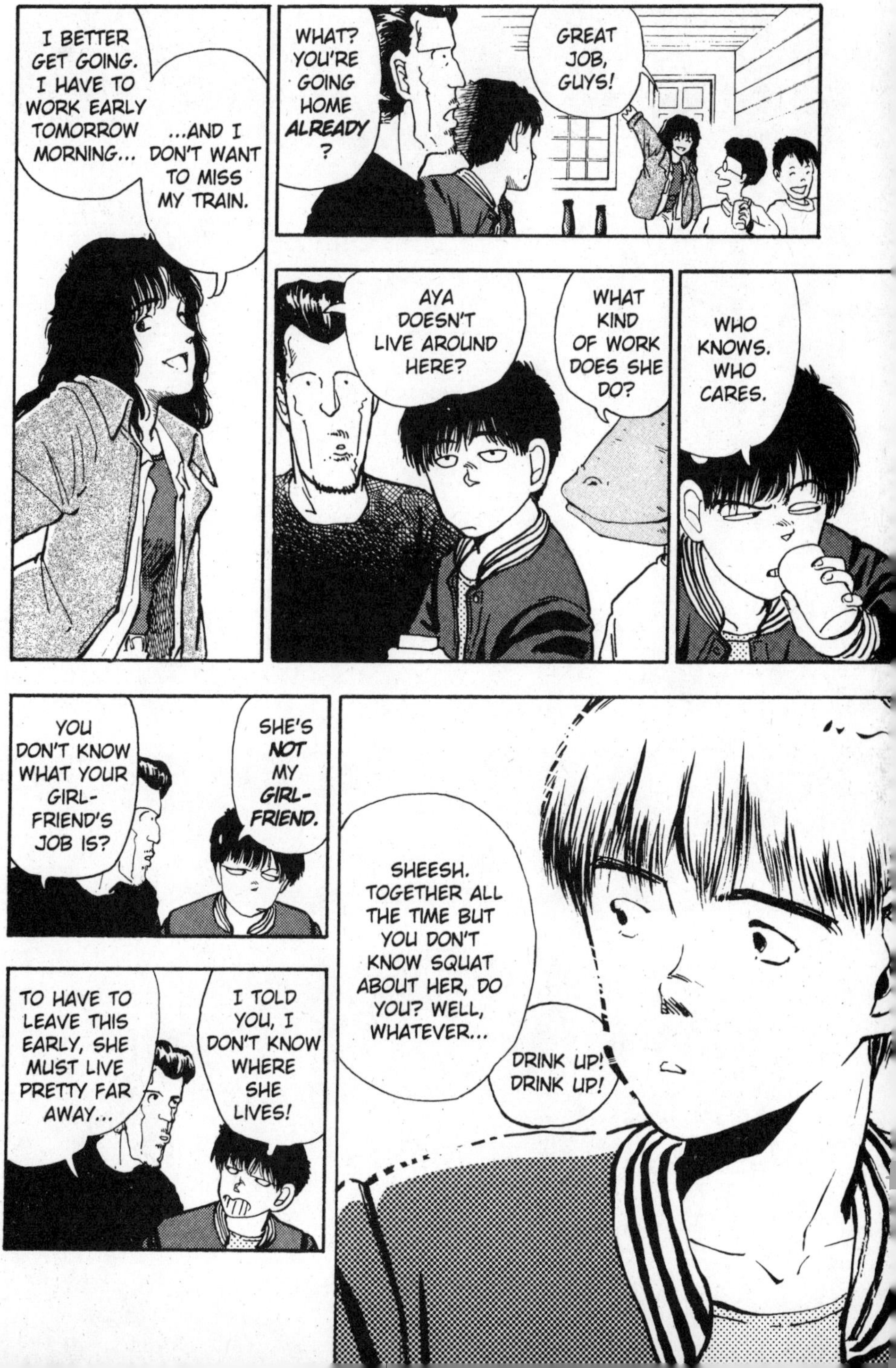
I BETTER GET GOING. I HAVE TO WORK EARLY TOMORROW MORNING...
...AND I DON'T WANT TO MISS MY TRAIN.
WHAT? YOU'RE GOING HOME ALREADY?
GREAT JOB, GUYS!
AYA DOESN'T LIVE AROUND HERE?
WHAT KIND OF WORK DOES SHE DO?
WHO KNOWS. WHO CARES.
YOU DON'T KNOW WHAT YOUR GIRLFRIEND'S JOB IS?
SHE'S NOT MY GIRLFRIEND.
TO HAVE TO LEAVE THIS EARLY, SHE MUST LIVE PRETTY FAR AWAY...
I TOLD YOU, I DON'T KNOW WHERE SHE LIVES!
SHEESH. TOGETHER ALL THE TIME BUT YOU DON'T KNOW SQUAT ABOUT HER, DO YOU? WELL, WHATEVER...
DRINK UP! DRINK UP!

MAN, ARE YOU EVER WASTED.

JUS' SHUDDUP 'N' POUR, IKEZU.

ARE YOU A BAD DRUNK, SUEKICHI?

MS. SHIMO-MURA!!

YES?

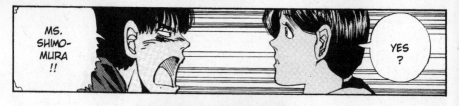

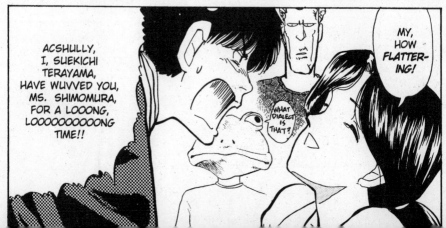

ACSHULLY, I, SUEKICHI TERAYAMA, HAVE WUVVED YOU, MS. SHIMOMURA, FOR A LOOONG, LOOOOOOOOOONG TIME!!

WHAT DIALECT IS THAT?

MY, HOW FLATTER-ING!

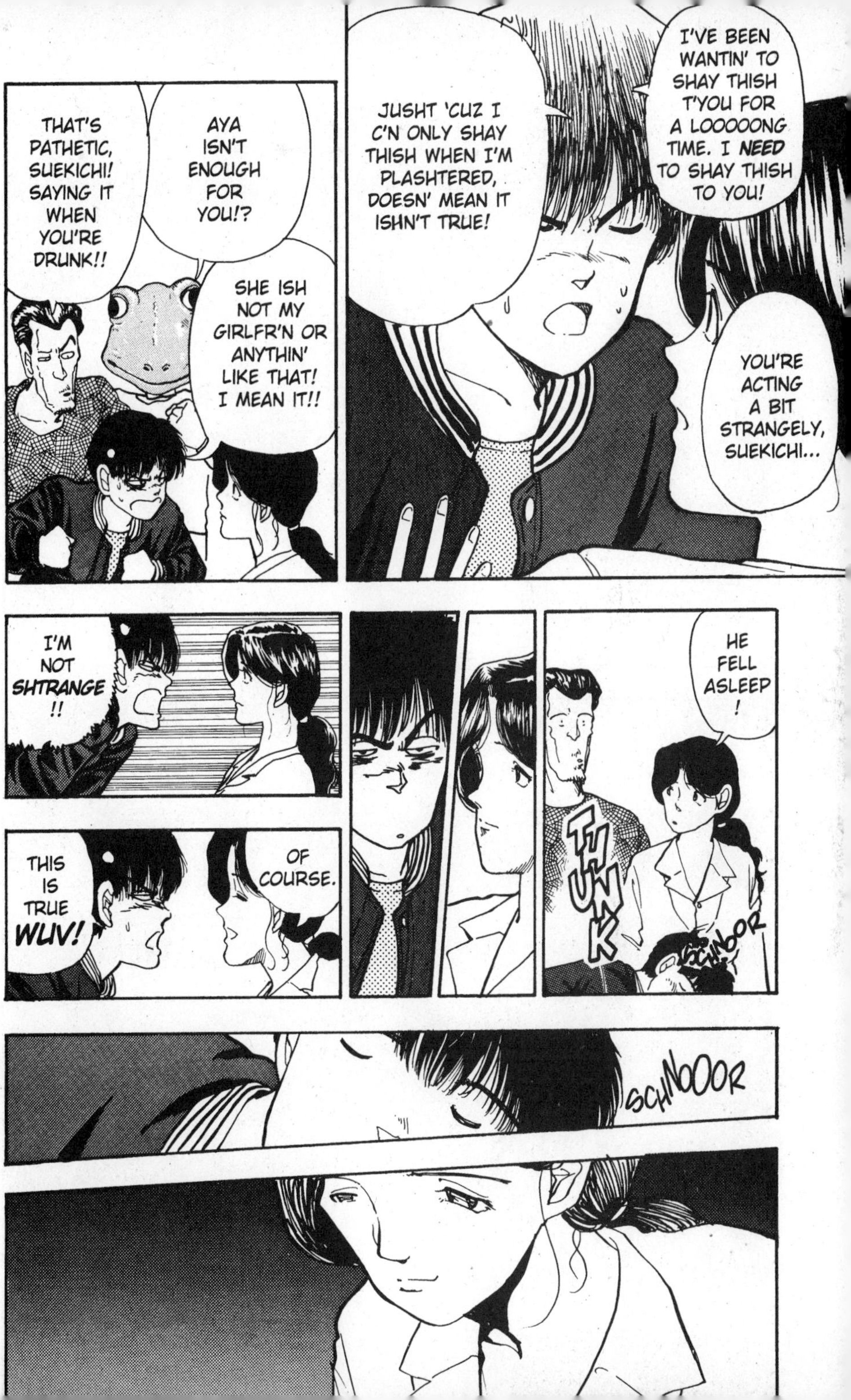
THAT'S PATHETIC, SUEKICHI! SAYING IT WHEN YOU'RE DRUNK!!
AYA ISN'T ENOUGH FOR YOU!?
SHE ISH NOT MY GIRLFR'N OR ANYTHIN' LIKE THAT! I MEAN IT!!
JUSHT 'CUZ I C'N ONLY SHAY THISH WHEN I'M PLASHTERED, DOESN' MEAN IT ISHN'T TRUE!
I'VE BEEN WANTIN' TO SHAY THISH T'YOU FOR A LOOOOONG TIME. I NEED TO SHAY THISH TO YOU!
YOU'RE ACTING A BIT STRANGELY, SUEKICHI...
I'M NOT SHTRANGE!!
THIS IS TRUE WUV!
OF COURSE.
HE FELL ASLEEP!
THUNK
SCHNOOOR
SCHNOOOR

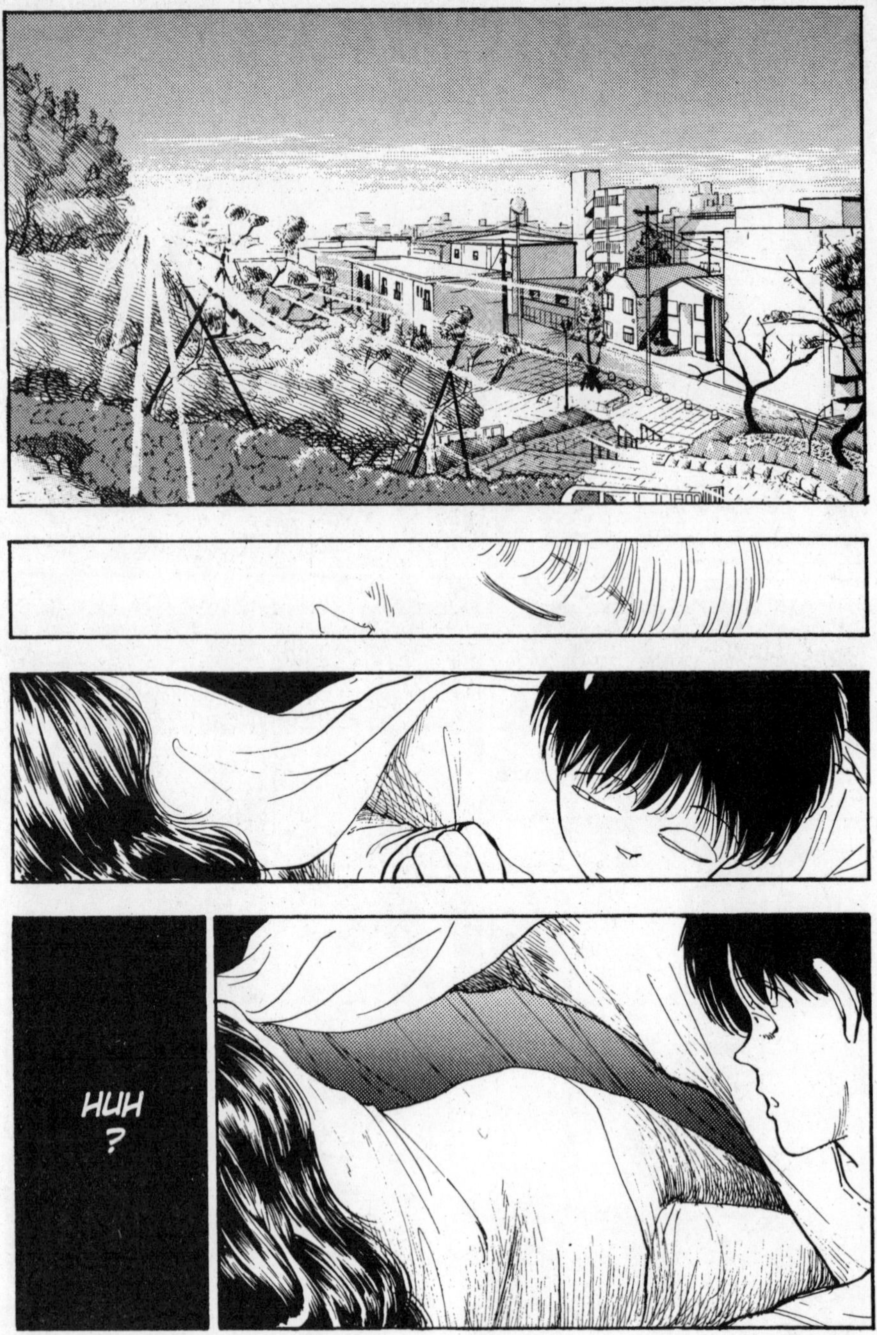
HUH ?

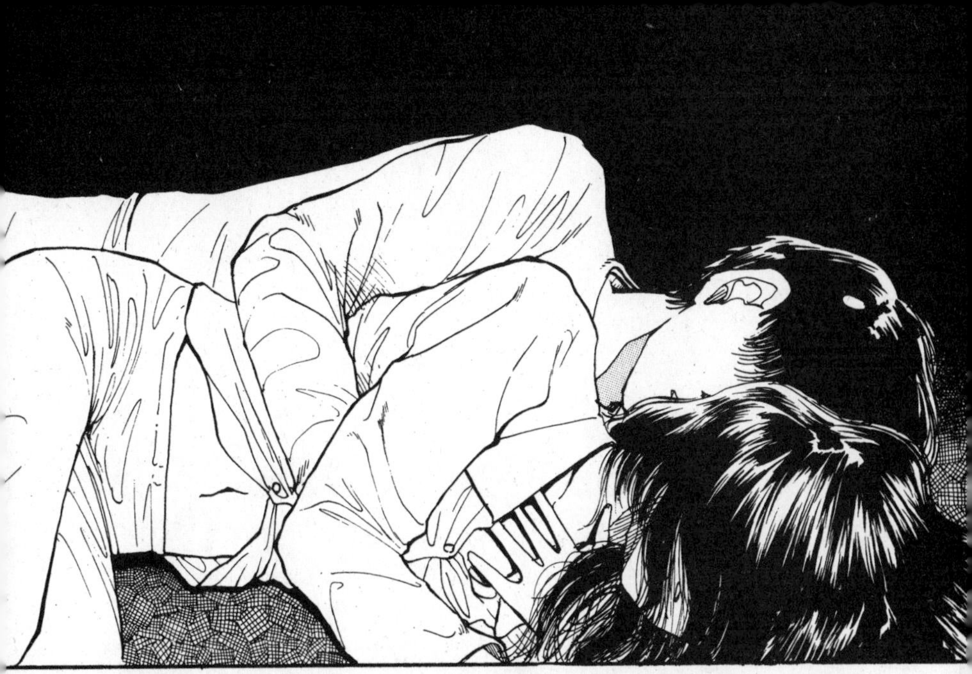

OH...
AYA'S HERE
AGAIN....

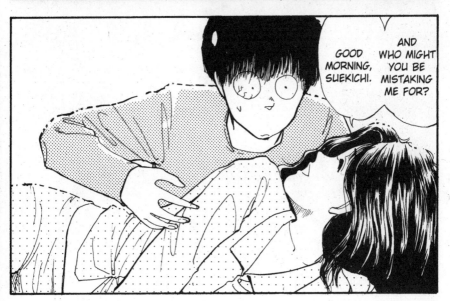

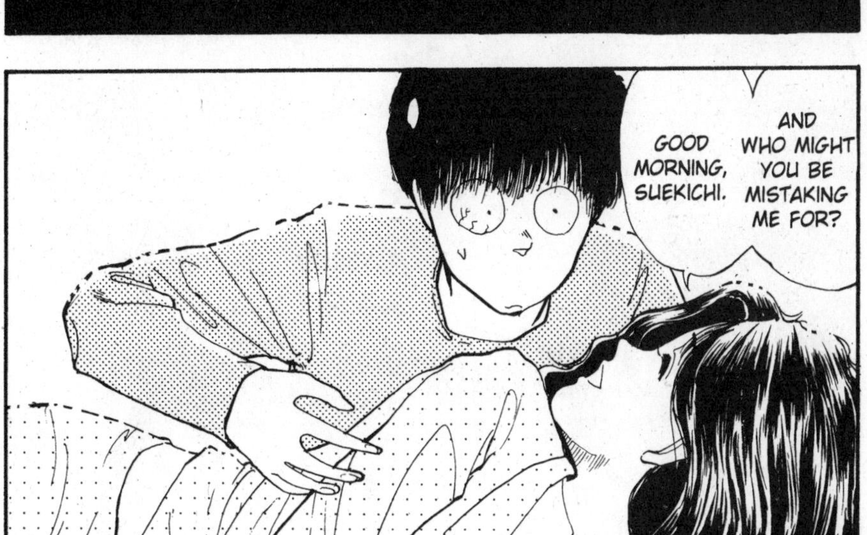
GOOD MORNING, SUEKICHI.
AND WHO MIGHT YOU BE MISTAKING ME FOR?

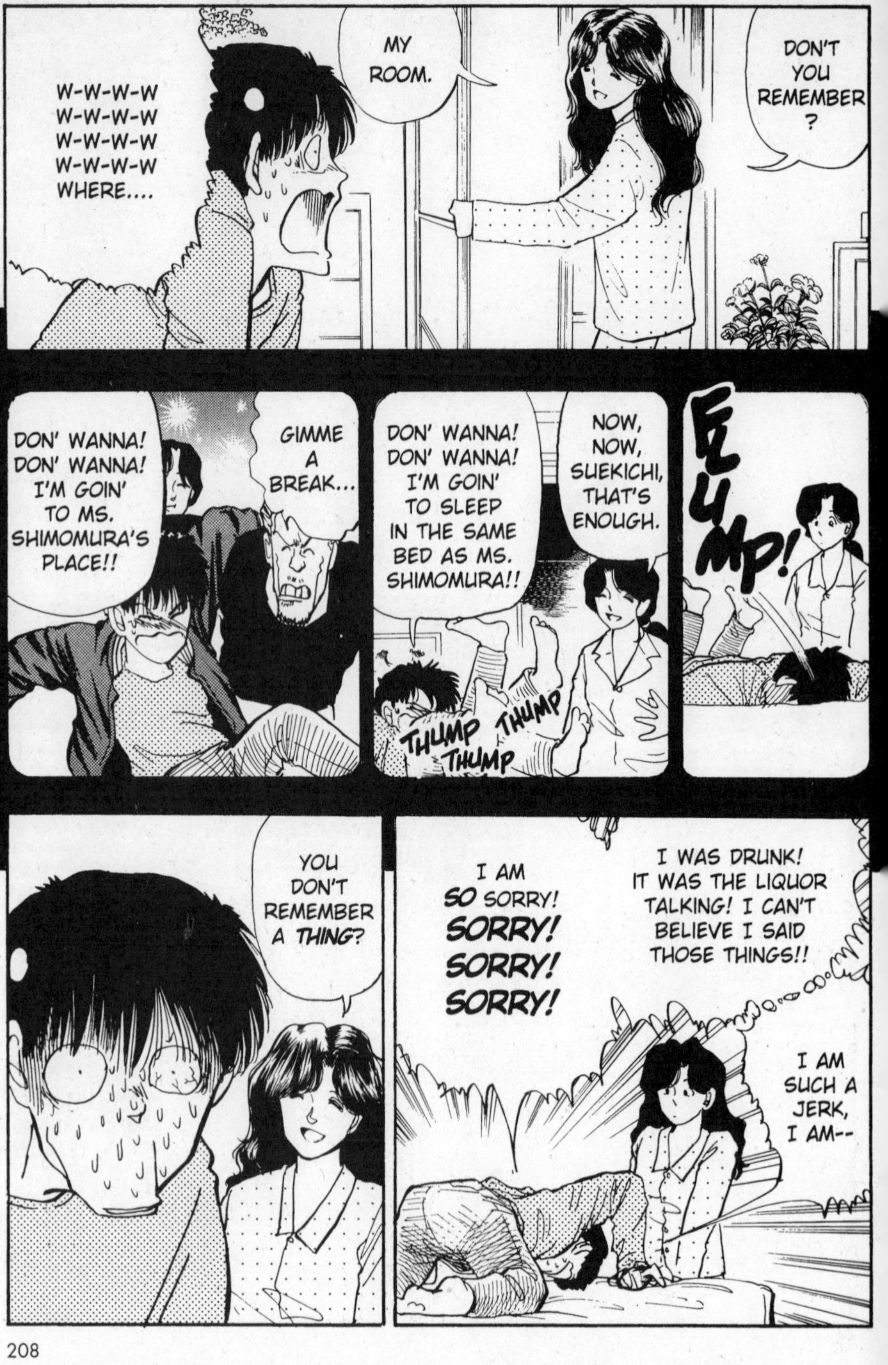
W-W-W-W W-W-W-W W-W-W-W W-W-W-W WHERE....
MY ROOM.
DON'T YOU REMEMBER ?
DON' WANNA! DON' WANNA! I'M GOIN' TO MS. SHIMOMURA'S PLACE!!
GIMME A BREAK...
DON' WANNA! DON' WANNA! I'M GOIN' TO SLEEP IN THE SAME BED AS MS. SHIMOMURA!!
NOW, NOW, SUEKICHI, THAT'S ENOUGH.
THUMP THUMP THUMP
FLUMP!
YOU DON'T REMEMBER A THING?
I AM SO SORRY! SORRY! SORRY! SORRY!
I WAS DRUNK! IT WAS THE LIQUOR TALKING! I CAN'T BELIEVE I SAID THOSE THINGS!!
I AM SUCH A JERK, I AM--

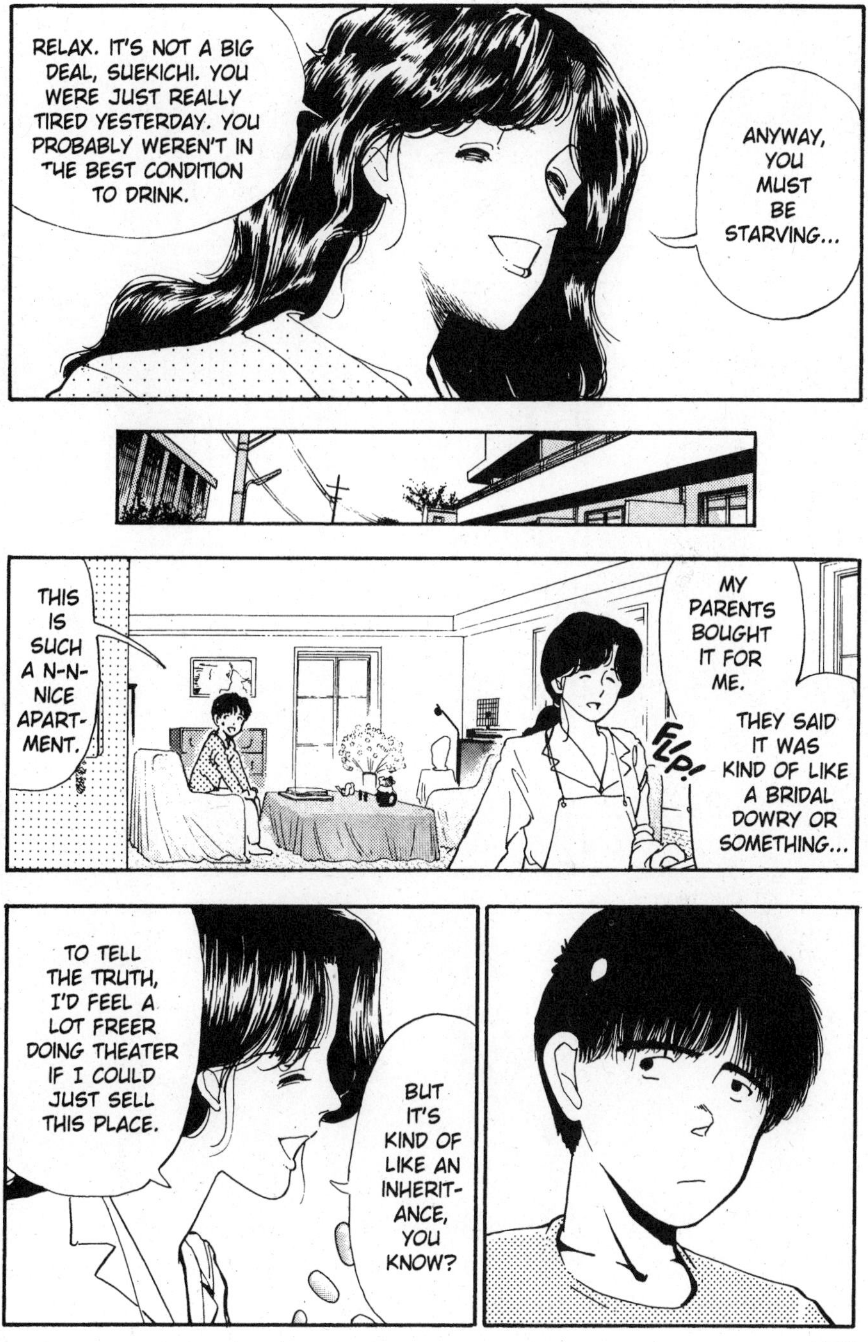
RELAX. IT'S NOT A BIG DEAL, SUEKICHI. YOU WERE JUST REALLY TIRED YESTERDAY. YOU PROBABLY WEREN'T IN THE BEST CONDITION TO DRINK.
ANYWAY, YOU MUST BE STARVING...
THIS IS SUCH A N-N-NICE APARTMENT.
MY PARENTS BOUGHT IT FOR ME.
FLIP!
THEY SAID IT WAS KIND OF LIKE A BRIDAL DOWRY OR SOMETHING...
TO TELL THE TRUTH, I'D FEEL A LOT FREER DOING THEATER IF I COULD JUST SELL THIS PLACE.
BUT IT'S KIND OF LIKE AN INHERITANCE, YOU KNOW?

TH-THANK YOU FOR BREAKFAST.

I'M GONNA JUMP INTO THE SHOWER, OKAY?

FSSHHH

DOES SHE EXPECT ME TO ...?

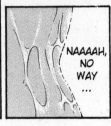

NAAAAH, NO WAY ...

WHY DON'T YOU TAKE A SHOWER, TOO, SUEKICHI. IT'S SO *REFRESHING!*

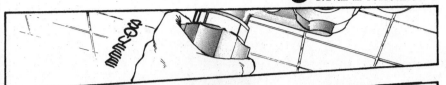

SHE BRINGS ME TO HER PLACE...

THEN SHE TAKES A SHOWER...

NOW SHE INVITES *ME* TO TAKE A SHOWER...

AND WE'RE BOTH GROWN-UPS...

MAYBE AFTER I GET OUT OF THE SHOWER I'LL FIND HER NODDING OFF ON THE SOFA...

YOU'LL CATCH COLD.

I'M JUST SO *TIRED* AFTER ALL THOSE PERFORMANCES...

SUE-KICHI, I...

YOU'RE THE FIRST MAN I'VE EVER ALLOWED IN MY ROOM...

YOU UNDERSTAND ABOUT...THE SHOWER, RIGHT?

MS. SHIMO-MURA...

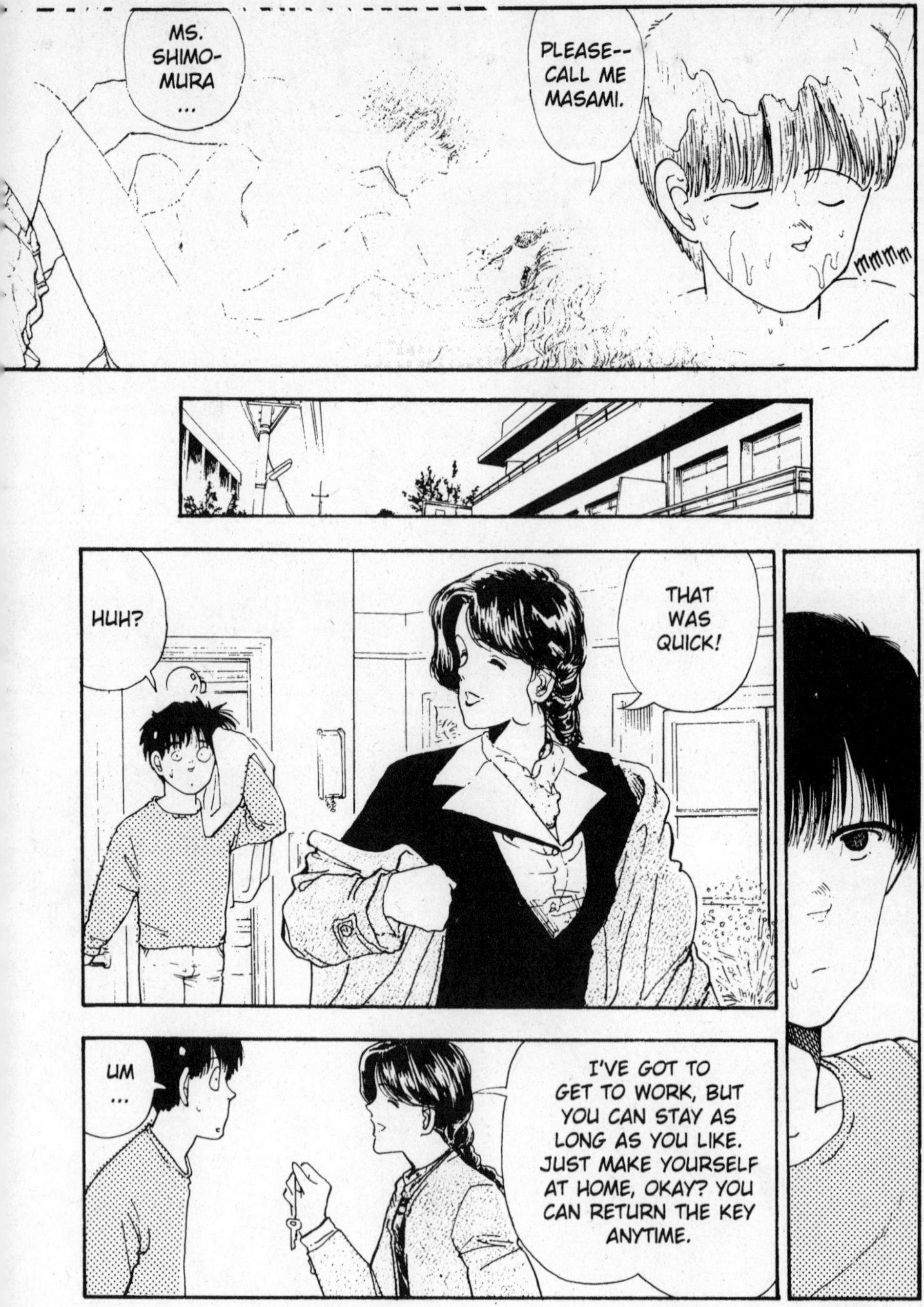
MS. SHIMO-MURA ...
PLEASE-- CALL ME MASAMI.
MMMM
HUH?
THAT WAS QUICK!
UM ...
I'VE GOT TO GET TO WORK, BUT YOU CAN STAY AS LONG AS YOU LIKE. JUST MAKE YOURSELF AT HOME, OKAY? YOU CAN RETURN THE KEY ANYTIME.

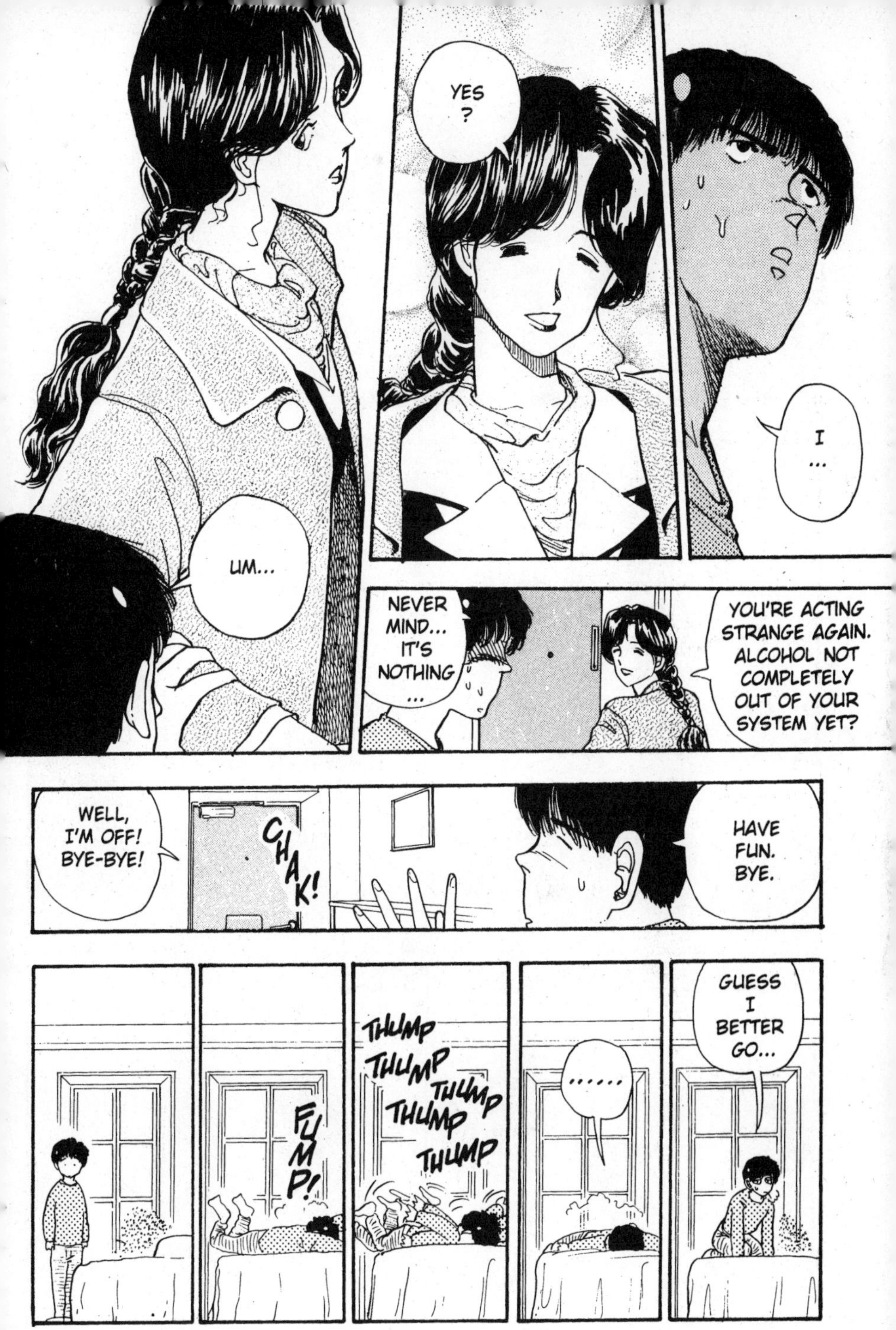
UM...
YES ?
I ...
NEVER MIND... IT'S NOTHING ...
YOU'RE ACTING STRANGE AGAIN. ALCOHOL NOT COMPLETELY OUT OF YOUR SYSTEM YET?
WELL, I'M OFF! BYE-BYE!
CHAK!
HAVE FUN. BYE.
FUMP!
THUMP THUMP THUMP THUMP THUMP
......
GUESS I BETTER GO...

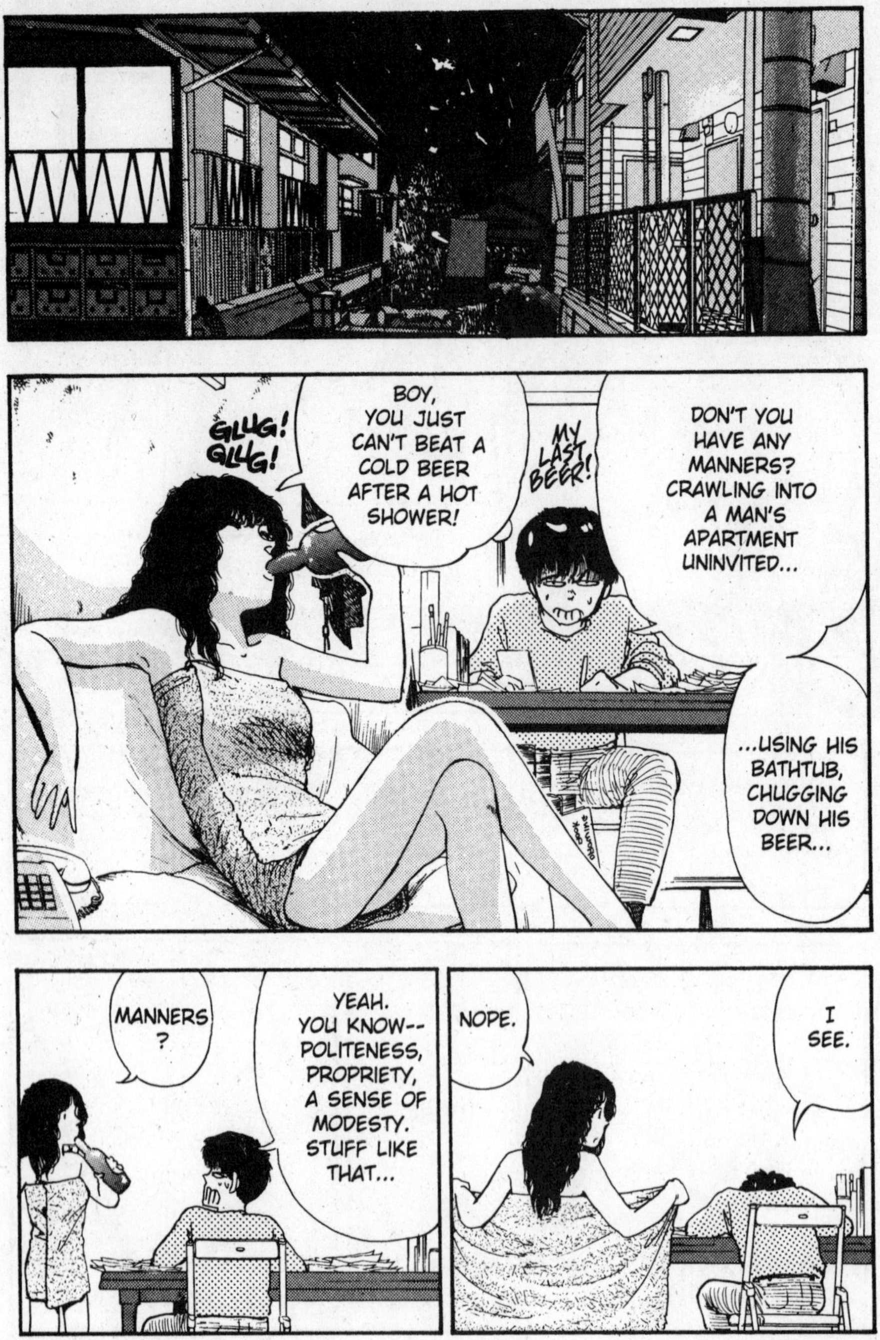
GLUG! GLUG!
BOY, YOU JUST CAN'T BEAT A COLD BEER AFTER A HOT SHOWER!
MY LAST BEER!
DON'T YOU HAVE ANY MANNERS? CRAWLING INTO A MAN'S APARTMENT UNINVITED...
...USING HIS BATHTUB, CHUGGING DOWN HIS BEER...
MANNERS ?
YEAH. YOU KNOW-- POLITENESS, PROPRIETY, A SENSE OF MODESTY. STUFF LIKE THAT...
NOPE.
I SEE.

To Be Continued

ABOUT THE ARTIST

NAOKI YAMAMOTO

DATE OF BIRTH: February 1, 1960
BIRTHPLACE: Hokkaido, Japan
BLOOD TYPE: AB
COLLEGE: WASEDA UNIVERSITY, TOKYO
PROFESSIONAL DEBUT: 1984

Naoki Yamamoto began drawing comics while attending Waseda University in Tokyo. As a senior, following in the footsteps of manga superstar **Rumiko Takahashi** (*Ranma 1/2, Maison Ikkoku, Inu-Yasha*), he studied under master manga artist **Kazuo Koike** (*Crying Freeman, Lone Wolf and Cub*). In 1984, Yamamoto's first professional work, *My Blue Sky*, debuted in *Just Comics* magazine. During the same time period, under the name **Toh Moriyama**, he produced a variety of popular erotic comics.

In 1986, under the name Naoki Yamamoto, he published the series *8 Times 8 Equals 64*, followed in 1987 by the series *Extreme Kamoshida*, the lighthearted story of a nerdy student who chases—not always fruitlessly—after all his female classmates. Both titles appeared in *Big Comic Spirits*.

Two of Yamamoto's manga series with more adult themes were turned into live-action movies. These were *Thank You* (1986), a realistic series about growing up in a dysfunctional family, and *We Are All Alive* (1993), the story of a Japanese businessman trapped in a Southeast Asian country during a *coup d'état*.

Dance Till Tomorrow, Yamamoto's only title translated into English to date, began serialization in *Big Comic Spirits* in 1989 and continued for a year and a half.

Q & A

Q: What made you decide to become a professional comic book artist?
Yamamoto: A friend told me to.
Q: If you hadn't become a comic artist, what profession would you have chosen?
Yamamoto: Teaching Japanese Literature.
Q: What are your current interests & hobbies?
Yamamoto: What kind of people my children will become when they grow up, why Japanese soccer teams are so weak [He may have changed his answer now that Japan made it to the World Cup Finals—Satoru, Editor-in-Chief], and whether Charles Barkley is going to win a championship ring this year.
Q: What's your plan for your next title?
Yamamoto: Ordinary stories about ordinary people—but they have to be erotic.
Q: Name your three favorite American comic artists.
Yamamoto: Robert Crumb [*Zap Comics, Mr. Natural, Self-Loathing Comics*] Gary Panther [*Jimbo*, published by **Zongo Comics**], Henry Dirger.
Q: How would you characterize the American comics industry?
Yamamoto: I don't know much about it, so I can't say much. But if by chance my titles become popular in America, I'll be happy because I can make more money.
Q: What message do you have for your American readers?
Yamamoto: Please support my title! Thank you!